Functional Grammar

Functional Grammar is a model of grammar based on a functional view of the nature of language. This book presents a critical account of Functional Grammar. The main characteristics and central issues of Functional Grammar are presented and the analyses of language structure it proposes are placed in the context of other currently available grammatical frameworks. This comparative approach brings out the strong and weak points of Functional Grammar in relation to other grammatical orientations and allows the reader to assess critically its position within linguistic theory.

Anna Siewierska is Lecturer at the Department of General Linguistics at the University of Amsterdam and is the author of *The Passive: A Comparative Linguistic Analysis* (1984) and *Word Order Rules* (1988).

Linguistic Theory Guides
General editor Dick Hudson

Relational Grammar
Barry Blake

Current Morphology
Andrew Carstairs-McCarthy

Functional Grammar

Anna Siewierska

London and New York

First published 1991
by Routledge
11 New Fetter Lane, London EC4P 4EE

Simultaneously published in the USA and Canada
by Routledge
a division of Routledge, Chapman and Hall, Inc.
29 West 35th Street, New York, NY 10001

© 1991 Anna Siewierska

Set in 10/12 pt Times by
Megaron, Cardiff, Wales
Printed and bound in Great Britain by
Clays Ltd., St. Ives plc.

All rights reserved. No part of this book may be reprinted or
reproduced or utilized in any form or by any electronic,
mechanical, or other means, now known or hereafter invented,
including photocopying and recording, or in any information
storage or retrieval systems, without permission in writing
from the publishers.

British Library Cataloguing in Publication Data
Siewierska, Anna
   Functional grammar. — (Linguistic theory guides)
   1. English language. Grammar
   I. Title. II. Series
   428.2

Library of Congress Cataloging in Publication Data
   Siewierska, Anna.
     Functional grammar / Anna Siewierska.
      p. cm. — (Linguistic theory guides)
     Includes bibliographical references and indexes.
     1. Functionalism (Linguistics) I. Title. II. Series.
   P147.S54   1991
   415—dc20   90-49937

   ISBN 0-415-02644-X
        0-415-02645-8 pbk

To Barry Blake

Contents

Series editor's preface	xi
Preface	xiii
Abbreviations and symbols	xvii

1 Functional grammar as a theory of natural language — 1
  1.1 *Introduction* — 1
  1.2 *The functional orientation* — 3
    1.2.1 *Linguistic explanations* — 3
      1.2.1.1 *A functional explanation of markedness* — 5
  1.3. *Some characteristics of FG* — 8
    1.3.1 *A note on terminology* — 8
    1.3.2 *The basic theoretical constructs* — 9
    1.3.3 *Constraints on the rule system* — 11
  1.4 *The scope of FG* — 13
    1.4.1 *The data base* — 15
  1.5 *Beyond FG* — 17

2 The organization of the grammar — 20
  2.1 *Overview* — 20
  2.2 *The Fund* — 20
    2.2.1 *Predicates and predicate frames* — 23
      2.2.1.1 *Predicate formation* — 27
    2.2.2 *Terms and term formation* — 31
  2.3 *From nuclear to fully specified predications* — 35
    2.3.1 *The underlying structure of the clause* — 36
    2.3.2 *Operators and satellites* — 38
    2.3.3 *The derivation* — 39
    2.3.4 *Expression rules* — 42

3 States of affairs and semantic functions — 43
- 3.1 Introduction — 43
- 3.2 A typology of SoAs — 45
  - 3.2.1 A brief comparison — 46
  - 3.2.2 The features — 47
    - 3.2.2.1 Control — 47
    - 3.2.2.2 Experience — 49
    - 3.2.2.3 Telicity — 51
    - 3.2.2.4 Dynamicity — 53
- 3.3 The argument/satellite opposition — 55
  - 3.3.1 Arguments and level-1 satellites (δ_1) — 56
- 3.4 Semantic functions — 62
  - 3.4.1 Predicate and argument features — 62
  - 3.4.2 Grammaticalization — 64
  - 3.4.3 One semantic function per argument — 66
- 3.5 The inventory of semantic functions — 67

4 Syntactic functions — 73
- 4.1 Introduction — 73
- 4.2 Perspective — 76
  - 4.2.1 Perspective in FG — 77
- 4.3 Subject assignment, the passive and the antipassive — 79
  - 4.3.1 The passive in Philippine-type languages — 82
  - 4.3.2 Ergative languages and the antipassive — 86
    - 4.3.2.1 Ergativity and the Philippine languages — 91
- 4.4 Object assignment — 93
  - 4.4.1 One object function — 95
    - 4.4.1.1 Double object in Bantu — 97
    - 4.4.1.2 Obligatory object assignment — 101
- 4.5 The Semantic Function Hierarchy — 104
  - 4.5.1 Behind the SFH — 105
  - 4.5.2 Extending the domain of the SFH — 107

5 The layered structure of the clause — 113
- 5.1 Introduction — 113
- 5.2. Tense, aspect and modality — 115
  - 5.2.1 Aspect and tense — 116
    - 5.2.1.1 Level-1 π_1 operators — 118
    - 5.2.1.2 Level-2 π_2 operators — 121
  - 5.2.2 Mood and modality — 123
    - 5.2.2.1 Modality — 124
    - 5.2.2.2 Illocution — 130
- 5.3 The layered structure of the clause vs X-bar constituency — 136
  - 5.3.1 Hierarchical structure and clausal complementation — 140

6	**Pragmatic functions and the pragmatics of discourse**		146
	6.1 *Introduction*		146
		6.1.1 *Pragmatic functions and formal expression*	147
	6.2 *Pragmatic functions and special positions*		148
	6.3 *Topicality*		153
		6.3.1 *Topicality and the given/new distinction*	155
		6.3.2 *The topic function subdivided*	160
		6.3.3 *The topic function and formal expression*	163
		6.3.3.1 *The coding of GivTop*	166
		6.3.3.2 *NewTop*	168
	6.4 *Focality*		173
		6.4.1 *The focus subdivided*	176
7	**Form-determining expression rules**		181
	7.1 *Introduction*		181
	7.2 *Interdependence between form and order*		182
	7.3 *Lexical priority*		183
	7.4 *Agreement*		186
		7.4.1 *Cross-reference*	191
		7.4.2 *A note on agreement in Achenese*	193
	7.5 *The English verbal complex*		195
8	**Linearization**		200
	8.1 *Introduction*		200
	8.2 *The universal principles of order*		201
		8.2.1 *Refining the Natural Serialization Principle (NSP)*	203
		8.2.1.1 *Head Proximity*	204
		8.2.1.2 *The relator principles*	207
		8.2.2 *Relative ordering of modifiers*	209
		8.2.2.1 *LIPOC*	212
	8.3 *The FG rules of order*		214
		8.3.1 *Functional patterns and placement rules*	218
		8.3.1.1 *The P_1 position*	220
		8.3.1.2 *The functional patterns of English*	224
	Notes		228
	References		249
	Language index		269
	Name index		271
	Subject index		275

Series editor's preface

The Linguistic Theory Guides have been commissioned with a rather special readership in mind – the typical linguist, who knows a good deal about a small number of theories in his or her area of specialism, but is baffled by the problem of keeping up with other theories even in that area, to say nothing of other areas. There just aren't enough hours in the day to read more widely, and even if there were it wouldn't help much because so much of the literature is simply incomprehensible except to the initiated. The result is that most of us cultivate our own garden reasonably conscientiously, but have very little idea of what is happening in other people's gardens.

This theoretical narrowing is a practical problem if you are expected to teach on a broad front – say, to give a course of lectures on syntactic theory – when you only know one theory of syntax. Honesty demands that one should tell students about alternative approaches, but how can you when you have at best a hazy idea of what most theories have to say? Another practical problem is the danger of missing pearls of wisdom which might be vitally important in one's research, because they happen to have been formulated in terms of some unfamiliar theory. There can be very few linguists who have not rediscovered some wheel in their area of specialism, out of ignorance about work in other theories.

However, there is an even more serious problem at the research level, because one of the main goals of our joint research effort is to work towards the best possible theory (or set of theories), and this can only be done if we constantly compare and evaluate all the available theories. From this perspective, it is simply pointless to spend one's life developing one theory, or some part of it, if it is already outclassed by some other theory. It is true that evaluation of theories is quite a subjective matter, and is far too complex for any kind of absolute certainty to be arrived at. All we can do is to make a reasonably dispassionate, though subjective, assessment of the strengths and weaknesses of the alternatives, in the full expectation that our colleagues may disagree radically with our verdict. Total ignorance of the alternative theories is clearly not a good basis for evaluating them – though it is arguably better than the misinformation that can be used to bolster one's confidence in one's favourite theory.

It is with these problems in mind, then, that we have planned the Linguistic Theory Guides. Each book in the series will focus on one theory that is currently prominent in the literature (or in a few special cases, on a range of such theories). The list of titles is open-ended, and new titles will be added as new theories come into prominence. The aim will be both to inform and to evaluate – to provide enough information to enable the reader to appreciate whatever literature presupposes the theory concerned, and to highlight its strengths and weaknesses. The intention is emphatically not to sell the theory, though the valuation will naturally be sufficiently positive to explain why the theory is worth considering seriously. Several of the theories are already well provided with textbooks which say a great deal about their strengths and very little about their weaknesses. We assume that our typical reader finds such books irritating at best. What they want is clear exposition at the right level of sophistication (i.e. well above first-year undergraduate level), and wise evaluation, both internally and in relation to other theories.

It is not easy to write a book with these qualities, and we have selected our authors with great care. What we have looked for in each case is essentially someone who is a sympathetic outsider, rather than a devotee of the theory – someone who has experience of working within other theories, but who is well-disposed to the theory concerned, and reasonably well-informed about it. We hope that this recipe will produce books which will be acceptably non-partisan in tone, but we have also taken steps to make them factually reliable as descriptions of the theories concerned. Each book has benefited from detailed comment by at least one prominent devotee (a term which we do not apply disparagingly – without their devotees theories would not come into being, still less develop, and there would be no theoretical linguistics), as well as by an outside reader. Needless to say, the authors have been allowed to stick to their evaluations if the protests of their devotee readers have failed to change their minds.

It is our sincere hope that these books will make a significant contribution to the growth and development of our subject, as well as being helpful to those who read them.

Richard Hudson

Preface

The first tentative outline of FG was presented in Dik's (1968) book *Coordination* in answer to a number of problems with the Standard Theory (Chomsky 1965) treatment of coordinate structures. A more comprehensive account of the proposed framework appeared ten years later as *Functional Grammar* (Dik 1978). The major developments in the theory within the ten years since the publication of *Functional Grammar* have been consistently documented in a series of book publications, articles, working papers and theses written by Dik himself and his increasing number of associates and students. Chief among the book publications are in order of publication:

> Dik, Simon C. (1980) *Studies in Functional Grammar*, London: Academic Press.
> Bolkestein, A. Machtelt, Combé, Henk A., Dik, Simon C. *et al.* (1981) *Predication and Expression in Functional Grammar*, London: Academic Press.
> Hoekstra, Teun, van der Hulst, Harry and Moortgat, Michael (eds) (1981) *Perspectives on Functional Grammar*, Dordrecht: Foris.
> Dik, Simon C. (1983) (ed.) *Advances in Functional Grammar*, Dordrecht: Foris.
> Bolkestein, A. Machtelt, de Groot, Casper and Lachlan Mackenzie, J. (eds) (1985a) *Syntax and Pragmatics in Functional Grammar*, Dordrecht: Foris.
> —— (1985b) *Predicates and Terms in Functional Grammar*, Dordrecht: Foris.
> Van der Auwera, Johan and Goossens, Louis (eds) (1987) *Ins and Outs of the Predication*, Dordrecht: Foris.
> Nuyts, Jan and de Schutter, G. (eds) (1987) *Getting One's Words Into Line*, Dordrecht: Foris.
> Hannay, Michael and Vester, Elseline (eds) (1989) *Working with Functional Grammar: Descriptive and Computational Applications*, Dordrecht: Foris.
> Connolly, John H. and Dik, Simon C. (eds) (1989) *Functional Grammar and the Computer*, Dordrecht: Foris.
> Dik, Simon C. (1989) *The Theory of Functional Grammar. Part I: The Structure of the Clause*, Dordrecht: Foris.
> Nuyts, Jan, Bolkestein, A. Machtelt and Vet, Co (eds) (1990) *Layers and Levels of Representation. A Functional View*, Amsterdam: John Benjamins.

The list of publications in or on FG numbers hundreds of titles with contributions from several hundred researchers stationed in academic institutes primarily in The Netherlands and Belgium, though by no means exclusively so. The bibliography of FG is kept up to date on a regular basis by Casper de Groot. The insights emerging from all the publications, various discussion groups, workshops and symposia (the latter are held every two years) have led to the successive restructuring of FG, the latest version of which is presented by Dik (1989) in *The Theory of Functional Grammar. Part 1: The Structure of the Clause*. Volume two of this work, devoted to complex and derived constructions, is to appear in 1991.

Given the existence of two comprehensive book-length presentations of FG, not to mention numerous short outlines, the task of providing an interesting and insightful account of the theory which would not be a simple rehashing of Dik's own words is not an easy one. The approach that I have adopted is to compare the FG treatment of several basic issues with other analyses currently available in the literature. In doing so I hope to bring out the strong and the weak points of the theory and to provide a frame of reference which will enable readers to relate the FG analyses to the solutions adopted within their own framework, and consequently to arrive at their own conclusions as to the degree of success of the FG proposals. My own background as a linguist is firmly entrenched within the Anglo-American tradition. Consequently, the repertoire of grammatical frameworks to which I compare FG is basically confined to exponents of this tradition. Of the insightful analyses offered within French, German or Slavic linguistic theory, only some work in dependency theory and on language universals and information structure will be taken into account.

As for the aspects of FG to be discussed in this book, the choice of topics was determined by my own knowledge and interests, by what I consider to be the strong and weak points of FG, and by the range of subjects covered by Dik's (1989) new version of the theory. This last consideration confined the subject matter of this book, like Dik's, to the simple clause; derived constructions will be mentioned only in passing, and complex ones will receive some attention only with respect to the hierarchical structure of the clause. Within the domain of the simple clause, I have concentrated on aspects of the predication (clause) rather than the term (noun phrase), as this coincides with my work in the area of morpho-syntax and information structure. The chapters on semantic, syntactic and pragmatic functions and on linearization are directly inspired by my prior research. The remaining two non-introductory chapters concerning the hierarchical structure of the clause and form-determining expression rules have been chosen because they represent two newly developed areas within FG which help to give a more complete idea of the working of the grammar and thus enhance the appeal of the model.

Returning to the matter of comparison with other theoretical frameworks, the grammatical models have been chosen largely on the basis of what they have to say about the area of FG under scrutiny in any given instance. Thus, for example, in discussing the FG treatment of states of affairs and semantic functions I have considered the analyses that have been proposed by Vendler (1967) and Dowty (1979) and the adherents of various versions of Case Grammar (e.g. Fillmore 1968, 1977; Anderson 1971, 1977; Starosta 1977, 1979). The FG argument/satellite distinction has been confronted with both the dependency and constituency (Chomskyan) tradition. The way syntactic functions are handled in FG has been juxtaposed primarily to the treatment of grammatical relations in Perlmutter and Postal's Relational Grammar (Perlmutter 1983a; Perlmutter and Rosen 1984), but also to Bresnan's (1982a) Lexical Functional Grammar (LFG), traditional grammar (e.g. Jespersen 1927) and the host of analyses offered within the domain of morpho-syntactic typology by linguists such as Comrie (1976, 1981, 1985), Keenan (1976, 1981), Nichols (1986), Thompson (1986) and others. The hierarchical structure of the clause is compared to Foley and Van Valin's (1984) analysis, and both their and the FG model are contrasted with the underlying constituent structure of Chomsky's (1986) *Barriers*. The FG approach to pragmatic functions is placed in the context of the work on information structure carried out by linguists such as Chafe (1976, 1980, 1987), Davison (1984), Givón (1983a, 1984), Gundel (1988), Halliday (1967/68, 1985), Reinhart (1982). And some of the rules of order proposed in FG are compared to the weighted linear precedence statements presented by Uszkoreit (1986) in the context of Generalized Phrase Structure Grammar. This is not intended to be an exhaustive list of the frameworks and linguists whose analyses have been confronted with those suggested in FG, but rather an illustration of the range of the comparison that the reader may expect.

My first contact with FG dates back to the early 1980s when I chose FG as one of the grammatical models for a cross-theoretical study of linearization rules. Subsequently, I participated in the Second FG Conference held in September 1986 in Antwerp and next, at the invitation of Simon Dik, spent ten months of 1988 in Amsterdam among functional grammarians on a research grant of the Dutch Science Foundation NWO (then ZWO). Part of the work on this monograph was carried out during my stay there. I would like to convey my thanks to Simon Dik and the NWO for providing me with such a marvellous opportunity to familiarize myself more closely with FG and other theoretical frameworks and to pursue my interest in pragmatics and text linguistics. For fruitful discussions of various topics connected with this book, and for their warmth, kindness and hospitality I would like to thank in particular: Dik Bakker, Machelt Bolkestein, Simon Dik, Casper de Groot, Kees Hengeveld, Peter Kahrel, Harm Pinkster and Jan Rijkhoff. The responsibility for all the interpretations proposed in this book is, of course my own. Additionally I would like to thank my husband, Peter Kahrel, for help in preparing the manuscript. Finally, I would like to express my thanks for helpful comments and suggestions to the editor, Richard Hudson, and the two reviewers.

Although much of Dik's previous work and also that of his associates is now available in the updated version of FG presented in Dik (1989), to help the reader find the relevant sources, both earlier and current references will be cited. The Working Papers on Functional Grammar can be obtained from the Klassiek Seminarium, University of Amsterdam, Oude Turfmarkt 129, 1012 GC Amsterdam.

Abbreviations and symbols

A	adjective
A^1	first argument
A^2	second argument
A^3	third argument
abl	ablative
abs	absolutive
acc	accusative
act	actor
AF	actor focus
Ag	agent
al	allative
anim	animate
AP	adjectival phrase
appl	applicative
a/p	antipassive
arg	argument
art	article
asp	aspect
aux	auxiliary
Ben	beneficiary/benefactive
C	complementizer position
caus	causative
cl	clitic
clf	classifier
Comp	complementizer/complementizer position
compl	completive
con	control
cond	conditional

cont	continuous
contr	contrast
d	definite
dat	dative
Dec	declension, declarative
Dem	demonstrative
DF	direction focus
Dir	direction
dl	dual
do	direct object
DO	direct object
DS	different subject
dub	dubitative
dyn	dynamic
e_i	event variable
E_i	utterance variable
EC	exceptional clause
erg	ergative
EST	Extended Standard Theory
evid	evidential
Exp	experiencer
f	feminine/finite
f_i	variable
FG	Functional Grammar
Fo	force
foc	focus
fut	future
G	genitive
GB	Government and Binding
gen	genitive
GF	goal focus
GivTop	Given Topic
Go	goal
GPSG	Generalized Phrase Structure Grammar
h	honorific
H	head
HPSG	Head-Driven Phrase Structure Grammar

i	infinite verb
I	inflection (GB)
IF	instrumental focus
Ill	illocution
Imp	imperative
imperf	imperfective
inan	inanimate
ind	indicative
Inf	infinitive
infer	inferential
ingr	ingressive
Instr	instrumental
irr	irrealis
iter	iterative
LF	locative focus
LFG	Lexical Functional Grammar
Loc	locative/location
M	modal
m	masculine
Man	manner
mod	modal
mp	masculine personal
N	noun
n	neuter
neg	negative
NewTop	New Topic
NLU	Natural Language Using System
nmp	nonmasculine personal
nom	nominative
nonfut	nonfuture
NP	noun phrase
NSP	Natural Serialization Principle
Num	numeral
O	object
obj	object
obl	oblique
OC	ordinary clause
P	preposition

p	person
PaP	past participle
part	participle/partitive
pass	passive
perf	perfective
PFG	Procedural Functional Grammar
pl	plural
Pos	position
Post	postposition
PP	prepositional phrase
pred	predicate
Prep	preposition
pres	present
PRO	pronoun
prob	probability marker
Proc	processed
Prog	progressive
prox	proximate
PrP	present participle
prt	particle
purp	purposive
Q	question
R	relator
Rec	recipient
refl	reflexive
RG	Relational Grammar
reinf	reinforcement marker
rel	relative
ResTop	Resumed Topic
RRG	Role and Reference Grammar
S	subject/sentence/clause
SC	small clause
SFG	Systemic Functional Grammar
SFH	Semantic Function Hierarchy
sg	singular
SoA	state of affairs
Sou	source
SS	same subject
Sub	subordinate

Abbreviations and symbols xxi

subj	subject
subjc	subjunctive
SubTop	SubTopic
t/asp	tense/aspect
tel	telic
Temp	temporal
TG	Transformational Grammar
tns	tense
top	topic
Top	topic
tr	transitive
V	verb
voc	vocative
VP	verb phrase
x_i	Individual variable
X_i	content variable
1	first person/level one (in hierarchical clause structure)
2	second person/level two
3	third person/level three
4	level four
P_1	special clause initial position
P_2	special position to the left of the predication
P_3	special position to the right of the predication
P_0	special focus position
β	variable denoting predicate type (verbal, adjectival or nominal)
δ	satellite
Ω	term operator
π	predicate, predication, proposition and clausal operators
X	variable
*	ungrammatical
#	inappropriate in the specified context
?	of dubious grammaticality or acceptability
§	section
∅	zero form/elided material
-	morpheme boundary/boundary between glosses
:	joins elements of a gloss

Further abbreviatory conventions are given in the text.

1 Functional Grammar as a theory of natural language

1.1 INTRODUCTION

FG is characterized by Dik as a general theory of the grammatical organization of natural language based on the functional view of the nature of language. It is a sentence grammar envisaged as part of a wider theory of verbal interaction and ultimately as a sub-component of a model of a natural language using (NLU) system in which the human linguistic capacity is linked to epistemic, logical, perceptual and social capacities. The functional orientation of FG is the key feature of the theory permeating all facets of the structure and workings of the grammar including the choice of language facts to be described, the nature of the descriptive apparatus and most importantly the range and form of explanations proposed for the observed language data and the suggested analyses of these data. Dik places FG firmly within the functional paradigm of linguistic theory which he repeatedly champions and unequivocally opposes to the formal paradigm as represented by mainstream American linguistics, in particular the grammatical tradition of Chomsky and his associates.

The exclusively functional affiliations of FG have been challenged by representatives of the formal camp (e.g. Koster 1982; Miller 1986; Muysken 1988) who see in the FG analyses of sentence structure clear parallels with their own more formally based analyses, or even correspondences suggestive of FG being a notational variant of Chomskyan generative grammar. And indeed there is no denying that FG has drawn from Chomskyan theory and its offshoots, and that there exist points of convergence in the treatment of language structure in both of these grammatical frameworks. Nonetheless, the real intellectual debt of FG is to the linguistic tradition of Jespersen, Bolinger, Greenberg and the Prague School, the representatives of an underlying philosophy that indisputably identifies the theory as belonging to the functional orientation. Thus functional grammarians see themselves, and it is also here within the functional paradigm that their contributions to linguistic theory lie.

The major factor distinguishing FG from the other functionally oriented approaches to language currently available (for example Foley and Van Valin's (1984) Role and Reference Grammar (RRG), Halliday's (1985) Systemic Functional Grammar and the host of analyses of linguists such as Comrie (1977, 1981), Givón (1983a, 1984), Haiman (1985), Kuno (1987), Nichols (1986), Shibatani (1985) and Thompson (1985, 1986), just to name a few) is that it offers a coherent and explicit model of grammar which aims to provide a complete account of sentence structure from the underlying semantic representation to the surface phonetic form. Most functionalists focus their attention on selected language phenomena and remain vague as to how the linguistic constructs and structures that they postulate link up into a coherent whole. Givón (1984: 25) even considers the very idea of attempting to present a grammar as methodologically unsound on the grounds that the required prior delimitation of the scope of the grammar and the necessary formalization 'bias one's perception of new facts and freeze one's explanatory intuition'. To my knowledge the only other functional approach to language comparable in scope to FG is Halliday's Systemic Grammar. Systemic Grammar, however, is not explicit enough in regard to the consecutive steps leading to the interpretation or generation of structures to qualify as a full-fledged model of grammar. Nor does it possess the internal consistency of FG, a matter readily acknowledged by Butler (1985) in his recent overview of systemic linguistics. The construction of an actual model of grammar, with a high degree of explicitness and consistency within the functional orientation, I take to be the single most significant aspect of FG which in itself constitutes an invitation to familiarize oneself with the theory.

The functional orientation, on the one hand, and the sentential character, on the other, have made FG rather an eclectic theory, vulnerable to the attacks of functionalists and formalists alike. As a sentence grammar it is anathema to many a functionalist. Formalists in turn find the theory lacking in formalizations and categorical as opposed to relative statements which in their eyes precludes assessment or comparison. Yet in presenting FG one has to compare it with formal theories, since often these are the only theories which have provided an alternative systematic account of the relevant data. I will try to show that FG stands up to scrutiny in the face of these comparisons.

1.2 THE FUNCTIONAL ORIENTATION

Since within the last decade the functional/formal opposition has received considerable attention in the linguistic literature,[1] I will refrain from a detailed exposition of functionalism and concentrate only on the points most essential to the understanding and appreciation of FG. Whereas adherents of the formal paradigm view language as a potentially infinite set of structural descriptions independent of matters of use, functionalists take the very opposite approach in considering all aspects of the structural organization of language in the light of its role in human social interaction. FG shares with other functionally oriented models all the major theoretical assumptions of the functional paradigm; chief among them is the priority of the communicative over the cognitive function of language, with the accompanying socio-cultural as opposed to psychological bias. The adoption of the communicative perspective entails extending the traditional domain of linguistic analysis consisting of semantic, syntactic, morphological and phonological rules to include the complex and often ill-understood pragmatic principles governing the patterns of verbal interaction. Moreover, the system of semantic, syntactic, morphological and phonological rules is seen as instrumental with respect to the communicative and interactional functions that it fulfils; and within the traditional rule system syntax emerges as instrumental in relation to semantics. The pragmatico-semantic bias of FG can be most readily appreciated by a brief consideration of the type of linguistic explanations invoked in the theory.

1.2.1 Linguistic explanations

One of the most striking aspects of functional models of grammar for linguists or students schooled in the formal tradition is the radical difference in the nature of linguistic argumentation and particularly in the type of information utilized in the construction of linguistic explanations. In formal approaches linguistic explanations are framed with reference to the hypothesized system of semantic, syntactic, morphological and phonological rules – the grammar – which, rather than the language, is considered to be the proper domain of linguistic inquiry. A typical explanation consists of demonstrating that a given phenomenon can be subsumed under or derived from a principle or rule which has already been established as belonging to the rule system. In the case of Chomskyan GB and its predecessors, linguistic explanations may also directly refer to the innate language faculty assumed to be responsible for language acquisition; a particular phenomenon, rule or constraint may be shown to be a necessary part of the innate mental organ of language. Functional explanations, on the other hand, refer not to the grammatical system or even to the language which the grammatical structures define, but to the extra-linguistic factors affecting language use.

Dik (1986: 9–10) traces the form of functional explanations to the following functional prerequisites: a) the aims or purposes for which natural language expressions are used; b) the means by which natural languages are implemented; c) the circumstances in which natural languages are used.

Given that the functional paradigm takes communication to be the primary function of language, type a) explanations involve the representational and relational aspects of the utterance bearing on the distinctions between directives, imperatives, interrogatives, declaratives, expressives, etc. Type b) explanations refer to the physiological and psychological constraints imposed on language use. The physiological constraints concern the limitations of the human vocal and auditory tracts; the psychological determinants may relate to matters of production, perception, comprehension, memorization and acquisition (with references to the innate genetic endowment only as a last resort). Explanations falling within type c) embrace the physical, socio-cultural and linguistic circumstances of use. By physical circumstances is meant primarily the features of the natural environment. Within the socio-cultural circumstances one may distinguish factors such as: prestige and stigmatization; politeness and deference; and solidarity. Finally the linguistic circumstances refer to the presence of other languages in a given speech community.

Adherence to the functional view of language does not presuppose a one-to-one form/function correlation. On the contrary, both *multifunctionality*, where one structure may serve several functions, and *redundancy*, where one function is served by several structures, are considered to be the linguistic norm. In fact without multifunctionality or redundancy as preconditions it is difficult to conceive of acquisition, innovation and thus language change. The impossibility of identifying or the non-existence of *the* function of one structure or another is the proverbial straw man attacked by formalists, as in Newmeyer (1983: 102). Real functional explanations, however, draw on several interacting principles, requirements or constraints, each with its own functional motivation, correlating with the superordinate communicative function of language. As a case in point let us consider the functionally based account of the typological marked/unmarked distinction recently advanced by Gundel *et al.* (1988), which draws on the just-presented body of assumptions shared by most functionalists, including the adherents of FG.

1.2.1.1 A functional explanation of markedness

The notion of *markedness* is used in the literature with reference to pairs of phonological, morphological and lexical oppositions as well as to construction types both within and across languages. Matters of theory notwithstanding, the unmarked member of the opposition is seen to denote what is taken to be a norm or standard, an expected or natural situation. This in turn is primarily affected by matters of frequency of occurrence and distributional restrictions.[2] Gundel *et al.* hypothesize that typological markedness is closely tied to the complementary yet distinct communicative tasks of the speaker/writer and addressee. They argue that though human language is geared to serve both speakers and listeners, 'the decoding task of the listener is intrinsically more difficult than the encoding task of the speaker, since the speaker "knows" in some sense, what is going to be said, but the listener does not' (Gundel *et al.* 1988: 287). Given this assumption, they suggest that an optimal communicative system should be biased towards the addressee rather than the speaker. If this is the case, we would expect the addressee-oriented properties to display a wider distribution and fewer constraints than the speaker-oriented ones. The forms reflecting a speaker bias, by contrast, should be more context dependent and hence preferred or used regularly only under specific conditions. These correlates of the speaker vs addressee bias tally with the characteristics associated with the marked/unmarked opposition described above. Thus, in short, the unmarked member of an opposition should be addressee oriented, the marked speaker oriented.

In phonology ease of articulation is taken to be the major parameter reflecting a speaker bias and perceptual distance the addressee bias. The morpho-syntactic counterparts of these two parameters are brevity, associated with marked speaker-sensitive constructions, and explicitness, overtness and redundancy characteristic of unmarked addressee-sensitive ones. One piece of evidence for this distinction from the domain of morphology is the overriding cross-linguistic dominance of additive as opposed to subtractive morphological processes (see e.g. Mayerthaler 1988: 84–85). In the area of morpho-syntactic coding the above parameters identify, for example, zero anaphora or pronominal coding by verb agreement as speaker-biased marked forms and nominal coding as unmarked, unless the context determines otherwise. It will be shown in §6.3.3 that the use of different forms of anaphoric coding is a complex matter dependent on a number of discourse variables. Pronominal forms are, however, clearly more context bound than nominal forms, which is what their positive markedness value under Gundel *et al.*'s analysis is intended to reflect.

The other major dimensions correlating with the marked/unmarked opposition in morpho-syntax suggested by Gundel *et al.* are conceptual prominence or salience in the mind of the speaker,[3] as the speaker-bound parameter, and iconicity, i.e. correspondence to the order of things in the real world, as reflecting addressee orientation.[4] There is ample evidence for the typologically unmarked nature of iconic patterns of grammatical coding involving the subject and object functions and linear order both within the clause and among sequences of clauses (see ch. 8). For example, the apparent universal tendency of humans to show an unqualified interest in themselves, their interlocutors and other humans over and above non-human entities or abstract situations and events, which is captured in the Personal Hierarchy (see e.g. Siewierska 1988a: 56–60) in (1), underlies the preference for clauses with human or animate subjects as in (2), rather than inanimate or abstract ones as in (3).

(1) The Personal Hierarchy
    1p > 2p > 3p human > higher animals > other organisms > inorganic matter > abstracts

(2) a. People are dying of starvation.
    b. The horse was killed by lightning.
    c. She was overcome with love.

(3) a. Starvation is killing people.
    b. Lightning killed the horse.
    c. Love overcame her.

The same iconic reflection of widely accepted perceptions of salience or dominance may be observed in the sequencing of conjuncts according to the social status or relative authority with which they are imbued in a society, the higher-ranking entities being always placed first, e.g.

(4) a. the President and the Secretary of State
    b. your highness, my lords, ladies and gentlemen
    c. God the father, the son and the holy ghost
    d. men, women and children.

Another type of iconic patterning involves matters of temporal order. This is manifest in a preference for examples such as (5a) as compared to (5b).

(5) a. We arranged to meet on the road from Florence to Sienna.
    b. ?We arranged to meet on the road to Sienna from Florence.

Note also that (6a) and (6b) would normally be depicted as representing a different sequence of events.

(6) a. They had another espresso and entered the museum.
    b. They entered the museum and had another espresso.

There is also considerable evidence suggestive of the fact that departures from iconic patterning typically require special pragmatic, textual or situational circumstances, such as contrast, emphasis, topic-shift or unplanned, spontaneous speech, as in face-to-face conversation among intimates. For instance, in many languages, including English, fronting of non-subject arguments typically involves contrast or some form of emphasis. Two cases in point are presented in (7) and (8).[5]

(7) Did you have hockey?
    No *tennis n basketball* we played.

(8) What was the headmaster like?
    Oh well, he's what you'd expect a headmaster to be, I s'pose ... I mean a headmaster's a pretty heavy sort of person.
    About the headmistress?
    She was heavier still. *Little Hitler* she used to be called. *Mrs Benno*, I'll never forget her.

The claim that the patterns of use in (2)–(5) are attributable to addressee vs speaker orientation is consistent with the Grice (1975) tradition which holds that in order to be as communicatively effective as possible, speakers adapt their communicative strategies in accordance with their assessment of the communicative needs of the addressees. The accepted line of reasoning is that to achieve this the speaker will first present information familiar to the addressee so as to provide a frame of reference for the interpretation of the utterance (see §6.3.1). This is seen to facilitate the processing task of the listener.

Considerable support for this view has been adduced by psycholinguistic research which is summarized in Bock (1982). Bock argues that adult language comprehension and production involves two syntactic processing modes; one that may be termed 'automatic' affecting easily accessible language data, and the other, which is more 'controlled', relating to less accessible language material. She cites a large body of psycholinguistic data from experiments on the nature of sentence production, sentence recall, sentence preferences and implicit picture description, all of which suggest that accessibility correlates with the parameters associated with iconic patterning. The presentation of accessible material prior to less accessible information is claimed to free both the speaker's and the addressee's processing resources for the controlled processing of the less accessible data. Thus such a presentation of information eases the task not only of the addressee, but also of the speaker. Bock (1982: 38) points out that there may be another factor influencing this sequencing of information apart from the adherence to the addressee's need for a prior perspective from which to interpret the utterance(s), namely the time necessary for the focusing of attention. Automatic processing is very fast and does not interfere with other processes. The activation of less accessible data, on the other hand, requires attention. Therefore, the speaker is likely to produce the already activated information first, inadvertently, since it does not demand the application of conscious attention. If this is so, in beginning with conceptually salient information and thus setting his or her own needs above those of the addressee, the speaker not only violates a cooperative norm, but also makes an extra demand on his or her own processing resources by exerting additional attention. One would expect these departures from the norm to require special motivation, which is exactly what is claimed.

Gundel *et al.*'s hypothesis as to the existence of a correlation between markedness and speaker vs addressee orientation is intended as a typological generalization, not as a prediction of the markedness values of structures in individual languages. In fact, as argued by Dik (1989: 41), within languages the markedness value of a particular item is subject to change along the diachronic dimension which typically finds reflection synchronically in different varieties or forms of language, for example dialectal distinctions, different styles, registers or text types. Typological correlations such as those suggested by Gundel *et al.* are aimed at providing a better understanding of what constitutes 'a possible human language' and are of relevance in the construction of a grammar of language *per se*, but not necessarily of a particular language.

1.3 SOME CHARACTERISTICS OF FG

1.3.1 A note on terminology

The differences in the nature of linguistic explanations recognized by formalists and functionalists noted in §1.2.1 find direct reflection in the type of terminology utilized in the respective theories. The rules, constraints or principles of formal theories are framed in absolute terms, and they either do or do not apply in any given instance. The functional approach, on the other hand, deals with tendencies, preferences, favoured and disfavoured solutions which may be seen as simpler, more effective or more efficient in relation to the discussed functional prerequisites.

The comparative lack of categorical statements in FG is thus not due to insufficient data or fear of commitment on the part of its proponents but is a direct consequence of the theory's functional orientation. This must be kept in mind in assessing the type of statements that feature in FG.

1.3.2 The basic theoretical constructs

Subscribing to a functional view of language entails that the rule system should, as far as possible, be described in terms of functional notions. Accordingly, in FG functional labels are assigned unquestionable priority over categorial ones. The structure of the clause is built around the semantic relation of predicate and argument to which may be assigned three levels of functions: semantic, syntactic and pragmatic. The *semantic functions* correspond to what in other grammatical frameworks are called semantic or thematic roles, relations or cases, e.g. agent, goal, recipient, beneficiary, instrument, etc. The *syntactic functions* are subject and direct object, though interpreted rather idiosyncratically (see §4.2). The *pragmatic functions* specify the informational status of language expressions. These include the Topic, Focus, Theme and Tail (see §6.2). Of the three levels of functions only the semantic ones are obligatorily present in underlying structure. Thus although FG is primarily a theory of syntax, its basic theoretical constructs are semantic. We will see in ch. 2 and ch. 5 that the other major structural distinctions within the clause and also the term (noun phrase) are based primarily on semantic considerations too. Pragmatic functions like the semantic ones are taken to play a role in the structural organization of the clause in all languages, though not necessarily to the same extent. Syntactic functions, by contrast, are not considered to be universally valid.

In addition to the three levels of functions, current FG makes use of the notions of *first* (A^1), *second* (A^2) and *third* (A^3) *argument* which denote the conventional argument positions specified in a given predicate frame (see §2.2.1) as well as the ordering of arguments in the Semantic Function Hierarchy (SFH) discussed in §4.5. This is an innovation relative to the (1978) model dictated by and large by the need to account for agreement (see §7.4) and case-marking phenomena which are sensitive to what in a multilevel theory of clause structure, such as Perlmutter and Postal's Relational Grammar (RG) (Perlmutter 1983a; Perlmutter and Rosen 1984), are regarded as underlying grammatical relations. In §4.5.2 it will be argued that in effect the three argument positions define such an additional underlying level of grammatical functions.

The final set of functional constructs employed in FG are the notions of *head* and *dependent* defined more or less as in standard dependency theory (see e.g. Hudson 1980). The only notable departure from standard treatments of these functions is that the head is necessarily lexical which is interpreted by Dik as excluding auxiliary verbs and adpositions from head status (see §7.5).

In FG each clause is characterized in terms of an abstract clause structure which is mapped onto actual linguistic expressions by a set of expression rules specifying form, order and intonation. This is shown schematically in (9).

(9)   underlying structure
           ↓
    expression rules
           ↓
    linguistic expressions

The schema in (9) should not be interpreted as suggesting that FG makes a clear distinction between syntax and semantics. On the contrary, Dik (1989: 7) maintains that such a distinction is not possible. The underlying clause structures posited in FG are indeed essentially semantic, while matters of form and order are dealt with by expression rules. Nonetheless, Dik (1989: 46) conceives of his underlying structures as representations not only of the semantic organization of clauses but also of aspects of their formal organization.[6] Therefore, in some sense, the FG underlying structures may be viewed as semantico-syntactic ones.[7]

Under the current version of FG (Dik 1989), the underlying structure of the clause is seen to consist of several nested *layers*, *levels* or *domains* (the three terms are used more or less interchangeably) of organization which correspond to the different communicative functions that a clause fulfils (see §2.3.1). The major layers in question are:

(10)   clause   – 'speech act'
       proposition – 'possible fact'
       predication – 'state of affairs'
       predicate   – 'property/relation'
       term   – 'entity/entities'

Accordingly, the structure of the clause is built up as follows: a predicate is applied to an appropriate number of terms (referential expressions) which results in a predication designating a given state of affairs (SoA); the predication is built into a proposition designating a 'propositional content', and finally, the proposition is built into an illocutionary frame defining a given speech act. Example (11) provides a first impression of the difference between the recognized levels, details of which will be discussed in §2.3.1–§2.3.3 and in ch. 5.

(11) clause   Has Mark returned?
     proposition   Mark returned.
     predication   Mark's returning.
     predicate   return
     term   Mark

The yes/no question *Has Mark returned?* contains the questioned proposition *Mark returned* which refers to the SoA of *Mark's returning* which in turn is the result of applying the predicate *return* to the single term *Mark*.

As regards the actual form of FG structures, the theory posits no graphic representation of structure, whether by means of constituency or dependency trees, arrow-headed arcs, relational networks or the like. The underlying structure of the clause is depicted by means of a schema, inspired by predicate logic, which takes the form of a predicate frame flanked by a series of brackets and parentheses depicting various levels of structure.[8] A simplified example is shown in (12).

(12) clause: $(E_i:[(X_i:\text{etc.}\ (X_i))]\ (E_i))$
     proposition: $(X_i:[(e_i:\text{etc.}\ (e_i))]\ (X_i))$
     predication: $(e_i:[\text{pred.}_B\ (x_i)^n]\ (e_i))$
     term: $(x_i:\text{pred.}_N\ (x_i))$

The details of this schema will be elaborated upon in the relevant sections in ch. 2 and ch. 5.

1.3.3 Constraints on the rule system

FG is a mono-level theory of clause structure in the sense that it postulates no intermediate levels of representation between the predicate argument-based layered underlying semantic structure and the visible or audible surface structure which we as users of a language are privy to. The derivation of fully fledged sentences is achieved by the gradual building up of structures rather than the mapping of one structure onto the other. Thus a predicate frame which is seen to contain only the predicate and its arguments (see §2.2.1) is successively expanded by specifications of, for example, aspect, tense, manner, time, place, reason, possibility, probability, evidentiality and illocutionary force into, first, an (extended) predication, then a proposition and finally a clause. All the information required for the surface realization of the clause is incorporated in its underlying structure. Consequently, the rules that determine form, order and intonation – the expression rules – can be construed in such a way as to enable the immediate derivation of well-formed linguistic expressions.

Given the nature of FG underlying structures, there is no need for movement or reordering transformations which effect changes in pre-established structures such as those familiar from Chomskyan theory.[9] Nor are there any filtering devices that would factor out the effects of overgeneration of one rule or another, as is the case in Bresnan's (1982a) Lexical Functional Grammar (LFG).[10] Analyses involving insertions are unequivocally preferred to those requiring deletion of elements. Consequently the phenomenon of missing pronouns commonly referred to as 'pro-drop', for example, is treated as a case of pronominal insertion rather than deletion under appropriate pragmatic conditions. Also avoided is the use of abstract semantic predicates to capture underlying semantic similarities between predicates and predications, an analysis used by Dowty (1979) and adopted by Foley and Van Valin (1984) in their typology of predicates (see ch. 3).

Dik justifies the above constraints on the FG rule system on nowadays widely accepted methodological and psychological grounds. Methodologically, the allowance for transformations, filters, deletions and abstract predicates gives rein to too many potential analyses of one and the same set of data and thus contributes little to our understanding of what structures fall within the scope of 'possible human language'. Psychologically, it seems implausible that large numbers of structures are created which never see the light of day: why should the human linguistic capacity be so inefficient? Needless to say, the positing of structures which by definition we have no direct access to confounds psycholinguistic testing.

The major grammatical rules of FG fall into four types: predicate formation rules; term formation rules; assignment rules; expression rules.

The predicate and term formation rules apply in the Fund (see §2.2) to extend the set of predicate frames and terms that may serve as input to the formation of sentences. The term formation rules derive non-basic terms from predicates in accordance with a general schema to be discussed in §2.2.2. The derived terms are subsequently inserted into the argument positions of predicates. The predicate formation rules (see

§2.2.1) perform deletion, insertion, re-evaluation and permutation operations on the predicate and its arguments (sometimes also satellites). These rules correspond to Chomsky's much-discussed lexical rules, though they do not cover exactly the same range of structural relationships as those assumed to fall within the domain of lexical rules by linguists working in transformational approaches.[11] Note that the operations performed by the predicate formation rules compensate in part for the absence of transformations in FG.

The assignment rules assign syntactic and pragmatic functions to the arguments and satellites in the underlying structure. The assignment takes the form of subscripts on the constituents in question. For example, the underlying structure of the active clause in (13a) will carry the subject subscript on the Agent and the object subscript on the Goal,[12] while the corresponding passive (13b) will have a subject subscript on the Goal, as shown in (13c,d) respectively.

(13)   a.   Plato affirmed the spirituality of politics.
        b.   The spirituality of politics was affirmed by Plato.
        c.   [Past e_i [[affirm$_v$ (Plato)$_{Ag/Subj}$ (the spirituality of politics)$_{Go/Obj}$)] (e_i)]
        d.   [Past e_i [[affirm$_v$ (Plato)$_{Ag}$ (the spirituality of politics)$_{Go/Subj}$)] (e_i)]

As mentioned above, the expression rules are responsible for the form, order and intonation of the constituents of the clause. All the form-determining expression rules are taken to conform to the general schema in (14), which will be discussed in ch. 7.

(14)   Operator [Operandum] = Value

Linearization is handled by means of assigning each language a number of functional patterns such as the one in (15) or templates (see §8.1) in which constituents are positioned by a series of placement rules.

(15) P_2, P_1 SVO(X)

In both the form- and sequencing-determining expression rules rule ordering is applied. This is another feature of FG which allows the theory to dispense with transformations. An attempt is made to provide independent motivation for the imposed ordering of the particular rules, but such motivation is not always forthcoming.

1.4 THE SCOPE OF FG

Dik is careful to point out that FG is not a theory of pragmatics, but rather a theory of linguistic expressions which seeks to be compatible with a wider theory of verbal interaction. He holds the view that FG can achieve the desired pragmatic compatibility without actually describing the pragmatic rules underlying the use of language structures. This position is rather difficult to reconcile with the precepts of functionalism and is therefore not shared by all functional grammarians (cf. e.g. Nuyts 1983: 383).

I do not wish to take issue with Dik's stance, my reason for raising this problem being the desire to forewarn the reader not to expect detailed FG expositions of standard pragmatic concerns, such as speech acts, presuppositions, conversational implicature, deixis, text and discourse structure, turn-taking, etc. These issues are dealt with only so far as they bear on the different structural realizations of predications. What finally determines the use of a given structure over all the other structures, lexicalizations or non-verbal means of communication that could have been used to convey the same or similar information content does not constitute the subject matter of FG. This does not mean, however, that no attention has been devoted to the place of FG within a system of verbal interaction. On the contrary. While restricting the scope of FG, Dik has simultaneously explored the ways in which the theory can be integrated into a wider cognitive framework of an NLU system. This system is currently being developed in the form of a computational model which draws heavily on the underlying structural representations of FG, both for its knowledge representation and inference rules. In parallel a Functional Procedural Grammar (FPG) is being elaborated by several linguists in Antwerp, most notably Nuyts and De Schutter. A few words about Dik's NLU system and FPG will be given in §1.5.

Having delimited the scope of FG, what does the theory have to offer within the boundaries that it defines for itself? As mentioned earlier, I take the most significant achievement of FG to be the construction of a coherent and systematic functionally based grammar. Of the areas of grammar that FG has so far dealt with, the analyses that are, in my opinion, of greatest interest in the context of the overall body of analyses encountered in the linguistic literature concern three areas: semantic functions, linearization and predicate formation. The FG account of semantic functions extends in scope any other grammatical framework that I am familiar with. It combines the insights achieved within the Case Grammar tradition with the typology of predicates initiated by Vendler (1967). None of the formal theories can boast of an equally well-worked-out typology of semantic functions, while functionally oriented ones such as SFG (Halliday 1985) or RRG (Foley and Van Valin 1984) have not applied theirs to as wide a range of data as FG. The treatment of linearization in FG is of interest chiefly in view of the fact that it is the only functional, rule-based approach to matters of order currently available. Within the functional paradigm and in particular within typological studies, matters of order have received an enormous amount of attention. The observations made have been captured in the form of hierarchies, tendencies and principles. However, there has been no attempt to integrate these observations into a system of explicit rules. Formalists, on the other hand, have provided different types of linearization rules, even some very compact ones with a high degree of descriptive power, but these are restricted to so-called unmarked linearization patterns. FG, by contrast, seeks to cover all forms of order. As regards predicate formation, FG shows how a wide range of structures can be handled in terms of operations directly performed on semantically labelled predicate argument structure, provides a taxonomy of the predicate formation rules thus defined, and combines them under several general principles with wide explanatory potential. Again, there is no comparable treatment of lexical rules which does not rely on additional constituency, and/or dependency or categorial relations. I will have little to say about predicate formation in this book, as it is one of the topics to be dealt with in the second volume of Dik's newer version of FG. Some idea of the workings of predicate formation rules can, however, be gathered from §2.2.1.1 and various comments made in ch. 4. The two other topics, semantic functions and linearization, receive detailed treatment in separate chapters.

1.4.1 The data base

So far FG has been concerned with an idealized corpus of language data. In fact the theory has been developed mainly on the basis of isolated sentences rather than stretches of discourse, the work on Latin, Greek, biblical Hebrew and the Papua New Guinea languages Usan, Kobon and Wambon being a notable exception. Consequently, there has been no discussion of sublanguages, varieties of language, text types, differences in style or register. In this way FG differs radically from Halliday's SFG which has devoted considerable attention to the relationship between language and social context and to actual language use. Owing to the sociological orientation of SFG, Halliday admits to linguistic analysis far less idealized language data than has been the practice to date in FG. Various forms of sub- or ungrammaticality are catered for, and use is made of the features distinguishing the degrees or differences in grammaticality between different manifestations of a given language. FG, by contrast to SFG and also to Chomskyan theory, has virtually ignored ungrammatical sentences. This, Dik now admits, needs to be remedied. In Chomsky's GB, ungrammaticalities play a significant role in determining the range of structures belonging to what is referred to as the core grammar. FG makes no comparable distinction between a set of universal core structures from which each language draws and a set of language-specific peripheral structures. Ungrammatical sentences are of relevance to the theory in that they constitute a major source of information as to the fluctuating status (diachronic and across different language varieties) of various grammatical constructions within a particular language system. Another factor that has contributed to the idealized nature of the linguistic data so far considered in FG is the focus on the written language. As a result matters of intonation have up to very recently been sadly neglected. This has had repercussions, particularly for the treatment of pragmatic functions and linearization which are inherently connected with accentuation (see ch. 6 and ch. 8).

It is difficult to assess exactly how the nature of the data base on which FG has been developed has affected the basic principles and structure of the theory. There has been considerable controversy on the linguistic features characteristic of the spoken vs the written forms of language, of different text types and registers.[13] Despite this, the current opinion is that it is unlikely that any absolute differences exist between these dimensions of language use. The distinctions that can be discerned between speech and writing or various text types involve tendencies or preferences but not categorical differences. And the parameters on which these tendencies and preferences are defined are the same as those following from the idealized data handled so far in FG. In any case, the rather narrow data base of FG in regard to intra-language varieties is to a large extent compensated for by the large number and typological diversity of the languages that have been investigated by adherents of the theory.

Typology is one of the strong points of FG. The goal of typological adequacy has been pursued persistently from the very beginnings of the theory. In fact all the developments within the grammar owe much to cross-language studies. This is something that FG has in common with RG, RRG, the various forms of Case Grammar, and the research of Givón, Comrie, Keenan and others. The theory has dealt with, more or less, all of the typological ground covered by the above linguists, its treatment of states of affairs, semantic functions, the operator system and linear order, both at the level of the predication and of the term phrase, being of particular interest.

Matters of typology are inherently connected with the quest for language universals. FG has been primarily concerned with providing universally valid taxonomies and establishing universally applicable analyses based on these taxonomies, but not with statistical or implicational universals in the sense of Greenberg (1963) or Hawkins (1983). The major area which has been investigated from the point of view of implication universals is word order (Dik 1983b; Kahrel 1985b; Limburg 1985; and Rijkhoff 1986, 1990). Currently an appropriate sampling technique according to the methodology first outlined in Bell (1978) is being developed (Rijkhoff *et al.* 1990) which will enable the formulation of more reliable implicational universals.

1.5 BEYOND FG

As mentioned in §1.4, FG is part of an NLU system which is intended to be a model of communicatively adequate natural language processing. The NLU system is outlined in several publications by Dik (1987a,b, 1988a) and various aspects of its computational implementation are discussed in Connolly and Dik (1989).

FG is seen as forming the basis not only for the linguistic module of the NLU system, i.e. of the generator and parser, but also as providing the primary constructs of the knowledge representation and inference mechanism. Dik diverges from the standard view of knowledge representation as consisting of some language-independent code expressed symbolically by trees, graphs, networks or the like in postulating a linguistically based means of storing knowledge.[14] He suggests that knowledge representation is structured around the actual content words of the language used to express that knowledge. The form of the postulated structures is that of FG underlying predications which are built up from language-specific predicates, but are taken to be structured in a largely language-independent way. The language-independent characteristics of FG underlying predications (the hierarchical structure, the semantic, syntactic and pragmatic functions, and the type of operators) are what make these constructs suitable for a representation of human knowledge irrespective of the type of language used. Dik suggests that the underlying predication may also serve as the locus of logical operations, deductive, inductive and probabilistic, all of which are involved in the drawing of logical inferences from pieces of knowledge. Thus the logical form of linguistic expressions is identified with grammatical form. This is another departure from orthodoxy, the traditional view being that the relation between grammatical and logical structure is not one of identity. To signal this difference the system of rules and principles governing the inferential capacities of the NLU is termed by Dik *Functional Logic*. In all FG underlying predications are taken to fulfil the following roles within the NLU model (Dik 1987a: 18):

(i) output of a parser;
(ii) input of a generator;
(iii) instrument of lexical definition;
(iv) vehicle for conceptual knowledge representation;
(v) input and output of a Functional Logic inferencing calculus;
(vi) input and output of translation module.

Various aspects of the NLU system are being tested and perfected in several computer implementations. Actual parts of FG are being put under scrutiny in the Functional Grammar Machine, a computer implementation of FG meant as a tool to formalize and test the rule system of the grammar and its potential linguistic and non-linguistic (e.g. data-base) applications (Bakker 1989). A program for randomly generating English sentences in terms of FG has been developed by Kwee (1979, 1987) and work is in progress on a parser. Another parsing process with FG predications as input is being researched in the context of a knowledge-base project LIKE (Dignum 1989). A translation procedure from English to French via the level of the FG predication has been implemented by Van der Korst (1986). Other projects are under way within the research program of the FG-Computational Model of the Natural Language User (FG-CMNLU) embedded within the Institute for Functional Research on Language and Language Use of the Faculty of Arts of the University of Amsterdam.

A different view of the place of FG within a wider cognitive system of discourse production is advanced by the proponents of the previously mentioned Functional Procedural Grammar (FPG). FPG is still in its infancy. Nonetheless, a detailed account of the outlines of the conceptual networks determining the speaker's and addressee's universe of interpretation, of the pragmatic superstructure underlying the act of communication and of the type of procedures potentially involved in the transposition of conceptual representations into linguistic patterns can be found in Nuyts (1988, 1989) and several earlier publications. The major difference between FPG and FG in regard to matters of cognition concerns knowledge representation; as presented above, FG holds that conceptual knowledge is stored in linguistic form, while FPG argues that knowledge representation is non-linguistic. As regards the actual theoretical constructs of FG, the main modification introduced in FPG involves the role of pragmatic functions. In FG pragmatic functions are assigned just prior to the application of expression rules. Thus they have nothing to do with the choices underlying the overall organization of information in a discourse, lexicalization or syntactic function assignment. FPG, on the other hand, takes pragmatic functions to be crucial at the pre-lexical stage of the structuring of information, to have a significant effect on the choice of lexical items to be used in a predication, and to bear on matters of subject and object assignment. Support for the need to give a more pervasive role to pragmatic information in the structural organization of predications has been provided in the context of FG mainly by the work of Bolkestein (1985a,b) and the computer implementations of the Functional Grammar Machine mentioned above. Bolkestein's findings on the discourse-bound nature of sentence-level concepts such as subject and object or type of subordinate or coordinate structure (Bolkestein 1988) have, however, only been partially integrated into Dik's (1989) current exposition of FG. In this newest presentation of FG, Dik attempts to provide a closer tie between the sentence-level pragmatic functions and the role that the constituents that implement them fulfil in the wider discourse setting (see §6.3). Nonetheless, he does not allow for pragmatic function assignments at several stages of the derivation, which is what would be required to do even partial justice to the effect of pragmatic factors on sentence structure.

2 The organization of the grammar

2.1 OVERVIEW

The overall structure of FG is shown in Figure 2.1, adapted from Dik (1989: 53). Assuming a generative mode, as represented by the arrows in Figure 2.1, an underlying predication is gradually built up from the elements in the Fund, then further developed into a fully specified underlying predication by means of operators (π), satellites (δ) and functions reflecting various aspects of its communicative value and finally mapped onto linguistic expressions via a number of different types of expression rules specifying matters of form, order and prosody. By way of clarification, the terms *operator* and *satellite* are used in FG for modifications and modulations of linguistic expressions effected by grammatical (operators) and lexical (satellites) means respectively. The major steps of the derivational process presented in Figure 2.1 will be elaborated on in the course of this chapter. However, a discussion of most of the finer points will be postponed to later sections of the book which the reader will be referred to whenever necessary.

2.2 THE FUND

The Fund consists of a lexicon containing the properties of lexical items that must necessarily be learnt and memorized and two rule components generating forms derivable by synchronically productive rules. The FG stance on lexical representation is thus a version of the fairly orthodox position, best exemplified by Hooper (1976), according to which irregular and unpredictable forms are stored in the lexicon while regular and productive ones are derived by word formation rules. This contrasts with the other widely held view (e.g. Vennemann 1974; Jackendoff 1972; Aronoff 1976) which places all words in the lexicon and seeks to account for productive processes by means of redundancy rules. Since regular

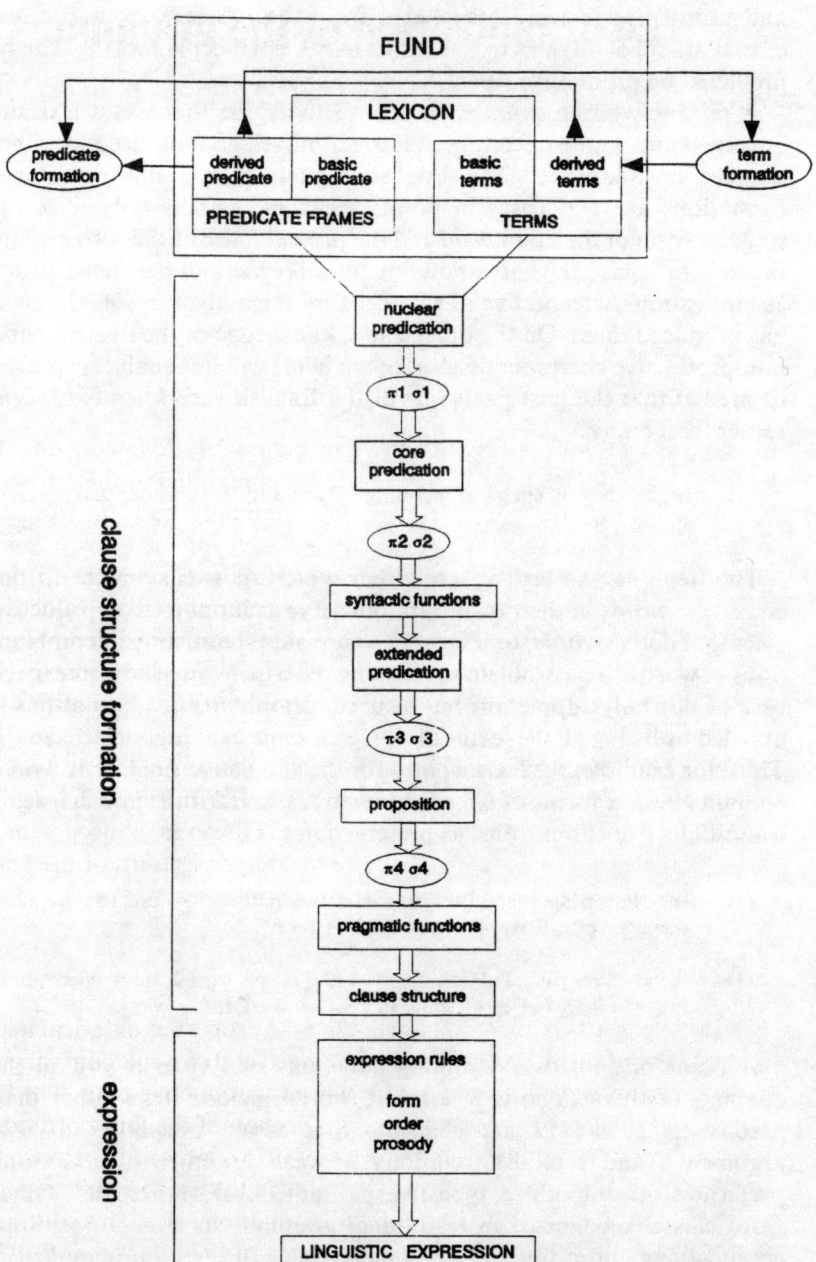

Figure 2.1 The schematic structure of FG

and productive forms are excluded from the FG lexicon, the lexical entries are rid of all inflectional and derivational morphemes that can be predicted by productive rules.

A productive rule is understood by Dik as one that is not lexically governed and whose effects, even if token-novel, go unnoticed by either speaker or addressee. The English regular plural and past tense formations are two cases in point; speakers familiar only with the singular form of the noun *bond* and the present tense of the verb *kiss* are unlikely to regard the corresponding plural *bonds* and past tense *kissed* as innovations, irrespective of whether they themselves or someone else has produced them. On the other hand, knowledge of the irregular and non-productive correspondences shown in (1) will not enable a speaker to predict that the past participle of the English verb *bring* is *brought* rather than *brung*.

(1) begin – begun; cling – clung; fling – flung; shrink – shrunk; stick – stuck; spring – sprung.

The items in the lexicon are either words or stems which do not constitute words in their own right but serve as input to the productive rules that derive words, or idiomatic expressions consisting of combinations of words.[1] The problem of selecting the base form of a lexeme in the case of not only suppletion but also morphophonemic alternations is avoided by listing all the forms of a given lexeme in a single lexical entry. Thus, for example, the lexical entry for the suppletive English *be* would contain all the x forms of *be*, as shown in (2), and for the Polish lexeme *wieść* all its five allomorphs, as presented in (3):

(2) {be-, Pres p1sg = am, Pres p3sg = is, Pres p2/Pres pl = are, Past p1/p3 = was, Past p2sg/Past pl = were, PaP = been}$_v$.

(3) {wiod-, Pres p1sg, PaP f, nmp = wiod, Pres p2,3sg,1,2,3pl = wiedz, Imp, PrP = wiedz, PaP m = wiód, PaP mp = wied, Inf = wieś}.

A point of controversy among adherents of FG in regard to the contents of the lexicon is whether it should include items other than predicates. *Predicates* are elements that assign properties to sole arguments, and establish relations between arguments. In FG all predicates fall into three types: verbal, adjectival or nominal. Other word classes recognized in traditional grammar such as adpositions, conjunctions, subordinators, demonstratives, articles, etc. are treated as the expression of operators (the first three as a subclass called relators) more or less on a par with typical inflectional categories such as tense, aspect, mood, case, gender, number and so forth. Dik holds the view that the form of operators is determined by the expression rules and that therefore they need not be listed in the lexicon. The alternative solution would be to allow the expression rules to select the appropriate form of an operator from a special, separate part of the lexicon. Given the different morpho-syntactic status of the class of operators, some being words and some inflectional morphemes displaying various degrees of fusion with the stem and with each other, neither of these scenarios is entirely satisfactory. Dik's approach is more compatible with the claim that bound morphemes are not learnt independently of the lexemes with which they co-occur, but denies ready access to operators or combinations of operators which have the status of words. Conversely, the alternative view provides a natural solution to the problem of the accessibility of both free and bound forms but makes false claims in regard to matters of learnability.

A lexicon of predicates entails not only the absence of inflectional affixes but also no listing of derivational ones. Derivational affixes that take part in synchronically productive processes are introduced in the predicate formation component as the output of specific predicate formation rules. These affixes can be accessed via comparing the input and the output of the relevant rules. Derivations that are irregular or unpredictable in form or meaning are simply listed as separate lexemes in the lexicon.

2.2.1 Predicates and predicate frames

FG shares with many other grammatical models, both functional and formal, the idea that clause structure is largely predictable from the semantics of predicates. Predicates are taken to define structures called *predicate frames* which specify the number and nature of arguments required by a given predicate. These predicate frames are like the subcategorization frames of Chomskyan generative theory and its offshoots, with the arguments corresponding to the subcategorized complements.[2] In formal theories, however, the structures defined by predicates are mapped onto theory-specific initial syntactic structures, be they constituency (GB, LFG, HPSG), dependency (Hudson's Word Grammar and Anderson's or Starosta's Case Grammar) or relational (RG) ones. Whereas in FG, as mentioned in §1.3.3, there are no configurational representations of utterances whatsoever. The predicate/argument structure specified in the predicate frame is the underlying structure; the initial structure is essentially a semantically based one. The arguments are characterized solely in terms of their semantic function and not according to categorial status, as in GB or HPSG, or syntactic function, as in LFG for instance. As an example of a predicate frame consider (4).[3]

(4)   give$_v$ (x$_1$: <anim> (x$_1$))$_{Ag}$ (x$_2$)$_{Go}$ (x$_3$: <anim> (x$_3$))$_{Rec}$

The most important information contained in the predicate frame is:

a) the form or forms (all the allomorphs) of the predicate presented in standard phonological notation with specifications of tone and characteristic accent position;
b) the category of the predicate (verbal, adjectival or nominal);
c) the argument positions associated with the predicate,[4] represented by variables: x$_1$, x$_2$, x$_3$ ... x$_n$;
d) the semantic functions of the arguments;
e) the imposed selectional restrictions;
f) the meaning postulates.

The first three points are self-explanatory. Semantic functions will be discussed in ch. 3.

As regards selectional restrictions, their presence in the predicate frame entails that Dik considers the syntagmatic relations between lexemes (collocations) to be the product of the semantics of the relevant lexemes rather than a reflection of knowledge of the world, as argued most recently by, among others, Johnson-Laird (1981: 115), Allan (1986: 293-306) and Nuyts (1988: 78). The FG conception of selectional restrictions differs, however, from the standard view in that their violation is not automatically equated with anomaly. In other words the selectional restrictions do not prohibit the insertion of terms with features other than those specified in the predicate frame; they only identify the features most compatible with the semantics of the predicate (such as those in the quote from McCawley on p. 25). Since the FG selectional restrictions are not charged with the task of separating out well-formed utterances from anomalous ones, they are not vulnerable to the major criticism that has been levelled at selectional restrictions, namely that the determination of the full set of selectional restrictions would involve the impracticable or even impossible task of testing every conceivable combination of lexemes in every conceivable context (within certain grammatical constraints).

Dik's basic motivation for making use of selectional restrictions is the desire to provide an account of the strategies involved in the understanding of metaphorical extensions. The assumption is that non-compliance with the selectional restrictions of a predicate triggers reinterpretation procedures which lead to metaphorical interpretations, the limits of which are presumably determined by the ingenuity of the speaker or addressee. Needless to say, before the relaxing of selectional restrictions can be treated as the source of certain metaphorical uses of language (or of anomaly) it is first necessary to determine what selectional restrictions a particular language manifests. Though of a practical rather than a theoretical nature, this is a problem that FG has not yet addressed. Attention was drawn to this issue over twenty years ago by McCawley (1968a,b), who demonstrated that in order to express the full range of selectional restrictions to be found in a language such as English an enormous range of features would be needed. By way of illustration, I quote McCawley (1968b: 134): 'the verb *diagonalize* requires as its object a noun phrase denoting a matrix (in the mathematical sense), the adjective *benign* in the sense "non-cancerous" requires a subject denoting a tumour, and the verb *devein* as used in cookery requires an object denoting a shrimp or a prawn.'

Turning now to the meaning or rather the sense[5] of the predicate, FG denies the need or even the possibility of providing a semantic definition for all predicates. Dik suggests that in the case of many a basic predicate all that can be achieved is a specification of some aspect of its sense. This is accomplished via a set of asymmetric implicational statements, termed *meaning postulates* by Carnap (1956), which characterize the sense (or part of the sense) of a predicate by relating it to one or more other predicates. As an example of a meaning postulate consider (5a).

(5) a. (x) (bachelor x → not married x)

This gives us some idea of the sense of the predicate *bachelor*[6] by relating this predicate to the predicate *married*. The meaning postulate which may be read as 'Every x who is a bachelor is not married' allows the inference in (5b), 'if x is a bachelor he is not married'.

(5) b. bachelor (x) → not married (x)

The converse inference, however, does not hold; an unmarried person is not necessarily a bachelor; if female, the person could be a spinster, or if a boy too young for matrimony, he would normally not be referred to as a bachelor. Since meaning postulates are asymmetric semantic implications, they do not amount to semantic definitions. To arrive at a meaning definition a unidirectional inference has to be converted into a bidirectional one, i.e. the defining predicates have to be such that they constitute a paraphrase of the defined predicate. In the case of *bachelor* all that is required is the addition of the predicate *man*, since a bachelor is an unmarried man.

(6) bachelor (x) ↔ unmarried man (x)

The symmetric implication in (6) is symbolized by the double-headed arrow. Dik refers to this type of meaning analysis – where the sense of a predicate is characterized in terms of the senses of other predicates whose senses in turn may be specifiable by yet other predicates – as *stepwise lexical definition*.

It is important to note that in FG the predicates used in the meaning postulates, semantic definitions and also selectional restrictions are predicates of the object language rather than special predicates of a metalanguage (Dik 1978). The use of the object language as a semantic metalanguage has several advantages, chief among them being the avoidance of the vicious circularity that results from defining (or characterizing) an object language expression by means of an identical metalanguage expression; for instance, defining *open* as 'open' rather than as 'not shut' (see Allan 1986: 269). The second major advantage of making use of the object language in the semantic representation of language expressions is that it is possible to exploit the rich resources of synonyms available in most languages, thereby, returning to the previous example, defining *open* as 'not shut' and potentially *shut* as 'not open', just as in a traditional dictionary.

Another important feature of the FG semantic predicates is that they are not confined to semantically simplex ones. Observe that both *unmarried* and *man* in (6) are complex predicates which may be defined as 'not having a spouse' and as 'an adult male person' respectively. Since most language expressions are not semantically primitive, it would be difficult to conceive of a stepwise lexical definition without allowing such complex predicates in meaning definitions or meaning postulates.

The second prerequisite for the success of stepwise lexical definitions is the recognition of the existence of predicates which cannot be provided with a definition themselves. It is to these predicates that the semantic definitions will ultimately lead, thus avoiding the otherwise inevitable circularity of the system. The positing of undefinable predicates is the major difference between the FG lexical analysis and other approaches. As shown above, such predicates receive a partial specification of their sense via meaning postulates. Dik suggests that there may also be predicates that will even have to be characterized ostensively, through pictures, as in standard dictionaries.

The arguments of the predicate frame are unordered, though by convention with a verb such as *give* the Agent is referred to as the first argument, the Goal as the second argument, and the Recipient as the third argument. We will see in §4.5 that this conventional order corresponds to the ordering of functions on the semantic function hierarchy (SFH). The fact that FG does not impose a linear order on the constituents of the predicate frame is seen by Dik to be a major advantage of the theory, since this permits languages displaying quite diverse linearization patterns to be analysed in terms of the same format of predicate frames. This and other benefits of the lack of an underlying order such as reducing or even dispensing with the need for reordering and movement rules are nowadays generally acknowledged within linguistic theory.[7]

Predicate frames may be basic or derived. *Basic predicate frames* are such that must be learned and memorized, while *derived* ones can be construed by synchronically productive processes of predicate formation. The two types of predicate frames, basic and derived, are together called *nuclear predicate frames*.

Predicate frames express the morpho-phonemic form and semantic and syntactic characteristics of concrete predicates. To capture generalizations across different predicates, structures called *predicate schemata* have been introduced (Junger 1987). Predicate schemata contain the same information as predicate frames, but pertaining to some, more or less narrowly defined class of predicates. They thus enable the capturing of derivational relationships whenever the exact form of the predicate is not at issue.

2.2.1.1 Predicate formation

The process of predicate formation takes a predicate frame as input and delivers a predicate frame as output (Dik 1980: ch. 2 and ch. 3, 1985, 1988b).[8] Though previously formulated exclusively in regard to predicate frames, currently predicate formation also includes operations on predicate schemata; either the input or the output or both may have the form of a predicate schema. Another more significant innovation is the extension of the domain of predicate formation rules from operations on arguments to certain satellites (Dik *et al.* 1990). Predicate formation may be applied recursively, i.e. the output of one predicate formation rule may constitute the input to some other predicate formation rule. In other words, both basic and derived predicate frames may form the input to predicate formation. Actual predicate formation rules may, however, be sensitive to the basic vs derived status of the input predicate frame. For example, De Groot (1989: 164) observes that in Hungarian it is possible to form intransitive verbal predicates from basic adjectival predicates such as *meleg* 'warm' or *szèp* 'pretty', but not from derived ones such as *tartós* 'durable'.

Any feature of the input predicate frame may be affected by predicate formation. De Groot (1989: 137), who provides an insightful account of predicate formation rules in Hungarian, lists the following as the major effects of predicate formation:

(7) (i) effects on the quantitative (number of arguments) valency of the predicate:
   - valency extension
   - valency reduction;
  (ii) effects on the state of affairs (SoA) the predicate designates;
  (iii) other effects on the input predicate frame:
   - semantic function shift of the arguments of the predicate (qualitative valency change)
   - semantic modification of the predicate
   - change in the syntactic category of the predicate.

To give a concrete example, the valency-reducing predicate formation rule in (9), adapted from Kahrel (1985a: 13), captures the relationship between the transitive clause (8a) and its inchoative counterpart in (8b).

(8) a. John broke the watch.
     b. The watch broke.

(9) Inchoative formation
     input: $pred_v (x_1)_{Ag} (x_2)_{Go}$
     output: $pred_v (x_2)_{Proc}$

The predicate formation rule in (9) suppresses the underlying Agent (quantitative reduction) and simultaneously transforms an activity predication into a process one (see §3.2). As a result of this change the underlying Goal argument is shifted to the position of first argument and undergoes semantic modification (qualitative valency change) from a Goal into a Processed argument.

Valency extension can be illustrated on the basis of the general schema for causative formation presented in (10) which relates pairs of clauses such as those in (11).

(10) Causative formation
     input: $pred_v (x_1) \ldots (x_n) [n > 1]$
     output: $pred_{v\text{-}C} (x_0) Causer (x_1) Causee \ldots (x_n)$
     meaning: x_0 brings it about that x_1 $pred_{vs} \ldots (x_n)$

Turkish (Comrie 1981: 169)
(11) a. Müdür   mektub-u   imzala-di
         director letter-acc sign-past
         'The director signed the letter.'

   b. Dişçi   mektub-u   müdür-e   imzala-t-ti
       dentist letter-acc director-dat sign-caus-past
       'The dentist got the director to sign the letter.'

The rule of causative formation introduces an extra argument (x_o) representing the Causer, adds to the first argument (x_1) the semantic function Causee, in addition to its original semantic function, and marks the verb as causative. The formal expression of these innovations is language specific. In Turkish the verbal marking is in the form of a causative suffix, the causer is in the nominative, and the causee (in underlying transitive clauses) takes dative marking. Dik (1985, 1988b) offers two general principles presented in (12) and (13) which specify the type of both formal and semantic readjustments that tend to occur cross-linguistically in various predicate formation processes.

(12) Principle of formal adjustment (PFA)
Derived constructions of type T tend to mould their expression after the typical expression model of non-derived constructions of type T.

(13) Principle of semantic adjustment (PSA)
To the extent that PFA is yielded to, the derived construction will also tend to adjust to the semantics of the non-derived constructions of type T.

In line with the PFA, the dative marking of the Causee in (11b) is the product of the adoption of the expression model for trivalent predicates such as *give* (see (4)). The above two principles have been shown to have considerable explanatory power with respect not only to causative formation, but also to various reflexive constructions (Dik 1983c) and nominalizations (Dik 1985).

It must be noted that the structural changes induced by predicate formation rules do not extend to the type of changes that can be achieved by Chomsky's current 'move α' transformation. Thus the predicate formation rules cannot, for example, be employed to relate pairs of predications (simple or complex) differing only in terms of displacement as found with relative, interrogative, comparative or topicalized clauses illustrated in (14) (where --- marks the source of the alleged displacement).

(14) a. John I don't like ---.
     b. A book --- has just appeared about FG.

c. This girl, I told Mark that John should meet ---.
d. What did you expect Mary to be pleased by ---?
e. What do you think the army believes the president is going to do ---?

I mention this in view of the fact that in Head-Driven Phrase Structure Grammar (HPSG),[9] the lexical rules apparently can perform such operations (Sag 1987: 317). Clauses related by such displacement phenomena are dealt with in FG with reference to syntactic and pragmatic function assignment applied to predications built on one predicate frame, or in some cases on two, not directly related, predicate frames. I will not be dealing with complex predications or displacement phenomena in this book. For further information I refer the reader to Bolkestein *et al.* (1981).

A recent innovation in the FG approach to predicate formation (Dik *et al.* 1990) is the extension of the scope of predicate formation from operations solely on arguments to certain δ_1 (see §2.3.2) satellites. Most of the operations in question involve incorporation of satellites into the predicate or 'acquisition' of argument status on the part of the satellite. This latter situation may be seen to underlie, for example, the ability of certain prepositional objects to function as passive subjects in English. Given contrasts such as the ones below, the prepositional object in (15a,b) could be regarded as an argument, the one in (15c,d) as a satellite.

(15) a. The participants arrived *at the following conclusion*.
b. *The following conclusion* was arrived at by the participants.
c. The tourists arrived at the town.
d. *The town was arrived at by the tourists.

An analysis along these lines is inherent in Chomsky's (1965) readjustment rule and the advancement to object account proposed in RG. The FG equivalent could take the form of a predicate formation rule involving absorption of the prepositional object into the predicate frame of the relevant predicate.[10] The derived predicate frame would then constitute the basis for the derivation of the passive via subject assignment (see §4.3).

It is not yet clear whether the range of effects of predicate formation rules on satellites should be the same as the ones for arguments stated in (7).[11] Another issue which needs to be addressed in connection with the extension of the domain of predicate formation rules is the formal status of the input and output of the rules. Note that satellites are by definition not included within predicate frames. Consequently either the domain of predicate frames has to be extended or the predicate formation rules must be allowed to operate also outside the Fund on core predications (see §2.3.3).

2.2.2 Terms and term formation

A *term* in FG is an expression with a referential potential in some world. Dik suggests that functionally speaking terms can be viewed as instructions from the speaker to the addressee aimed at facilitating the latter's identification of the entity about which certain future things will be predicated.

The entities referred to by terms are divided along the lines proposed by Bunt (1985) into three basic types: ensembles, sets and masses. According to Bunt, an ensemble may be partitioned into 'parts' which correspond to subsets of sets; but they do not have constituents which correspond to members of sets. Thus Dik (1987d) takes ensembles to be neutral in regard to the set/mass distinction. Sets are composed of discrete individuals, i.e. members, while masses are perceived as an undifferentiated unity and thus consist of parts which have measures. Individuals are treated as singleton sets. The distinction between individuals, sets and masses is illustrated in (16) below.

(16) a. There is a lamb in the field. (individual)
b. There are three lambs in the field. (set)
c. We're having lamb for dinner. (mass)

As for ensembles, Dik (1987d, 1989: 143) suggests that such is the status of nouns, like those underlined in the Thai examples in (17), that take sortal classifiers (Lyons 1977: 463) which individuate an entity according to 'unit type' in classifier languages.

Thai (Allan 1977: 286)
(17) a. *khru* lâ j khon
'teacher three person' = 'three teachers'
b. *ma* sì tua.
'dog four body' = 'four dogs'

The relevant nouns when used without an accompanying classifier carry no suggestion of individuation or number. Yet they differ from mass nouns in not occurring with classifier expressions specifying measure (mensural classifiers). Dik therefore argues that they cannot be simply considered as mass nouns, but rather as ensemble nouns whose referents are unspecified in terms of individuation and quantification.

In addition to the taxonomy of entities, terms are divided into basic and derived. The *basic* terms, listed in the lexicon, are restricted in number, being confined to personal pronouns and proper names. The vast majority of terms are therefore *derived* via term formation. The general format of derived terms is:

(18) $(\Omega x_i : \phi_1(x_i) : \phi_2(x_i) : \ldots : \phi_n(x_i))$.

Here x_i stands for the intended referent of the term; Ω indicates one or more term operators (e.g. number, definiteness, quantification); each $\phi(x_i)$ is an open predication in x_i (a predicate frame in which all the term positions but that of x_i have been filled with terms); ϕ is a predicate (nominal, adjectival or verbal) called a *restrictor*; the colon is to be read as 'such that'. The colon indicates that the set of potential referents of x_i is restricted by the nature of the information contained in the open predication $X(x_i)$. The presence of more than one $X(x_i)$ allows for recursion and thus for the progressive narrowing down of the set of the potential referents of the term.[12] To take a concrete example, the term *the girl who kissed the silly man* has the structure in (19).

(19) (d1 x_i: girl$_N$ (x_i): kiss$_v$ (x_i)$_{Ag}$ (d1 x_j: man$_N$ (x_j): silly (x_j)$_{Go}$).

It is important to note that restrictors are 'stacked' onto each other, as indicated by the symbol ':', not as in the analysis traditionally adopted in logic conjoined with each other.

Any predicate or predication, irrespective of its complexity, may be used as a restrictor, as long as one of the term positions is left free for the term variable x_i. Witness the italicized complex term in (20), for example.

(20) Last week I saw *a film that had been recommended to me by the wife of the man who had promoted the actor who played the part of a director who makes a film about his own career that ends up exposing him as a fraud.*

The eligibility of an open predication for restrictor status in a given term structure is subject to two constraints, namely those of predicability and expressibility. Predicability refers to whether or not the property specified by the restrictor can be meaningfully assigned to the entity in question. It is determined by the nature of the head noun and the already applied restrictors. Compare, for example, *pregnant man* with *pregnant professor*, on the one hand, and *pregnant male professor*, on the other.[13] By expressibility is meant the structural well-formedness of the particular restrictor and head combination. This is by and large a language-specific matter. In English, for instance, it is not always possible to 'extract' a PP qualifying an object NP. Compare the examples in (21).

(21) a. What does Fred collect pictures of?
 b. Which doors do you have the key to?
 c. *Who did Bob destroy a book about?
 d. *Which country did you meet a refugee from?

Consequently, a relative clause built on a PP such as that in (21) cannot be used as a restrictor, as evinced by the ungrammaticality of (22).

(22) *John met a man who Bob destroyed a book about.

Within terms restrictors may function either as *heads* or as *modifiers*. The head is not explicitly identified in the underlying structure, the convention being that the first restrictor will become the head. The modifiers may take the form of nominal, adjectival and participial phrases and relative clauses depending on the properties of the restrictors that implement them in the underlying term structure.

Following Lyons (1977: 442–447), the internal complexity of terms is seen to correlate partially with the ontological classification of the type of entities they refer to, i.e. with whether they implement first-, second-, third- or also fourth- (not as such distinguished in Lyons) order entities. First-order entities are taken to be entities that exist in the physical world, i.e. physical objects or individuals; second-order entities are those located in time rather than space and are spoken of as 'occurring' rather than 'existing'; third-order entities refer to propositions which are outside both space and time, and fourth-order entities are the acts via which propositions are implemented. This distinction of 'different order' of entities plays a key role in the current model of FG and will be elaborated in greater detail in §2.3.1. The structural realizations of terms manifesting different order entities will be discussed in connection with the FG typology of clausal complements in §5.3.1.

Turning to term operators, these are grammatical elements which take the form of determiners, quantifiers and inflections. Rijkhoff (1989b) suggests that the operators within terms[14] may be divided into three groups: quality, quantity and location operators. To the quality term operators belong the sortal classifiers co-occurring with ensemble nouns, mentioned on p. 31. The presence of such classifiers is obligatory if the relevant noun is to be used in a term phrase containing a cardinal numeral, as in (17b) above. Therefore the classifier is taken to effect a change in the quality of the given noun, converting an undifferentiated ensemble noun into a discrete entity permitting countability. The quantity operators embrace the various non-lexical means of indicating size (cardinality and measure) in the term phrase. Such operators take the form of number inflections or quantifiers, the latter including all sorts of numerals. The treatment of quantifiers as term operators rather than predication-level ones in FG constitutes a radical departure from traditional analysis.[15] The last group of term operators covers markers of definiteness and indefiniteness. Rijkhoff's use of the term *locational* to describe such operators is motivated by the fact that matters of identifiability which underlie the definite/indefinite distinction (see §6.3.1) centre on whether or not a given entity can be located at a particular space and time region (Rijkhoff 1989a).[16]

The three types of term operators are taken to differ not only semantically, but also with respect to matters of scope. Since quality operators refer to the essential characteristics of an entity, Rijkhoff takes the scope of such operators to be confined to the lexical head. Quantity operators in turn are seen to have scope over a simple term, i.e. the intended referent x_1 proper without additional embeddings of possessor phrases or restrictive relative clauses. That quantity marking of the simple term is independent of the marking of the embedded term and vice versa is evidenced by the different number-marking possibilities illustrated in examples such as the following:

(23) a. the child in front of the house   (sg-sg)
      b. the children in front of the house   (pl-sg)
      c. the child in front of the houses   (sg-pl)
      d. the children in front of the houses (pl-pl).

Locational operators are considered to have scope over the whole complex term. This can be appreciated on the basis of the fact that an embedded term may provide the motivation for the definiteness marking of the complex term. Consider the examples in (24).

(24) a. #We went to the bar.   (What bar?)
      b. We went to the bar next to my house.   (#What bar?)

Rijkhoff (1989a) argues that the definiteness marking of *the bar* in (24b) as compared to (24a) does not depend on whether or not the hearer knows *the bar*, but rather on the hearer's ability to identify the speaker's *house*. Thus the location of the intended referent *the bar* can be inferred on the basis of its semantic relation to the identifiable entity in the embedded term.

Rijkhoff (1989b: 24) contends that the above typology of term operators and in particular the different scope relations that they exert define several additional layers of structural organization not expressed in the structure of terms presented earlier in (19). On the basis of his typology of term operators he proposes the complex structure of the term phrase shown in (25), where the 'boxes' denote scope boundaries and Ω_1, Ω_2 and Ω_3 stand for quality, quantity and location operators respectively.

(25) $(\Omega_3 \mid \Omega_2 \mid x_i : \mid \Omega_1 \phi_1 \mid (x_i): \phi_2(x_i): \ldots : \phi_n(x_i)))$

The order of the elements in the underlying structure of the term is taken to reflect the existing semantic dependencies, but not necessarily surface linear order. The scope boundaries defined by the three different types of term operators, however, are claimed by Rijkhoff to correspond to the surface order of actual linguistic expressions in mirror-like fashion with respect to the head, e.g. *abcHcba*. We will see in ch. 5 that the same claim is made in regard to the relative ordering of operators at the level of the clause. This issue will be resumed briefly again in §7.5.

As a final comment on the nature of terms in FG, it needs to be noted that any term can be turned into a one-place predicate over another term. This is achieved via a process called *term-predicate formation*, illustrated schematically in (26).

(26) Term-predicate formation
      input: any term (t)
      output: {(t)} (x_1)

Term-Predicate-Formation supplemented with a special rule of 'copula support' (Dik 1980: 94f, 1989: 166) accounts for the predicative use of terms, as shown in (27) for instance.

(27) a. John is a perpetual adolescent.
      b. That's the official who helped me get the passport on time.
      c. Sue is a woman with a purpose in life.

The FG treatment of non-verbal predicates will not be discussed in this book. The reader is referred to Dik (1980, 1983a, 1989) and Hengeveld (1990a,b).

2.3 FROM NUCLEAR TO FULLY SPECIFIED PREDICATIONS

A nuclear predication is formed by the insertion of terms into the argument slots of a nuclear predicate frame. In order to have a better understanding of the steps leading from such a nuclear predication to a fully specified one, let us first briefly consider the overall conception of clause structure adopted in FG.

2.3.1 The underlying structure of the clause

Inherent in the functional approach to language is the recognition of several layers of the structural organization of the clause corresponding to the multiple functions that the clause fulfils in the act of communication. In the Halliday (1967/68, 1970) tradition the clause is viewed in relation to what are taken to be the three macro-functions of language: the ideational, dealing with matters of propositional content; the interpersonal, concerned with the interaction between speaker and addressee; and the textual, involving the structuring of information in discourse. Accordingly, the clause is seen as a representation of processes (patterns of experience), an exchange (of information or goods and services) between speaker and addressee, and an organized message. This overall conception of clause structure is also adhered to in FG though expressed in different terms and enriched by subdivisions of the representational and interpersonal layers.

In the earliest versions of FG as presented in Dik (1978, 1980) little attention was given to other than the representational structure of the clause, which was identified with the predication. Subsequently (De Jong 1981; Moutaouakil 1984) an attempt was made to relate explicitly the predication to its function as a communicative act between speaker and addressee by including the illocutionary force of utterances, in the sense of Searle (1969), in the underlying clause structure; a clause was taken to consist of an illocution represented as an illocutionary operator and a predication. Increased interest in the interpersonal features of the clause and in particular the desire to provide a satisfactory treatment of modality led to the recognition of an additional propositional level of structural organization.

Currently (Hengeveld 1989; Dik 1989; Rijkhoff 1989b, Nuyts *et al.* 1990) the utterance is analysed as a multi-layered structure with the levels shown in (28).[17]

(28)	level	structural unit	type of entity	variable
	4	clause	speech act	$E_i, E_j \ldots$
	3	proposition	possible fact	$X_i, X_j \ldots$
	2	predication	state of affairs	$e_i, e_j \ldots$
	1	predicate	property or relation	$f_i, f_j \ldots$
		applied to terms	entity/entities	$x_i, x_j \ldots$

Dik conceives of this hierarchical structure as correlating closely with the previously mentioned (§2.2.2) distinction of 'different order' of entities drawn by Lyons (1977: 442–445). First-order entities are taken to correspond to level 1, second-order entities to level 2, and third-order entities to level 3, with entities of the fourth order as an FG innovation.

The structures at levels 1 and 2 are associated with the representational function of the predication, while those at levels 3 and 4 are connected with its interpersonal properties. Matters of information structure (the textual function) are considered at level 4, but with reference to different descriptive categories, in conjunction with the distribution of pragmatic functions across the whole clause.

In FG the representational function of the predication is characterized in terms of the notion 'state-of-affairs' (henceforth SoA), this being defined as a state or event, or more precisely as 'the conception of something that can be said (to occur, take place or obtain) in some world'. A predication is seen as designating a particular type of SoA, i.e. an action, process, position or state; but crucially it cannot in itself refer to a specific SoA, to an actual event, until it is provided with a spatio-temporal reference point in the act of utterance. In its interpersonal function the predication takes the form of a proposition. It becomes something that can be affirmed or denied, doubted, contradicted, agreed to, disagreed with, insisted on, accepted, rejected, qualified, regretted, remembered and so forth. Propositions as expressions of belief (knowledge or thought) designate not SoAs but possible facts. The interpersonal function of the predication is not, however, confined to the expression of propositional content. In the wake of the pioneering research of Austin (1962) and Searle (1969), it is nowadays generally acknowledged that in every utterance the speaker performs an act such as stating a fact, asking a question, issuing an order or a warning, making an offer or a promise, giving advice or permission and so on. The clause is therefore seen as designating a speech act.

The variables corresponding to each of the levels distinguished in (28) provide the means of both identifying and distinguishing the different types of entities designated at that level of clause structure. Thus, for example, anaphoric reference can be made to each of the proposed levels via the appropriate variable, as exemplified in (29)–(32) below, where A stands for an anaphora.

(29) a. Allegedly, there is a region of The Netherlands that is quite hilly.
    b. Yes, *it* is called Limburg.   (Ax_i)

(30) a. I've finally managed to sell my car.
    b. *That's* good.   (Ae_i)

(31) a. Your friend is an extremely good liar.
    b. Yes, *that's* true, I'm afraid.   (AX_i)

(32) a. Can I see you for a moment?
    b. Is *that* a request or an order?   (AE_i)

In (29b) reference is made to a term designating a first-order entity, a particular individual. In (30b) the anaphor is to the whole SoA of *my selling the car*, a second-order entity. Example (31b) refers to the truth value of the propositional content (a third-order entity) expressed in (31a) rather than to the SoA, and (32b) is anaphoric to the preceding speech act (a fourth-order entity). The use of the above variables in distinguishing different types of complements will be illustrated in §5.3.1.

Though this is not shown in (28), as mentioned in §2.2.2, the entities referred to by terms may also be of different orders. The proposed layered model of the clause thus extends into term structure. This holds not only for complex terms but also, as in Lyons (1977: 446), for those based on simple noun predicates. For example *Cindy* and *table* are seen to designate first-order entities, *mistake* and *visit* second-order entities, *idea* and *fact* third-order entities, and *order* and *question* fourth-order ones.

2.3.2 Operators and satellites

Essential to the building up of a fully specified predication is the semantic contribution of operators and satellites. Each of the recognized levels of clause structure is taken to have its own operators and satellites. In fact it was the behaviour of operators and satellites, more specifically the evident differences in the type of semantic contributions effected by different operators and satellites, that provided the initial motivation for developing the multi-layered model of the clause.

Level-1 (predicate) operators and satellites are characterized as specifying additional internal properties of the SoA designated by the nuclear predication (consisting solely of a predicate and its arguments). In the case of predicate operators the relevant properties are the internal temporal organization of the SoA as reflected in, for example, the imperfective/perfective distinction and predicate negation. The satellites are those of manner, speed and instrument.

Level-2 (predication) operators and satellites are seen to define the spatial, temporal and cognitive location of an SoA in a real or imaginary world without affecting the properties of the SoA itself. The distinctions captured by predication operators include tense (both absolute and relative, as defined in Comrie 1985), what Dik (1989: 204) calls *quantificational* aspect, i.e. semelfactive and iterative aspectual categories specifying the frequency of an SoA, objective modality expressing the likelihood or degree of obligation of a particular SoA, and finally polarity of the actual/non-actual type. Most of these distinctions can be rendered lexically by the appropriate satellites of time (e.g. *yesterday*), place (e.g. *in Australia*), frequency (e.g. *often*), probability (e.g. *probably*), etc.

Level-3 (proposition) operators and satellites are claimed to reflect the speaker's evaluation of and attitude towards the content of the expressed proposition. The term *epistemological* modality is sometimes used in this context. The modifications in question concern the extent to which the speaker is committed to the truth of the expressed proposition (*subjective* modality), and specifications of the source of the proposition and circumstances under which knowledge of it was acquired (*evidentials*).

Level-4 (illocutionary) operators and satellites are considered to modify the force of the basic illocution of the utterance. As mentioned on p. 36, in Dik's (1989), as compared to Hengeveld's (1989), exposition of the layered model of the clause the illocutionary operators also provide the basic illocution. The most common modifications effected by illocutionary operators are *mitigation* and *reinforcement*. The satellites may be used in a similar way, but also to provide other clues relating to how speakers would like their speech acts to be interpreted by their addressees. Greenbaum's (1969) 'style disjuncts' are included in this category.

2.3.3 The derivation

A *nuclear predication* which is arrived at by the insertion of terms into the argument slots of nuclear predicate frames is extended by predicate operators and level-1 satellites into a *core predication*:

nuclear predication = pred $(arg)^n$
core predication = π_1 pred $(arg)^n (\delta_1)^n$.

A core predication provided with an SoA variable e_i and supplemented with predication operators and level-2 satellites is transformed into an *extended predication*:

extended predication = $\pi_2\ e_i$: [[core predication] $(\delta_2)^n$] (e_i).

At the level of the extended predication the syntactic functions of subject and object are assigned to terms (for details, see ch. 4). Thus, unlike in Halliday's (1985: 32–37) SFG, in which the subject is treated as part of the interpersonal structure, the FG subject belongs to the representational organization of the clause. In accordance with the spatio-temporal character of level-2 categories (see §2.3.2), subject and object assignment is not considered to affect the internal structure of the

SoA, but only the camera angle from which it is presented. The subject is seen to define a primary, and the object a secondary, perspective for the interpretation of the SoA designated by the predication.

The extended predication is built into a *proposition* which when modified by level-3 operators and satellites results in an *extended proposition*:

proposition = X_i : [extended predication] (X_i)
ext. proposition = $\pi_3 X_i$: [[extended predication] $(\delta_3)^n$] (X_i).

This structure, in turn, is built into a *clausal* structure which may be elaborated into an *extended clause* structure by means of level-4 operators and satellites:

clause = E_i: [extended proposition] (E_i)
extended clause = E_i: [π_4 Ill [extended proposition] $(\delta_4)^n$] (E_i).

The final stage of this derivational process is the assigning of pragmatic functions to the elements of the clause in accordance with their informational status relative to the speaker's evaluation of the pragmatic information of his addressee. Since communication by definition involves effecting changes in the pragmatic information between speaker and addressee, the assignment of pragmatic functions, in contrast to syntactic function assignment, is obligatory. The pragmatic functions recognized in FG centre on the notions of topicality and focality, understood more or less in the traditional way; the topic is what the utterance is primarily about; by focus is meant the most salient information between speaker and addressee, as perceived by the speaker. Any element of the clause may bear focus, but topic functions are assigned only to terms.

To get a better idea of the above-outlined derivational process, consider the derivation of the utterance in (33). For purposes of exposition the structure of the terms will be ignored.

(33) In case you haven't heard, Marilyn allegedly gave the letter to Rob surreptitiously during the staff meeting.

The nuclear predication underlying (33) is built on the predicate *give* which has the predicate frame in (4), repeated here as (34):

(34) $give_v (x_1: <anim> (x_1))_{Ag} (x_2)_{Go} (x_3: <anim> (x_3))_{Rec}$.

After inserting terms into the argument slots in (34) we arrive at the nuclear predication in (35):

(35) give$_v$ (Marilyn)$_{Ag}$ (the letter)$_{Go}$ (Rob)$_{Rec}$.

The adverb *surreptitiously* specifies an additional property of the SoA designated by the nuclear predication and as such qualifies as a δ_1 satellite. The addition of this adverbial specification to the nuclear predication leads to the core predication in (36):

(36) [[give$_v$ (Marilyn)$_{Ag}$ (the letter)$_{Go}$ (Rob)$_{Rec}$] (surreptitiously)$_{Man}$].

The core predication is located in time by the past tense operator and in space by the δ_2 satellite *during the staff meeting* which results in the extended predication in (37):

(37) [Past e$_i$ [[give$_v$ (Marilyn)$_{Ag}$ (the letter)$_{Go}$ (Rob)$_{Rec}$] (surreptitiously)$_{Man}$] (during the staff meeting)$_{Loc}$ (e$_i$)].

The perspective for the interpretation of the SoA designated in (37) is imposed by assigning the subject function to the agentive argument *Marilyn* and the object function to the goal *the letter*, as indicated by the subscripts in (38):

(38) [Past e$_i$ [[give$_v$ (Marilyn)$_{Ag/Subj}$ (the letter)$_{Go/Obj}$ (Rob)$_{Rec}$] (surreptitiously)$_{Man}$] (during the staff meeting)$_{Loc}$ (e$_i$)].

The structure in (38) is built into a proposition which is qualified by the attitudinal δ_3 quotative satellite *allegedly*, expressing that the speaker has come upon the propositional content indirectly, and thus cannot be held responsible for its ultimate veracity. It is thus turned into the extended proposition in (39):

(39) [X$_i$ [Past e$_i$ [[give$_v$ (Marilyn)$_{Ag/Subj}$ (the letter)$_{Go/Obj}$ (Rob)$_{Rec}$] (surreptitiously)$_{Man}$] (during the staff meeting)$_{Loc}$ (e$_i$)] (allegedly)$_{Man}$ (X$_i$)].

The extended proposition is expanded into a clause structure and assigned a basic illocutionary force which in the case of (33) is that of a declarative.

(40) [E$_i$: Dec [X$_i$ [Past e$_i$ [[give$_v$ (Marilyn)$_{Ag/Subj}$ (the letter)$_{Go/Obj}$ (Rob)$_{Rec}$] (surreptitiously)$_{Man}$] (during the staff meeting)$_{Loc}$ (e$_i$)] (allegedly)$_{Man}$ (X$_i$)] (E$_i$)].

The clause is elaborated into the extended clause structure in (41) where the illocutionary δ_4 satellite *in case you haven't heard* mitigates the illocutionary force of the utterance by querying the felicity of the speech act relative to the hearer's knowledge:

(41) [E$_i$ [Dec [X$_i$ [Past e$_i$ [[give$_v$ (Marilyn)$_{Ag/Subj}$ (the letter)$_{Go/Obj}$ (Rob)$_{Rec}$] (suureptitiously)$_{Man}$] (during the staff meeting)$_{Loc}$ (e$_i$)] (allegedly)$_{Man}$ (X$_i$)] (in case you haven't heard)] (E$_i$)].

Finally, the location of the utterance in the context of the discourse relative to the pragmatic information shared by the speaker and hearer is signalled by the assignment of pragmatic functions, indicated by the placement of subscripts on the relevant terms. The pragmatic function assignment shown in (42) is arbitrary, though given the form and order of the main clause in (33), the agent/subject is highly likely to be the topic and the recipient is a good candidate for focus.

(42) [E$_i$ [Dec [X$_i$ [Past e$_i$ [[give$_v$ (Marilyn)$_{Ag/Subj/Top}$ (the letter)$_{Go/Obj}$ (Rob)$_{Rec/Foc}$] (surreptitiously)$_{Man}$] (during the staff meeting)$_{Loc}$ (e$_i$)] (allegedly)$_{Man}$ (X$_i$)] (in case you haven't heard)] (E$_i$)].

2.3.4 Expression rules

A fully specified predication such as that in (42) is mapped onto actual language expressions by means of expression rules specifying matters of form, order and prosody. There is no a priori order of application of the form-determining and linearization rules relative to each other; even interweaving of the two types of rules is permitted in cases of interdependencies between form and order.

Of the three types of expression rules posited in FG, so far the rules connected with the prosodic contour of utterances have received the least attention (but see Dik 1989: ch. 18). I have nothing to contribute in this regard, and therefore matters of prosody will not receive any further consideration in this book. The form-determining expression rules will be discussed in ch. 7, and the sequencing rules, which have featured prominently from the outset of FG, in ch. 8.

3 States of affairs and semantic functions

3.1 INTRODUCTION

The FG typology of SoAs is a typology of situations and events that a nuclear predication may designate, viewed from the perspective of internal temporal constituency and a restrictive conception of agentivity.[1] Thus it includes within its scope the range of considerations discussed under the labels of '*Aktionsart*'[2] or 'mode of action' as well as selected facets of participant involvement, which constitute the traditional domain of investigations of semantic role relationships. An SoA designates the conception of something that may be the case in some world. Significantly, SoAs are taken to represent not patterns of experience as they exist in the real world, but rather the codified view of reality built into the grammar of a language. Examples of the different ways in which real-world phenomena can be encapsulated in language are not hard to find. Thus while in English a winning streak at the card table can be expressed as in (1a), Polish uses the construction in (1b), and Russian the structure in (1c).

(1) a. I was lucky at cards.
 b. Miałam szczeęście w kartach.
    had:1sg luck   in cards
    'I had luck in cards.'
 c. Mne   v karty vezlo.
    I:dat in cards was:lucky:3sg:neuter
    'To me there was luck in cards.'

To give another example, the falling of rain is rendered in English by the construction in (2a) rather than the one in (2b), the equivalent of which is in turn the structure utilized for this purpose in one of the Chinese dialects.[3]

(2) a. It's raining.
 b. The sky is dropping water.

As a final[4] illustration of the different language configurations used in the expression of what may be a single aspect of experience, consider the possibilities in (3) (not all of which are actually possible in English or any other one language) cited in Dik (1989: 107).

(3) a. John was very scared of the dog.
    b. John scared enormously because of the dog.
    c. John had great fear for the dog.
    d. Great fear came to John from the dog.
    e. There was great fear for John because of the dog.
    f. Great fear for the dog ate John.
    g. The dog scared John enormously.
    h. The dog made great fear in John.

Although all the predications in (3) express the same real-world situation – John's fearing the dog – in FG each of the predications is seen to represent a different SoA. The FG literature does not provide any discussion of what constitutes a difference in SoA as opposed to a difference in the type of SoA. The latter is primarily associated with a different configuration of semantic functions in the underlying predicate frame (see §3.2). It may also be effected by the semantic features of the arguments (e.g. definiteness and countability) and by the presence of a δ_1 (level-1 satellite), say an instrumental or a benefactive (see §3.3.1). Since an FG SoA is defined on a nuclear predication, we can presume that differences in SoAs of the same type must be the product of differences in any features of the predicate frame other than semantic function, i.e. lexical choice, semantic features, categorial properties and selectional restrictions (see §2.2.1). In (3) the lexical nature of the terms is constant. Therefore the differences in SoAs are due to differences in types of SoA and to the use of distinct lexical predicates.

The typology of SoA plays a central role in FG. It provides the basis for the argument/satellite distinction. It serves as the cornerstone for the determination of nuclear semantic functions. It helps to define the permissible combinations of nuclear and satellite functions. And finally, it determines the overall approach to aspect and tense adhered to in FG by specifying the nature of the interplay between lexically expressed distinctions (*Aktionsart*) and grammatical aspect. In this chapter we will be looking at only the first three points, leaving matters of aspect to ch. 5. The discussion will start with a presentation of the SoA types and characterization of the parameters defining this typology (§3.2). Then we will pass on to the argument/satellite dichotomy (§3.3) and consider how this distinction fares in relation to analogous distinctions drawn in other theoretical frameworks. In §3.4 we will be concerned with several issues pertaining to the nature of the semantic functions borne by arguments, including the constraint against assigning more than one semantic function per term. And in §3.5 the inventory of semantic functions of both arguments and satellites will be reviewed.

3.2 A TYPOLOGY OF SoA

The types of SoA distinguished in FG and the major parameters determining them as presented in Dik (1989: 98) are shown in the matrix in (4).

(4)
SoA type				[dynamicity]	[control]	[telicity]
◆	Situation			−		
◆	◆	Position		−	+	
◆	◆	State		−	−	
◆	Event			+		
◆	◆	Action		+	+	
◆	◆	◆	Accomplishment	+	+	+
◆	◆	◆	Activity	+	+	−
◆	◆	Process		+	−	
◆	◆	◆	Change	+	−	+
◆	◆	◆	Dynamism	+	−	−

The feature [dynamic] is taken to distinguish Situations from Events, both of which are in turn subdivided in terms of the property [control] resulting in a four-way classification of SoAs into States, Positions, Actions and Processes.[5] Within Actions and Processes a further distinction is made on the basis of telicity, the outcome of which is the following subclassification: Accomplishment, Activity, Change, and Dynamism. Examples of each of the six SoAs distinguished in (4) are given below:

(5) a. The river and forest system covers 2.7 square miles. (State)
 b. Biologists keep specimens under observation. (Position)
 c. People destroyed the plant life in just one generation. (Accomplishment)
 d. The government is building a system of roads. (Activity)
 e. The rubber trees withered under the assault of sun, rain and pests. (Change)
 f. The river meanders for 4,000 miles. (Dynamism)

In addition to the six SoAs presented in (5), Dik posits two supplementary distinctions by means of the features [momentaneous] (corresponding to [punctual] of other typologies) and [experience]. The former is taken to apply only to telic SoAs (see §3.2.2.3), whereas all SoAs are considered to have an experiential option. For example:

(6) a. Alice longed for the holidays. (State)
    b. Alice suspected a snag. (Position)
    c. Alice imagined a knight in shining armour. (Accomplishment)
    d. Alice wondered about the real meaning of the game. (Activity)
    e. Alice forgot about the past. (Change)
    f. Alice dreamed about her homeland. (Dynamism)

The SoA types emerging from this subclassification are not supplied with names.

3.2.1 A brief comparison

There are evident parallels between Dik's typology of SoAs, the verb classification proposed by Chafe (1970) and the event typologies initiated by Vendler (1957, 1967)[6] and developed by Dowty (1979).[7] Due to the similarity in aims the Vendler/Dowty typologies are closer to Dik's than Chafe's case-oriented classification. Nonetheless, there are enough overall similarities among all the typologies to warrant a brief comparison.

Chafe distinguishes four main classes of predicates: States, Processes, Actions and Action-Processes. Vendler's typology consists of: States, Activities, Achievements and Accomplishments. Dowty, adopting Vendler's basic classification, imposes a hierarchy over the distinguished event types analogous to Dik's. It is important to note that the features [dynamic], [telic] and [momentaneous] employed in Dik's typology enter into a hierarchical relationship with each other, which is cross-cut by the feature [control]. The corresponding features in Dowty's classification are [change], [definite change] and [complex change], all subdivided by agentivity. By way of contrast, Vendler's typology is non-hierarchical, consisting of a matrix of simultaneously applying features. Such an approach has been advocated in the context of FG by De Groot (1985). The hierarchical nature of Dik's and Dowty's features as compared to Vendler's and also Chafe's is another source of the different classifications of particular SoAs across the typologies. Additional differences stem from the consideration or non-consideration of the effect on SoA of argument features (of subjects as well as objects), aspect and tense. In view of the above, the following correspondences are by no means absolute. However, for readers familiar with Chafe's classification and/or the Vendler/Dowty one, a presentation of the major correspondences with Dik's typology should prove instructive and facilitate understanding of the FG system.

Vendler/Dowty	Chafe	Dik
State	State	Situation
Activity	Action	Activity
Achievement	Process	Process
Accomplishment	Action-Process	Accomplishment

The major differences in classification will be pointed out in the next section.

3.2.2 The features

The justification for the choice of features used in defining the typology of SoAs and simultaneously for the validity of the SoA types thus distinguished is sought in their differential semantic and syntactic properties, in particular in their selectional restrictions and co-occurrence possibilities. As mentioned at the beginning of the chapter, the features belong to two different frames of reference, the internal temporal structure of the SoA and agentivity. The features pertaining to temporal organization are motivated primarily by the interaction of the given type of SoA with the aspectual and tense systems, whereas the relevance of [control] and [experience] is evinced basically in the area of semantic function assignment. The operational tests used in support of the proposed SoA reflect the two interacting domains.

3.2.2.1 Control

The FG notion of control is a dichotomous one, with a uniform cross-linguistic status, and as such it needs to be distinguished from the scalar and relative conception of control featuring in recent discussions of the typology of voice phenomena (Klaiman 1988: 71). Dik defines an SoA as controlled if the first argument has the power to determine whether the SoA will obtain. Compare the (a) with the (b) and (c) examples in (7) and (8).

(7) a. John hid the present.
    b. John mislaid the present.
    c. John lost the present.

(8) a. Tracey listened to a funny story.
    b. Tracey heard a funny story.
    c. Tracey overheard a funny story.

Reflected in the above characterization of control is the prevailing, but apparently not universal,[8] world view as to the necessary convergence of control with source of action (but not vice versa). A controller is thus an instigator or effector; hence the common interchangeable use of the terms control and agentivity. The potential for control, however, is typically seen necessarily to involve animacy (Foley and Van Valin 1984: 32); and this is also the FG position, while agentivity, more often than not, carries no similar restriction (see Fillmore 1971: 42; Chafe 1970: 109). The animacy requirement imposed on the first arguments of controlled predications raises the question of the relationship between control and intentionality (volition). This is not discussed in the FG literature, but I presume that control, while not necessarily entailing intention, is incompatible with 'unintended result', it being difficult to control something one is not aware of doing. This is another difference between control and agentivity, as the term is most commonly applied. The correctness of the above correspondence between control and intentionality is suggested by the behaviour of the (b) and (c) clauses in (7) and (8) in relation to the operational tests used to distinguish controlled from non-controlled SoAs. The tests include the possibility of occurring in imperative constructions with and without *may* (9a,b,c,d), as the complements of the predicates *force* or *persuade* (10a,b), and with manner adverbials such as *deliberately* or *intentionally* (11a,b).

(9) a. Hide the present!
    b. *Mislay the present!
    c. *May you hide the present.
    d. May you mislay the present.

(10) a. I persuaded Tracey to listen to a funny story.
     b. *I persuaded Tracey to hear a funny story.

(11) a. John hid the present deliberately.
     b. *John mislaid the present deliberately.

Observe that all three nuclear predications in (7) and (8) may be taken to differ with respect to intentionality. In the (a) examples all the events leading up to the final effect, including the final effect itself, are carried out intentionally; in the (b) clauses only the events preceding the end result are intended; and in the (c) clause there is no intention.[9] One of the manifestations of these differences in intentionality is the tautology arising from the use of *deliberately* with intentional predicates like *hide* in (11a), and conversely of *accidentally* with non-intentional ones such as *mislay* and *lose* in (12).

(12) I accidentally mislaid/lost the book.

The occurrence of such adverbials with neutral predicates as in (13b,c) does not produce analogous tautologies.

(13) a. I tore the cover.
b. I accidentally tore the cover.
c. I deliberately tore the cover.

While (13a) is ambiguous or vague in regard to matters of intention, (13b) can receive only the unintended and (13c) only the intended reading. A similar difference can be observed between the ambiguous (14a) and the necessarily accidental reading of (14b).

(14) a. I killed the snail by hitting it with my hand.
b. I killed the snail in hitting it with my hand.

The FG literature does not specify whether the presence of satellites such as *accidentally*, *by chance* or the like cancels the control property of an SoA or not. I would expect this to be the case, since, if (7b) and (8b) are classified as [− control], so should (13b) and (14b) be. We will see in §3.5 that this has important consequences for semantic function assignment in FG.

It is worth noting that the above differences identify intentionality as a potential independent SoA parameter. The need for such a parameter is obviated in FG by subsuming intentionality under control.[10] However, in typologies that take agentivity rather than control as an SoA parameter, intentionality would warrant independent recognition.

3.2.2.2 Experience

Experiential SoAs are those that obtain through the sensory or mental faculties of some animate being. FG adopts the position that experiences do not constitute an independent SoA type, but are conceptualized and expressed within the models used for non-experiences. The argument is that there tend not to be any regular cross-linguistic manifestations of [+ experience] SoAs *per se* which would justify positing an independent SoA type. Dik (1989: 98) rightly observes that the characteristics attributed to experiential SoAs in fact hold only for [− control] [+ experience] SoAs. This, however, suggests that the relevant SoA parameter is perhaps [affect] rather than [experience]. Note that uncontrolled experiences tend to be conceived of as the product of outside influences, which makes the experiencing entity simultaneously an affected one.

The fact that distinct behavioral characteristics accrue only to uncontrolled as compared to controlled experiences can be illustrated on the basis of the pan-South Asian phenomenon of 'dative subjects' (Masica 1976: 160), commonly found in constructions representing events occurring in the body or mind of the experiencer, though not exclusively so. Consider the following examples from Kannada (Sridhar 1976: 132).

Kannada
(15) a. Avanu   ī   suddi   (-yannu) tilidukondanu.
         he:nom   this   news   (-acc)   learnt:3sg:m
         'He learnt this news.'

     b. Avanige   ī suddi   tiliyitu.
         he:dat   this news became known:3sg:n
         'He came to know this news.'

Example (15a) is patterned like a non-experiential SoA with the subject in the nominative and the object optionally in the accusative; in (15b) the term corresponding to the nominative of (15a), the would-be subject, is in the dative, and the second term is in the nominative. Cross-referencing in Kannada is confined to nominative terms, thus whereas in (15a) it is the subject *avanu* that is cross-referenced on the verb, in (15b) *ī suddi* is cross-referenced. The necessarily controlled interpretation of (15a) as compared to the non-controlled reading of (15b) comes out neatly in the English translation in the use of different lexical verbs. As in English, the difference in the control properties of the respective predications is confirmed by behavioral tests, in the ability to occur in commands as compared to wishes, and in the admission of adverbials expressing volition (see Sridhar 1976: 132). Although these behavioral differences follow from control, the coding properties are specific to [− control] [+ experience] SoAs. Consequently in order to be able to deal with these facts the relevant SoA type needs to be identified in the underlying predication. This in essence is the justification for including the feature [experience] in the typology of SoAs and for recognizing the previously rejected (Dik 1978: 41f.) Experiencer function, though not as a function in its own right. Dik (1989: 101–102) regards Experiencer as a subsidiary function, which is assigned to an argument only in conjunction with another semantic function. Significantly it can be borne not only by a first argument, but also by a second or third one (see §3.5). Such a treatment of the Experiencer is a direct reflection of the FG claim as to the 'parasitic' nature of experiential predications *vis-à-vis* non-experiential ones. The feature [experience] and the semantic function Experiencer therefore have a different conceptual status from the other SoA features and semantic functions.[11]

3.2.2.3 Telicity[12]

Telicity is an evident property of predications rather than predicates, and as such it is not used in Chafe's or other verb typologies.[13] Drawing on the analogy with the feature [control] which, as mentioned on p. 47, is always associated with the first argument of a predicate, De Groot (1989: 41) suggests that telicity may be seen to be associated with the participants or entities bearing the semantic functions of Goal or Direction. This is a direct reflection of the fact that telic SoAs are taken to have an inherent endpoint and are considered to be fully realized only upon reaching this end point. Atelic SoAs, on the other hand, are seen to lack a terminal point and consequently are completely realized whenever they obtain. The telic/atelic distinction can be most readily appreciated on the basis of the different pragmatic implications following from an SoA in the progressive *X (is/was) V-ing*; an atelic SoA pragmatically entails the perfect *X has/will have V-ed*, while a telic SoA carries no such implication. For example:

(16) a. He's living in Tucson. → He's lived in Tucson.
     b. They're writing an ms on euphemism and dysphemism. ↛
        They've written an ms on euphemism and dysphemism.

A controversial aspect of Dik's approach to telicity is the treatment of momentaneous SoAs as telic. Vendler labels such SoA Achievements, using telicity to distinguish Activities from Accomplishments. A momentaneous SoA is conceived of as having no inherent duration,[14] its beginning coinciding with its endpoint (Comrie 1976: 45 note 3). The following may serve as examples.

(17) a. The door slammed.
     b. The bubble burst.
     c. The bomb exploded.

The major diagnostic for the [+/− momentaneous] distinction is taken to be the possibility of the SoA co-occurring with so-called aspectual verbs specifying various stages of the development of an event (beginning, middle, end); acceptability with these verbs is viewed as an indication of a non-momentaneous SoA, non-acceptability of a momentaneous one.[15] Compare (18a) and (18b).

(18) a. There started/continued/stopped developing a misunderstanding.
     b. There *started/*continued/*stopped erupting a terrible argument.

Whereas momentaneous events lack time, the telic/atelic opposition centres on time, definite vs indefinite time. The realization of a telic SoA necessarily involves some given limited time span. The realization of an atelic SoA, on the other hand, does not depend on time; it may go on indefinitely or alternatively be broken off at any point. Assuming a hierarchically based typology of SoAs as in Dik or Dowty, no time may be associated with definite or indefinite time. Both Dik and Dowty opt for the former solution, while Comrie (1976: 42) embraces the latter. Significantly, the above entailment test is either inapplicable to momentaneous SoAs (19) or identifies them as non-telic (20).

(19) a. *Ben was reaching the summit.
　　 b. *The teacher was noticing the mistake.

(20) a. The child was coughing. → The child has coughed.
　　 b. The man was kissing Mary. → The man has kissed Mary.

The non-ambiguity of momentaneous SoAs with *almost* is another of the commonly cited behavioral tests for telicity that momentaneous events fail. With telic SoAs, as in (21), *almost* can refer to the inception or the terminal point, whereas with atelic SoAs, as in (22a), it has only one reading, that of non-realization of the SoA.

(21) He has almost finished the sculpture.

(22) a. They almost walked along the beach.

As evinced by (22b), since momentaneous SoAs have no time span, *almost* always entails that the SoA has not been realized, just as with atelic SoAs.

(22) b. They almost signed the accord.

Mourelatos (1981: 193–194) argues that contrary to what is often claimed, momentaneous SoAs do involve time, as evidenced by their admission into contexts of the form *It took him N Ts to V* (where *N* is a count expression and *T* a unit of time).

(23) a. It took him five minutes to notice the picture.
　　 b. It took him all of thirty seconds to sneeze.

Rijksbaron (1988: 5) in turn suggests that the scope of the temporal modifier in such cases is not the SoA but the preparatory phase leading up to the SoA. Thus in (23a), *five minutes* is the time before the noticing. The contradictory claims in regard to the telicity of momentaneous SoAs can be reconciled by means of a non-hierarchical relationship between these two features along the lines of Vendler (1967). I see no reason why the FG typology of SoAs should not be represented by an n-dimensional grid rather than a hierarchy of features.

3.2.2.4 Dynamicity

Dynamicity is characterized in FG in relation to the notion of change; non-dynamic SoAs do not involve any change; they remain constant at all points of time, whereas dynamic SoAs describe some sort of change. As pointed out by Taylor (1977: 171), there is no state of affairs in the real world which is completely unchanging and endless. However, FG SoAs do not exist in the real world, but are rather conceptualizations of what happens in the real world. Therefore what is taken to constitute change is open to interpretation. Dik, like Dowty (1979), takes a very broad view of change to include SoAs such as those in (24) which Dowty characterizes as describing indefinite change, i.e. a change in physical properties or an internal movement that is manifest in some visual, audible or tactile way.

(24) a. Morris strolled along the canal.
     b. Mark kissed Alice.

The validity of the notion of change thus conceived as a typological parameter has been recently called into question within FG by Rijksbaron (1988) who, drawing on the Aristotelian distinction between *kineseis* and *energeiai*, argues that the notion of change is truly applicable only to kineseis, i.e. telic SoAs. He reasons that since a clear determination of change requires an initial and final reference point, and only telic SoAs have a natural endpoint, it follows that only such SoAs can be seen to undergo change in the strict sense. Thus whereas telicity is used by Dik to subclassify dynamic SoAs, Rijksbaron would have it as the initial typological parameter. Dynamism, which Rijksbaron associates with some kind of movement, is ousted from his basic classification of SoAs.

Though non-dynamic SoAs, Dik's Situations (Vendler's, Dowty's and Chafe's States), are seen to form a separate category opposed collectively to Events or individually to Actions and Processes, there is in fact very little unequivocal semantico-syntactic evidence for such a firm distinction.[16] The only factor that Dik (1989: 92) cites to differentiate his Situations and Events is the co-occurrence with adverbs of speed. As shown in (25a,b) Situations cannot be qualified by such satellites but Events (25c,d) can.

(25) a. *Thomas was tall quickly.
     b. *They sat quickly.
     c. Thomas grew tall quickly.
     d. They sat down quickly.

Dowty (1979) maintains that the distinction between [+/−change] predications is reflected in English by means of the *do-so* and *do*-pseudo-cleft tests. However, the feature determining the possibility of these *do*-constructions is [control] rather than [change] as evidenced by the similar behaviour of Actions (26a) and Dik's Positions (26b) with respect to the *do*-tests.

(26) a. What she liked to do was sit quietly.
     b. What she liked to do was dance all night.

The same holds for the other syntactic and semantic differences seen to distinguish Situations from Events, such as agentivity, the admission of the progressive, modification by manner adverbials, passivization and the ability to function as the complements of *persuade, force* or *make*, all of which apply equally well to Positions.

There are, on the other hand, several behavioral properties common to atelic Events and Situations supporting Rijksbaron's (1988) proposal of an SoA typology with an initial telic/atelic distinction. Observe that in view of the fact that telicity is treated as relevant only to dynamic SoAs, Situations, which are by definition atelic, are not identified with non-telic Events as constituting an SoA type in the FG SoA typology in (4) on p. 45. Brinton (1987), for example, lists among the characteristics of atelic SoAs (including Situations) in English:

(a) the admission of durative punctual time adverbials (e.g. *for ten years*) as compared to time adverbials with *in*, such as *in an hour*, required by telic SoAs;
(b) accompanying the durative adverbs, the so-called continuative perfects describing SoAs which began at some time in the past, continuing into the present and potentially into the future;
(c) in conjoined or sequential clauses in the narrative past, concurrent or overlapping readings rather than successive ones;
(d) co-occurrence with mass as opposed to count quantifiers in nominalizations.[17]

Assuming a division of SoAs along the telic/atelic distinction, Rijksbaron suggests distinguishing Situations from atelic Events (Activities and Dynamism) with reference to time. This is in accordance with Vendler who characterizes States (Dik's Situations) as denoting SoAs that may endure or persist over stretches of time. The distinction between the semi-permanent time of States and the indefinite time of atelic Event, as Rijksbaron himself admits, rests on real-world knowledge rather than conceptual knowledge, which again suggests the surprisingly tentative nature of the category of States.

3.3 THE ARGUMENT/SATELLITE OPPOSITION

The distinction between arguments and satellites (or their equivalents in other theoretical frameworks) bears on numerous facets of clause structure, which in the case of FG include:

(a) the assignment of semantic functions, particularly in regard to the interpretation of Fillmore's (1968) one-case-per-clause principle and the treatment of related matters such as term coordination, reiteration and stacking;
(b) the correlation between semantic functions and syntactic functions as reflected in the SFH (§4.5);
(c) the operation of the expression rules in the area of case and adpositional marking, agreement and cross-reference (§7.4), and ordering relations.

FG (Dik 1978, 1989; Dik *et al.* 1990) presents the argument/satellite opposition as a universal semantic distinction rather than as either a syntactico-semantic one, as originally conceived by Tesnière (1959), or as a syntactic division. This latter syntactic approach is dominant in the German Valency tradition (see, e.g., Helbig and Schenkel 1973) and reflected in Anglo-American linguistics in the complement/adjunct dichotomy[18] of, for example, Chomskyan theory and its offshoots.

FG seeks to provide a characterization of arguments and satellites in relation to the notion of SoA. *Arguments* are terms which are required by the semantics of a given predicate and whose presence is necessary for the definition of the SoA designated by the nuclear predication. *Satellites* are not required by the predicate and are not essential to the integrity of the SoA; they only provide optional further specifications of the SoA. There are two problems with the FG characterization of satellites. The first is the circularity involved in defining a nuclear predication as a predication with no satellites (see §2.3.2), and a satellite as a term not involved in the definition of the SoA designated by the nuclear predication.[19] The second problem concerns the distinction between arguments and level-1 satellites (δ_1). Since this is the most contentious point of the FG analysis of the argument/satellite distinction I will consider it in some detail.

3.3.1 Arguments and level-1 satellites (δ_1)

While not integral to the SoA, δ_1 are nonetheless seen to contribute to its internal features. In fact, as a general criterion for distinguishing δ_1 from other satellites Dik (1989) suggests whether or not the SoA is somehow different with the δ_1 from without it, an affirmative answer entailing δ_1 status. Thus, for example, the Manner and Instrument satellites in (27) and (28) clearly affect the nature of the dancing and the killing.

(27) Mary danced beautifully/clumsily.

(28) Mary killed her husband with a knife/with a hammer.

The contribution of δ_1 to the SoA may even extend to the determination of the type of SoA. For example (29a) is an atelic SoA, (29b) a telic one, the difference in telicity being a function of the nature of the directional term, which Dik treats as a satellite.

(29) a. The tourists walked (in the park).
b. The tourists walked to the station.

To give another example, the presence of the Beneficiary satellite in (30b) is seen by Dik to entail a controlled SoA (a Position) as compared to the non-controlled State of (30a).

(30) a. Mary was beautiful.
b. Mary was beautiful for the guests.

Recall also the change in control determined by the presence of the Manner satellites in (13), p. 49. If SoAs are defined on nuclear predications, we would not expect satellites, which do not belong to the nuclear predication, to affect the nature of the SoA. Yet δ_1 do.[20] There is thus an obvious inconsistency in Dik's characterization of the general relationship between satellites and SoAs and the recognized effect of δ_1 on SoAs.

The terms constituting the class of δ_1 hamper all attempts to achieve a neat argument/satellite dichotomy.[21] They behave erratically with respect to the recognized diagnostic tests for argumenthood, displaying sometimes argument, sometimes satellite properties. For example, under approaches to the argument/satellite distinction more directly tied to the semantic structure of the predicate, as reflected in the semantic decomposition of the sense of the predicate, δ_1 emerge as arguments. Karolak (1984: 54, 58), for instance, analyses the verbs *buy, lend* and *reward* in (31) as all taking four arguments.

(31) a. This afternoon, Philip bought a bunch of roses *for Carole for only $5*.
b. Jane lent her camera to me *for a month* last year (and I still have it).
c. In the park, Susan rewarded her admirer *for his efforts with a smile*.

Observe that the italicized terms belong to the semantic characterization of the respective predicates; one *buys* something for someone for a price; one *lends* something to someone for some period of time; and one *rewards* someone for something with something. Consequently, on the grounds of the semantic decomposition of the predicates, all of the italicized terms qualify as arguments. The extra specifications of time and place, on the other hand, emerge as non-arguments, since they can occur with any predicate. Dik imposes an upper limit on the number of possible arguments, three for non-derived predicates and four for derived ones (e.g. causatives). The above analysis of the argument structure of the verbs *buy, lend* and *reward* is not therefore a possible one in FG. *Lend* is seen to be trivalent and the other two predicates are bivalent. The italicized terms in (31) are δ_1, the extra time and locational adverbials δ_2.

As regards the argument-like behavioral characteristics of δ_1 satellites, the following are listed in Dik *et al.* (1990) as particularly significant: (a) availability for syntactic function assignment; (b) participation in predicate formation rules; (c) susceptibility to specific semantic constraints. Syntactic function assignment will be discussed in detail in ch. 4. The FG claim is that only arguments and δ_1 satellites are accessible to syntactic function assignment (but see p. 105). Therefore if a particular satellite can, for example, be subjectivized via the passive it is treated as a δ_1. On the basis of this criterion the status of the locative term in (32a) is ambiguous between that of an argument or a δ_1, under the (i) interpretation and that of a δ_2, under the (ii) interpretation. Only in the former case can it function as a passive subject.

(32) a. John was writing on the terrace.
(i) 'John inscribed something on the terrace.'
(ii) 'John was writing something while being on the terrace.'
b. The terrace was written on by John.

Turning to predicate formation, the inclusion of operations on satellites within the scope of predicate formation rules is a direct reflection of the dual argument/satellite status of δ_1. Recall from §2.2.1.1 that the type of predicate formation rules that δ_1 participate in involve incorporation of the δ_1 into the predicate, absorption into the predicate frame and removal of the δ_1 from the core predication. As for semantic constraints, on the whole the semantic requirements imposed on satellites, unlike those imposed on arguments, are not specific to particular predicates, but to features of the predication as a whole. This is captured in the FG typology of SoAs. For instance, Beneficiary, Instrument, Quality, Reason and Purpose satellites demand a [+ control] SoA, while a Manner satellite requires either a [+ control] SoA or a [+ dynamic] one. Nonetheless, in the case of δ_1 satellites there may be some additional specific constraints. One case in point cited in Dik *et al.* (1990: 51) is the inability of intrinsically benefactive verbs in Greek such as 'eat' or 'drink' to co-occur with a Beneficiary. Another example is the classification of Manner adverbs in English according to the specific type of SoA which they co-occur with.

The fact that δ_1 display argument-like characteristics is not at issue; this is universally recognized. The problem that linguists are still trying to solve is how to draw a distinction between δ_1 and bona fide arguments.

Dik uses two supplementary criteria for distinguishing δ_1 from arguments: omissibility and detachment. The assumption underlying the omissibility test is that arguments as opposed to satellites cannot be left out without affecting acceptability or without semantic effects. According to this criterion, all of the italicized terms in (31) are indeed satellites since their omission does not entail unacceptability or involve a change in semantic interpretation; the only difference would be the non-specification of certain additional information. By contrast, the removal of the postverbal term in (33a) introduces a meaning difference.

(33) a. Witek lives in Warsaw.
     b. Witek lives.

Example (33b) means that *Witek* is alive rather than dead or that he enjoys an enviable life-style. Thus *in Warsaw* is identified as an argument.

Dik draws attention to the well-known fact that the reliability of omissibility as a test for argumenthood is undermined by the phenomena of contextual and indefinite or unspecified deletion which delete arguments without necessary semantic effects. Consider, for instance, the following examples, adapted from Allerton (1982: 68–70).

(34) a. Oliver passed the salt [to Charles].
b. Oliver was listening [to the music].
c. Oliver taught French (to school children).
d. Oliver is concentrating (on something).

Allerton employs the convention of square brackets for weakly optional arguments, which he defines as necessarily definite and easily retrievable contextually. The arguments within parentheses are called strongly optional; they are indefinite and therefore may be supplied on the basis of the meaning of the predicate or knowledge of the world. In both cases the missing argument is assumed to be present semantically, though not specified lexically. The degree of the semantic presence of the parenthesized arguments particularly in (34) is strikingly reminiscent of the δ_1 italicized in (31).

The detachment test, also known as the backformation test (Sommers 1987: 14), rests on the difference in bondedness of arguments and satellites relative to the predicate. Arguments are seen to enter into a direct relationship with the predicate while satellites relate not to the predicate, but to the nuclear and core predications, the proposition and the clause.[22] The claim therefore is that satellites can be detached from the nuclear predication, while arguments cannot. This in effect means that satellites may serve as the basis for a separate, complete or reduced predicate argument structure (Karolak 1984: 56). Compare (35a,b) with (35c).

(35) a. *Charles passed the salt and he did it to Anne.
b. *Charles passed to Anne and he did it the salt.
c. Charles passed the salt to Anne and he did it quickly/with a smile/for his mother's sake.

The major problem with this test is that it is not always clear what criteria to use in choosing the appropriate form of the verb and subject in the backformation. Nor is it easy to judge whether the basic meaning is maintained in the backformation. Consider (36) and (37).

(36) a. *Jane lent her camera to me and she did it for a month.
b. Jane lent her camera to me and she let me have it for a month.

(37) a. #Susan rewarded her admirer and she did it with a smile.
b. ?Susan rewarded her admirer and it was with a smile.

In (36a) *for a month* is identified as an argument, as in Karolak's analysis (see 31b), while in (36b) it is a satellite. In (37a) *with a smile* is a satellite, but this is not the reading corresponding to (31c). While (37b) has the relevant reading, I am dubious about its acceptability.

The difference in semantic bonding of arguments and satellites with the predicate also has a formal, categorial reflex, discussed in the transformational-generative literature under the label of subcategorization. Even under the most semantically based of the current approaches to subcategorization, as in Chomsky's (1981) GB and its predecessors,[23] the distinction between (strictly) subcategorized elements (complements) and non-subcategorized ones (adjuncts) does not completely coincide with Dik's argument/satellite one.[24] Nonetheless, it is in regard to constituency-based subcategorization that the distinction between arguments and δ_1 most clearly emerges. Predicates impose subcategorization restrictions on the semantic features and categorial features (NP, PP, VP, S, S') of their arguments, but not on their satellites. Satellites are subject to semantico-pragmatic requirements which become less restrictive the higher the level at which the satellite is attached. Consider, for instance, some of the differences in the categorial requirements (and also semantic features) of the predicates *tell, say* and *admit* (adapted from Radford 1981: 142).

(38) a. He tells the same story to all his friends. (NP PP)
　　 b. He tells all his friends the same story. (NP NP)
　　 c. *He won't tell that/whether he is ill to his friends. (*that/*whether PP)
　　 d. He won't tell his friends that/whether he is ill. (NP that/whether)
　　 e. *He won't tell that/whether he is ill. (*that/*whether)

(39) a. He says the same thing/*story to all his friends. (NP PP)
　　 b. *He says all his friends the same thing. (*NP NP)
　　 c. *He won't say that/whether he is ill to his friends. (that/whether *PP)
　　 d. *He won't say his friends that/whether he is ill. (*NP that/whether)
　　 e. He won't say *that/whether he is ill. (*that/whether)

(40) a. He admits his shortcomings/*the same story/?the same thing to his friends. (NP PP)
　　 b. *He admits his friends his shortcomings. (*NP NP)
　　 c. He won't admit that/whether he is ill to his friends. (that/whether PP)
　　 d. *He won't admit his friends that/whether he is ill. (*NP that/whether)
　　 e. He won't admit that/*whether he is ill. (that/*whether)

No comparable formal requirements are imposed on satellites, including δ_1. For example, all the above grammatical predications can take the same type of Manner (e.g. *in the same chaotic manner*), Purpose (e.g. *in order to gain/avoid/maintain (their) sympathy*) or Reason (e.g. *for his mother's sake*) satellites.

Dik does not offer subcategorization as a diagnostic for distinguishing arguments from δ_1 because in FG predicates are subcategorized for semantic function, not for constituent structure.[25] And as far as semantic functions are concerned, there is no clear distinction between arguments and δ_1 (see §3.5); note for example that the locative in (31c) is a satellite, while the one in (33a) is an argument. A categorial approach to subcategorization, on the other hand, is excluded by the functional nature of the theory which restricts (reduces) all references to categorial information to the absolute minimum. It is therefore somewhat of a paradox that the very categories that FG rejects (constituent structure categories) provide the relatively clearest evidence for the syntactic validity of the FG argument/satellite distinction.[26] This in turn casts doubt either on Dik's claim as to the semantic rather than syntactic nature of this dichotomy[27] or alternatively on the dichotomy itself.

A number of linguists (e.g. Matthews 1981: 140; Nichols 1986: 106; Sommers 1987: 25) have argued that the conflicting properties of δ_1 (or their equivalents) stem from the fact that the binary argument/satellite (complement/adjunct, actants/circumstantials) opposition misleadingly conflates two distinct though related phenomena: verbal semantics and syntactic structure. The former is reflected by semantic (sometimes implicit) presence, the latter by overt presence and morpho-syntactic form. Nichols refers to this distinction as one between subcategorization and government. Matthews and Sommers propose a semantic split into non-peripheral (central) items and peripheral ones, and a syntactic valency-based division into complements (valency-bound) and non-complements (non-valency-bound). Since δ_1 are implied by the semantic structure of the verb (though not as strongly as arguments), but neither their overt presence nor their form is determined by the verb, in terms of these classifications δ_1 emerge as subcategorized but non-governed, or non-peripheral non-valency-bound, as shown in (41).

(41)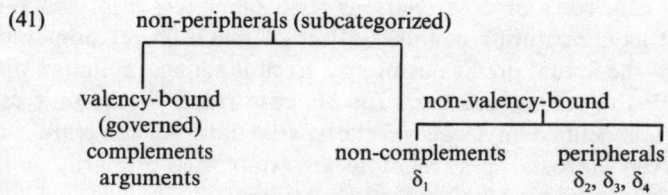

Sommers argues that the in-between nature of δ_1 warrants recognizing a separate category of *middle* elements. He also suggests subdivisions among the peripherals, more or less corresponding to the FG ones. Consequently the traditional two-way distinction of complements and adjuncts is expanded into a multi-level one. The resulting system is *de facto* like the layered structure of FG, the major difference being that it is taken to constitute a conflation of two intersecting classifications rather than a single semantic one. The other difference is essentially one of terminology. FG expresses the special status of δ_1 vis-à-vis other satellites in the definition of the δ_1; Sommers provides an independent label.

3.4 SEMANTIC FUNCTIONS

The approach to semantic functions adopted in FG is based on three fairly widely held general assumptions:

(a) semantic functions are inferred from the intersection of the primitive semantic properties of predicates and their arguments;
(b) semantic functions capture only those semantic inferences that are formally reflected in the grammar of a language;
(c) each argument bears only one semantic function.

Let us consider each of these points in turn.

3.4.1 Predicate and argument features

Implicit in the first assumption is a derivational approach to semantic functions which follows from the general requirement that a linguistic theory should recognize as few primitive relations as possible (see e.g. Stockwell 1980: 361). The adoption of a predicate-based typology of semantic functions places FG in the tradition of Gruber (1976), Halliday (1967/68) and Chafe (1970), and in opposition to linguists such as Fillmore (1968, 1977), Anderson (1971, 1977) and Starosta (1977, 1979), who view case roles or case relations (two other terms for semantic functions) as constituting a universal set of semantic relations independent of the actual predicates of any given language. Fillmore does not specify the conceptual basis for his case roles. Anderson's case relations are defined in terms of the spatial notions of 'place' and 'source'. And Starosta's case relations are established primarily on the basis of differential morpho-syntactic behaviour.

One of the consequences of an approach to semantic functions centring on the properties of predicates is that the assignment of semantic functions is independent of the paraphrase relations obtaining between predications. The semantic function borne by a term in a closely related predication is a common criterion used in the assignment of semantic functions, even if in a given theoretical framework the capturing of paraphrase relations *per se* is not considered to be the major task of semantic functions. Starosta (1977), Blake (1979b) and Perlmutter and Postal (1984a: 91–92), for instance, on the basis of the sense similarities between the (a) and the (b) clauses in (42)–(44), analyse the subjects in the (b) examples as bearing the locative (42b), time (43b) and instrumental (44b) semantic functions.

(42) a. Good tomatoes grow in this soil.
     b. This soil grows good tomatoes.

(43) a. Kirchner moved to Berlin in 1911.
     b. The year 1911 saw Kirchner moving to Berlin.

(44) a. One could buy a Kokoschka with/for $5,000 then.
     b. $5,000 could buy you a Kokoschka then.

In FG all of the (b) examples are interpreted as stative and the subjects are seen to bear the Zero semantic function characteristic of the first argument of State predications (see §3.5). The assignment of the Zero semantic function to the terms in (42b)–(44b) is a reflex of the distinction between semantic features and semantic functions in the technical sense (Dik 1989: 105), a distinction which is easy to make, but more difficult to define and apply systematically.

Which differences in the interpretation of predications attributable to the semantic features of terms should be regarded as a matter of knowledge of the world, and which as a manifestation of the grammar of the language, is one of the key questions raised by any typology of semantic functions that considers the conditioning effect on predicates of the changing properties of terms. The nature of the problem can be illustrated on the basis of the examples below.

(45) a. Martha hit her daughter.
     b. Martha hit the computer.

(46) a. Marcia received the parcels.
     b. Marcia received the guests.

In both (45) and (46) the second arguments differ in regard to animacy which has an effect on the interpretation of the respective predications. The differences in interpretation can be attributed to our knowledge of the world (to our understanding of what human beings are and what computers and parcels are), in which case the same semantic functions will be assigned to the (a) and (b) examples of each pair.

Alternatively the semantic distinction between the (a) and (b) examples can be viewed as grammaticalized in the assignment of different semantic functions to the terms in the two sets of predications. The first of these solutions is generally applied to the clauses in (45), the first argument being treated as an agent, the second argument as either objective, patient, locative or Goal (FG), depending on the theory in question. The clauses in (46), however, tend to be distinguished in terms of the semantic function of the first argument; *Marcia* in (46a) is assigned the function recipient, goal, locative or Processed (FG), while in (46b) *Marcia* is considered to be an agent. The grounds for making such a distinction between the examples in (45) and (46) are captured in the second assumption characterizing the FG approach to semantic functions.

3.4.2 Grammaticalization

The grammaticalization condition specifies that the semantic functions postulated must have systematic repercussions in the grammar. In English the animacy contrast in (45a) and (45b) has no morphosyntactic reflexes; all the behavioral properties of (45a) are paralleled by (45b). On the other hand, (46a) and (46b) differ with respect to control, a difference which, as discussed in §3.2.2.1, is made manifest by a number of semantico-syntactic properties.

Though the grammaticalization requirement is adopted in one form or another in most if not all theoretical frameworks, there are vast differences in the range and type of formal properties that are taken to be associated with, or considered to be manifestations of, the recognized semantic functions. In theory practically any morphological, syntactic, semantic or pragmatic similarity, or conversely discrepancy, in the behavioral patterns or co-occurrence possibilities of two terms can be used as evidence for or against a common semantic function. Therefore, on its own, the principle of grammaticalization as a constraint on the nature of possible semantic functions is virtually vacuous. It acquires substance only if coupled with other independently based principles specifying the parameters deemed relevant for the typology of semantic functions adhered to in a given theoretical framework. In the case of FG the major principles in question are those defining the typology of SoAs. Though strictly speaking the typology of SoAs bears directly only on first arguments, it has an indirect effect on other semantic functions too. This will become obvious in the course of the discussion.

Of prime significance for matters of grammaticalization is also the postulated interplay between semantic functions and syntactic functions captured in FG in the Semantic Function Hierarchy (§4.5),[28] and/or any other semantic or categorial distinctions recognized in a given model of grammar. This can be immediately appreciated by comparing the semantic and morpho-syntactic properties attributed to semantic vs syntactic functions in FG and RG. RG postulates the universal validity of at least four syntactic functions (or rather grammatical relations), i.e. the subject, direct object, indirect object and chômeur (a relation assigned to former subjects, direct and indirect objects), and in some languages as many as nine grammatical relations are distinguished. The recognized relations are identified at several different levels of structure. The initial grammatical relations are assigned primarily on the basis of semantic functions; an agent, experiencer or cognizer is an initial subject, a patient an initial direct object, and a recipient an initial indirect object. Other semantic functions such as instrument, locative or manner are associated with initial oblique relations. Non-initial grammatical relations are determined on the basis of morpho-syntactic behaviour. Since the theory has at its disposal not only several grammatical relations but also a number of different levels of grammatical representation, differences in the morpho-syntactic properties or behavioral characteristics of constituents bearing the same semantic function can quite easily be attributed to the nature of the grammatical relation that they bear and to the level at which they bear it. The same holds for behavioral similarities among constituents bearing different semantic functions. Consequently, there are few restrictions on the type of semantic functions recognized and the way that they are assigned to arguments. Moreover, the relationship between semantic functions and grammatical relations is much less constrained than in FG, grammatical relations at levels other than the initial one being by and large determined by morpho-syntactic coding and behavioral properties.[29]

As a final point about grammaticalization, it must be mentioned that theoretical frameworks differ in the weight assigned to syntactic as compared to semantic or conceptual criteria in the determination of semantic functions. It was remarked earlier that in Starosta's (1977, 1979) Lexicase, syntactic criteria are given primacy. This is also the position of many linguists working in the area of typological studies such as Blake (1979b) or Comrie (1981) who consider differential syntactic behaviour as a sufficient, though not necessary, criterion for distinguishing case relations. Dik (1989), while stressing the importance of form in semantic function assignment, seeks to maintain a basically notional characterization of semantic functions. This I take to be one of the reasons why FG does not recognize a semantic function corresponding to the category of absolutives (encompassing intransitive subjects and direct objects) which, Halliday's (1985: 145) unsuccessful semantic characterization notwithstanding, is basically a syntactic relation. I mention this in view of the host of common properties displayed by absolutives even in English (summarized in Keenan 1984), and the unavailability of means to capture this in FG.

3.4.3 One semantic function per argument

The third assumption affecting the FG position on semantic functions, the 'one semantic function per argument' principle formulated by Fillmore (1968: 24),[30] restricts the conceptual basis of semantic functions to a shallow (near-surface) level and excludes the possibility of representing, by means of semantic functions, situations and events from the point of view of several conceptual systems simultaneously. The fact that a particular situation or event may be conceived of simultaneously on a number of conceptual planes is typically illustrated on the basis of verbs of transfer and communication[31] (e.g. Fillmore 1972; Longacre 1976; Talmy 1985a) which have been characterized in terms of both the control or instigating domain of agent/patient relations and the motion/direction plane of source/goal. Consider, for instance, the predicates *buy* and *sell*.

(47) a. Jan bought an old Lancia from Peter for $1,000.
b. Peter sold an old Lancia to Jan for $1,000.

As discussed in Fillmore (1972), assuming a situationally based role analysis centring on the notion of *transfer*, the initiator of the transfer is the agent in both (47a) (*Jan*) and (47b) (*Peter*). In terms of the direction of transfer the original possessor is the source *Peter*, the subsequent possessor the goal *Jan*. If the nature of the transferred item is considered, say a distinction is drawn between the transfer of goods and of payment (to distinguish *buy/sell* from *pay/charge*, for instance), the same argument can be both a source and a goal. Thus *Jan* in (47a) could be assigned three roles: agent, goal (of the goods) and source (of payment). Adherence to the one semantic function per argument principle necessitates the assignment of only one set of semantic functions which precludes the capturing of the fact that the agent of *buy* is the goal, while the agent of *sell* is the source.

Such considerations have led a number of linguists representing various theoretical frameworks (e.g. Anderson 1971, 1977; Talmy 1985a; Jackendoff 1987; Sommers 1987; Schlesinger 1989) to abandon Fillmore's constraint in favour of an analysis recognizing several layers or tiers of semantic functions dealing with direction and location, action, time, cognition, experience, etc.[32] However, in FG, since the assignment of nuclear semantic functions, particularly those of first arguments, is tied to an action-based typology of SoAs, the first arguments in (47a) and (47b) are assigned only the Agent function. The distinction between *buy* and *sell* is achieved with reference to the third arguments; *Peter* in (47a) is seen to bear the semantic function Source, while *Jan* in (43b) is analysed as a Recipient (see §3.5). The fact that there is a relationship between predicates such as *buy* and *sell* can be captured by meaning postulates.

The enrichment of the basic SoA typology by the feature [experience] sanctions the introduction of dual semantic functions involving the experiential dimension. This, however, is the only concession in regard to double semantic functions that Dik makes. We will find out in due course whether there will be others.

It must be pointed out, however, that the assignment of only one set of semantic functions to the arguments of predicates which designate situations or events amenable to several conceptual interpretations is consistent with the FG approach to SoAs. Recall that FG SoAs are not intended to directly reflect extra-linguistic relationships, but only the intra-language representations of these relationships. Thus, though the participants in a particular situation or event may be variously conceived of, this does not mean that all of these conceptualizations are coded linguistically. With a given predicate, a language may choose to code one set of participant roles as opposed to another.

3.5 THE INVENTORY OF SEMANTIC FUNCTIONS

Dik (1989: 103) distinguishes eleven nuclear semantic functions, four of which may form doublets with the additional Experiencer. The following semantic functions may be borne by the first argument of a predicate frame:

(48) Agent: the entity controlling an Action (Activity or Accomplishment);
Positioner: the entity controlling a Position;
Force: the non-controlling entity instigating a Process (Dynamism or Change);
Processed: the entity that undergoes a Process;
Zero: the entity primarily involved in a State;
Processed[Exp]: the entity that experiences a [+ exp] Process;
Zero[Exp]: the entity that experiences a [+ exp] State.

Relevant examples are provided in (49).

(49) a. Chico Mendes fought deforestation.
b. The Indians remained in the jungle.
c. The river flooded the valley.
d. The level of the water rose.
e. The house stood on a hill.
f. The people sweated in the sun.
g. The child is hungry.

These semantic functions are tailored to the typology of SoAs on the control, dynamism and experiential dimensions. As discussed on p. 62, from the point of view of models of grammar that do not seek to conflate verb and noun features in the assignment of semantic functions, for example Case Grammar, the FG semantic functions are somewhat opaque precisely because they repeat information predictable from the inherent features of nouns and verbs while failing to capture the underlying similarities in the semantic roles of closely related predications.

Particularly striking is the restrictive nature of the Agent which is confined not only to animate entities, but also to dynamic and intentional acts. Consequently all five of the basic first argument functions are used in FG to designate entities that in one framework or another would be classified as Agents. This is most obvious in the case of the Positioner by virtue of its controlling properties. The semantic function Force, taken over from Huddleston (1970: 504), is the inanimate counterpart of the Agent (but see below) and is used in FG in a similar way to Fillmore's (1968) Instrument. It therefore includes so-called 'inanimate agents' such as machines and natural forces. Instrument itself is only a satellite rather than a nuclear semantic function in FG. It is used to denote tools or aids employed by a controller, as in (50a) as compared to (50b).

(50) a. Oliver opened the door with a key.
b. The key opened the door.

The restriction of the Instrument function to controlled predications entails that in clauses such as those in (51), where a Process is brought about by two inanimate entities in a whole–part relationship to each other, the first argument has to be reinterpreted as an Agent, or alternatively the Instrument as a Manner.[33]

(51) a. The car broke the window with its fender.
b. The sandstorm covered everything in its wake with a centimetre layer of dust.

Coming back to Force, owing to the identification of control with intentionality discussed in §3.2.2.1, Force could also be the function of the first argument of unintended actions, which according to FG terminology would qualify as Processes.[34] Thus in the examples in (7) and (13), which I repeat for convenience, the (a) clauses would take an Agent as a first argument and the (b) ones a Force.

(52) a. John [Agent] hid the present.
  b. John [Force] mislaid the present.

(53) a. I [Agent] deliberately tore the cover.
  b. I [Force] accidentally tore the cover.

Such an assignment of semantic functions runs counter to most conceptions of agentivity. It finds its parallel, though, in Foley and Van Valin's (1984: 51) approach which, like the FG one, is based on the Vendler/Dowty typology of predications. Foley and Van Valin also reserve the agent for controlling (necessarily animate) entities using the effector function in cases such as (52b) and (53b).

The Processed function is primarily associated with semantic undergoers corresponding in most instances to the intransitive manifestations of Fillmore's (1968) objective, Chafe's (1970) patient and Gruber's (1976) theme. More about this use of Processed will be said in connection with the Goal function, below. As regards the Zero function, the connotation of semantic vacuity is rather unfortunate. However, as FG does not postulate a default semantic function,[35] and the use of any other of the functional labels recognized in the theory to capture the distinction between Processes and States and Situations would require redefining the given semantic function, the term 'zero' is just as good as, say, 'neutral' or 'essive' which are two other labels for this function that have been used in the literature. The conflation of the Processed and Zero functions with the Experiencer is used in [− control] [+ experience] SoAs such as those in (6a,e,f) and (15b) cited on pp. 46, 50.

Turning to the second and third arguments, the relevant semantic functions are:

(54) Goal: the entity affected or effected by the operation of some controller (Agent/Positioner) or Force;
  Goal[Exp]: the entity that experiences the effect of the operation of some controller or Force;
  Recipient: the entity into whose possession something is transferred;
  Recipient[Exp]: the entity that experiences the effect of some transfer;
  Location: the place where something is located;

Direction: the entity towards which something moves/is moved;
Source: the entity from which something moves/is moved;
Reference:[36] the second or third term of a relation with reference to which the relation is said to hold.

The Goal is the exclusive domain of the second argument. The remaining semantic functions may be borne either by the second argument or the third; in this latter case the second argument is always a Goal.

All of the labels in (54), except for Goal and the double ones (Goal[Exp], Recipient[Exp]), are used in more or less the standard way, and therefore require no illustration. The FG Goal denotes not the direction or recipient roles as is commonly the case (recall the discussion concerning *buy* and *sell*), but the second argument counterpart of the Processed function, i.e. the transitive (and arguably primary) reflex of Fillmore's objective, Chafe's patient and Gruber's theme. According to these linguists and most other analyses that I am familiar with, the same semantic function is borne by *the vase* in both (55a) and (55b).

(55) a. Pamela broke the vase.
     b. The vase broke.

Dik (1989: 105), on the other hand, assigns to *the vase* in (55a) and (55b) the semantic functions Goal and Processed respectively. He seeks justification for his analysis in the fact that semantically the status of *the vase* in the two clauses is not the same, since the condition in which the vase is in (55a) is brought about by an external participant, while (55b) involves no outside operation. The semantic difference between the predications in (55a) and (55b) is universally recognized. However, under the canonical analysis the fact that the process in (55a) as compared to (55b) is not self-engendered is captured by the overt presence of the Agent in (55a). So why should the existence of an outside 'cause' be coded twice, by the semantic function of the first and of the second argument, as it is by Dik? Note that the typology of SoAs to which the assignment of nuclear semantic functions is tied does not include a feature pertaining to external influences or participants although this is an important consideration in Chafe's (1970) typology and also in Halliday's (1985) transitivity and ergativity systems. Therefore the double coding of an outside participant cannot be argued for with reference to the typology of SoAs, as in the case of the Positioner vs Agent distinction mentioned above. In fact the parameters defining the typology of SoAs provide another argument against Dik's analysis and for the canonical one. As pointed out by Halliday (1985: 145), external participants notwithstanding, in both (55a) and (55b) it is *the vase* that undergoes some sort of change in state or location. As an example of the latter consider (56) from Keenan (1984: 208).

(56) a. The ball rolled/bounced/fell into the pool.
      b. Bill rolled/bounced/dropped the ball into the pool.

Change is part of the definition of dynamicity (see §3.2.2.4), one of the features of the typology of SoAs. Therefore the assignment of the same semantic function to the non-controlling entity undergoing a change irrespective of whether it is a first or a second argument would be far more consistent with Dik's overall approach to semantic functions than is his current analysis.

The double Goal [Experiencer] and Recipient [Experiencer] functions are assigned to animate arguments in experiential predications with a stimulus, an FG Force, as a first argument, for example:

(57) a. The book upset the Islamic community.
      b. Heat soothes me.
      c. A wonderful idea occurred to him.
      d. That has also happened to me.

Another likely candidate for these double functions is the so-called 'possessive-dative' found in many languages in constructions such as (58).

Polish
(58) a. Obcieli   nam   pensje.
          cut:3pl   us:dat   wages:acc
          'They cut our wages.'

      b. Piotr   zepsuł   Januszowi   zegarek.
          Peter:nom   broke   John:dat   watch:acc
          'Peter broke John's watch.'

In many grammatical frameworks, the equivalent of the FG Goal is the only nuclear (inner, complement, argument, etc.) semantic function that does not double up as a satellite (Sommers 1987: 194–195). This also holds for FG, though not in the case of languages that have a productive passive. Owing to the FG treatment of the passive as not involving a reduction in valency (see §4.3), in languages such as English with a productive passive, none of the first argument functions in (48) is a possible satellite function. Most of the semantic functions that do occur as satellites were mentioned in the introductory discussion of the layered structure of the clause in §2.3.2. They are listed again in (59), for the sake of completeness.

(59) Satellite semantic functions
    (a) further specification of the SoA: Manner, Quality, Instrument;
    (b) additional participants: Beneficiary, Company;
    (c) the temporal dimension: Time, Duration, Frequency;
    (d) the spatial dimension: Location, Source, Direction, Path;
    (e) cause and motivation: Circumstance, Cause, Reason, Purpose, Result.

The distribution of the non-nuclear semantic functions is partially determined by the typology of SoAs, in that certain satellites demand a particular type of predication, and by the layered structure of the clause (see §2.3.2 and ch. 5).

An important distinction between nuclear and non-nuclear semantic functions is that the former are subject to Fillmore's (1968: 21) one case per clause constraint, which is nowadays standardly interpreted as applying solely to nuclear predications rather than to simplex predications *per se*. In line with this constraint only the italicized temporal and locational terms in (60) are seen to belong to the nuclear predication.

(60) a. I waited *for an hour* yesterday.
      b. The press meetings lasted *half an hour* every Tuesday.
      c. In Amsterdam, I lived *on the Singel*.
      d. They arrived *in Paris* at Roissy.

The stacking up of satellites appears to be subject only to processing limitations. Witness the examples in (61).

(61) a. She is knitting a sweater for my husband for me.
      b. He sat in an armchair on his sunny veranda at Summervile house in Kent (and dared to complain, mind you).
      c. Trains leave every fifteen minutes from 7 a.m. Monday to Friday throughout the summer.

In closing the discussion on semantic functions, it needs to be mentioned that Dik does not view his inventory of semantic functions as exhaustive, or the semantic functions postulated as definitive. FG is ready to accommodate additional distinctions if they are necessary to capture cross-linguistic regularities.

4 Syntactic functions

4.1 INTRODUCTION

FG offers a very restrictive view of syntactic functions as compared to both traditional grammar and other current grammatical frameworks, most notably RG. It aims to provide a characterization of syntactic functions consistent with the functional orientation of the theory which would reflect their contribution to the organization of the utterance and would simultaneously enable them to be distinguished from pragmatic functions, these being seen to constitute a higher-level functional domain of clause structure. Only two syntactic functions are recognized, the subject and object. These functions are regarded as neither primitive nor universal. Nor in the case of languages actually manifesting syntactic functions are subjects and objects considered to be necessarily present in all the structures of the language. Furthermore, syntactic functions are potentially distinguishable only at one level of representation.

In traditional grammar the subject and object are characterized in relation to the notion of transitivity, which itself receives no independent definition. The subject is identified as the nominal constituent of a transitive verb which has the same grammatical properties, i.e. position in the clause, case or adpositional marking, and control of verbal agreement, as that of the sole argument of an intransitive verb. The object is typically considered to be the non-subject argument of a transitive verb. A transitive verb is in turn characterized as a verb that takes a direct object, and an intransitive verb as one that does not.[1] The circularity inherent in the above characterization of subject and object is by and large replicated in current grammatical theory, though typically disguised in one form or another, be it by a model-specific definition (e.g. GB or Anderson's Case Grammar) or by the treatment of syntactic functions as linguistic primitives (e.g. RG, LFG). In either case, in practice linguists tend to rely on word order, morphological marking, syntactic behaviour (e.g. the ability to relativize, passivize or function as a controller of covert arguments) and semantic characteristics (e.g. control and affect) to identify subjects and objects.

A morpho-syntactic approach to subject and object is not compatible with the functional orientation of FG. Although termed syntactic, the subject and object functions are defined notionally in relation to a theory-specific interpretation of the notion *perspective* (see §4.2). The subject is taken to determine the primary and the object the secondary perspective for the interpretation of the predication. Therefore Dik (1989: 25) suggests that strictly speaking the subject and object functions are not syntactic but rather perspectival.

The FG approach to subjects and objects constitutes one of the most controversial aspects of the theory. As far as subject assignment is concerned, the FG analysis draws heavily on the Philippine language type of clausal organization, for which the very recognition of subjects has been hotly disputed. As a result, many more languages emerge as lacking a subject than under any other current analysis. The object function, in terms of the FG approach, becomes a cross-linguistic rarity. Paradoxically, even in some of the Bantu languages renowned for their extensive object assignment possibilities, the recognition of an object function requires some manipulation of the basic tenets of syntactic function assignment. Another consequence of the FG interpretation of subjecthood and objecthood is the theory's characterization of transitivity directly in terms of semantic functions rather than syntactic functions. A transitive verb in FG is a verb with two or three arguments where the A^1 is an Agent, Positioner or Force and the A^2 is a Goal. This characterization of transitivity fares no better than the traditional one based on the presence of an object, since there is no independent semantic characterization of 'goalhood'. On the whole the FG and traditional approaches to transitivity converge in identifying the same class of predications as transitive, passive predications being the major exception (see §4.3). It must be mentioned that in the FG literature, the notion of (quantitative and qualitative) *valency* tends to be used in preference to transitivity. This produces a number of descriptive problems particularly in relation to ergative languages, and necessitates a certain amount of circumlocution which even adherents of FG do not employ consistently.[2]

The treatment of syntactic functions is also one of the most confusing areas of FG. Most of the problems encountered in the understanding of the FG position on syntactic functions stem from the fact that the class of items identified as bearing the subject or object functions in FG overlap virtually but not completely with the more familiar morpho-syntactically defined set of subjects or objects. This near, yet not total, identity makes it difficult to pinpoint where exactly the difference in the FG handling of syntactic functions lies. The problem is compounded, on the one hand, by Dik's supplementing of the perspective-based definition of syntactic functions with morpho-syntactic criteria, and on the other, by the general (cross-theory) recognition of perspective as a determinant (or consequence) of subject and object selection (see §4.2 and §4.2.1).

I take the specificity of the FG approach to syntactic functions to be primarily a matter of a difference in focus. While recognizing that subject and object are multi-facet concepts, Dik seeks to explicate their perspectivizing role at the cost of their morpho-syntactic characteristics, and from the many facets of perspective, he again singles out the sphere of semantic functions, downplaying the established discourse correlates of subjecthood and objecthood. He specifically rejects the view, espoused by Comrie (1981) and Givón (1984), that the subject and object are grammaticalized primary and secondary topics. The syntactic functions are therefore neither syntactic nor pragmatic, but represent a distinct level of structural organization which is seen to contribute to the interpretation of the predication. One cannot help but sympathize with this attempt to isolate a level of structure corresponding to the complex array of interacting features which are seen to underlie the recalcitrant notions of subject and object. Whether the path chosen by FG is the optimal one is, of course, another matter.[3]

Dik's overall conception of syntactic functions has not changed since his 1978 exposition of FG, but his handling of particular issues connected with subject and object assignment has undergone various modifications. Of special interest is the current (Dik 1989) role ascribed to the argument positions, i.e. A^1, A^2 and A^3, which are used in a way reminiscent of the initial- and intermediate-strata subject and object relations of RG (see §4.2.1). Though there is no one-to-one relationship, in the main, the FG A^1, A^2 and A^3 correspond to RG initial or intermediate subjects, and direct and indirect objects respectively. Thus some of the changes in initial relations involving advancement to subject or direct and indirect object in RG find their analogue in FG in the acquisition of argument status (in the case of satellites) or shifts in argument position, say from A^3 to A^2 or A^2 to A^1. From the perspective of a morpho-syntactic approach to syntactic functions, as in RG, it could be argued that shifting the subject and object functions from the syntax to a special perspectival level of clausal organization in FG has led to the emergence of a new set of syntactico-semantic functions.

However, given the semantic bias of FG, the status of a term as an A^1, A^2 or A^3 is more fundamental to the semantics of the predication than its potential syntactic function. Consequently, from the point of view of FG, it is the failure to recognize the role of argument positions which has induced the proliferation of syntactic functions in a theory such as RG.

Given the significance of the notion of perspective for the FG treatment of syntactic functions, our discussion of the major issues connected with syntactic function assignment will begin with a consideration of perspective (§4.2). The controversial analysis of the passive necessitated by the FG perspective-based view of subject assignment will be the topic of §4.3. In §4.4. we will deal with object assignment and we will draw special attention to the treatment of non-objects. And the final section §4.5 will deal with the FG version of the representation of the relationship between semantic functions and syntactic functions as captured in the Semantic Function Hierarchy (SFH).

4.2. PERSPECTIVE

Most theorists readily acknowledge a relationship between the subject and object functions and perspective (point of view, orientation, vantage point, viewpoint, point of departure, camera angle, anchoring point) or the related concepts of empathy (Kuno 1987), focus of interest (Zubin 1979), familiarity (Ertel 1977), semantic focus (Van der Auwera 1981) or attentional focus (DeLancey 1981). FG is unusual in being the only theory to elevate perspective to the level of a defining criterion of the subject and object functions.

The notion of perspective, as used in linguistics, draws heavily on both the everyday and literary uses of the term.[4] In its non-technical sense, perspective refers to the presentation or viewing of situations and events through the eyes, literally or figuratively, of one of a range of potential parties. The possibility of choice is typically considered to be crucial, it being difficult to recognize the imposition of a perspective if no alternatives can be envisaged. In literary studies considerations of point of view involve both the nature of the adopted perspective, whose perceptual or world view is being advanced, and the identity of the person (e.g. real or implied author, narrator, character or any combination of these) presenting it.[5] Investigations of perspective in literary studies concern primarily matters of lexical choice as well as tense and aspectual distinctions, the use of anaphoric devices and indexicals, and the sequencing of events. All these factors also play a role in linguistic approaches to perspective. For linguists, however, the notion of perspective is primarily tied to the coding of participant roles via morphological marking, agreement and order, all of which are inherently intertwined with the subject and object functions. This narrow approach to perspective involves both inter- and intra-language considerations. The former, typological, considerations centre on the conceptual bias or cognitive profile of languages as reflected in typological distinctions such as accusative vs ergative vs active language. Within a given language, differences in perspective are sought in structural oppositions which include alternations between actives/passives, ergatives/antipassives, alternative predicate frames, and converse or reciprocal predicates. It is with this range of oppositions that the FG notion of perspective is concerned.

4.2.1 Perspective in FG

The FG conception of perspective is not outlined in sufficient detail to enable one to state unequivocally that the relation between two predications does or does not constitute an instance of a difference in perspective. Therefore the discussion in this and later sections of this chapter contains a certain degree of speculation. The following account of perspective represents what I take to be the FG prototype of perspective. Already authorized and potential departures from the prototype will be commented on in the body of the chapter.

The key notion in the FG view of perspective is *sameness of SoA*. Differences in perspective are taken to obtain solely between predications depicting the same SoA. As discussed in §3.1, since an FG SoA is defined on the nuclear predication, two or more predications can only qualify as realizations of the same SoA if they have identical predicate frames. This identity must involve all the component parts of the predicate frame (§2.2.1), i.e. not only argument structure and semantic functions, but also semantic features, categorial properties, selectional restrictions, lexical choice, etc. Such an approach to perspective excludes from the FG domain of perspectivizing, in the sense just outlined,[6] most of the earlier-mentioned alternations typically cited as exemplars of the notion of perspective, such as oppositions involving:

(a) reciprocal predicates (1):

(1)   a.   Sam met Cindy at the station.
        b.   Cindy met Sam at the station.
        c.   Sam and Cindy/Cindy and Sam met at the station.

(b) converse predicates (2):

(2) a. Jill sold the car to Jack.
    b. Jack bought the car from Jill.

(c) so-called ergative predicates (3):

(3) a. Fred rolled the ball down the hill.
    b. The ball rolled down the hill.

(d) lexical passives (4):

(4) a. The result surprised me.
    b. I was surprised at/with the result.

(e) semantic antipassives (5):

(5) a. I believe that man.
    b. I believe in that man.

(f) locative and instrumental alternations with trivalent predicates of the 'load' type (6):

(6) a. Max loaded hay onto the wagon.
    b. Max loaded the wagon with hay.

(g) deictic distinctions (7):

(7) a. The door opened and a woman came in.
    b. The door opened and a woman went in.

(h) anaphoric distinctions (8):

(8) a. Jack hit the man.
    b. My brother hit the man.

In fact the only differences between predications which the FG notion of perspective is intended to capture are those involving the internal organization of semantic functions within a given predicate frame. These permutations, if accompanied by the transfer of certain morpho-syntactic properties from one semantic function to another, are taken as defining subject and object assignment. Perspective in FG is thus solely a matter of the mapping between semantic functions and syntactic functions.

This is captured in the postulated interdependence between perspective and subject and object assignment. The subject is taken to define the primary, and the object the secondary, perspective for the interpretation of the SoA depicted in a given predication. The two perspectives, primary and secondary, are defined ostensively on the basis of the active/passive opposition as in (9) in the case of the primary perspective, and in terms of the so-called dative-shift opposition as in (10) in the case of the secondary perspective.

(9) a. Jeff hit the child.
    b. The child was hit by Jeff.

(10) a. Charles gave a rose to Anna.
     b. Charles gave Anna a rose.

In (9a) the act of hitting is claimed to be depicted from the point of view of the Agent *Jeff*, in (9b) from the perspective of the Goal *the child*. And analogously in (10); the secondary perspective in (10a) is that of the Goal *a rose*, in (10b) that of the Recipient *Anna*. The active/passive and dative-shift oppositions are used in FG not only to exemplify differences in perspective, but also to define subject and object assignment. The existence of a productive active/passive opposition and the occurrence of dative-shift constructions in a given language are necessary conditions for recognizing, respectively, subject and object assignment in that language. In other words, for languages which lack either or both of these oppositions no subject or object functions are posited. Thus syntactic functions both determine and are determined by perspective. More specifically, the possibility of choosing among alternative perspectives is indicative of the existence of syntactic function assignment, while the actual syntactic function assignment imposes one of the potential perspectives.

As one would expect, the choice of the secondary, object perspective is conditional on the prior selection of the subject perspective. Therefore object assignment in a language automatically entails subject assignment (though not necessarily to the same range of semantic functions), whereas the converse does not hold.

4.3 SUBJECT ASSIGNMENT, THE PASSIVE AND THE ANTI-PASSIVE

Given that in FG considerations of perspective are restricted to predications based on the same underlying predicate frame, and that the major diagnostic for subject assignment is the active/passive opposition, actives and passives are taken to display identical argument structure. Such a conception of the passive is widely accepted. However, though semantically bivalent, the passive is typically viewed as syntactically monovalent; the passive actor[7] is seen to function not as a syntactic argument of the predicate, but as an adjunct. Under the FG approach, by contrast, actives and passives differ only in regard to subject assignment; the quantitative (number of arguments) valency, as well as the qualitative (nature of the arguments) valency, are the same.

The fact that the actor is semantically present in passive constructions is universally recognized (e.g. Perlmutter and Postal 1977; Keenan 1981; Siewierska 1984a; Shibatani 1985; Roeper 1987). The underlying presence of an actor is what is seen to distinguish the passive clauses in (11) from the related derived intransitive structures (called middles, ergatives or anticausatives) in (12).

(11) a. The watch was broken deliberately.
b. Polish books were sold well.

(12) a. The watch broke (*deliberately).
b. Polish books sold well.

Support for a covert actor in (11) comes from the possibility of using an agentive adverb such as *deliberately* in (11a) as compared to (12a). Note also the difference in the interpretation of the manner adverbial *well* in (11b) and (12b); in the passive the adverb is interpreted as qualifying the actor, while in the derived intransitive it qualifies the event designated by the verb. Moreover, the implied actor of the passive can function as a controller[8] into purposive clauses as illustrated in (13b).

(13) a. *The boat sank to collect the insurance.
b. The boat was sunk to collect the insurance.

And finally, the implicit actor of the passive can even be referred to anaphorically, as shown in (14).

(14) The game was played without stepping on *each other's* toes.

Equally widely accepted is the syntactic adjunct status of the passive actor. The passive actor, unlike a typical argument, is generally covert rather than overt. More significantly, however, the morphological marking of passive clauses, even those with a lexical actor, is identical to that of intransitive clauses. This is most evident in morphologically ergative languages in which the subject of a transitive verb appears in the ergative case, while the subject of an intransitive verb takes absolutive marking. Greenlandic Eskimo (Woodbury 1977: 323–324) is a case in point.

Greenlandic Eskimo
(15) a. Aŋut-ip araŋq-∅ taku- vaa.
man-erg woman-abs see- ind:3sg:3sg
'The man saw the woman.'

b. Aŋut-∅ autlar -puq.
man-abs go away -ind:3sg
'The man went away.'

As shown in (15c) the passive subject is also in the absolutive, just like the subject of the intransitive clause (15b).

c. Araŋq-∅ aŋuti-mit/mut/mik taku-tuu/niqar-puq.
woman-abs man-abl/al/instr see-pass-ind:3sg
'The woman was seen by the man.'

The intransitivity of the passive (15c) is also indicated by the cross-referencing pronoun on the verb. In Greenlandic Eskimo the cross-referencing pronouns are phonologically fused with the particular mood suffixes. There are separate suffixes for intransitive subject terms, and other portmanteau forms for all the possible person and number combinations of the transitive subject and direct object. A comparison of (15b) with (15c) reveals that the cross-referencing pronoun used in the passive clause (15c) is the same as in the monovalent (15b).

In grammatical frameworks which adhere to a multi-level theory of clause structure, the semantic presence of the passive actor is reconciled with its syntactically peripheral status by deriving passives from an underlying structure where the actor is an argument (either left unfilled or filled by an empty or unspecified term), and subsequently reducing it to a subsidiary status by some theory-internal procedure such as semantic function absorption (GB) or demotion (RG). The FG equivalent of such an analysis would be to treat the passive as an instance of predicate formation. The relevant predicate formation rule would take an active predicate frame with an unspecified A^1 as input and derive a passive predicate frame in which the A^1 of the active has been reduced, as shown in (16).

(16) Potential passive predicate formation rule
input: predicate$_v$ $(x_1)_{Ag(Un)}$ $(x_2)_{Go}$
output: predicate$_{pass}$ ∅ $(x_2)_{Go}$

Actives and passives receive an analysis along the lines of (16) in Bresnan's (1982a) LFG. For FG, however, (16) does not constitute a possible means of capturing the relationship between actives and passives in the context of subject assignment, since it would destroy the whole conception of syntactic functions advanced by the theory. The essence of the FG syntactic functions is that they impose different perspectives on the same predicate frame. The predicate formation analysis, on the other hand, defines a distinct passive predicate frame. Needless to say, there is no way of reconciling the contradictory claims entailed by the two analyses. If the passive were to be derived via predicate formation, then actives and passives cannot be seen to depict the same SoA, and therefore cannot be related by a notion of perspective based on sameness of SoA. There is also another reason for rejecting a predicate formation account of the active/passive opposition in FG. A predicate frame, be it basic or derived, is a representation of the semantic structure of a predication. Therefore, in view of the obligatory semantic presence of the actor in the passive, the actor must be specified as being a semantic argument of the predicate. Given the valency-reducing predicate formation analysis, this in turn would require referring to the input predicate frame, which in effect would be tantamount to recognizing levels of derivation, a procedure in conflict with the FG approach to clause structure.[9]

4.3.1 The passive in Philippine-type languages

The debate on the most appropriate analysis of clause structure in the Philippine-type languages is not yet closed. There are two major points of controversy: whether these languages lend themselves to an analysis in terms of the syntactic function subject (cf. Schachter 1976; Foley and Van Valin 1984 with De Wolf 1988; Shibatani 1988b) and whether they are nominative/accusative (Bell 1983; Perlmutter and Postal 1984a; Shibatani 1988b) or ergative (Payne 1982; De Guzman 1983; Cooreman *et al.* 1984; Blake 1990). FG adopts the nominative/accusative analysis. As for the subject, the Philippine languages are seen to have a subject par excellence in that it is open to a wide range of semantic functions and thus provides the best exemplification of the FG approach to subject assignment. Given that the passive is the major diagnostic for subject assignment in FG, the Philippine languages also play an important role with respect to the FG view of subject assignment in relation to the analysis of passive constructions, particularly in regard to the proposed treatment of the passive actor. It is this issue which I will concentrate on below, postponing a consideration of a potential FG analysis of subject assignment under the alternative ergative view of Philippine clause structure to §4.3.2.1.

Under a nominative/accusative analysis of the Philippine languages, the basic transitive clause is the so-called actor focus clause, as in (17a) adapted from Shibatani (1988b: 88).

Cebuano
(17) a. Ni-hatag si Juan sa libro sa bata.
AF-give act/foc Juan goal book rec child
'*Juan* gave the book to the child.'

Assuming the basic nature of (17a), if we take the grammatical subject in Philippine-type languages to be the entity often referred to by Philippinists as the 'topic' or 'focus'[10] identified morphologically by particles such as *ang/si* (Cebuano, Tagalog, Hiligaynon), *ti* (Ilocano), *ing* (Kapampangan) or *say/si* (Pangasinan), the clauses in (17b)–(17d), also from Shibatani (1988b: 89), can be seen as instances of the passive.

(17) b. Gi-hatag ni Juan ang libro sa bata.
GF-give act Juan goal/foc book rec child
'Juan gave *the book* to the child.'

c. Gi-hatag-an ang bata ni Juan sa libro.
DF-give rec/foc child act Juan goal book
'Juan gave *the child* the book.'

d. I-hiwa ang kutsilyo sa mangga ni Maria.
IF-cut instr/foc knife goal mango act Maria
'Maria cut the mango *with a knife*.'

In terms of the FG analysis, each of the clauses in (17) is viewed as manifesting different subject assignment; in (17a) the subject is an Agent, in (17b) a Goal, in (17c) a Recipient and in (17d) an Instrument. Most of the Philippine languages also permit subject assignment to the Beneficiary, Direction, Source and Location. The semantic function, strictly speaking the macro-semantic function of the subject term, is in each case indicated by affixation on the verb. In Cebuano, as shown in (17), actor focus constructions are marked by the prefix *ni*, goal focus clauses by the prefix *gi-* (17b), recipient focus (17c) as well as direction and location focus take the circumfix *gi-an*, and instrumental focus constructions require the prefix *i-* (17d).

Though (17b)–(17d) meet some of the general characteristics of the familiar Indo-European personal passive (see e.g. Siewierska 1984a: 79–86), they differ from such passives in regard to text frequency and agent defocusing. In most languages passives are rare. In the Philippine languages, on the other hand, the number of passives is either greater than or about equal to that of actives. Cooreman *et al.* (1984) state that 76% of the transitive clauses in their Tagalog corpus were goal focus constructions. The corresponding figure given by Shibatani (1988b) for Cebuano is 46%. The high text frequency of the Philippine non-actor focus constructions is attributable to the wide range of semantic functions accessible to subject, to the requirement (Tagalog) or strong preference (Cebuano) for subjectivizing definite Goals, and to the fact that several grammatical processes such as relativization and certain types of question formation are constrained to subject terms. Another reason for the surprisingly frequent occurrence of the non-actor focus constructions in texts is provided by Hopper and Thompson (1980) who argue that the Philippine languages utilize voice as a means of discourse foregrounding and backgrounding where by *foreground* is understood the material which supplies the main points of discourse, and by *background* the part of the discourse that does not immediately contribute to the speaker's goal, but merely assists, amplifies or comments on it. According to Hopper and Thompson the Philippine languages represent an extreme case where the statistical correlation between definite Goals and foreground has resulted in a specialization of non-actor focus to denote foregrounding.

Turning to the matter of actor defocusing, in English the vast majority of passive clauses are actorless. The statistics vary, depending on the nature of the text, from 80% (Svartvik 1966: 41) to 97% (Weiner and Labov 1983). Similar statistics are cited for other languages. In the Philippine languages, on the other hand, non-actor focus constructions, particularly goal focus ones, display a very high incidence of overt actors. Shibatani (1988b: 93) states that in his text counts of non-actor focus clauses in Cebuano, 40 out of 49 had a specified actor. In Matthew Dryer's investigation of Tagalog, referred to in Hopper and Thompson (1980), there was an expressed actor in 57 out of the 67 goal focus constructions. These statistics suggest that the actor in the Philippine passive, unlike in English, is not a peripheral term.

As regards morphological marking, the passive actor receives the same marker as the Goal in a transitive clause. This is obscured in the examples in (17) because proper names in non-actor focus constructions occur with the preposition *ni*, while common nouns take *sa* or, if non-referential, *ug*. The common marking of the passive actor and transitive Goal can be seen by comparing the examples in (17) with both the actor focus (18a) where *Pedro* is the Goal, and the goal focus (18b) where the actor *magdadaro* is a common noun.

Cebuano (Shibatani 1988b: 107; Bell 1983: 157)
(18) a. Ni-kumusta si Juan ni Pedro.
AF-greet act/foc Juan goal Pedro
'Juan greeted Pedro.'

b. Gi-palit sa magdadaro ang karabao.
GF-buy act farmer goal/foc buffalo
'The farmer bought *the buffalo*.'

The verbal marking identifies all the focus constructions, including the actor focus ones, as equally marked or unmarked.[11] Therefore there is no morphological evidence either from nominal or verbal marking suggesting that the passive actor has lost its argument status.

On the contrary, the syntactic behaviour of the passive actor lends strong support to an analysis under which it continues to function as a verbal argument. Unlike in English, the Philippine passive actor can serve as the antecedent of a reflexive subject pronoun, control deletion into a coordinate or complement clause, and itself delete in imperatives or under co-reference of a main clause controller. The first of these phenomena is illustrated in (19), which is a locative focus clause (Foley and Van Valin 1977: 308), the second in (20) (Shibatani 1988b: 107–108).

Tagalog
(19) I-b-in-ili ng lalake ng isda ang kaniyang sarili.
LF-buy act man goal fish ben/foc him self
'A/the man bought some fish *for himself*.'[12]

Cebuano
(20) Gi-bunal-an ni Juan si Pedro ug ni-lakaw-∅.
DF-hit act Juan dir/foc Pedro and AF-leave
'Juan hit *Pedro* and left.' (∅ = Juan.)

Shibatani observes that if the actor *Juan* in the (first) non-actor focus clause of (20) were like the actor in the English passive *Pedro was hit by Juan*, the person leaving in the second clause could only be interpreted as being *Pedro*, while in Cebuano it is *Juan* who leaves.

In sum, the near-obligatory presence of the passive actor coupled with its syntactic properties is fully compatible with its maintaining its argument status as under Dik's subject assignment analysis. However, as Dik himself admits, the Philippine languages are exceptional in displaying a remarkably wide range of subject assignment possibilities, and as such must be placed at one extreme of a potential subject assignment continuum. Therefore it is somewhat of a paradox that the languages classified as atypical in regard to the eligibility of semantic functions to subject simultaneously provide the best illustration of the validity of the FG treatment of the passive actor.

The tying of passivization to subject assignment in FG, coupled with the fact that subject assignment relates predications with the same quantitative and qualitative valency, entails that only passives that are amenable to an analysis involving no change in valency enter into considerations of subject assignment.[13] This excludes various constructions which are commonly referred to as 'passive', such as lexical passives (a change in semantic function), reflexive passives (typically clear evidence for argument reduction) and, by definition, impersonal passives (no overt subject), from being potential diagnostics of subject assignment. Such 'passives' are dealt with in FG by several kinds of valency-changing predicate formation rules (Dik 1983c; Kahrel 1985a).[14] It follows that languages possessing only these latter type of passives (e.g. Amharic, Choctaw, Hungarian, Hindi, Lardil, Mojave, Nani, Tigre and Ute) and of course languages lacking passives altogether (e.g. most of the languages of the Australian continent, see Blake 1987: 64–67) are not considered to have subjects in FG.

4.3.2 Ergative languages and the antipassive

The passive is generally seen to be characteristic of morphologically accusative languages, while its structural analogue in morphologically ergative languages is often taken to be the antipassive. Whereas the passive is a means of downgrading the A^1 of a transitive predicate, the antipassive is considered to be a strategy for backgrounding the A^2 – the Goal.[15] Moreover, the antipassive parallels the passive in that it allows the marked argument of a transitive predicate (the accusative in the case of the passive, and the ergative in the antipassive) to occur in the unmarked nominative/absolutive slot.

In terms of Heath's (1976) functional typology, there are two main subtypes of the antipassive, semantic and syntactic. The semantic antipassive is common cross-linguistically, if not universal (see Tsunoda 1988). It is used when the Goal is indefinite or non-specific to emphasize the nature of the activity rather than its possible effects on the A^2. The following example (21) is from an Australian Aboriginal language of north-east Queensland, Warungu (Tsunoda 1988: 598, 613).

Warungu
(21) a. Pama-ngku   kamu-ø   yangka-n.
        man-erg   water-abs   search-pres/past
        'The man looks/looked for water.'

b. Pama-ø   kamu-wu   yangka-kali-n.
   man-abs water-dat search-a/p-pres/past
   'The man looks/looked for water.'

c. Pama-ø   yani-ø.
   man-abs go-pres/past
   'The man goes/went.'

Warungu is a fairly typical ergative language in that the A^1 of a transitive predication such as (21a) is marked in the ergative case, the A^2 in the absolutive. The absolutive is also the case of the intransitive A^1, as in (21c). We see that in the antipassive (21b) the A^1 appears with absolutive rather than ergative marking, and the A^2 occurs in the dative. The former Goal may also take instrumental marking and in other languages locative, ergative or even absolutive marking. The semantic antipassive often exhibits aspectual or modal differences (e.g. habit, inclination, non-completion, careful attention, etc.) from the corresponding active.

By contrast, no additional meanings are attached to the syntactic antipassive which Heath (1976) characterizes as occurring in dependent clauses to mark co-reference relations. It is this syntactic antipassive that is primarily associated with ergative languages. As an illustration, consider one of the uses of the antipassive in another Australian Aboriginal language.

Yalarnnga (Blake 1987: 149)
(22) a. Karlu   ngali   ngani-mu wartatyi-wu pirnpa-li-(ny)tyarta.
        father   we:dl   go-past   orange-dat   fetch-a/p-purp
        'My father and I went to get some wild oranges.'

   b. Nga-thu ngapa-mu waya pirlapirla pulytyuru-wu miya-li-nytyarta.
      I-erg   tell-past that child   chip-dat   get-a/p-purp
      'I told that kid to pick up the chips.'

   c. Nga-thu miya-nytyarta yimarta ngathi-nytyarta.
      I-erg   get-purp   fish   cook-purp
      'I'll get some fish to cook.'

The antipassive, marked by the verbal suffix -li, is obligatory in this purposive construction if the transitive A^1 of a dependent clause co-references a Goal or an intransitive A^1 of the governing clause. The dependent transitive A^1 is co-referential with the governing intransitive A^1 in (22a), with the governing Goal in (22b), and hence the antipassive and 'chip' in the dative. In (22c), by contrast, no antipassive is required, thus 'fish' is in the absolutive, as the co-reference relations obtain between two transitive A^1.

Since ergative languages that have the syntactic antipassive typically lack a passive, the question arises of whether there is a connection between subject assignment and antipassivization comparable to that of subject assignment and passivization. Due to the fact that in the antipassive it is the A^2 that is downgraded and not the A^1, the antipassive may at first sight seem to be of potential value only to object assignment, not subject assignment. And indeed the question of the relationship between subject assignment and the antipassive pertains only to the small number of languages such as Warungu, Yalarnnga, Yidin^y, Kalkatungu and the celebrated Dyirbal that in addition to morphological ergativity display a measure of syntactic ergativity (Blake 1979a). In these languages a number of morpho-syntactic phenomena single out the transitive Goal and the intransitive A^1 for preferential treatment to the exclusion of the transitive A^1.

It is debatable whether the notion subject should be extended to cover the transitive Goal and intransitive A^1 in such languages. Some linguists maintain that it should (see Dixon 1972; Blake 1979a; Dowty 1982; Marantz 1984). Others (e.g. proponents of RG; Blake 1990) argue that the term subject should be reserved for a (primary) identification of transitive and intransitive A^1, while the grouping of a transitive Goal and an intransitive A^1 should be covered by a separate grammatical relation or function, namely the *absolutive*. In FG, given the availability of the notion A^1 which is independent of transitivity, there seems little motivation to reserve the notion *subject* for a primary grouping of the transitive and intransitive A^1. Therefore assuming that the notion *subject* is allowed to embrace the transitive Goal and intransitive A^1 in FG, the choice of using an ergative construction over an antipassive one or vice versa can be interpreted as involving an alternation of semantic functions, which is, as the reader will recall, the criterion underlying the FG notion of subject assignment.

In terms of such a subject assignment analysis, subject assignment to the Goal would result in an ergative clause, subject assignment to an Agent or one of the other A^1 semantic functions would produce an antipassive. Dik does not, however, consider the ergative/antipassive opposition to be an instance of different subject assignment. After our discussion of the passive, the reason for this should be fairly obvious. The change in the quantitative valency of the predicate in the antipassive as compared to the ergative suggested by the oblique marking of the A^2, and the absolutive marking of the A^1 is incompatible with the claim that subject assignment relates predications depicting the same SoA. Dik (1978: 169, 1983c) therefore suggests capturing the relationship between the ergative and the antipassive by the detransitivizing predicate formation rule in (23) as a result of which the Goal is combined with the predicate.

(23) Predicate formation antipassive rule
input: predicate$_v$ (x1)$_{Ag}$ (x2)$_{Go}$
output: (predicate$_v$ (x2)$_{Go}$)$_v$ (x1)$_{Ag}$

Though appropriate for the semantic antipassive, (23) is a questionable representation of the syntactic antipassive, since in constructions such as (22b) there is no evidence of Goal incorporation into the predicate. Note that the dative Goal in (22b) receives a definite interpretation. Furthermore, in some languages, for instance Warungu, the Goal in an antipassive may occur in the focus of a question (24) or undergo focal fronting (25b) which is completely at odds with its alleged incorporated status.

Warungu (Tsunoda 1988: 625, 643)
(24) [Tasaku Tsunoda's informant, who had weak eyesight, saw a man working nearby, and asked him:]
Ngani -ngku papa -kali-n? Kalpa? Kalpa papa-n?
what -instr dig -a/p -p/p sand:abs sand:abs dig-p/p
'What is [he] digging? Sand? Is [he] digging the sand?'

(25) [From the myth about the blue tongue lizard. 'I asked the blue tongue lizard; where do you get water from? No, there is no water here.']
a. Ngana yaku mutya-n.
we:nom grass:abs eat:p/p
'We eat grass [to get moist from it].'

b. Yaku- nguku ngana mutya-kali-n yarru-n-ta.
grass- instr we:nom eat-a/p-p/p here-lig-loc
'We eat *grass* here.'

In grammatical frameworks which recognize demotions, such as RG, the Goal in the antipassive is treated as a chômeur, i.e. a term which formerly bore the subject or object relation to the predicate. In FG this is not a possible analysis, since predicate formation operates on predicate frames which constitute the input to predications, whereas syntactic function assignment is applied to predications. Consequently, as far as argument structure is concerned, predicate formation may only change the qualitative or quantitative valency of the predicate. The FG equivalent of demotion is thus argument reduction. An alternative FG account of the syntactic antipassive could therefore involve a predicate formation rule deriving an intransitive predicate via reduction (rather than incorporation) of the Goal and subsequently introducing the Goal as a predication satellite, as in the case of the Agent of a reflexive passive mentioned in note 14. This would require relaxing the restriction precluding Goals from bearing a satellite function.[16] The only other possibility open to FG is an analysis in terms of a change in qualititive valency. In the case of the antipassive, this is not, however, a promising option because there is no evidence, other than the atypical morphological marking of the Goal, of a change in semantic functions.[17]

The major problem with a predicate formation treatment of the syntactic antipassive is that it belies the functional nature of this process. The syntactic antipassive is used for clause linkage: subordination, coordination and sentence sequencing. Therefore it is much more naturally viewed as a predication-level than a predicate-level phenomenon. And the only operations on predications recognized in FG involve syntactic or pragmatic function assignment. One may therefore conclude that the relationship between subject assignment and the antipassive deserves more detailed consideration in FG.

Interestingly enough Dik's rejection of a subject assignment analysis of the antipassive does not prevent him from recognizing a subject comprising the two absolutive arguments in Dyirbal (Dik 1980: 123–125) and presumably in the other syntactically ergative languages mentioned. He (Dik 1989: 244) argues that the ergative construction in Dyirbal should be considered to be an obligatory passive which lacks a corresponding active. Despite the fact that there is no alternation of semantic functions to satisfy the requirement of the perspective-based definition of syntactic functions adopted in FG, the absolutive Goal in this obligatory passive is considered to be a subject. Dik seeks justification for this analysis in his typological scenario of a passive-to-ergative-to-active drift where the ergative construction is a transitional stage leading from the passive to the active. Considerable support can be found for the feasibility of such a passive-to-ergative reanalysis (see e.g. Estival and Myhill 1988). In fact such a reanalysis is claimed to have taken place in the Philippine languages by those who maintain that these languages are ergative. It is highly questionable whether this type of diachronic explanation should be incorporated in a synchronic analysis. For FG, however, the obligatory passive treatment of Dyirbal transitive clauses represents the optimal way of recognizing a subject in the language within the constraints imposed by the perspectival approach to syntactic functions.

Dik's analysis of Dyirbal could also be extended to the Philippine languages if they were to be treated as ergative in FG. In view of the fact that the ergative interpretation of Philippine languages is currently

Syntactic functions

gaining ground, it is worth briefly considering the form that this analysis takes and also the potential FG treatment of the Philippine languages in the context of such an approach.

4.3.2.1 Ergativity and the Philippine languages

The nominative/accusative interpretation of Philippine clause structure sketched in §4.3.1 is based on the following assumptions. The actor focus constructions as in (26a) are the basic transitive constructions.

Tagalog
(26) a. Bumasa   ng   libro   ang   propesor.
        read:AF goal   book   act/foc   professor
        'The professor read a book.'

The transitive Agent *propesor* in (26a) and the sole argument of an intransitive clause *propesor* in (26b) receive the same nominative marking (*ang* or with proper names *si*), while the transitive Goal *libro* appears with a different marker (*ng*), the accusative.

(26) b. Tumakbo   ang   propesor.
        ran:AF   act/foc   professor
        'The professor ran.'

The subject is the nominative (*ang*) marked term. The non-actor focus constructions as in (26c) are passive.

(26) c. Binasa   ng   propesor   ang   libro.
        read:GF   act   professor goal/foc   book
        'The book was read by the professor.'
        'The professor read *the book*.'

Under the ergative analysis the goal focus constructions (26c) are the basic transitive constructions and the actor focus (26a) is a detransitivized antipassive with the Goal functioning not as a syntactic argument but as an oblique relation. Support for the syntactically oblique status of the Goal in such constructions comes from the fact that, as mentioned in §4.3.1, it is typically indefinite, and unlike other nominals, including 'passive' actors, it cannot participate in inversion and topicalization. According to this ergative analysis, the *ang* marking is absolutive rather than nominative since it groups together the sole argument of an intransitive clause *propesor* in (26b) and the transitive Goal *libro* in (26a) as opposed to the transitive Agent *propesor* in (26a) which in turn takes ergative (*ng*) marking. The absolutive *ang* marked terms are not interpreted as subject, but are assigned a special absolutive relation or function. The two analyses are contrasted in (27).

(27) a. Accusative analysis
verb-$_{AF}$ Agent nom (*ang*)   Goal acc (*ng*)   active
verb-$_{GF}$ Agent obl (*ng*)   Goal nom (*ang*) passive

b. Ergative analysis
verb-$_{GF}$ Agent erg (*ng*)   Goal abs (*ang*) (active)
verb-$_{AF}$ Agent abs (*ang*)   Goal obl (*ng*)   (antipassive)

In terms of the ergative analysis in (27b) there is no passive if the notion is understood in the traditional Indo-European way, i.e. as involving Agent demotion and promotion of some other semantic function to subject. Instead the recipient focus, direction focus, etc. constructions such as the one in (28) and the previously cited (17b)–(17d) and (18b) are seen as involving the promotion of a Recipient, Beneficiary, Location, etc. to the favoured absolutive slot and the demotion of the Goal from that position. The Agent is unaffected by this process.

Tagalog
(28) Binilhan   ng   propesor   ang   tindahan   ng   libro.
     bought:LF   act   professor   loc/foc shop   goal book
     'The professor bought a book at *the shop*.'

The derivation of the clause in (28) is reminiscent of object assignment (advancement to A^2) rather than subject assignment.

In the light of Dik's interpretation of Dyirbal, the above ergative analysis of the Philippine languages can be accommodated in FG by treating the absolutive category as the subject. The recipient focus, location focus, etc. constructions such as (28) can then be considered as involving subject assignment. Assuming such an analysis, if by analogy with Dyirbal, the ergative, i.e. goal focus, constructions are treated as obligatory passive, the Philippine languages would emerge as lacking subject assignment to the Agent. This would not, however, make them a typological oddity, since such a situation is sanctioned for Dyirbal and perhaps other ergative languages. Consequently, the lack of subject assignment to the Agent in the Philippine languages would simply be one of the manifestations of their underlying ergativity.

The alternative would be to treat the goal focus constructions as active rather than obligatory passive and to posit subject assignment to the Agent on the basis of the active/antipassive alternation. As discussed earlier, such an analysis cannot be reconciled with, on the one hand, a predicate formation treatment of antipassives, and, on the other, the FG view of subject assignment obtaining between predications designating the same state of affairs. Note, however, that under the nominative/ accusative analysis, antipassive clauses such as (26a) or the earlier (17a) and (18a) are considered to be transitive rather than intransitive. Therefore, a case could be made in FG for treating the Philippine antipassive analogously to the passive, i.e. as involving a change in morphological marking but no change in argument structure. The difference between the active and the antipassive would then be solely one of subject assignment, but unlike in nominative/accusative languages subject assignment to the Agent would constitute the marked option.

The major advantage of an ergative analysis of Philippine languages over a nominative/accusative one is that it provides an explanation for the high text frequency of goal focus constructions relative to passives in other languages. Moreover, in most theoretical frameworks, though not in FG, the behaviour of the Agent in non-actor focus constructions discussed in §4.3.1 can be more easily reconciled with an ergative than a passive analysis. Observe that under the ergative analysis, while not being in the privileged absolutive slot, the Agent in non-actor focus constructions is nonetheless a syntactic argument, while under most treatments of the passive it is not. For FG the behaviour of the Agent is not at issue as it is considered to be an argument under the passive analysis as well. As for matters of text frequency, Shibatani (1988b: 113) points out that the natural explanation for the high text frequency of goal focus constructions that follows from the ergative analysis is to a large extent eclipsed by the inability of this analysis to explain the high number of actor focus constructions, i.e. antipassives. In languages that have antipassives, these constructions have an extremely low text frequency. For example, Kalmàr (1979: 121) gives the figure 4.9% for Eskimo, and Tsunoda (1988) 11% for Warungu, whereas in Philippine languages the occurrence of actor focus clauses is significantly higher; Cooreman et al. (1984) cite the figure 24% for Tagalog while in Cebuano according to Shibatani (1988b: 112) the corresponding figure is 52%.

In all, as far as FG is concerned, an ergative analysis of the Philippine clause has little to recommend itself. It is, of course, significant that the theory can accommodate such an analysis, particularly in view of the fact that typological adequacy is one of the three major aims that FG sets for itself.

4.4 OBJECT ASSIGNMENT

The most immediate consequence of taking the existence of a dative-shift opposition as a diagnostic for object assignment is that comparatively few languages emerge as manifesting an object function. None of the following languages, for example, has an object as defined in FG: the Slavic languages, the Romance languages, Hungarian, Modern Hebrew, Sherpa, Japanese and the Philippine languages. Constructions reminiscent of dative-shift such as in (29) are found in many of these languages, but since object assignment in FG is envisaged as relating predications built on the same predicate frame, the pairs of clauses in (29) are excluded from the domain of object assignment.

Polish
(29) a. Wylała   kawę   na   nowy   obrus.
        spilt:3sg:f coffee:acc on   new   tablecloth
        'She spilt coffee onto the new tablecloth.'

   b. Oblała   obrus   kawą.
        spilt:3sg:f tablecloth:acc coffee:instr
        'She wet the tablecloth with coffee.'

The relationship between such structures is captured in FG by means of a qualitative valency-changing predicate formation rule which shifts the semantic function Goal from the A^2 to the A^3, as shown in (30).

(30) input V $(x_1)_{Ag}$ $(x_2)_{Go}$ $(x_3)_{Loc}$
       output V $(x_1)_{Ag}$ $(x_3)_{Go}$ $(x_2)_{Instr}$
       meaning: '(x_1) pred v's (x_3) completely with (x_2)'.

An analogous predicate formation rule would be posited for the Recipient or Beneficiary/Goal oppositions with verbs such as supply or provide, as in (31) and similar structures in other languages.

(31) a. Pakistan supplies weapons to/for Afghanistan.
     b. Pakistan supplies Afghanistan with weapons.

Dik (1980: 29–39, 1988b: 22) offers two additional arguments for a predicate formation analysis rather than an object assignment one of pairs of clauses such as those in (29) and (31). The first is that such structural pairs tend to exhibit semantic differences which need to be coded in the underlying predication (the underlying predication being a representation of the semantic structure). In the case of (29) and its English translation the difference in meaning is one of 'completeness'.[18] The second argument concerns the morphological marking of the verb which, though not present in the English translation of (29b) or in (31b), is common in this construction type cross-linguistically. Dik suggests that the morphological marking of the relationship between the (a) and

(b) clauses is typical of lexical rather than syntactic rules. This is particularly clear in a language such as Polish in which the nature of the verbal affix is in part semantically, in part lexically, determined. The most common affix is the prefix *ob-*, as in (29b);[19] other affixes include: *po-*, *na-* and *za-*. We will see below that object assignment may also be accompanied by verbal marking. This type of marking does not, however, tend to display the lexical idiosyncrasies found in constructions such as (29).

4.4.1 One object function

The other major consequence of the perspectivizing approach to syntactic functions in regard to object assignment is that in contradistinction to traditional grammar and most current grammatical theories, FG posits only one object relation. As under many other analyses, including the ones advanced in GB, RG, LFG and Categorial Grammar, in trivalent predications such as the ones in (32) the object function is associated with the Goal *Japanese scroll* in (32a) and with the Recipient *Ken* in (32b).

(32) a. I'll give the Japanese scroll to Ken.
     b. I'll give Ken the Japanese scroll.

Since only one object function is recognized, neither the prepositionally marked Recipient in (32a) nor the Goal in (32b) receives special recognition in the form of some additional syntactic label. This contrasts with analyses that assign an indirect object function to the prepositionally marked Recipient in (32a) and/or identify the Goal in (32b) by means of a grammatical relation such as the 'chômeur' in RG or the 'secondary object' suggested by Kaplan and Bresnan (1982), Dowty (1982) or Dryer (1986). The FG analysis of double object constructions and the solutions adopted by the other linguists mentioned all diverge from the traditional approach as represented by, for instance, Jespersen (1927), Halliday (1967/68) and Ziv and Sheintuch (1979), according to which the Goal is taken to bear the direct object function in (32b) as well as in (32a), and the Recipient in (32b) rather than the prepositionally marked one in (32a) is considered to be an indirect object.[20]

An indirect object treatment of neither the prepositional Recipient in (32a) nor the prepositionless Recipient in (32b) is compatible with a perspective-based approach to syntactic functions, in view of the fact that no choice of semantic functions underlies the putative indirect objects. Note that the would-be indirect object in (32a) does not enter into alternations with satellite functions such as Beneficiary, Location or Instrument. Nor does the putative indirect object in (32b) display an alternation between the argument functions of Recipient and Goal. The only way of reconciling a perspective-based treatment of syntactic functions with a tertiary perspective is if the Goal/Recipient contrast is taken to define both a direct object and an indirect object. This would entail recognizing a direct object encompassing the Goal in (32a) and the Recipient in (32b), and an indirect object embracing the prepositional Recipient in (32a) and the Goal in (32b). However, whereas considerable evidence can be adduced for the first step of such an analysis, the prepositional Recipient and the Goal do not share any morpho-syntactic characteristics, apart from linear order, that would warrant grouping them under the label of indirect object.[21] Thus, given the interdependence between perspective and syntactic function assignment in FG, the identification of only one object function in FG is fully justified.

The recognition of only one object function places the burden of accounting for the morpho-syntactic properties of the two non-subject arguments in double object constructions on semantic functions and the argument positions. This can be conveniently illustrated on the basis of English. The above-mentioned controversies surrounding the grammatical status of the four non-subject terms in pairs of clauses such as (32) are due to the distinct morpho-syntactic characteristics that each of these terms displays. Although FG assigns the direct object function to both the Goal in (32a) and to the Recipient in (32b), Recipient direct objects differ from Goal direct objects in that they cannot be:

(a) tough-moved:

(33) a. It is easy to please this girl.
b. This girl is easy to please.

(34) a. It is easy to tell this girl a story.
b. *This girl is easy to tell a story.

(b) appear in the 'of' phrase of gerundive nominals:

(35) a. They read books.
b. the reading of books

(36) a. They give people presents.
b. *the giving of people presents

(c) relativized according to the same strategies as Goals:

   (37) a. The girl/∅/that/whom/who you met in the park is here.
        b. The girl*∅/*that/*who/?whom I gave flowers is here.

(d) moved to the right by heavy NP-shift:

   (38) a. Fred sent to his clients several brochures with all the accommodation details.
        b. *Fred sent the brochures his new South-East Asian clients.

(e) questioned:

   (39) a. What did you give to Max?
        b. *Who did you give the book?

Because FG, in contrast to RG, does not aim to provide an analysis of clausal structure in terms of syntactic functions, it can handle the above differences in the behavioral properties of the two direct objects simply by referring to the semantic function of the direct object.

Turning to the properties of the Goal in (32b), implicit in the analysis which treats this term rather than the Recipient as a direct object is the fact that it retains, so to speak, some direct object-type characteristics. These include: the lack of adpositional marking, the ability to be relativized (40a) and questioned (40b) like monotransitive direct object Goals, and in some regional variations of English the possibility of being passivized (40c).

   (40) a. The books/∅/that/which Mary gave John were mine.
        b. Which books did Mary give John?
        c. No explanation was given them.

The passivization property is particularly common when the Recipient is a pronoun (Oehrle 1975: 177) and there is no overt actor, as in (40c). The fact that the Goal in (32b) shares some characteristics with the direct object can in FG be attributed to its status as an A^2. Note that though in RG the Goal is treated as a chômeur, unlike in the case of the passive actor, there is no controversy as to its continuing argument status.

4.4.1.1 Double object in Bantu

It is not quite clear how languages in which in double object constructions both Recipients and Goals appear to display object-like characteristics are to be treated in FG. Such a situation occurs in certain ditransitive clauses in the Bantu language Kinyarwanda. For example, in the clause in (41) from Kimenyi (1988: 364) both the Recipient and Goal lack prepositional marking, can be pronominalized by the same strategy, reflexivized, passivized and relativized.[22]

Kinyarwanda
(41) Umugóre a- r- éerek-a ábáana amashusho.
woman she- pres- show-asp children pictures
'The woman is showing pictures to the child.'

Identical facts hold for predications with a Goal and a Beneficiary (42) (Gary and Keenan 1977: 93), Goal and Instrument (43a) and Goal and Manner (44a) (Kimenyi 1988: 368, 369).[23]

Kinyarwanda
(42) Maria y- a- tek- e- ye abana inoko.
Maria she- past-cook-ben-asp children chicken
'Maria cooked a chicken for the children.'

(43) a. Umugóre a- ra- andik-iish- a íbarúwa íkarámu.
woman she- pres- write-instr- asp letter pen
'The woman is writing a letter with a pen.'

(44) a. Umugóre a- rá- kôr-an- a akazi umweête.
woman she- pres- do- man-asp work enthusiasm
'The woman is working with enthusiasm.'

The expression of a Beneficiary with a trivalent predicate in Kinyarwanda can only be achieved as in (42) where the Beneficiary occurs without prepositional marking and the verb takes the benefactive suffix *i-/e-*. Instrumental and Manner terms, on the other hand, can also be expressed as in (43b) and (44b) in which case they are marked by prepositions and take neither an instrumental *iish* nor manner *an-* suffixed on the verb.

(43) b. Umugóre a- ra- andik-a íbaarúwa n'ííkarámu.
woman she- pres- write-asp letter with pen
'The woman is writing a letter with a pen.'

(44) b. Umugóre a- rá- kôr- a akazi n'ûmweête.
woman she- pres- do- asp work with enthusiasm
'The woman is working with enthusiasm.'

Only prepositionless Instrument and Manner terms, as in (43a) and (44a), possess the above-mentioned direct object characteristics. The phenomenon of having several terms with virtually the same morpho-syntactic characteristics is also displayed in other Bantu languages such as Haya (Hyman and Duranti 1982), Chichewa (Trithart 1979), Mashi and Luyia (Gary 1977) though not necessarily with exactly the same range of terms as in Kinyarwanda.

For some linguists, for example Gary and Keenan (1977), the object-like properties of several terms in the same clause constitute an argument for recognizing two or even three direct object functions. Other linguists argue for treating the Goal as a direct object and the Recipient, Beneficiary, Manner, etc. as another type of object, indirect (Perlmutter and Postal 1983) or primary (Dryer 1986). Under the FG approach to syntactic functions both of these analyses are ruled out. The clauses in (41), (42), (43a) and (44a) must be analysed either as having Recipient, Beneficiary, Instrument and Manner direct objects or as displaying no object assignment at all. Note that in the context of FG, a direct object treatment of the Goal destroys the basis for recognizing an object function, the existence of which is dependent on the possibility of semantic function alternations.

The choice between the above two analyses depends on whether the clauses in question may be viewed as involving a change in perspective. On the basis of the characterization of perspective outlined in §4.2, we are led to expect that a change in perspective is accompanied by the loss of certain morpho-syntactic properties on the part of one term and the acquisition of these properties by another term. In the case of (41)–(44a) only the second of the above characteristics holds; the Goal does not lose its object properties. Whether the acquisition of properties is a sufficient criterion for recognizing a change in perspective is not an issue which has been directly addressed in FG. However, on the basis of Dik's (1978: 102–103, 110; 1989: 240) analysis of Kinyarwanda, we may presume that it is, since in the most recent version of FG (Dik 1989: 227) Kinyarwanda is listed as exhibiting object assignment to the Goal, Recipient, Beneficiary, Instrument and Location.

If the Goal in (41)–(44a) is not an object, the question arises of how to account for the fact that it displays similar morpho-syntactic properties to an object. A possible solution is to reinterpret the 'object' properties as properties not of objects but of non-subject verbal arguments. Such an analysis would, however, deprive the notion of object of much of its relevance. Moreover, the reinterpretation of object properties as argument properties does not provide a satisfactory account of the complex distribution of properties among prepositionless terms in triple or quadruple 'object' constructions.

The common properties of the Goal and Recipient, or Beneficiary or Instrument or Manner, listed above hold only in double object constructions. Thus, for example, when there are three prepositionless terms, say a Goal, Recipient and Beneficiary as in (45), the Recipient, in contrast to the other two terms, can no longer passivize, pronominalize, relativize, etc. (Kimenyi 1988: 366).

> Kinyarwanda
> (45) Umugóre y- a- sab-i- ye úmwáana umugabo amafaraanga.
> woman she-past-ask-ben- asp child man money
> ('The woman asked money to the man for the child.')

And in the presence of both a Location and a Beneficiary, neither the Goal nor the Recipient displays the relevant object characteristics while the Beneficiary and the Location do (Kimenyi 1988: 374). This holds for constructions both with three (46) and with four (47) terms, though in the latter case one of the terms must be a pronominal clitic.

> (46) Umukoôbwa a-ra- andik-ir- á- ho ámééza umuhuûngu íbarúwa.
> girl she-pres-write-ben- asp- on table boy letter
> ('The girl is writing a letter for the boy on the table.')

> (47) Umugabo a-rá- (ha) -h- éer- á- ho umugóre ábáana ibíryo.
> man he-pres- it -give-ben- asp- on woman children food
> ('The man is giving food to the children for the woman on it.')

Clearly some distinction among the relevant terms is called for, though the FG object assignment analysis, which assigns the object function solely to one term, does not appear to be the optimal one. For example, an analysis of (45) which treats the Beneficiary as the object, and the Goal and Recipient as arguments, does not account for the difference in the behavioral properties of the Goal relative to the Recipient. In (46), on the other hand, taking the object to be the Beneficiary leaves the object properties of the Location unexplained, and vice versa. Needless to say, under a potential no-object assignment analysis, the problem of distinguishing among the terms in constructions such as (45), (46) and (47) would be compounded. In Dryer's (1986) version of RG, which recognizes a primary and secondary object in addition to a direct and indirect one and to the chômeur relation, the above distinctions can be handled by a composite assignment of the relevant relations. Such a proliferation of syntactic functions is, of course, impossible in FG.

We will return to the problem of choosing the most appropriate analysis of double objects in Bantu after considering other data bearing on the issue.

Syntactic functions 101

4.4.1.2 *Obligatory object assignment*

The situation in Bantu with respect to the behavioral properties of the non-subject arguments is undoubtedly atypical from the typological point of view. More common are languages which lack the (a) member of the dative-shift opposition in (32), and in which it is always the Recipient (or Beneficiary), not the Goal, that displays direct object properties in double object constructions. Such a situation is found in Huichol, for example, in which the identification of the Recipient or Beneficiary as the object is expressed by the cross-referencing pronouns. As shown in (48) it is the Beneficiary rather than the Goal that is cross-referenced on the verb.

Huichol (Comrie 1982: 110)
(48) Eekɨ nawazɨ tɨɨri pe-wa- rutinanairi.
you knife children 2sg-3pl bought:ben
'You bought the children the knife/the knife for the children.'

And it is also only the Recipient or Beneficiary that may function as the subject of the corresponding passive. Other languages which exhibit the same phenomenon include Nez Perce (Rude 1982), Manam (Lichtenberk 1982), the Bantu languages Chi-Mwi:ni (Kisseberth and Abasheikh 1977) and Shona (Hawkinson and Hyman 1974), and the Mayan languages Quiche, Cakchiquel, Tzeltal (Norman 1978) and Tzotzil (Aissen 1982). A conservative interpretation of the conditions underlying the recognition of object assignment entails no object assignment in such languages as well.

The absence of an object function in the described circumstances is problematic for FG owing to the difficulty in accounting for the characteristics shared by the Goal of a monotransitive predication and the Recipient of a ditransitive one. A possible solution would be to claim that in ditransitive predications the Goal is not an A^2 but an A^3, in which case whatever behavioral properties are common to Goals in monotransitive predications and Recipients in ditransitive ones could be attributed to their status as A^2. The feasibility of analysing the Recipient in double object constructions as more intimately linked to the verb than the Goal finds support in the treatment of double object constructions proposed by Chomsky (1955) and recently revived by Larson (1988). Larson, working within the framework of GB, presents a number of arguments for deriving structures such as (32) in English from an underlying structure in which the verb and the Recipient make up a constituent that excludes the Goal. Most of the arguments for this analysis are specific to the theory of GB and therefore cannot be easily transposed to other theoretical frameworks. A point worth mentioning, though, is that the exact semantic interpretation of the Goal in ditransitive clauses may depend on the contribution of the verb and Recipient combination, as in (49), adapted from Larson (1988: 341).

(49) a. Beethoven gave the Fifth Symphony to the world.
b. Beethoven gave the Fifth Symphony to his patron.

Larson suggests that (49a) is roughly synonymous with *Beethoven created the Fifth Symphony*, while (49b) is understood as involving a simple transfer. In the context of FG an analysis of English involving a reinterpretation of a prepositional Recipient as an A^2 rather than an A^3 introduces only unnecessary complications. But for languages in which the Recipient is, to use RG terminology, obligatorily advanced to direct object such a solution is a promising one.

Dik (1978, 1989) allows for the possibility of obligatory object assignment. Part of his motivation for doing so is undoubtedly the fact that some of the languages which have obligatory object assignment to the Recipient or Beneficiary exhibit alternations involving prepositional and prepositionless Instrument, Manner or Locational terms which are prime candidates for an analysis involving object assignment. The Bantu languages are a case in point, leaving aside the type of complications mentioned in connection with the Kinyarwanda data. Thus in the context of object assignment to a wide range of semantic functions, the most natural way to view the non-existence of pairs of clauses involving alternations of a Goal and a Recipient or Beneficiary is indeed as a simple (though perhaps pragmatically determined) gap.

Dik makes the obligatory object assignment analysis conditional on the presence of morphological marking on the verb. In the Bantu languages the advancement of various constituents to object is accompanied by the appearance of the so-called applicative affix, as in the Kinyarwanda examples (42)–(47). The distribution of the affix is subject to language-internal variations, but on the whole it does not occur with obligatory Recipient (41) as compared to Beneficiary (42) advancement, and is always present in cases of optional advancement such as in (43a) and (44a). We find a similar situation in Huichol and Nez Perce. Dik suggests that the lack of verbal marking in the case of obligatory Recipient advancement may be interpreted as indicating that what appears to be a Recipient is in fact a Goal. This analysis draws on the Goal status of the semantic recipient in the predicate frame (or one of the predicate frames) of predicates such as *supply*, *present* and *reward*. Recall from §4.4. that in English these predicates enter into oppositions

Syntactic functions 103

involving a Recipient or Beneficiary and a Goal, as in (31) repeated for convenience below.

(50) a. Pakistan supplies weapons [Go] to/for Afghanistan [Rec/Ben].
b. Pakistan supplies Afghanistan [Go] with weapons [Instr].

The argument is that under the pressure of the personal hierarchy (see §1.2.1.1 or §4.5.1) a language may model the SoA of *giving, sending* or *showing* on the pattern of *present*-type verbs with the receiver as an A^2 Goal rather than an A^3 Recipient. Assuming such an analysis, the language in question will emerge as having either no object assignment or, if there are grounds for recognizing object assignment with respect to other semantic functions, as having simply no object assignment to Recipients. The latter is the analysis that Dik now favours for Bantu. As mentioned on p. 99, despite the retention of direct object properties on the part of the Goal, the alternations of prepositional and prepositionless terms such as in (43) and (44) are treated in terms of object assignment rather than by means of predicate formation.

If this is so, then a complication arises in connection with double verbal marking in passive clauses. Consider the passive counterparts of (43a) and (44a) presented below.

Kinyarwanda
(51) Ikarámu i- ra- andik-iish- w- a íbaarúwa n'ûmugóre.
pen it- pres- write-instr- pass- asp letter by woman
'The pen is used to write a letter by the woman.'

(52) Umweête u- rá- kôr-an- w- a akazi n'ûmugóre.
enthusiasm it- pres- do-man-pass- asp work by woman
'It is the woman who is working with enthusiasm.'

We see that the verbs in (51) and (52) are marked both by the applicative instrumental and manner affixes, which are generally interpreted to be an advancement to object affixes, and by a passive, advancement to subject affix. In models of grammar such as RG the presence of two advancement affixes in passive clauses such as (51) and (52) is a consequence of the fact that object assignment, or rather advancement, is assumed to feed the passive. In FG, however, subject assignment is independent of object assignment in that the subjectivization of a term does not involve the intermediate step of advancement to object. Therefore the presence of the advancement to object marker in the passive (51) and (52) cannot be attributed to an earlier level of object assignment, but must be interpreted as due to subject assignment alone. The subject assignment marker in (51) and (52) is thus not -*w*- but the combination of -*iish*- or

-*an*- and -*w*-. Consequently the occurrence of, say, the verbal affix -*iish*- in (51) and (43a) is a product of two independent factors, subject assignment and object assignment.²⁴ Under a predicate formation analysis of the relationship between pairs of clauses such as (43a) and (51), and (44a) and (52), the applicative instrumental or manner affix marks predicate formation (the increase in the valency of the basic predicate), not object assignment. The predicate frame with the verb marked by the applicative affix then constitutes the input to subject assignment. The necessity of imputing a double function to the applicative affixes entailed by the object assignment analysis may be regarded as an argument in favour of the predicate formation treatment of some apparent instances of object assignment in Bantu. The matter is left open to further consideration.

4.5 THE SEMANTIC FUNCTION HIERARCHY

The assignment of the FG syntactic functions to semantic functions is constrained by the SFH presented in (53).

(53) The Semantic Function Hierarchy²⁵

	Ag	>	Go	>	Rec	>	Ben	>	Instr	>	Loc	>	Temp
subject	+	>	+	>	+	>	+	>	+	>	+	>	+
object		>	+	>	+	>	+	>	+	>	+	>	+

The SFH is conceived of as a language universal (for languages displaying syntactic function assignment), with different cut-off points for different languages. It predicts a decrease both in the ease with which a given semantic function can be selected for subject or object and its likelihood of being thus chosen, as we proceed from left to right. Thus the Agent is predicted as being the most likely and frequent candidate for subject, and the Goal for direct object; the next least-marked choice for subject or object is the Recipient, then the Beneficiary, and so on. The SFH is interpreted as reflecting the continuity principle whereby only continuous segments of the hierarchy are accessible to subject or object. This means that if in a given language an oblique constituent, say a Beneficiary, can be subjectivized or objectivized, then so should the Recipient and Goal.²⁶

Since syntactic function assignment is applied in FG at the level of the core predication which consists of the basic predicate frame expanded by level-1 satellites (δ_1), in principle only argument and δ_1 semantic functions should be accessible to syntactic function assignment. If strictly adhered to, this theory-internal correlation would make of syntactic function assignment a major diagnostic for argument and δ_1

status. The dangers inherent in this are all too familiar from discussions of the relationship between passivization and direct objecthood, the bottom line of which is frequently a definition of direct objecthood in terms of passivization and of passivization in terms of direct objecthood (see e.g. Siewierska 1984a). Dik permits syntactic function assignment to δ_2 to accommodate in particular the subjectivization of outer locatives in the Bantu languages (e.g. Kinyarwanda and Hibena). He claims that such a departure from the norm tends to be motivated by language-specific grammatical requirements connected with relativization, question formation, clause linkage and the like. Though the SFH is extended to outer satellites, we shall see in §4.5.2 that FG does not manage to avoid entirely the circularity involved in the specification of the relationship between argumenthood and syntactic function assignment.

The SFH differs from other eligibility to subject and object hierarchies presented in the literature (see Fillmore 1968: 33; Givón 1984: 139) primarily in scope; the range of predications that it covers is comparatively narrow. To ensure wider applicability of the SFH Dik (1989) has introduced a number of modifications. By way of background to the discussion of these modifications in §4.5.2 let us consider the underlying motivation for the SFH.

4.5.1 Behind the SFH

The underlying motivation for the SFH is sought, on the one hand, in the psychologically based prototypical directionality of predicates, i.e. in what DeLancey (1981), for example, calls natural 'attention flow', and on the other in the personal hierarchy, both of which are manifestations of iconicity (see §1.2.1.1). Natural attention flow, as conceived of by DeLancey, refers to the actual development of events in the real world, the basis for the perception of naturalness being temporal order. In the case of an action event the natural progression is from Agent to Goal, for motion events it is from Source to Goal; and for an act of 'giving', from giver to receiver. The claim embodied in the SFH, or more precisely in the priority of the Agent over all other semantic functions, is that speakers exhibit a preference for presenting situations and events in line with the natural attention flow. In other words, the natural attention flow is the unmarked *linguistic* attention flow, the preferred starting point for the linear mapping of linguistic expressions.

Natural attention flow interacts in obvious ways with the personal hierarchy[27] cited in §1.2.1.1 and repeated in (54) p. 106, which is a reflection of what is often termed the 'Me-first principle' (Cooper and Ross 1975; Silverstein 1976; Lakoff and Johnson 1980):

(54) The personal hierarchy:
1stp > 2ndp > 3rdp human > higher animals > other organisms > inorganic matter > abstracts.

The personal hierarchy expresses the fact that human beings show an unqualified interest in themselves, their interlocutors and other humans. Consequently, events and situations tend to be interpreted from the point of view of the persons involved rather than in terms of the events themselves or non-human or inanimate entities participating in these events. The relationship between the personal hierarchy and the SFH is most transparent in the case of the left end of the two hierarchies. Recall that in FG Agents are by definition animate, and since the potential agenthood of non-human animates affects only a limited sphere of human experience, human beings are the most frequent Agents due to both the nature of agenthood and the human bias expressed in the personal hierarchy. The second most likely semantic function for humans is not, however, the Goal, as the juxtaposition of the two hierarchies would lead us to expect, but rather the Recipient.

There is a standing controversy concerning the location of the Goal relative to the Recipient[28] in the SFH and its equivalents. As far as subject assignment is concerned the situation is clear,[29] the Goal is evidently more easily accessed to subject than the Recipient, since there are many languages that allow the subjectivization of Goals while not permitting the subjectivization of Recipients (e.g. the Romance and Slavic languages), but the converse situation does not occur. The standard argument for positioning Recipients prior to Goals in connection with object assignment is the existence of languages in which it is the Recipient rather than the Goal which is obligatorily singled out for preferential treatment in double object constructions (see §4.4.1.1). In the context of FG, however, such obligatory 'advancement' to object does not necessarily qualify as an instance of object assignment, since, as discussed in §4.4.1.2, the Recipient may be reinterpreted as a Goal. Another piece of evidence for the priority of the Recipient over the Goal in relation to object assignment concerns the greater frequency of Recipient over Goal objectivization. For instance in Givón's text-study of English double object constructions cited in Givón (1984: 174), 84% of the objects (as defined in FG) were Recipients and only 16% were Goals. A compelling argument for the contrary view, i.e. for placing the Goal before the Recipient on the SFH, is that in bivalent predications, which are statistically dominant, the Goal is typically the only possible object. Needless to say, this line of reasoning is not open to FG, by virtue of the absence of choice underlying the notion of perspective.

There is also some degree of correspondence between the positions towards the right end of the personal hierarchy and the SFH in that instrumental and locative terms are typically inanimate, barring elliptical genitives such as *at Mike's* in the case of locatives; and temporal terms are by definition abstract. If one concedes that instruments are likely to be perceived as partners in the perpetration of an act (and hence within the sphere of ego), the placement of Instrument higher up on the continuum than Location or Time can also be attributed to the personal hierarchy or alternatively to familiarity (see below) with which the personal hierarchy interacts.

Primarily by way of the personal hierarchy the SFH is affected by the host of parameters which comprise the domain of linguistic perspectivizing in the more typical non-FG sense of the term referred to in §4.2. The mediating role of the personal hierarchy[30] is most evident in connection with those parameters that fall under what I, following Ertel (1977), call 'familiarity', a notion more or less coterminous with Kuno's (1987) 'empathy' or Zubin's (1979) 'focus of interest'. Familiarity encompasses topicality, givenness, definiteness, referentiality and temporal priority, but crucially also purely idiosyncratic factors such as personal preference, emotive involvement, expertise in a given field, etc. Also of relevance in regard to subject and object selection and therefore to the SFH are the more specifically discourse-based aspects of perspectivizing discussed in the literature under the label of 'cohesion' (Halliday and Hassan 1976) or 'cohesiveness' (Bolkestein and Risselada 1987) which include more detailed considerations of the discourse significance of syntactic functions. Of prime importance for our present discussion, however, is the multiplicity of factors that may be seen to affect directly or indirectly the choice of syntactic functions. The SFH attempts to reduce all these factors to the level of semantic functions. But, clearly, to capture even some of the relevant distinctions the SFH has to be both refined and extended to cover more semantic functions.[31]

4.5.2 Extending the domain of the SFH

The domain of the SFH is subject and object assignment as defined in FG. This, as we have seen, is a very restricted domain in comparison to what falls under standard conceptions of subject and object assignment, say as in Fillmore (1968) or Givón (1984). For example, whereas English is typically regarded as a language whose subject assignment possibilities extend right across the spectrum of the SFH, in terms of the FG analysis the cut-off point for English is after the Beneficiary. The source of this difference is that Instrument, Location and Time are not possible A¹ semantic functions in FG, and more significantly that the SFH, as presented in (53), encompasses only predications that are both transitive (in the unhappy traditional sense, where transitive means admitting the passive) and actional. Recall from the discussion in §3.5 that the A^1 in (55), for instance, are in FG taken to be not Instrument, Location and Time, but Force, Zero and perhaps Processed respectively.

(55)   a.   The wind broke the glass.
        b.   The cabin sleeps twenty people.
        c.   Five hours have elapsed since he left.

The absence of these latter semantic functions from the SFH in (53) brings us to the second point, or rather to two related points. The fact that the SFH does not cover intransitive predications is a direct consequence of the perspectivizing approach to syntactic functions. This is something which is often overlooked by critics or reviewers of FG (e.g. Watters 1980: 167; Sommers 1987: 107) who cite intransitive predications such as (55b,c) as evidence for subject assignment beyond the cut-off point for English adopted in FG.

Regarding the action orientation of the SFH, to accommodate the full range of types of SoAs distinguished in FG, Dik (1989: 233–234) suggests substituting the first position on the SFH by the set of mutually exclusive A^1 semantic functions, i.e. Agent, Positioner, Force, Processed [Experiencer] and Zero [Experiencer]. This explicitly ties the SFH to the inherent directionality of predicates, partially obscuring the discussed correspondences between the SFH and the personal hierarchy. The first position on the SFH becomes coterminous with the notion of A^1. An analogous expansion of the second position on the SFH is also found to be necessary to account for the fact that subject assignment to some semantic functions may not apply across the board but be dependent on the argument status of the given semantic function. As a case in point Dik cites Ancient Greek, which permits the subjectivization of only certain kinds of Recipients, namely those occurring with a small class of bivalent (as opposed to trivalent) predicates such as *help* and *impress*. According to Berman (1982: 116, note 6), the same situation is found in Modern Hebrew. FG analyses the A^2 of predicates such as *help* and *impress* in English as bearing the Goal[Exp] semantic function rather than the Recipient one. In Ancient Greek and Modern Hebrew, however, these A^2 appear with dative as compared to accusative marking.[32] Therefore to provide a basis for an account of the difference in morphological marking and other behavioral distinctions, the dative A^2 are assigned the Recipient and not the Goal[Exp] function. If the SFH is to capture the fact that in Ancient Greek and Modern Hebrew, unlike in English, regular A^3 Recipients do not participate in subject assignment while these A^2 Recipients do, subject assignment to Recipients must be made sensitive to the argument status of the Recipient.

A similar argument could be advanced in regard to locatives in Maori. According to Chung (1978: 174), Maori permits subject assignment only to what she calls 'affected' locatives, as in (56), which contrasts with the directional locative in (57).

Maori
(56) a. Ka haere au i te māunga.
t/asp go I on the mountain
'I walk on the mountain.'

b. Ka haere- tia te māunga e au.
t/asp go- pass the mountain by me
'The mountain has been walked on by me.'

(57) a. Ka haere au ki te māunga.
t/asp go I to the mountain
'I go to the mountain.'

b. *Ka haere- tia te māunga e au.
t/asp go- pass the mountain by me
*'The mountain has been gone to by me.'

The possibility of passivizing the locative in (56), but not in (57), is viewed by Chung as suggestive of the former's as opposed to the latter's surface direct objecthood. If the two locative terms are not assigned different semantic functions in FG, their distinct behaviour with respect to subject assignment could be dealt with by the equivalent of Chung's RG analysis, namely by treating *the mountain* in (56) as an A^2, and *the mountain* in (57) as a δ_1.

A case can also be made for substituting the third position on the SFH by the set of possible A^3 semantic functions. In the Bantu language Chichewa (Trithart 1979) the subjectivization possibilities of A^2 and A^3 Recipients are the converse of those of Ancient Greek and Modern Hebrew: A^3 Recipients can be passivized, A^2 ones cannot. Compare (58) and (59).

Chichewa
(58) a. John a- na- lankhul-a kwa mkazi.
John he- past -talk-ind to woman
'John talked to the woman.'

b. *Mkazi a- na- lankuhul -idw-a   ndi John.
    woman she-past-talk-   pass-ind   by   John
    'The woman was talked to by John.'

(59) a. John a- na- pats-a   nthochi kwa mai   ache.
         John he- past-give-ind   banana   to   mother his
         'John gave a banana to his mother.'

   b. Mai   ache a John a- na- pats-idw- a nthochi ndi John.
       mother his of John she-past-give-pass-ind banana by   John
       'His mother was given a banana by John.'

Incidentally, if *to me* in *The girl matters to me* is treated as a Recipient, the same facts hold for English. Applying the line of argumentation given for Greek and Hebrew, in order to eliminate incorrect subject assignment, the Recipient on the SFH has to be marked as an A^3. In view of the fact that in Bantu in general only prepositionless terms can be assigned the subject function, the semantic functions borne by these terms need to be distinguished from those borne by their prepositional counterparts. As discussed in §4.4.1, the relevant distinction is typically seen to be one of argument and satellite. In the Kinyarwanda examples in (43a) and (44a) the Instrument and Manner terms qualify as A^3.

Assuming an expansion of all the argument positions, the revised SFH would look something like (60).

(60) A^1 > A^2 > A^3 > Rec > Ben > Instr....
      Ag   Go   Rec
      Pos   Rec   Ben
      Fo   Ben   Instr
      Proc   Instr Loc
      Zero   Loc   Dir
             ...   ...

Unlike the earlier version, the SFH in (60) makes the explicit prediction that all argument semantic functions are more accessible to syntactic function assignment than the satellite ones, and, of the argument semantic functions, the A^1 are more accessible to subject than the A^2, and the A^2 than the A^3. As typological generalizations these predictions are fine, but at the level of individual languages they are evidently incorrect. The plotting of individual languages on this new SFH cannot simply involve different cut-off points, as in the case of the old SFH in (53), but crucially requires a specification of different sets of semantic functions (including no expansions at all) under the A^2 and A^3 positions. For example in English, of all the semantic functions capable of functioning as A^2, only the Goal and Goal[Exp] are accessible to subject. The same applies to the A^3 semantic functions relative to either subject or object assignment; only the Recipient (Reference?) can be accessed for either function. Furthermore, the Beneficiary, which in FG is treated as a satellite function, can be a subject or object, while the Location A^3 of verbs such as *put* or *place* cannot. Consequently, in the version of the SFH for English, the second and third positions on the hierarchy must remain unexpanded.

The SFH specifies the preferential order of semantic functions for subject and object assignment as well as the relative frequency with which the particular choices are made, both cross-linguistically and within individual languages. The predictions incorporated in the SFH cannot, however, be automatically transposed to the level of concrete predications since the strength of the association between a semantic function and subject or object in a given instance will depend on:

(a) the range of semantic functions accessible to subject and object;
(b) the impact of the personal hierarchy and the familiarity-based determinants of subject and object selection;
(c) the nature of the predicate.

The first point is fairly obvious; one would expect the degree of bonding between a semantic function and subject and object to be inversely proportional to the number of semantic functions in the predication eligible for subject and object. The second and third points are closely related. In discussing the factors underlying the SFH in §4.5.2, we noted that some semantic functions are much more likely than others to display characteristics known to favour the choice of subject or object, such as humanness, animacy and familiarity. It follows that the eligibility of a semantic function for subject or object will be reinforced or reduced relative to the nature and number of subject- or object-oriented features of the terms by which the semantic function is borne. Thus the position of the Goal relative to the Agent as a candidate for subject will increase when the former is more familiar than the latter.

Given the 'Me-first' orientation, a human Goal and especially a Goal[Exp] will be a particularly strong candidate for subject in non-controlled SoAs, which in FG take a Force, Processed or Zero A^1. The preference for the (b) clauses over the (a) ones in (61) and (62) is one of the standard pieces of evidence cited in support of the personal hierarchy. (See also the examples in §1.2.1.1.)

(61) a. Lightning killed her first husband.
b. Her first husband was killed by lightning.

(62) a. The book impressed me.
b. I was impressed by the book.

In English, as in most if not all other languages, so-called 'affect' or 'mental process' predicates can be lexicalized with the experiencer/ affectee as an A^1 and the stimulus as an A^2, or vice versa. Though some of the most colloquial predicates such as *like, love, hate, want* and *fear* belong to the former type, the dominant pattern for English appears to be the latter. Talmy (1985a: 41), for example, lists over 100 predicates with a stimulus (Zero or Processed in FG) A^1, as compared to 65 predicates with an experiencer (Zero[Exp] or Proc[Exp] in FG) A^1. As predicted by the personal hierarchy, the Goal[Exp] A^2 co-occurring with Zero or Processed A^1, as in (62), are particularly prone to be subjectivized in English (Halliday 1985: 110). Such Goal[Exp] are even strong candidates for subject in the presence of a human stimulus (Agent or Positioner in FG), as in (63).

(63) a. He delighted me.
b. I was delighted by him.

We can thus observe a weakening of the A^1 semantic functions for subject, and a comparable strengthening of the claims of the A^2 semantic functions, particularly in the case of the Goal[Exp], as we move from the Agent to Positioner, then Force, Processed and Zero.

5 The layered structure of the clause

5.1 INTRODUCTION

As outlined in §1.3.2 and §2.3, the current version of FG views the clause as a hierarchical structure consisting of several levels, rather than as a flat structure. The innermost level is the nuclear predication composed of the predicate and its arguments. By the addition of level-1 operators π_1 and satellites δ_1, the nuclear predication is extended into a core predication. The core predication supplemented with π_2 and δ_2 is transformed into an extended predication. The extended predication is built into a proposition. The proposition modified by π_3 and δ_3 is built into a clause structure elaborated by means of π_4 and δ_4 into an extended clause.

Following Vet (1986), the representation of the structure of the predication and of all the subsequent levels leading to the utterance is modelled on the schema for term structure presented in §2.2.2. The intended referents of the predication, proposition and clause are symbolized by variables, just like the intended referent of the term phrase. And like the predicate in the term phrase, the predication, proposition and clause are interpreted as restrictors on these variables, providing information about the entities symbolized by them. The relevant variables and restrictors are shown in (1), and the resulting structure of the utterance in (2), both of which are adapted from Hengeveld (1989: 130–131).

(1)

Variable	Reference of variable	Restrictor	Designation of restrictor
E	utterance	clause	speech act
X	content	proposition	possible fact
e	event	predication	state of affairs
x	individual	predicate	property/relation

(2)

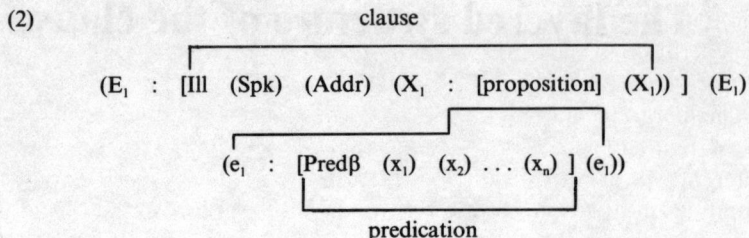

In (2) the basic illocution of the utterance is represented in an abstract illocutionary frame (Ill stands for illocutionary force; Spk for speaker; and Addr for addressee), while in Dik (1989: 256) it is treated as an operator.

The structure in (2) is to be understood as follows: when a predication designating a particular type of SoA is inserted into an event slot it acquires referential potential, the referent being the situation or event in the mind of the speaker; on inserting this predication into the proposition slot of an illocutionary frame, the referent becomes the propositional content conveyed in a speech act; and finally when a clause is inserted into the speech act slot, i.e. endowed with an illocutionary force, a speaker, addressee and a spatio-temporal location, it becomes an actual speech act, an utterance.

The FG model of clause structure is an extension of the layered structure of the clause proposed in Foley and Van Valin's (1984) RRG.[1] Foley and Van Valin postulate three levels of structure: the *nucleus* (nuc) consisting of the predicate and predicate operators (aspectual inflections and certain adverbials), the *core* comprised of the nucleus and the verbal arguments together with certain modal operators, and the *periphery* (per) encompassing the adjuncts (satellites), tense, markers of subjective and evidential modalities and indicators of illocutionary force. This model, in simplified form, is shown in (3) (adapted from Foley and Van Valin 1984: 187).

(3) per[(Oblique NPs) core[NP(NP nuc[Predicate]nuc]core]per
     periphery   core   nucleus

Foley and Van Valin's core predication subsumes the nuclear and core predication levels of FG, while the periphery embraces the extended predication, proposition and clause.[2] Foley and Van Valin seek the primary justification for their tripartite division of clause structure in the distribution of expressions of tense, aspect and modality, the so-called TAM-system.[3] This too is a major area from which FG draws evidence for its more elaborate (as compared to RRG) model of clause structure.

The body of this chapter (§5.2–§5.2.2.2) will therefore be devoted to a consideration of the FG treatment of the TAM system as it bears on the adopted layered structure of the clause.

The hierarchical analysis of the clause adopted in FG is semantically based in that each of the recognized layers is taken to represent a different type of entity: a speech act, proposition or SoA. No comparable semantic motivation underlies the layers of constituent structure recognized in the phrase structure rules of Chomsky's (1981, 1982, 1986) GB (and its predecessors and offshoots). There are, however, evident correspondences between the levels of semantic structure recognized in FG and the predicate-argument-based underlying (D-structure) constituency relations of GB. This is hardly surprising, since one of the determinants of constituency relations is the preservation of the semantic integrity of groups of lexical and grammatical items. This tendency is known in the literature as Behagel's First Law, which is that the most important law is that what belongs together mentally (semantically) is placed close together syntactically. By the same token, in FG support for the semantically based levels of clause structure is sought in certain syntactic phenomena. Consequently, there is a certain degree of overlap in the criteria used in determining the multi-layered structure of the clause in the two grammatical models, which in turn leads to some areas of convergence in regard to the multi-layered structures posited. In view of the import of GB constituency structure relations on linguistic theorizing, §5.3 will be devoted to a brief comparison of the levels of structure postulated in GB with those suggested in FG. The discussion will close with a consideration of how the levels of structure recognized in FG and GB are reflected in the typologies of clausal complementation advanced within the two theoretical frameworks.

5.2 TENSE, ASPECT AND MODALITY

The FG analysis of tense, aspect and modality draws heavily on the insights achieved by Foley and Van Valin (1984)[4] and Bybee (1985) who investigated the expression of these three categories on a cross-linguistic basis. Their investigation led them to the claim that the preferred order of application of tense, aspect and modality operators relative to the verb nucleus is either verb-ATM or MTA-verb. In either case aspect markers occur closest to the verb nucleus, followed by tense,[5] with modal operators constituting the outermost layer. A closer look into the distributional characteristics of aspect, tense and modality indicators reveals a slightly more complex picture with variants and subcomponents of each of the three categories displaying different ordering preferences and scope relations. Dik (1989) adopts the schema worked out by Hengeveld (1989) according to which the TAM categories operate over the four basic levels of clause structure (see Table 5.1, taken from Hengeveld 1989: 132). The subdivisions within the category of aspect and modality, and the arguments for the stratification shown in Table 5.1, will be discussed in the relevant sections below.

Table 5.1 The classification and distribution of operators over the structure of the clause

Semantic domain	Grammatical category
Predicate operators	

internal temporal constituency
presence or absence of
    property or relation
    expressed by predicate
	imperfective/perfective
	phasal aspect
	predicate negation

Predication operators	
time of occurrence frequency of occurrence actuality of occurrence	tense quantificational aspect objective modality/polarity
Proposition operators	
source of proposition proposition	subjective modality evidential modality
Illocutionary operators	
weakening strategy strengthening strategy	mitigating mode reinforcing mode

5.2.1 Aspect and tense

The aspectual distinctions covered by predicate and predication operators pertain to grammatical as opposed to lexical aspect (*Aktionsarten*). Grammatical aspect receives overt morphological coding, while lexical aspect is a matter of the type or class of predicate, and as such falls under the FG typology of SoAs discussed in §3.2. Both aspect and tense are generally seen to be grammatical reflections of our experience of time.[6] Comrie (1976: 3), for example, defines aspect as a way of viewing the internal temporal constituency of a situation. By contrast, tense is seen to depict the distribution of situations in time, as points in a linear sequence (Givón 1984: 272). The distinction between aspect and tense may be illustrated on the basis of the following examples adapted from Majewicz (1985: 79).

Polish
(4) a. W młodości przeczytałam   wiersze Miłosza.
       in youth   perf:read:past:3sg:f poems Miłosz
       'In my youth I read (all of) Milosz's poetry.'

    b. W młodości czytałam   wiersze Miłosza.
       in youth   read:imperf:past:3sg:f poems Miłosz
       'In my youth I read Milosz's poetry.'

    c. W młodości czytywałam   wiersze Miłosza.
       in youth   read:iter:past:3sg:f poems Miłosz
       'In my youth I used to read Milosz's poetry.'

All three clauses depict the same situation anterior to the current point in time and are therefore in the past tense, but presented from different internal temporal perspectives: the perfective (4a), imperfective (4b) and iterative (4c).

In the literature, the distinction between the (typically) temporal relations covered by aspect and tense is often explicated with reference to Reichenbach's (1947) three time points:[7] *speech time* – the time of speech; *event time* – the set of times in which various events take place that may be mentioned in the speech act; *reference time* – all the times other than the speech time which may serve as alternative points of reference for the speaker. Though Reichenbach regarded these three times as points in time, nowadays in the wake of the observations of Bennett and Partee (1972), event time is considered to be an interval rather than a point in time, and reference time may be either an interval (when it is identical to event time) or a point (when it is an alternative to speech time).

Tense categories are seen to relate reference time to speech time from the perspective of speech time.[8] The reference time may be anterior (past), simultaneous (present) or posterior (future) to the time of speech. Aspectual categories, on the other hand, relate event time to reference time. The nature of this relationship is not always straightforward, as will be shown below.

Dik subdivides the category of grammatical aspect into three groups: the perfective/imperfective distinction, phasal aspect and quantificational aspect. The *perfective/imperfective* distinction is described along traditional lines as reflecting whether an SoA is depicted from the outside as a complete whole (perfective), or from the inside as non-complete and on-going. Though no reference to time is made in the above characterization, in order for an SoA to be viewed as complete, the reference time must coincide with the time of the whole event including its completion, as in (4a). Conversely, if an SoA is conceived as on-going, as in (4b), the event time must be seen to extend beyond the speaker's point of reference. Therefore the perfective/imperfective contrast does in fact involve a facet of the time dimension. Nonetheless, it is with respect to phasal aspect that the difference in the relation between reference time and event time is most evident.

Phasal aspect is taken to emphasize different phases of the development of an SoA through time, such as: the time (immediately) preceding the SoA (prospective), the beginning of an SoA (ingressive), an SoA in progress (progressive), the final phase of an SoA (egressive), the result of an SoA (resultative), etc. In each case the time of the event is related to the reference time: before, at the beginning, in the middle, at the end, or after the event. For quantificational aspect, of relevance is some subperiod of time. Dik uses the term *quantificational aspect*[9] for distinctions involving habit, frequency, continuity and intensity, which typically bear aspectual labels such as semelfactive, iterative, frequentative, distributive, etc.

According to Table 5.1, perfectivity/imperfectivity and phasal aspect are π_1 operators, while quantificational aspect and tense are π_2. The π_1 status of perfective/imperfective aspect follows from the fact that it affects the internal dynamics of the SoA. Phasal aspect also contributes to the specification of a given SoA, but significantly with reference to another SoA whose internal constituency is not affected by the aspectual operator. Dik is therefore much more tentative in his classification of phasal aspect as an operator over the predicate than he is in the case of the predication. Quantificational aspect, on the other hand, is evidently a π_2, since it does not contribute to the definition of the SoA, but merely quantifies it in some way.

5.2.1.1 Level-1 π_1 operators

One piece of evidence that Dik suggests for π_1 status is the frequently noted interaction of such operators with a particular type of SoA. He notes that in languages that have the perfective/imperfective opposition, the semantic incompatibility of the perfective or imperfective with a given type of SoA tends to be resolved by inducing a particular type of interpretation of the SoA. For instance, in the case of the imperfective and telic SoAs (the imperfective is unbounded, non-complete; telic SoAs are by definition bounded) the imposed reading is often a conative (attempted but not finished), iterative or distributive one. We see this in the Polish (5) and (6) which, as indicated, receive a conative and iterative interpretation respectively.

Polish
(5) Marek pisał ten list przez godzinę (i nie skończył).
    Marek wrote:imperf this letter for hour (and not finished)
    'Mark spent an hour writing the letter (and didn't finish it).'

(6) Jacek pił ziółka przez cały rok.
    Jack drank:imperf herbs for whole year
    'Jack drank herbal mixtures for a whole year (regularly).'

The conflict between the inherent boundness of perfectivity and the open-endness of non-dynamic SoAs is in turn often countered by means of assigning an ingressive or terminative interpretation which imposes some sort of boundary on the state or position. For example, (7) receives an ingressive reading, while (8) is interpreted as temporally restricted but non-punctual.

Polish
(7) Andrzej pokochał Jolę za jej temperament.
    Andrew fell in love:perf Yoland for her temperament
    'Andrew fell in love with Yoland for her liveliness.'

(8) Basia posiedziała z mamą (chwilę).
    Barbara sat:perf with mother (moment)
    'Barbara sat with mother for a while.'

Comrie (1976: 19, 20) cites similar examples from Ancient Greek, Spanish, Mandarin and Russian.

Dik is careful to point out that the different interpretations of the perfective or imperfective have to be distinguished from the actual phasal or quantificational aspectual forms. Polish, for instance, has an inflectional perfective/imperfective opposition with some groups of verbs, as shown above, but no separate marker for phasal aspect, and arguably[10] only one quantificational aspectual morpheme – *yw*, the iterative, as in (4c) cited on p. 117. The meanings associated with both phasal and quantificational aspect are rendered by different interpretations of the perfective and imperfective. The imperfective is used not only to convey a conative or iterative meaning, as in (5) and (6) above, but also to express the progressive (9a), immediate prospective (9b), the perfect (9c) and the habitual (9d).

Polish
(9) a. Ona teraz pisze list.
       she now write:imperf letter
       'She is writing a letter now.'

      b.   A   teraz   piszę   zadanie domowe.
          and now   write:imperf:1sg homework
         'And now I'm just about to do my homework.'

      c.   Już   jadłem.
          already ate:imperf:3sg
         'I've already eaten.'

      d.   Pisał   do   niej   bardzo dużo.
          wrote:imperf:3sg to   her   very   much
         'He wrote to her a lot.'

The perfective in turn is typically resultative (a perfect), as in (10a), sometimes semelfactive (10b,) distributive (10c), cumulative (10d) and, as mentioned before, ingressive.

Polish
(10) a.   Marek   spoważniał/(*poważniał)   ostatnio.
          Mark   matured:perf/matured:imperf   recently
        'Mark has matured recently.'

      b.   Paweł   kopną/kopał   piłkę.
          Paul   kicked:perf/kicked:imperf ball
        'Paul kicked (a single time)/was kicking the ball.

      c.   Zołnierze   pozdejmowali/ zdejmowali   czapki.
          soldiers   took off:perf/took off:imperf caps
        'Each of the soldiers took off his cap./The soldiers took off their caps.'

      d.   Naczytałam się   kryminałów./ Czytałam   kryminały.
          read:perf:1sg refl   detective stories read:imperf:1sg detective stories
        'I have had my fill of detective stories./I have read detective stories.'

English, in contrast to Polish, does not have a morphological perfective/imperfective distinction. The progressive and the perfect are phasal aspects. Phasal aspects may also be seen to interact with the basic properties of a given SoA. The English progressive, for instance, may change a dynamic SoA into a non-dynamic one (11), a momentaneous SoA into an iterative state (12), and a State into a Process (13).

(11) a.   She read the book.
       b.   She was reading the book.

(12) a.   I noticed the poverty.
       b.   I was still noticing the poverty then.

(13) a.   He is a fool.
       b.   He is being a fool.

The non-dynamic nature of (11b) and (12b) is suggested by their interpretation in the presence of point adverbials such as *when I arrived*, *at two o'clock*, etc. (Comrie 1976: 30; Vlach 1981: 273–274). A non-dynamic SoA, when accompanied by such adverbs, is interpreted as being already in progress at the time specified by the point adverbial. For example:

(14) He was eight when I was born.

A dynamic SoA, on the other hand, is interpreted as eventuating after the time stated in the adverbial. For example:

(15) Dorothy spoke when I entered.

The progressives in (11b) and (12b) behave just like the stative (14) in this respect.

5.2.1.2 Level-2 π_2 operators

The major argument for the π_2 nature of quantificational aspect is that it may quantify over any element of the core predication including a δ_2. For instance, according to Kucera (1981: 182), the iterative in Czech, which is derived from imperfective stems by the infix *-va-*, may quantify not only the predicate, but also a temporal adverb (16) or a subject (17).

Czech
(16) V   sobotu   Pavel   sedává   v   hospodě.
      on   Saturday Paul   sit:iter   in   pub
      'On Saturdays Paul (usually) sits in the pub.'

(17) Němci   mluvívají   spatně   česky.
      Germans   speak:iter   bad   Czech
      'Germans tend to speak Czech badly.'

Example (16) means that Paul sits in the pub most Saturdays, rather than that he sits there several times every Saturday. And (17) states that of all the Germans who speak Czech, the majority speak it badly, not that most of the times that they speak it they do so badly. Additional support for treating quantificational aspect as a π_2 comes from the fact that it can be specified independently of perfective/imperfective or phasal aspect. The English habitual, for instance (indicated by the *used to* construction), can combine freely with the progressive (Comrie 1976: 30). For example:

(18) When I visited John, he used to be reciting his latest poems.

Consider also the following Polish example, from Majewicz (1985: 49), in which *po-* denotes completion of the whole chain of events, *przez-* marks perfectiveness implying the completion of every single event in the sequence, and *yw-* is the iterative morpheme.

Polish
(19) Po-   prze-czyt-yw -a-łam   wszystkie jej   kśiążki.
     compl- perf-read-iter -past   all   her   books
     'I have read all her books, reading them occasionally, from time to time or one after another, and right through.'

The π_2 nature of tense is manifest primarily in the ordering preferences mentioned earlier, i.e. in the tendency for tense markers to occur further away from the verb nucleus than aspect. Two examples are given below, from the PreAndine Arawakan language Campa (Wise 1986: 587) and the Australian language Walmadjari (Hudson 1976: 656).

Campa
(20) h -ow -ak- a-   -ri.
     3m -eat -perf- nonfut:refl -3m
     'He ate it.'

Walmadjari
(21) yan- an- ku   mana.
     go- cont- fut I
     'I will keep on going.'

Also suggestive of the π_2 status of tense is the fact that in mono-clausal serial verb constructions and other constructions with complex verbs no independent choice of tense is possible for the individual verbs (Foley and Van Valin 1984; Foley and Olson 1985). This is illustrated on the basis of the examples in (22) from Luiseño (Langacker 1988: 97–98) in which the tense marker *-q* attaches not only to a single verb, but to the verb with the widest semantic scope.

Luiseño
(22) a. noo ŋee- q.
         I   leave-tns
         'I am leaving.'

     b. noo ŋee- viču- q.
         I   leave-want-tns
         'I want to leave.'

c. noo   poy   ŋee- ni-   q.
    I   him   leave-make-tns
    'I made him leave.'

d. noo   poy   ŋee- vicu- ni-   q.
    I   him   leave-want-make-tns
    'I made him want to leave.'

e. noo   poy   ŋee- vicu- ni-   vicu- q.
    I   him   leave-want-make-want-tns
    'I want to make him want to leave.'

5.2.2 Mood and modality

In the linguistic and logical literature the terms *mood* and *modality* have been used with reference to a number of apparently disparate phenomena. Logicians restrict considerations of modality primarily to matters relating to the propositional expression of necessity and possibility, whereas linguists view modality more widely, as also encompassing the expression of the speaker's opinion or attitude towards the proposition that the sentence conveys or the situation that the proposition describes, and even his or her communicative intention in producing the given utterance. Nowadays it is generally acknowledged that the notion of modality, as used in linguistics, does not define a unified conceptual domain. Therefore it is usual to discuss modality with reference to several subareas.

Dik adopts the subdivisions proposed by Hengeveld (1987a,b, 1989), who, drawing heavily on the insights of Lyons (1977) and Foley and Van Valin (1984) in particular, divides the semantic distinctions typically subsumed under the label 'modality' into three groups: inherent modality, objective modality and epistemological modality. These three subareas of modality pertain in one way or another to the propositional content of the clause; in FG terminology, to the core and extended predication and the proposition. What are often referred to as sentence-type modalities and other means used to transmit and modify the speaker's communicative intention are treated as a matter of illocution (see Table 5.1), rather than modality *senso stricto*. In the following discussion, this division of semantic distinctions into modal (§5.2.2.1) and illocutionary (§5.2.2.2) will be maintained.

In line with FG practice, the term *mood* will be used in the traditional sense to denote a grammatical category, not necessarily identifiable in all languages, employed to code some subset of the semantic distinctions covered by the label 'modality'. It needs to be emphasized that though mood in FG is recognized as one of the most common means of signalling sentence type, it is not equated with sentence type or illocutionary force, unlike under the analyses of the philosophers Austin (1962) and Searle (1969) or in Halliday's (1985) Systemic Functional Grammar. We will see in §5.2.2.1 and 5.2.2.2 that the grammatical category of mood may be used both to mark modal distinctions and to qualify illocutions.[11]

5.2.2.1 Modality

The term *inherent modality* refers to the speaker's estimate of the relationship between a participant in the SoA and the realization of that SoA. Inherent modalities are taken to belong to the internal structure of the SoA, the nuclear predication (core predication in RRG). The type of modal distinctions conveyed by inherent modalities include: ability, willingness, obligation, permissibility and volition. The same semantic distinctions fall within the domain of objective and epistemological modalities. However, in the case of inherent modality these distinctions are realized lexically (e.g. in English by the use of constructions with: *can, want, be able to, be allowed to, have to,* etc.), not grammatically. Hengeveld (1987a: 11–12) suggests that there is also a semantic difference between inherent and objective modality in that by means of the former speakers merely present their knowledge of a given situation, while by means of the latter they offer an evaluation of the situation in terms of this knowledge. For many linguists this difference excludes inherent modality from the proper domain of modality. Dik recognizes inherent modality as a subarea of modality mainly because diachronically, the lexical items used in the expression of inherent modality typically give rise to bona fide modal forms. A case in point is the frequently attested reinterpretation of ability predicates (e.g. *can* in English) as expressions of objective epistemic possibility.

Objective modality is characterized in FG as involving the evaluation of an SoA in terms of the speaker's knowledge of its likelihood of occurrence (actuality). Following Chung and Timberlake (1985: 241), FG includes within the set of actually modalized distinctions not only expressions of non-actuality, which are generally regarded as constituting the subject matter of objective modality, but also explicit markers of actuality used by speakers to indicate a direct correspondence between a given SoA and their experience of the here-and-now. In line with conventional linguistic analysis, the evaluation of non-actual SoAs is assumed to be carried out either with reference to the factuality of the SoA relative to the nature of SoAs in general, or with reference to a system of moral, legal or social conventions. The former type of modality is referred to as *epistemic*, the latter as *deontic*. The two types of modality are illustrated in (23a) and (23b), respectively.

Polish
(23) a. W   Gdańsku może być spokojnie.
           in   Gdańsk   can   be   calm
           'It can be calm in Gdańsk.'

       b. We Francji można się pobrać w   lokalnej karczmie.
           in   France can   refl marry   in local   pub
           'In France you can get married in a local pub.'

Example (23a) may be paraphrased as: 'In view of what is generally known I conclude that it is not excluded that it is calm in Gdańsk.' Example (23b) is self-evident. Epistemic modality is assumed to be quantifiable on a scale of possibility (24a), deontic modality on a scale of permissibility (24b).

(24) a. certain – probable – possible – conceivable – impossible.
       b. obligatory – customary – permissible – acceptable – forbidden.

The encoding of objective modality may take the form of verbal mood or embedding predicates. The latter include modal auxiliaries, as in the Polish examples in (23) and their English translation, and modal adjectives, such as *certain, possible, likely*, etc. Bybee (1985: 180) notes that the fine grading of epistemic modality shown on the scale in (24a) is a feature of non-inflectional manifestations of modality.[12] Epistemic inflections tend to cover the possibility–probability range of the scale, and there is generally no more than one such inflection in any given language. This is consistent with the overall greater generality of the semantic distinctions coded inflectionally as compared to the lexical mode of expression.

The term *epistemological modality* is proposed by Hengeveld (1987a: 10) to cover subjective modalities and evidentials. Subjective modalities are divided into two types: subjective epistemic modality and volitional (boulomaic) modality. Subjective epistemic modality is seen to specify the degree of the speaker's commitment with regard to the truth of the presented proposition, while volitional modality is taken to convey the emotional commitment – the wishes, hopes and desires – of the speaker to the proposition. The factor uniting the two modalities is the relevance of the source of the information contained in the proposition. As an illustration of these two subjective modalities consider the examples in (25) and (26).

Polish
(25)   Może   przyjdzie.
       may   come
       'He/she may come.'

(26)   Oby   przyszedł.
       prt:optative   come
       'I hope he comes./He better come.'

Observe that in both Polish and English, as well as in other languages, the modal auxiliaries are open to an objective and a subjective epistemic reading. According to Lyons (1977: 797–809), subjectively modalized utterances, unlike objectively modalized ones, are statements of opinion rather than fact. In the uttering of a subjectively modalized utterance the speaker expresses his doubt about the factuality of the proposition. By means of an objectively modalized utterance, on the other hand, the speaker performs an act of telling. Lyons therefore concludes that the illocutionary force of subjectively modalized utterances is like that of a question.

Whereas subjective modalities mark the truthfulness of the proposition from the point of view of the speaker, evidentials indicate the factuality of the proposition in terms of how the speaker has obtained knowledge of it. The relevant distinction may be a simple binary one reflecting whether or not the speaker has witnessed the given event or has direct as opposed to secondhand knowledge of it. In Bulgarian, for example, such a distinction is coded inflectionally on the verb. Compare (27a) and (27b) from Radewa (1984: 222).

Bulgarian
(27)   a.   Pólskijat   fútboljen   otbór   pobjedí   bylgarskija.
            Polish   football   team   defeated:ind   Bulgarian.
            'The Polish football team defeated the Bulgarian.'

       b.   Pólskijat   fútboljen   otbór   pobjedíl   bylgarskija.
            Polish   football   team   deafeated:evid Bulgarian
            'Allegedly, the Polish football team defeated the Bulgarian.'

Finer evidential distinctions are also possible. The most common are inferential, quotative and experiential modalities which characterize the depicted event as inferred from evidence, reported from another source, and experienced by the source, respectively.

A language which has all of these is Pawnee (Macro-Siouan); there is a quotative prefix, a prefix for unwitnessed events about the nature of which there is no doubt, a dubitative prefix for unwitnessed events of doubtful nature, and an inferential prefix. The last two of these are illustrated in (28), adapted from Parks (1976) via Bybee (1985: 181–182). (Bybee gives a morpheme-by-morpheme gloss of the verb only.)

Pawnee
(28) a. tih- ra- ku:tit-∅ ku:ruks.
infer- abs- kill- perf bear
'He must have killed a bear.'

b. kuh- ra -u -∅ pi:ta a ku capat.
dubit-abs-be-perf
'It was either a man or a woman.'

In most European languages evidentials are marked by adverbs, such as *evidently, allegedly, supposedly, apparently* etc., as in the English translation of (27b).

As shown in Table 5.1, objective modalities are considered to operate on the predication, epistemological modalities on the proposition. Considerable evidence for this distribution of the two types of modality has been adduced both by the linguists who have elaborated the layered structure of the clause currently under discussion, i.e. Bybee, Foley, Hengeveld, Olson and Van Valin, and by those working in the general area of modality, such as Halliday (1970), Lyons (1977), Palmer (1983), Doherty (1987), Kiefer (1987) and others. The first, relatively minor point is that since objective modalities qualify the SoA as a whole rather than some facet of it, they must be SoA-external. All of the remaining arguments for assigning objective and epistemological modalities to different levels of clause structure involve the significant behavioral differences between objectively and epistemologically modalized utterances. It is frequently noted that the logical operations which normally can easily be performed on a proposition are blocked in the case of epistemologically modalized utterances, but not in the case of objectively modalized ones.[13] This follows from an analysis under which objective modalities by virtue of being π_2 belong to the proposition, while epistemological modalities, as π_3, stand outside the proposition modifying the speaker's assessment of the truth value of the expressed propositional content. The relevant logical processes, illustrated in (29)–(32), include:

a) questioning

(29) a. Is it possible that Mark will forget?
b. *Possibly will Mark forget?

b) negation of the marker of modality

(30) a. It is impossible that Mark will forget.
b. *Impossibly Mark will forget.

c) coordination

(31) a. It is impossible and inconceivable that Mark will forget.
b. *Mark is possibly and conceivably sick.

d) the possibility of occurring in the premise (*if*-clause) of a conditional

(32) a. If it is probable that the doctor will be late, I'm not going to wait.
b. *If the doctor is probably late, I'm not going to wait.

In addition to the above, the temporal reference of subjectively modalized utterances in contrast to objectively modalized ones is almost exclusively restricted to speech time. Witness the examples in (33).

(33) a. Given the conditions in Lubyanka then, it was possible to go mad in a very short time.
b. Given the conditions in Lubyanka then, *possibly one went mad in a very short time.

Halliday (1970: 336, 347), who originally made this observation, assumed that the binding of subjective epistemic modality to speech time affected all the English modal auxiliaries and modal adverbs alike. Subsequent investigations have revealed differences between the various modals in this respect. On the whole English subjective epistemic modals with past tense inflection (e.g. *might, could, had to*, etc.) do not refer to the past, but are used as a mitigating device expressing a certain degree of caution on the part of the speaker. Nonetheless, Leech (1971: 91) provides examples with *could* and *had* where they clearly do have past time reference. Bolkestein (1980: 69, 114) observes similar facts in Latin. For instance, in (34) the modal *necesse est*, which carries a subjective epistemic meaning, refers to a point in time anterior to speech time.

Latin
(34) magna pars deperiit ... quod accidere tot proeliis fuit necesse.
'a great part died, something which had to happen in so many fights'
(Caesar, *Civ.* 3,87)

Examples such as (34) aside, while objective modalities do, subjective modalities do not tend to fall within the scope of tense. Given that tense is a π_2, as argued in §5.2.1.2, and objective modality is external to the SoA, in order for the two to interact with each other, objective modality must be regarded also as a π_2. By the same token subjective modality must be outside the scope of tense.

A further source of support for the higher level of epistemological relative to objective modalities comes from the ordering preferences displayed by the two types of modality. In French (Schlyter 1982: 231), for example, in which – unlike in English – modal adverbs may be used both in a subjective and an objective epistemic sense, when the modal adverb is placed initially, as in (35a), it receives a subjective interpretation, whereas in the post-auxiliary position, as in (35b), the objective reading is strongly favoured.

French
(35) a. Probablement, Pierre a raté son examen – parce qu'il a l'air si triste.
b. Pierre a probablement rat son examen – parce qu'il a répondu à peu de questions.

The different interpretations accompanying the two sentential locations correlate with the fact that *probablement* as an objective modal adverb is tied more closely to the verbal nucleus than in its role as a subjective modal adverb. Similar facts hold for English with respect to δ_1 and δ_3 adverbials. Jackendoff (1972: 75–76) gives evidence that though a subjective epistemic adverb or an evidential may be placed after the first auxiliary, it cannot occur after subsequent auxiliaries or immediately before the verb, positions reserved for δ_1 manner adverbs which modify 1the nuclear predication. Compare (36) and (37).

(36) {Probably / Evidently} the newlyweds {probably / evidently} must {probably / evidently} have {*probably / *evidently} left early.

(37) {*Quickly / *Cleverly} Martha {*quickly / *cleverly} must {*quickly / *cleverly} have {quickly / cleverly} packed all the silver.

Moreover, in constructions with the two types of modality, epistemological and objective, epistemological modality always has the wider scope. In other words, whereas objective modalities can fall within the scope of subjective ones, the reverse does not hold.[14] We see this in (38) on the basis of the relative positioning of the modal adjective and modal adverb, in (39) with respect to the modal adverb and negation[15] (a π_2), and in (40) in relation to a modal adverb and a quantifier.

(38) a. Certainly, it is possible that the boss will be late.
b. *It is possible that certainly the boss will be late.

(39) a. Probably, Janice isn't sick.
b. Janice is probably not sick.
c. *Janice isn't probably sick.

(40) a. Probably, mother is often tired.
b. *Mother is often probably tired.

Evidence for the wider scope of epistemological relative to objective modality from the ordering of bound forms is hard to come by. Hengeveld (1989: 142) cites the example in (41) from the Yuman language Diegueño (Gorbet 1976) where an objective modal affix is followed by an evidential one.

Diegueño
(41) w - a:- m -x- kx.
3sg- go- away -irr- infer
'It must be that he will go.'

Easier to find are examples of affix or particle order where an expression of epistemological modality follows a marker of quantificational aspect or tense (π_2) and/or is itself followed by an illocutionary indicator or qualifier (π_4). Two cases in point are illustrated in (42) and (43).

Hidatsa (Siouan; Matthews 1965)
(42) wio i hirawe ki ksa c.
woman she sleep ingr iter prob
'The woman fell asleep again and again.'

West Greenlandic (Inuit, Fortescue 1984)
(43) Aki-nngil-aanga luunniit.
reply-neg-3sg:1sg:ind reinf
'He didn't even reply to me.'

The location of the evidential between the π_2 and π_4 operators corroborates its status as a π_3.

5.2.2.2 Illocution

The term *illocution* or *illocutionary force* is used to denote the function of the clause as an illocutionary (speech) act, in the sense of Austin (1962) and Searle (1969), i.e. as an act of asserting, informing, denying, predicting, questioning, requesting, promising, etc. Given the communicative function of language, every utterance is assumed to have an illocutionary force, though not necessarily a unique one. The determination of the illocutionary force of an utterance is seen to involve three major considerations: (a) the communicative intention of the speaker;[16] (b) the linguistic form of the utterance; (c) the interpretation of the utterance by the addressee.

The main point of contention in regard to these considerations has been the question of which aspects of the speaker's communicative intention and the addressee's interpretation belong to the realm of linguistic theory and which to a wider theory of pragmatics or communication. Nowadays the prevailing view is to consider as part of the linguistically relevant illocutionary force of an utterance only what the addressee can be assumed to construe reasonably as being the speaker's communicative intention on the basis of properties of the utterance. This excludes any speaker intentions inaccessible to the addressee, for instance an interpretation of the statement in (44) as a warning, and also any effects (perlocutions) on the addressee not predictable by the speaker, such as the addressee's interpretation of (44) as a request for the loan of his or her car.

(44)   We're going to Sienna.

What remains at issue is the nature of the information reconstructible by the addressee that should be seen as pertinent to the determination of the illocutionary force of the utterance, in the linguistically relevant sense of the term. This matter will be resumed below.

The linguistic means used to code illocutionary force are termed by Searle (1969: 20–21) *illocutionary force indicating devices* (ifids). The ifids regularly found across languages include: the markers of sentence type, namely word order, intonation, stress and mood, as well as performative verbs, tag questions, various particles and elements such as *please*. The sentence type plays a special role in that it is taken to identify the primary or basic illocution of the utterance.[17] In addition to the basic illocution all utterances may have one or more other indirect illocutions determined by different ifids or the pragmatic context. It is in regard to the linguistic status and treatment of the pragmatically determined illocutions that the opinions of linguists differ.

Scholars who seek to connect matters of illocutionary force with Grice's (1975) theory of meaning maintain that the identification of (45) and (46) as a request and a promise respectively, rather than as just statements, and of (47) as a threat as opposed to simply a question, is possible by conventional procedures of interpretation.

(45) I'll take a black coffee.

(46) I'll come back on Monday.

(47) Would you like your face smashed in?

They argue that the relevant indirect illocutions can be deduced from the pragmatic context of utterance shared by the speaker and addressee, the definitions of particular illocutionary acts, and crucially the general powers of rationality, inference and cooperation such as Grice's (1975) maxims or Brown and Levinson's (1978) face affects.[18]

Consequently they view the indirect illocutions of (45), (46) and (47) as falling within the scope of linguistic analysis. For other linguists, however, only the indirect illocutions that are coded linguistically, as the request and promise in (48) and (49) for instance, constitute the proper domain of grammatical inquiry, while the inferentially established illocutionary forces of (45)–(47) are seen to belong to a wider pragmatic theory of verbal interaction.

(48) I'll take a black coffee, please.

(49) I promise to come back on Monday.

Dik belongs to this second group.

In FG each utterance is assigned one of four basic illocutions (declarative, interrogative, imperative and exclamatory) corresponding to the sentence type via which it is realized. As mentioned in passing in §5.1, these basic illocutions are treated as illocutionary operators by Dik, and as constituting an illocutionary frame by Hengeveld. Indirect illocutions of the relevant kind are attributed to a process of illocutionary conversion achieved either lexically, for instance by a performative verb, or grammatically via illocutionary operators (π_4) such as mood inflection or various particles.

The direct and indirect illocutions of an utterance are subject to different forms of modification. Chief among the semantic effects exerted by illocutionary modifiers are mitigation and reinforcement (see Table 5.1), used to decrease or conversely heighten the directness or impact of an illocutionary act. What is involved in mitigation or reinforcement is the qualification of so-called *felicity conditions*, i.e. the contextual (situational and pragmatic) conditions underlying the successful performance of a given illocutionary act. The felicity conditions are classified into preparatory conditions which specify the real-world prerequisites to each illocutionary act, and sincerity conditions which concern the beliefs, feelings and desires of the speaker and addressee.

Mitigation and reinforcement may be implemented again by lexical (δ_4) or grammatical (π_4) means. English favours the lexical expression of both mitigation and reinforcement primarily, though by no means exclusively, via performative verbs, illocutionary adverbs and clausal satellites. The first two are used mainly for reinforcement. Performative verbs lend force to the illocution by spelling out what otherwise is expressed only on the grammatical plane. Illocutionary adverbs comment on the manner in which the speaker is performing his illocutionary act. As an illustration consider the examples below.

(50) a. Frankly, I don't like him.
b. I tell you frankly, I don't like him.

(51) a. Honestly, did you do it?
b. I ask you to tell me honestly, did you do it?

(52) a. Bluntly, piss off.
b. I tell you bluntly, piss off.

Clausal satellites in turn typically fulfil a mitigating function implementing such mitigating strategies[19] as:

a) the expression of the speaker's doubt as to the satisfaction of the preparatory conditions of his or her illocutionary act, from his or her own or the addressee's point of view:

(53) a. I promise to finish it, if I can.
b. If I hurt you, I apologize.

b) the appearance of giving the addressee the option of refusing or disagreeing:

(54) a. Come with me, if you don't mind.
b. Sit down, please (if you please).

c) rhetorically asking permission of the addressee:

(55) a. May I say what a delight it has been staying with you.
b. Let me tell you that I enjoyed your book enormously.

d) the appeal to the addressee's knowledge or interest:

(56) a. As you know, Bill is away.
b. The book is on the second shelf, if you are interested.

e) providing the circumstances underlying the execution of the illocutionary act:

(57) a. Just so I won't be late again, what is the exact time?
b. To get things straight, is it John or Mr Brown?

The clausal satellites in (53)–(57) provide specifications of reason, purpose and condition for the illocutionary acts.

The semantic effects achieved via mitigation and reinforcement are in many instances comparable to the modal distinctions discussed in §5.2.2.1. Observe that the felicity conditions and in particular the sincerity conditions which are qualified via mitigation or reinforcement relate to the speech act participants' knowledge, beliefs, wants and abilities, i.e. the same factors that are involved in objective and epistemological modality. Unlike these modal distinctions, however, which affect the propositional content of the clause or the speaker's attitude to it, the π_4 and δ_4 modify the illocutionary act itself. This is evidenced by the fact that π_4 and δ_4 can occur with sentences displaying all types of basic illocutions. Thus, for example, mitigation via the use of the conditional mood in Polish, coded by the preterite form of the verb and the clitic *by*, can be applied to a declarative (58a), interrogative (58b) and imperative (58c).

Polish
(58) a. Napiła-by-m się kawy.
drink-cond-1sg refl coffee
'I'd like some coffee.'

b. Czy poszedł- by-ś ze mną na spacer.
Q go- cond-2sg with me for walk
'Would you go for a walk with me?'

c. Wpadł- by-ś do mnie jutro.
drop in- cond-2sg to me tomorrow.
'Why don't you drop in to see me tomorrow!'

Note also the analogous distribution of the English illocutionary adverbs and performative verbs in the pairs of clauses in (50), (51) and (52). The near-paraphrase[20] relationship obtaining between the (a) and (b) sentences of examples such as these corroborates the fact that the scope of the illocutionary adverb in the (a) member of each pair is the illocutionary act. In (50) and (52) the adverbs modify the illocutionary act of the speaker, in (51) the part of the speaker's illocution which invites the addressee to give a verbal reply. Significantly, in either instance it is not the proposition asserted in the performance of the illocutionary act that is modified, but the current or future (requested) act of performing the illocution. The semantic parallelisms between the pairs of sentences in (50)–(52) is brought out by a comparison with examples such as (59) in which the expressed proposition is a complement of a descriptive verb of saying.

(59)   Hillary told me frankly that I was to blame.

Lyons (1977: 783) observes that (59) asserts the fact that Hillary was frank in the manner in which he performed the act of telling. In (51a,b), on the other hand, the manner adverbials function as a parenthetical comment on the way the illocutionary act was performed. The adverbs qualifying an explicit performative are parenthetical in regard to the proposition by virtue of belonging to the higher performative predication. In terms of the FG layered model of clause structure, however, these adverbials are nuclear-level manner adverbials just like the adverb of manner in (59). The illocutionary adverbs, by contrast, are parenthetical to the proposition owing to their independent status as modifiers of the illocution. In short, despite the semantic correspondences between the (a) and (b) clauses in (50)–(52), the two sets of adverbs belong to quite different levels of clause structure. FG does not consider the scope of the illocutionary adverbs in (50a)–(52a) to warrant the postulation of an underlying performative verb in these or any other sentences, an issue known in the literature under the heading of the performative hypothesis.[21] The recognition of a basic illocution attached to clause type counters the need to postulate an underlying performative verb in (50a)–(52a) because the illocutionary adverb, as a δ_4, by definition has the illocution within its scope, which is precisely what an implicit performative is meant to account for.

To return to the motivation for distinguishing illocutionary from modal operators and satellites, it is worth noting that illocutionary adverbs in English cannot be indirectly reported, (*saying that X* vs *saying X*). Witness the ungrammaticality of (60a) contrasted with (60b) in which the epistemological adverb is part of the message contained in the illocution.

(60)   a.   *She said that confidentially, it is certainly possible that John has AIDS.
       b.   She said that it is certainly possible that John has AIDS.

This follows from the fact that, as mentioned above, an illocutionary adverb as opposed to an epistemological one does not constitute part of what is being asserted. Another piece of evidence suggestive of the whole clause being in the scope of illocutionary modifiers is that their expression may affect all the inflectional forms of the predication including a subjective epistemic modal. Hengeveld (1987a: 56) offers the following example from Spanish in which the subjunctive mood is one of the forms of mitigation used in the language.

Spanish
(61) a. Quizás *es* seguro que la ceguera *puede* ser venicida.
maybe is:ind certain that the blindness can:ind be cured

b. Quizás *sea* seguro que la ceguera *pueda* ser vencida.
maybe is:subjc certain that the blindness can:subjc be cured
'It may/might be possible that blindness can be cured.'

The difference in scope of English epistemological and illocutionary adverbs is also manifest in matters of order. The examples in (62) below illustrate that the illocutionary adverb must precede the epistemic one, the reverse order being ungrammatical.

(62) a. Frankly, probably there is nothing that I can do about it.
b. *Probably, frankly, there is nothing I can do about it.

The same facts are claimed to hold in relation to affix order. Witness the following examples from Turkish in which the reinforcing affix *-dir* occurs utterance-finally.[22]

Turkish (Lewis 1967, cited in Hengeveld 1987a: 57)
(63) Bu, Türkçe gazete degil - dir.
this Turkish newspaper not-reinf
'This is not a Turkish newspaper at all.'

5.3 THE LAYERED STRUCTURE OF THE CLAUSE VS X-BAR CONSTITUENCY

Foley and Van Valin's (1984) model of the layered structure of the clause with the distinction between the core and periphery corresponds to the early TG constituency division of VP (verb phrase) and S (sentence), whereas the extra levels recognized in FG are reminiscent of the elaborate constituent structure representation characteristic of the current formulation of X-bar theory.[23]

The X-bar theory of clause structure allows each head X, where X is either a lexical category (noun, verb, adjective or adposition) or an abstract category such as inflection (I), to project n levels of phrase

The layered structure of the clause 137

structure. Currently, the maximal level of n for English is taken to be two. This does not mean, however, that there are only two layers of constituency relations. Recursions and, in the case of Chomskyan theory, abstract Xs result in very complex constituent structures. The underlying (D-structure) of the clause as represented in *Barriers* (Chomsky 1986) is shown in (64).

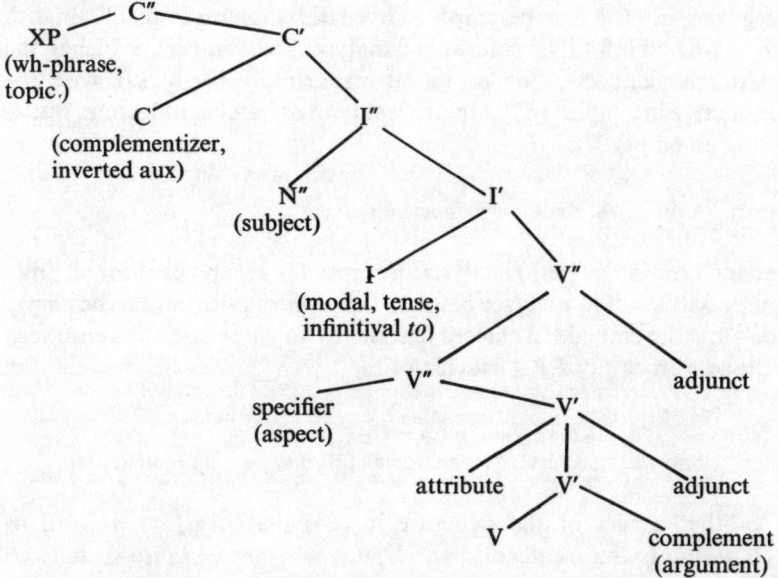

(64) V = verb, V" = verb phrase (VP), I = inflection, I' = predicate phrase, I" = clause (S); C = complementizer, C' = complementizer phrase, C" = main clause (S'), N" = full NP

Figure 5.1 The underlying structure of the clause

GB recognizes four functional categories: complements, adjuncts, attributes and specifiers. The complements are the arguments of X (with the exception of the subject, see below); the adjuncts are the satellites that follow X; the attributes are the satellites that precede X; and the specifiers are the determiners of X. A complement expands X into X'. An adjunct or attribute recursively expands an X' into another X', or potentially an X" into another X". And a specifier expands an X' into X" (the maximal projection). The structure of the clause presented in (64) is built up from the projections of three X categories: V – the basic predicate, I – inflection, and C – complementizer. Though only V is indicated as having attributes and adjuncts, I and C may co-occur with these categories too. In conformity with the claim that the maximal level of X^n projections is two, the VP is a V″, the S a I″, and S′ a C″.

The appropriateness of (64) as a representation of the underlying constituent structure of sentences rests on the recognition of empty (covert) categories. An empty category is characterized in GB as structurally present but phonologically invisible. Virtually any of the categories in (64) can be empty. Given this assumption, all English indicative and infinitival clauses are analysed as having a C which in the case of main clauses or *for*-less infinitives is simply empty. Likewise, the subjunctive in English (65) is interpreted not as lacking inflection, but as having an empty I.

(65) Mother will insist that we come for dinner.

Under Chomsky's (1986) analysis an empty I is also posited for all finite clauses without a modal (see below). The subject position can be empty too. Thus the embedded clauses in (66) are not subjectless, but are seen to possess an empty *PRO* subject.

(66) a. The students want [PRO to strike].
b. Karajan persuaded the woman [PRO to play in his orchestra].

Another aspect of the structure in (64) that begs for a word of explanation is the I category. I indicates whether a clause is finite or infinitival; finite clauses have a finite I carrying tense and agreement; non-finite clauses feature a non-finite I, and are by definition tenseless and agreementless. Significantly, both finite and non-finite clauses have an I. Modals are generated under a finite I, the infinitival *to* under a non-finite I. The infinitival *to* is not, however, just a marker of non-finiteness, but the non-finite analogue of a modal verb.[24] Witness the structural parallelism between (67a) and (67b).

(67) a. I am anxious that [Peter should arrive by midnight].
b. I am anxious for [Peter to arrive by midnight].

Note also that modals do not occur in infinitival clauses. In clauses with a modal, tense and agreement are realized on the modal. When there is no modal, I, as mentioned above, is empty. In such cases either the first aspectual auxiliary or in the absence of such an auxiliary, the verb stem is raised into I where it acquires the properties of tense and agreement.

Needless to say, the correspondences between the elaborate constituent structure representation in (64) and the FG layered structure of the clause are not perfect. Standard phrase structure (PS) representations as in (64) depict both dominance and precedence relations. The FG layered structure of the clause, on the other hand, reflects only dominance relations; each outer layer encloses the inner layers. This difference, however, disappears once the ordering relations of PS-rules are factored out into a separate linearization component as suggested by, for instance, Falk (1983) or Gazdar et al. (1985), or dealt with by some set of general ordering principles.[25]

The other most significant difference between hierarchical constituent structure and the FG levels of structure concerns the treatment of the subject. In GB, as in FG, the underlying structure of the clause is assumed to reflect predicate–argument relations. However, in Chomsky's theory of grammar, the first argument (A^1) is considered to be an argument not directly of the predicate, as in RRG, FG and even Bresnan's LFG, but of the abstract category inflection. To put it another way, the subject is considered to be an argument not of V, but of the VP.[26] Consequently there is no phrase structure constituent equivalent to the FG nuclear predication (or RRG core predication) which includes just the predicate and its arguments.

Apart from the treatment of the subject, however, just as in FG, the arguments (complements) are seen to form a close unit with the predicate. The attributes and adjuncts of V correspond to FG δ_1 (e.g. manner adverbials such as *cleverly, gently, wisely*) or δ_2 (e.g. time and place adverbials), some of the δ_2 potentially forming a higher V', and others being direct daughters of V". The I and C attributes and adjuncts cover the higher-level satellites. Thus, for example, the vast group of so-called sentence-adverbials[27] comprising attitudinal adverbs (e.g. *fortunately, happily, sadly*), evaluative adverbs (*wisely, cleverly, oddly*), subjective epistemic adverbs (e.g. *certainly, possibly, surely*), degree of precision adverbs (e.g. *exactly, precisely, essentially*) and evidentials (e.g. *apparently, evidently, seemingly*), all of which are considered as propositional (level-3) modifiers in FG, qualify as daughters of I". Given the various semantic and syntactic differences among these adverbs (see e.g. Greenbaum 1969; Dik 1975; Quirk et al. 1985; Ernst 1984), some of them, for instance the attitudinal ones, as suggested by Nakajima (1982), could be assigned to I", others to I', or perhaps even to V". FG δ_4 satellites, in turn, such as the illocutionary adverbs discussed in §5.2.2.2 and other style disjuncts like the ones exemplified in (68), adapted from Greenbaum (1969: 165) and Quirk and Greenbaum (1973: 243) are constituents of C" or C'.

(68) a. *Technically*, that means getting rid of the iambic pentameter.
b. The committee interviewed the two writers. *Generally*, the writers were against censorship.
c. *With respect*, none of them is competent to give an opinion on the matter.

Worthy of note is the fact that in both frameworks adverbs such as *cleverly, wisely, rudely, oddly*, etc. are assigned to different underlying levels of clause structure, i.e. V'/δ_1 and I''/δ_3 respectively, depending on whether they receive a manner reading (69a) or an evaluative interpretation (69b).

(69) a. Rudely, Sandra answered back.
b. Sandra answered back rudely.

Moreover, both FG and GB seek confirmation for the distinction between the two types of adverbs in the criteria proposed by Greenbaum (1969) and Quirk *et al.* (1972) for distinguishing adjuncts from disjuncts, such as the ability to carry focus (i.e. be questioned, clefted and otherwise contrasted) and behaviour under negation. Regarding negation, we see in (70) that an evaluative adverb takes negation within its scope, while a manner adverb falls within the scope of negation.

(70) Cleverly, she didn't answer stupidly this time.

Two other points of convergence between the GB and FG layers of structure are the treatment of aspectual auxiliaries as belonging to a lower-level constituent than tense and the modal auxiliaries (see §7.5), and the placement of the markers of basic illocutions (see §5.2.2.2) such as wh-constituents and inverted auxiliaries at the highest C'' level of constituent structure.

Leaving aside the internal configurations of the constituents in (64), which in any case are assumed to be subject to parametric variation, there are thus clear parallels between the V' and the nuclear predication, the V'' and the core predication, the I and the extended predication, the I'' and the proposition, the C' and the clause, and the C'' and the extended clause. These parallels find reflection in the way the hierarchical representation of clause structure is utilized in the primary classification of clausal complements in the two frameworks. Let us consider this issue briefly.

5.3.1 Hierarchical structure and clausal complementation

In what follows no attempt will be made to outline the intricate and varied semantic and syntactic properties of clausal complements, or to do justice to the many contributions to the field within Chomskyan theory. The intention is only to exemplify one area of grammar in which the levels of structure recognized in FG and GB are applied in a similar though by no means identical way. By clausal complementation is meant the embedding of sentence-like constructions as verbal arguments. The distinctions that will be discussed apply not only to complements but to subordinate clauses in general. However, due to limitations of space, we will be looking only at complements.

In both FG and GB the primary classification of clausal complements is carried out with reference to the highest layer that the complement contains. In the case of GB, the layers involved in distinguishing different complement types are claimed to be the maximal projections of which the sentence is comprised, V″, I″ and C″. FG is still in the process of developing its own typology of clausal complementation (see Dik 1987e; Dik *et al.* 1990; Bolkestein 1988, 1990). Therefore, at this stage, it is not clear whether all the levels that the theory has at its disposal, i.e. the predication (nuclear, core and extended), proposition (plain and extended) and clause (plain and extended), will ultimately be found to be directly reflected in a classification of clausal complements. As in GB, obviously relevant are the three basic levels, the predication, proposition and clause.

The GB typology of clausal complements involves a basic division into ordinary clauses (OC), exceptional clauses (EC) and small clauses (SC), exemplified in (71a,b,c) respectively.

(71) a. I believe that Hillary is capable of anything.
 [C I″]

 b. I believe Hillary to be capable of anything.
 [NP to VP]

 c. I believe Hillary capable of anything.
 [NP XP]

OCs are characterized as containing a C and an I, ECs have an I but no C, and SCs have neither a C nor an I. Given that C and I may be filled by an empty category, most main and subordinate finite and non-finite clauses fall under the label of OC. ECs comprise constructions known as accusative plus infinitive, analysed in early formulations of generative transformational grammar as involving raising and in earlier GB (Chomsky 1981) as undergoing S′ deletion. SCs consist of an NP, considered to be a subject and a predicative NP, VP, AP or PP. Under the traditional analysis the NP and XP are not viewed as forming a constituent in underlying structure, but rather the predicative noun, adjective, verb or prepositional phrase is considered as forming a secondary predication qualifying the main predication. This latter analysis in the current version of generative grammar is advocated by Williams (1980, 1983) and is also espoused by FG.

Hengeveld (1989) exemplifies the relevance of the FG layered model of the clause for a typology of clausal complementation on the basis of the complements involving direct speech reports, indirect speech reports, cognitive predicates and perceptual predicates. Complements rendering direct speech are considered to be full clause E-complements. (Recall that the variables E, X and e stand for the speech act, proposition and SoA, respectively.) Complements presenting indirect speech are treated as variants of either E-complementation or alternatively of propositional X-complementation. Cognitive predicates are seen to co-occur with propositional X-complements. And perceptual predicates are analysed as taking (extended) predicational complements. The four types of complements are illustrated in (72) below.

(72) a. Celia said, 'Honestly, I loved him once, didn't I?'
b. Celia asked whether I would go with her.
c. Celia believed that Hillary would certainly go to Paris.
d. Celia saw that Hillary caught the dog.

Secondary predications (71c) constitute a fifth type of complement the status of which may be taken to correspond to the nuclear predication.

Considering the many different semantic relations[28] obtaining between main-clause predicates and their clausal complements on a cross-linguistic basis (Noonan 1985: 91–133), the four-way distinction exemplified in (72) is rather limited. On the other hand, the four classes of complement taking predicates distinguished by Hengeveld are, according to Noonan, the most likely actually to take clausal complements in any given language. Moreover, it is precisely these types of complements that tend to manifest syntactic and semantic distinctions most amenable to an analysis in terms of different levels of structural representation.

Complements rendering direct speech qualify as E-complements since they may express all the different kinds of distinctions contained in the original utterance including illocutionary force and the various illocutionary modifiers discussed in §5.2.2.2, such as the illocutionary adverb and question tag in (72a). The unclear status of (semi-)indirect speech complements is a consequence of the fact that though they typically do not allow the expression of the illocutionary force of the original utterance by exactly the same means as in an independent clause, they do possess means of indicating the original illocutionary force. It may be indicated by, for instance, word order, as in the case of English semi-indirect speech (73), the choice of complementizer, as in the Polish examples in (74), or the finite/non-finite form of the complement clause, as in the English translation of the Polish sentences in (74).

(73) John wondered would she come on time.

Polish
(74) a. Powiedziałam mu, że ma wrócić o 8.
told:3sg:f him that is return at 8
'I told him that he is to return at 8.'

b. Powiedziałam mu, żeby wrócił o 8.
told:3sg:f him that return at 8
'I told him to return at 8.'

In both Polish and English, (74a) is the closest indirect rendering of an original declarative, (74b) of an original imperative. There are also languages such as Kom (Western Grassfields Bantu) in which, according to Chia (1986), indirect speech complements differ from direct speech complements only in the presence of an initial complementizer (*na*) and the use of special logophoric pronouns, but apparently not in relation to ifids. This suggests that such complements could be regarded as a subtype of E-complementation (Hengeveld's tentative proposal). Yet in English indirect speech complements cannot take illocutionary operators, such as illocutionary adverbs or question tags, which argues in favour of analysing them as variants of X-complementation.

Turning to cognitive predicates, the observation that the complements of cognitive and attitudinal predicates express propositions rather than predications is originally due to Vendler (1967).[29] In terms of the FG analysis of the TAM system, their propositional status is evidenced by their ability to occur with expressions of subjective epistemic modality, such as the modal *would* and the adverb *certainly* in (72c). By contrast, the complements of perception verbs cannot take such modifiers (75), which is suggestive of their predicational rather than propositional character.

(75) John saw that the man (*certainly/*surely) caught the dog.

It is obvious that there is little direct overlap between the GB and FG classifications of clausal complements. Nonetheless, it is of interest to observe the correspondences that do obtain. Both typologies reflect a decrease in the relative sententiality[30] or 'clausiness' of the complement, the highest level of complements being most similar (if not identical) and the lowest the least similar to main clauses. In the case of FG, the decrease in sententiality is evinced in the just-discussed distribution of TAM operators over the complement types. Similar facts hold for the GB complement types. Observe that GB OCs by virtue of possessing both a C and an I can express the illocutionary and/or modal distinctions associated with E- and X-complements in FG. The lack of C in ECs, in turn, correlates with the propositional status of X-complements of cognitive predicates which can express modal and tense distinctions, but not illocutionary ones. And the absence of an I in SCs corresponds to the lack of tense specification in secondary predications (see Hengeveld 1989: 155) which constitutes the fifth complement type in FG.

FG ties the decrease in the sententiality of clausal complements, from full clauses to nuclear predications, directly to the semantics of the main-clause predicate. This is also the long-term goal of GB (see e.g. Radford 1988: 389). And indeed despite the fact that the category of OCs is so broad that it subsumes most of the complement types recognized in FG, there is some correlation between the semantic distinctions which serve as a basis for the FG classification of complements and the OCs, ECs and SCs of GB.

Beginning with direct speech reports, Noonan (1985: 111) states that in all languages the most sentential (S-like) complements are those of direct utterance predicates. In fact complements rendering direct speech may even be the only true S-like complements in a language, as is claimed to be the case in Sherpa. Consequently, direct speech complements will always qualify as OCs in GB. Indirect speech complements are claimed also to favour S-like expression, though not as consistently so as direct discourse complements. Noonan notes that some languages may use subjunctive and other reduced complement types for expressing indirect discourse instead of or in addition to indicative forms. Indirect discourse complements too will constitute OCs in GB as will also the complements of a large number of the diverse range of cognitive predicates. Cognitive predicates, however, are the major class of predicates taking ECs. So in fact in both GB and FG an evident reduction in complement sententiality is associated with cognitive predicates.

The predicational as opposed to propositional nature of the complements of perception verbs noted in FG also finds its GB analogue. Noonan (1985: 119, 130) states that cross-linguistically complements of perception predicates tend to differ depending on whether they denote general awareness, as in (76), or immediate perception, as in (77).

(76) a. I see that Otto has left.
　　　b. I saw that Otto was leaving.

(77) a. I saw Otto leave.
　　　b. I saw Otto leaving.

The former tend to be coded by indicative complements which have independent time reference, the latter by reduced complements whose time specification is co-current with that of the main-clause predicate. As suggested by the contrast between (76) and (77), GB SCs depict the complements of immediate-perception predicates.

The points of similarity that may be discerned in the overall approach to clausal complementation in FG and GB follow from the fact that both typologies of complements are established in relation to the hierarchical status of the complements in the structural representation of the clause. The differences in turn result from the nature of the factors used in the determination of hierarchical structure in the two frameworks. On the whole, these factors are not dissimilar. The major difference is one of emphasis. GB, like other constituency-based frameworks, focuses on structural criteria, particularly on matters relating to the continuity requirement imposed on items forming a constituent such as distribution, permutability, interruptability and omissibility. FG by contrast stresses semantic criteria, and especially the scope relations reflected in the TAM system which has been amply illustrated in this chapter.

6 Pragmatic functions and the pragmatics of discourse

6.1 INTRODUCTION

FG is basically a sentence grammar primarily concerned with the predication. The predication, however, is viewed not in isolation but in context, as part of an act of communication between speaker/writer and addressee. The relationship between the constituents of the predication and the context of utterance is represented by pragmatic functions conceived of as functions specifying the informational status of constituents relative to the wider communicative setting in which they are used (Dik 1989: 265).

A distinction is made between extra-clausal and intra-clausal pragmatic functions. Extra-clausal pragmatic functions are expressed by so-called extra-clausal constituents (ECCs), which are typically set off from the predication by a disjuncture or a special intonation contour, less often by special morphological marking. The ECCs include various parentheticals, vocatives, forms of address, question tags and *Themes* and *Tails* which correspond to what are more commonly referred to as left- and right-dislocands (see §6.2). The clause-internal pragmatic functions are seen to pertain to two dimensions, topicality and focality, where topicality is characterized as a relation of 'aboutness', and focality as informational salience (within the predication) relative to the pragmatic information between speaker and addressee.

So far, with the exception of Theme and Tail, the extra-clausal pragmatic functions have received relatively little attention in FG. The clause-internal pragmatic functions, on the other hand, have undergone various modifications, the details of which will emerge in the course of the chapter. Central to these modifications is the postulated relationship between pragmatic functions and formal expression in FG which I outline directly below.

6.1.1 Pragmatic functions and formal expression

FG pragmatic functions are assigned to pieces of information of underlying predications (specifically extended clauses), not to actual linguistic expressions as they occur in the output of expression rules. The assignment of pragmatic functions, however, is taken necessarily to have effects on formal expression. This is a natural consequence of the fact that it is only by means of surface structure that the contents of predications and the discourse function of their constituents can be accessed. The assumption is that one of the functions of variation on the expression plane is to facilitate the speaker/addressee in the semantic interpretation of sentences, and in relating them to the context and the repertory of referential indices available. In other words, the features of surface syntax must be such as to enable, in conjunction with the semantic and pragmatic properties of predicates and terms, the postulated pragmatic functions to be recognized.

How exactly surface syntax interacts with contextual knowledge and other semantic and pragmatic information to define pragmatic functions is a matter of continuing debate. The issue has been approached both from the perspective of contextual knowledge, i.e. the discourse setting of a given utterance, and from the point of view of surface syntax. The first approach, reflected in the Prague School analyses of Functional Sentence Perspective (FSP) and most recently championed by Givón (1983a) and his colleagues, seeks to establish the informational status of the constituents of predications in a given discourse relative to the pragmatic information between speaker and addressee and relative to the nature and structure of the discourse. It then examines how these varying information statuses of discourse elements are reflected in surface syntax. The second approach, exemplified by, for instance, Davison (1984) and Gundel (1988), tries to determine, on the basis of variations in surface syntax, which constituents of the predication are singled out for special treatment, i.e. are identified by the morpho-syntax as salient. It then imbues these salient constituents with special informational significance, for which subsequently confirmation is sought in the discourse setting. The two approaches are complementary rather than mutually exclusive. Nonetheless, the choice of basic methodology determines whether it is the syntax or the pragmatics that plays the decisive role in defining pragmatic functions.

The current FG position on pragmatic functions draws heavily on matters of formal expression and thus is closer to the second of the above methodologies than to the first. In previous formulations of FG, the analysis of pragmatic functions was concentrated at the level of the utterance. Pragmatic functions were characterized notionally and were assigned to clausal constituents which met the defining criteria for the pragmatic function in question, subject to constraints concerning the number of instances of a given pragmatic function in a single predication. Crucially, the assignment of pragmatic functions was not deemed to be dependent on the peculiarities of morpho-syntax. In the present version of FG an attempt is made to link utterances more explicitly to their discourse setting. This has resulted in subdivisions within the clause-internal pragmatic functions, the nature of which in the case of the Topic[1] corresponds fairly closely to the scalar conception of pragmatic functions arrived at by linguists such as Givón (1983b) or Lambrecht (1987).

Topicality in FG is not, however, coterminous with the assignment of the topic pragmatic functions. The assignment of pragmatic functions is conditioned by matters of surface form. The relationship between pragmatic functions and formal expression is such that only constituents that 'are singled out for special treatment with respect to form, order and prosodic properties are assigned pragmatic functions' (Dik 1989: 266).[2] In other words, though a constituent may be topical or focal on discourse grounds, unless its topical or focal status is coded in the structure of the clause, there is no basis for recognizing a special clause-bound level of pragmatic organization distinct from the semantic and syntactic levels of clause structure. Given this approach to pragmatic functions, the question arises of which aspects of formal expression are to be considered indicative of pragmatic functions. This is the central issue which this chapter addresses.

The discussion will begin with the important distinction between pragmatic functions and special positions (§6.2), the very existence of which is endangered by the current changes, especially in the FG approach to topicality. Mention will be made of both extra-clausal and intra-clausal pragmatic functions. The body of the chapter (§6.3) will be concerned with the notion of topicality and the changes in the FG treatment of this issue. There will be discussion of the recent insights into relative givenness and newness (§6.3.1), of a topic scale (§6.3.2) and of the morpho-syntactic correlates of topicality (§6.3.3). Then §6.4 will deal with focality and the subdivisions within the focus function proposed by FG.

6.2 PRAGMATIC FUNCTIONS AND SPECIAL POSITIONS

One of the most frequent observations (e.g. Dezső 1977: 7; Harries-Delise 1978) in discussions of the syntactic effects of information structure is the existence of a close relationship between a language's basic syntactic order and its positional strategies for the topic and focus, the subject position being the most common location for the topic, and the direct object position the characteristic location of items in focus. This correlation, attributable to the apparently cross-linguistic tendency to merge the subject and topic, and object and focus, has given rise to a linguistic tradition which equates pragmatic functions with the sentential locations that they characteristically bear. Owing to the overwhelming dominance of subject-first languages (see §8.2.2) and the variable location of the object relative to the verb, the correlation which has gained the greatest currency is that between topic and initial position. Thus, for example, in Chomskyan generative grammar and its offshoots the topic is identified with the initial position in the sentence. Likewise in Halliday's (1967/68, 1985) Systemic Functional Grammar, in which the term *theme* is used rather than topic for the initial constituent.[3]

FG, while recognizing the existence of positional preferences for pragmatic functions, seeks to make a clear distinction between pragmatic functions and sentential locations. The *Topic* is not identified with the first constituent in the predication, but is defined as what the utterance is primarily about or, more fully, as the entity about which the predication predicates something in a given setting (Dik 1978: 130). The *Focus* is considered to be the relatively most important or salient piece of information with respect to the pragmatic information between speaker and addressee, from the point of view of the speaker (Dik 1978: 130). Focus is not equated with stress or accentuation, the claim being that constituents identified as focal by morpho-syntactic means need not simultaneously receive special prosodic marking (see §6.4). Moreover, topics may be stressed too. In English, for example, constituents which qualify under most analyses as topics (e.g. *this one* in (1d) below) are often stressed (Bardovi-Harlig 1983; Keijsper 1985).[4] A point worth noting is that in FG, Topic may be assigned only to terms, while Focus may be borne by any constituent.

The fact that the Topic and Focus, defined as above, cannot be seen to occupy invariant clausal locations can be illustrated on the basis of the responses to the question in (1a).

(1) a. Who painted this one?
    b. Jasper painted it.
    c. It was painted by Jasper.
    d. This one Jasper painted.
    e. It was Jasper who painted it.

Given the nature of the question (see §6.4), *Jasper* represents the most salient information in (1b)–(1e). It is therefore Focus. The item that is being predicated something of is the painting, *it/this one*. Thus it qualifies as Topic. The above examples show that the initial position in the utterance cannot be seen to fulfil a unified pragmatic function in English. This does not mean, however, that the initial position is of no pragmatic significance. On the contrary. Cross-linguistic analyses of sentence structure reveal that the first position is used for special purposes in all languages. FG recognizes this by regarding the initial position in the predication as a special pragmatic position referred to as P_1. All languages are taken to utilize P_1 for special purposes, though not in exactly the same way. This will be discussed at length in ch. 8.

In addition to P_1, FG posits two other special positions, to the immediate left and to the immediate right of the predication, called P_2 and P_3 respectively. P_2 is closely aligned with the pragmatic function Theme, and P_3 with the Tail. The *Theme* is defined as specifying the universe of discourse with respect to which the subsequent predication is presented as relevant (Dik 1978: 130). The *Tail* is characterized functionally as an 'after-thought' to the predication, i.e. as information meant to clarify or modify some constituent in the predication (Dik 1978: 130). As mentioned in §6.1, the FG Theme and Tail correspond to what are commonly referred to as left- and right-dislocands, as in (2) and (3) below.

(2) So what I confess to is a certain . . . feeling of dissatisfaction . . . in some of the habits 'n' expressions of students that come to me particularly English expression, spelling, punctuation. Once again, *very basic skills*, I'm often very dissatisfied *with them*.

(3) Both of my brothers came back, uh but one went up to New Guinea and was uh shot through the throat 'n' the bullet came out in his out his back. . . . Yes *it* was there a long time, *the bullet*, in fact and he had to have *it* removed, *the bullet*.

In left-dislocated structures, the initial constituent, *very basic skills* in (2), is resumed in the main predication by a co-denotational item, typically a pronoun as in (2), or a clitic, but also occasionally a noun. In right-dislocations, the final constituent, *the bullet* in (3), is co-denotational with an entity, again typically a pronoun, but not exclusively, in the preceding predication. The FG Theme also covers initial constituents such as those in (4), which correspond to Li and Thompson's (1976) topics.

(4) a. As for entertainment, I prefer Woody Allen.
     b. Concerning your sabbatical, you may go this year.

The Tail too need not be a further spelling out of information within the predication; it may just provide additional circumstantial information, as in (5).

(5) a. We'll be back, tomorrow or the next day.
    b. She stood up and told him what she thought of him, loud and clear.

The distinction between the Topic, on the one hand, and the Theme and Tail, on the other, to which Dik (1978) devotes considerable attention, centres on the extra-predicational nature of the two latter pragmatic functions. Thus the Theme, for example, is typically offset from the main predication prosodically (by a short disjuncture), often appears in absolute form (without any overt case marking) and lies outside the performative modalities of the main predication. The last point is illustrated in (6) below from Modern Standard Arabic in which the Theme occurs in the nominative case.

Modern Standard Arabic (Moutaouakil 1989: 110)
(6) a. Zaydun,   ʔa   najaḥa   mašrūʕuhu.
       Zayd:nom   Q   succeeded   plan:nom:3sg
       'Zayd, did his plan come off?'

    b. Zaydun?   qad   najaḥa   mašrūʕuhu.
       Zayd:nom   certainly succeeded   plan:nom:3sg
       'Zayd? His plan certainly came off.'

In (6a) we see that the Theme precedes the illocutionary force marker, and in (6b) that the Theme may have its own illocutionary force. Significantly, though a Topic may also be separated from the remainder of the predication by a disjuncture, as in (7a), it cannot precede an illocutionary force operator; (7b) is ungrammatical.

(7) a. Zaydan,   ṣafaḥtuhu.
       Zayd:acc   greeted:1sg:3sg
       'Zayd, I greeted.'

    b. *Zaydan,   ʔa   raʔaytahu.
       Zayd:acc   Q   saw:2sg:3sg
       'Zayd, did you see (him)?'

The above differences notwithstanding, subsequent investigations of Topics and Themes have shown that the distinction between the two pragmatic functions is not always a discrete one. In fact De Groot (1981) argues that in Hungarian some Themes must be viewed as being incorporated into the predication. The distinction between Topics and Themes is thus still in need of further refinement (see also §6.3.3.2).

Another issue that requires more detailed investigation is the exact relationship between P_2 and P_3 and Theme and Tail. In Dik (1978, 1980) and other FG publications, the terms P_2 and Theme, and P_3 and Tail, are used interchangeably, creating the impression that the special positions P_2 and P_3 are in fact pragmatic functions rather than designated locations which fulfil certain pragmatic functions. This latter view is advocated by De Schutter (1985, 1987), who maintains that in Dutch constituents placed in P_2 and P_3 respectively do not fulfil a unified discourse function. De Schutter argues that both thematic (contextually recoverable) and rhematic (non-recoverable) material in the FSP sense of the terms,[5] may be placed in either P_2 or P_3. For example, the P_3 in (8a) contains recoverable, and that in (8b) non-recoverable, information.

Dutch (De Schutter 1987: 105)
(8) a. Ik zou *met 'm* wel eens over dat probleem
I would with him mod-prt about that problem
willen praten, *met die man.*
like speak with the man.
'I would like to talk with him about that problem, with that man.'

b. Met die man zou ik *er* wel eens over willen
with that man would I there mod-prt about like
praten, *over dat probleem van jou.*
speak about that problem of you
'I would like to talk about it with that man, about that problem of yours.'

The same observation has been made in relation to English left-dislocands (Prince 1984). Compare (2) above with (9).

(9) The fact is that the promiscuous age was just as bad then as what it is now, possibly if not worse. *One girl, she* married very well, I understand, later, but at school she had quite a reputation. She used to. ...

Whereas the referent of the dislocated item in (2) represents given information (see §6.3.1), the left-dislocated item in (9), *one girl*, is newly introduced into the discourse. De Schutter also notes that in Dutch the P_2 position is frequently the locus of conditional and commentative clauses. Some of these clauses may be placed in either P_1 or P_2. The pragmatic factors underlying placement in P_2 are compatible with the general characterization of the Theme, as specifying an overall frame in which the main predication is to be interpreted. Nonetheless, De Schutter argues that in view of the various semantic characteristics of modifying clauses, they cannot be simply subsumed under the Theme function. Therefore in order to accommodate the positioning of the modifying clauses in question, P_2 cannot be considered as coterminous with Theme. One could, of course, argue that different types of Theme are involved. The same holds for the left-dislocands in (2) as compared to (9) and the Tails in (5a) and (5b).

The three P-positions P_1, P_2 and P_3 are considered to be pragmatically relevant on a cross-linguistic basis. Individual languages may have additional special positions. For example, to account for the location of vocatives in Modern Standard Arabic such as *ya Zaydu* in (10a,b), Moutaouakil (1989: ch. 5) posits an additional predication external (P_4) vocative position placed to the left of P_2 (*?aḣuka* in (10a)) and to the right of P_3 (*sulukuhu* in (10b)).

Modern Standard Arabic (Moutaouakil 1989: 150)
(10) a. ya Zaydu, ?aḣuka, zārahu ᶜAmrun.
O Zayd:nom brother:nom:2sg visited:3sg Amr:nom
'Zayd, your brother$_i$, Amr visited him$_i$.'

b. ?aᶜjabanī ?aḣuka, sulūkuhu, yā Zaydu.
pleased:1sg brother:nom:2sg behaviour:nom:3sg O Zayd:nom
'I liked your brother's behaviour, Zayd.'

As regards extra predication-internal positions, in Basque and Hungarian possible to discern a special preverbal focus position (P0); in written Czech, Polish and Russian a clause-final focus location; in Dutch an extra final topic/focus slot. There are also languages that have several additional special positions, such as Aghem (Watters 1979) which has one immediately before and one immediately after the verb, or Serbo-Croatian which, apart from an immediately preverbal focus position, has a strongly defined clause-second clitic position. In principle there is no limit to the number of special positions that may be posited for a language. There are, however, restrictions on how these positions can be utilized. These matters plus the details of the relationship between pragmatic functions and special positions and the way the special positions are used in the specification of order will be discussed in ch. 8.

6.3 TOPICALITY

The definition of topic presented in §6.2 as what the utterance is primarily about characterizes the topic as a relation between a discourse entity and a predication. This conception of topicality, closely tied to the subject/predicate distinction, has in recent years been supplemented by an approach which views topicality primarily as a relation between a discourse entity and, not the predication, but the overall structure of discourse.[6] Under this wider discourse-based approach, the topic emerges not as a discrete or atomic entity, but as a scalar notion reflecting the various contributions of a discourse entity to the development of the discourse. This non-unitary treatment of the topic finds reflection in Dik's (1989) newest version of FG, though not directly in a scalar approach to topicality, but rather in the form of several distinct topic functions.

The origins of the change in emphasis from an atomic to a scalar (e.g. Givón) or non-unitary (FG) view of topicality may be traced to the desire to provide a better understanding of the relationship between the topic of discourse and the topic of a single utterance, where by *topic of discourse* is meant the concern or set of concerns of an unspecified series of utterances constituting a discourse, and by *utterance topic* what an individual utterance is primarily about. The general assumption is that in a coherent discourse there is always some relationship between the various utterance topics and the overall topic of discourse. The specification of the exact nature of this relationship, however, has proved to be highly problematic. Utterance topics are linguistic objects and must correspond to an expression or expressions in the utterance (or to some grammatical form of coding). Discourse topics, on the other hand, as characterized by Van Dijk (1977), Reinhart (1982) and Brown and Yule (1983), among others, though expressible linguistically, are not considered to be linguistic objects, since their status as topics of discourse is not purely a function of their linguistic properties, but rather of a host of factors determining the subject matter of various forms of communicative behaviour. Nonetheless, situations in which a discourse topic is not overtly expressed within the discourse occur only sporadically (Brown and Yule 1983: 71-72), the principles of successful communication demanding that what is being talked about be made explicit, preferably at the outset of the discourse (Grice 1975). Therefore, typically a discourse topic does in fact receive lexical or grammatical expression in the discourse, and, what is more, often coincides with an utterance topic.

Conversely, any utterance topic is a potential topic of discourse. Whether it ends up fulfilling such a role depends to a large extent on whether it is pursued or elaborated on in the following utterances. It is rather rare to find a discourse, other than a very short one, in which there is no elaboration of some utterance topic or other in the subsequent stretch of discourse. The common situation is for a discourse to consist of several chains of clauses each united by a common topic of discourse which in turn somehow bears on an overall topic of discourse. The organization within the wider stretch of discourse of the discourse topics defined by each topic chain may be hierarchical, some discourse topics being evidently more central than others, or purely sequential, as in a series of episodes. The attention lavished on the notion of topicality within clause-centred grammatical theory is due to the fact that the various relationships that the discourse topics of each chain bear to each other and to the overall topic of discourse are expressed at clause level by differences in the structural organization of the clause, and in particular in different formal realizations of the utterance topic. It is the attempt to relate these different formal realizations of utterance topics to the type of discourse topic that they implement or are most closely associated with that has led to the scalar conception of topicality of linguists such as Givón, and to the recognition of different topic functions in FG.

For the scalar approach to topicality, of prime importance is the determination of the cognitive parameters underlying the scale. As suggested by the discussion in §1.2.1.1, unquestionably relevant is the given/new distinction and especially its more refined variants elaborated by Prince (1981) and Chafe (1987). The other major dimensions that have been regarded as significant are identifiability (*per se*, referential and contextual), newsworthiness, relative importance and the elusive 'aboutness'.

By contrast in FG the subdivisions of the topic function are achieved primarily in regard to the expression plane. Consequently the cognitive underpinning of the proposed subdivision is less of an issue. The major discourse correlate of topicality is 'aboutness', while the actual topic functions recognized are seen to reflect relative givenness and newness. Crucially, however, though the recognized topic functions are seen to correlate with different degrees of givenness and newness, they are not defined in terms of the given/new distinction. By way of introduction to a consideration of Dik's subdivision of Topic in §6.3.2, we will review the recent claims concerning the nature of the given/new opposition and how it is seen to interact with topicality.

6.3.1 Topicality and the given/new distinction

The notions *given* and *new* have been conceived of in two distinct though related ways which, following Gundel (1988), I will refer to as relational and referential, respectively. In the relational sense the terms *given* and *new* refer to the value of the information conveyed by a particular element or elements in the utterance. The given/new status of an item depends on whether it is informative to the addressee or not, which in turn is a reflection of the nature of the proposition shared by the speaker and addressee. Thus, for example, *I* in (11b) represents new information in the context of the proposition 'someone broke the window'.

(11) a. Who broke the window?
     b. I broke it/I did.

In (12b), however, both *I* and *her* (Sandra) constitute given information relative to the shared proposition 'I met Sandra sometime', the new information being *last year* and *Bologna*.

(12) a. Where did you meet Sandra?
     b. I met her last year in Bologna.

The notions *given* and *new* in the relational sense are tied directly to the pragmatic functions topic and focus. The topic is given relative to the focus, and the focus is new in relation to the topic. The necessary givenness of the topic follows from the fact that for something to be predicated of an entity in a given setting, the entity must in one way or another be already present in that setting. Assuming Grice's (1975) communicative maxims, the focus, on the other hand, must be new relative to the topic, since otherwise there would be no point in producing the utterance. This relational sense of given and new prevailed in earlier versions of FG, while currently the referential use is dominant.

In the referential sense the notions *given* and *new* reflect the cognitive status of discourse referents in the mind of the speaker.[7] This cognitive status is taken to be a reflection of the location of the referent or concept in both short-term and long-term memory. Relative status in short-term memory is frequently referred to by the notion *activation*,[8] the fullest explication of which is offered by Chafe (1987).[9] Chafe (1987: 25) suggests that a discourse referent may occur in one of three activation states: active, semi-active and inactive. An *active* referent is taken to be one 'that is currently lit up, a concept in a person's focus of consciousness at a particular moment'. A *semi-active* referent is one 'that is in a person's peripheral consciousness, a concept of which a person has a background awareness', but which is not being paid direct attention. And an *inactive* referent is one 'that is currently in a person's long-term memory, neither focally nor peripherally active'.

Discourse entities identified as active correspond to Chafe's (1976) earlier, widely accepted definition of givenness, while the inactive fall under what he previously referred to as new information. In terms of this referential conception of given and new, *I* in (11b) represents given information rather than new; speech act participants are normally assumed to be in the foreground of the hearer's consciousness. Referential newness and further examples of referential givenness are presented in the following extract from Chafe's (1980) famous 'pear stories' which I have adapted from Okamoto (1981: 223–224).

(13) 1. Okay, there's a farmer. 2. He looks like a Chicano American. 3. He is picking pears.... 4. A little boy comes by on his bicycle. 5. He sees that there are baskets of pears there. 6. Meanwhile, there are three little boys, up on the road a little bit, 7. and they see this little accident.

The referents of all the pronouns are referentially given, having been mentioned in the immediately preceding utterances, and therefore, presumably, still in the foreground of the addressee's consciousness. The referentially new referents, mentioned in the discourse for the first time, are: *a farmer* in sentence 1, *a little boy* in 4, *baskets* in 5 and *three little boys* in 6.

Semi-active referents constitute the in-between category, the given/new status of which has been variously interpreted. Terms used to describe such referents other than simply *given* or *new* are: *accessible*, *recoverable*, *derivable* and *discourse-bound*. Semi-active referents comprise two types. The first type includes those that were formerly active but have through lack of recent overt mention fallen into peripheral consciousness and may subsequently either pass into an inactive state or conversely be reactivated. To this category belong the referents of *the farmer* and *baskets* in (14), which is the continuation of (13) after a short episode concerning *the boy* and *the three boys*.

(14) 8. And then he [i.e. the boy on the bicycle] goes off, 9. and that's the end of that story. 10. But then it goes back to *the farmer*. 11. Finally he comes down from his tree. 12. He looks at *the baskets*.

It goes without saying that the line between semi-active and inactive referents is rather difficult to draw. This also holds for the second type of semi-actives which involve referents associated with a particular conceptual schema in the sense of Schank and Abelson (1977) and which in the terminology of Prince (1981: 236) constitute the category of inferables, i.e. referents inferentially related to some evoked entity, or in a salient set relation to such an entity. The relation of inference, which in the context of FG has been discussed by Hannay (1985b), may take a host of forms among which he (Hannay 1985b: 58) lists: *part of*, *member of*, *subset of*, *instance of*, *copy of*, *aspect of*, *opposite of*, *projection of* and *associated with*. The first three and the last of these inferential relations are illustrated in (15), taken from Hannay.

(15) a. It's a nice house, but the kitchen is too small.
 b. The team played quite well I suppose, but one or two of them are still a bit unfit.
 c. I was hoping to catch a bus so I could get there on time but when I arrived at the station one had just left.
 d. John and Bill came to see me yesterday. Fred's just acquired a new car.

Example (15d) deserves special mention owing to the fact that it can be construed as a felicitous discourse only provided the addressee can make a specific inference corresponding to Clark and Haviland's (1974) 'bridging assumption' as to the relation between the first and second utterance.

Hannay suggests that inferables should not be considered as necessarily semi-active, but only as potentially so. The same point is made by Lambrecht (1988: 169).[10] Both linguists maintain that speakers are free to assume the level of activation of an inferable entity as being either semi-active or inactive (actually unused, see below) and will code their utterances accordingly. Addressees in turn will draw the inference if the form of the utterance constitutes a request for them to do so. The potentially dual status of inferables can be illustrated on the basis of the two prosodic realizations of the second clause in (16).

(16) We're having a wonderful time in the department. The boss is away.

In one realization the subject takes secondary stress, while the primary stress falls on the predicate *away*. In the other, there is only a primary stress falling on the subject. The first type of accentuation identifies the subject as semi-active, the second as inactive.[11] It will be shown in §6.3.2 that in FG these two realizations of the subject are associated with two distinct pragmatic functions, namely that of Subtopic and Focus.

The notion of activation covers referents which the addressee has some previous knowledge of, that fall within the scope of his or her long-term memory. Consequently it cannot be used to distinguish such referents from those which are completely unknown to the addressee – *brand new* (Prince 1981), so to speak, and therefore not retrievable from memory. The parameter reflecting the cognitive status of discourse referents relative to long-term memory is *identifiability* conceived of as a binary opposition, as in Chafe (1976).[12] A referent may be considered to be *identifiable* if the speaker assumes that the addressee is capable of uniquely selecting from among a set of referents covered by some linguistic expression the one intended in any given instance.[13] A referent which cannot be thus selected is *unidentifiable*. The principal correlate of identifiability thus conceived is *definiteness*; identifiable referents are definite, unidentifiable ones typically, though not exclusively, indefinite. Identifiability in the binary sense interacts with activation in a predictable way; unidentifiable referents are necessarily inactive, while identifiable ones may be in any of the three states of activation, inactive, semi-active and active. In short, the two parameters, identifiability and activation, define four cognitive statuses of discourse referents: identifiable active (given), identifiable semi-active (inferable), identifiable inactive (unused) and unidentifiable (brand new).

Under the traditional definition of topic as an 'aboutness' relation between a discourse referent and a predication, these four cognitive statuses of referents may be taken to determine a scale of topic acceptability or 'goodness', such as that shown in (17), adapted from Lambrecht (1988: 147).

(17) The Topic Acceptability Scale

active	most acceptable
semi-active	↕
inactive	
brand new	least acceptable

Assuming that retrieving referents from memory requires time and effort, which affects the speed and ease of processing as discussed in §1.2.1.1 in relation to the two modes of processing suggested by Bock (1982), the best candidates for topic from the cognitive point of view are active referents. This follows from the fact that such referents are already in the foreground of the addressee's consciousness and therefore the understanding of the utterance is not impeded by a chain of inferences or the need to retrieve a referent from long-term memory as is required in the case of semi-active and unused referents. Of these two latter type of referents, the semi-active constitute far better candidates for topic than the unused, since, being in short-term memory, they are assumed to be more easily accessed than the unused referents which are in long-term memory. In fact unused discourse referents are primarily associated with the focus function. Brand new referents, in contrast to the other three categories, are unacceptable as topics, or at best only marginally acceptable, identifiability being a precondition for felicitous topic-hood. As stated earlier, if unable to identify the referent of the topic, the addressee is not in a position to assess whether what is predicated of this referent holds.

Evidence for this correlation between the cognitive status of discourse referents and the felicity of these referents as topics can be adduced from the statistical analyses of spoken and written texts and from various characteristics of morpho-syntax involving topic selection, topic marking and also topic avoidance. Some of these morpho-syntactic correlates of the topic acceptability scale will be illustrated in connection with Dik's subdivision of the Topic function, to which we now turn.

6.3.2 The topic function subdivided

The unitary Topic function of earlier formulations of FG is currently subdivided into four pragmatic functions which correspond fairly closely to the cognitive statuses of discourse referents as determined by the activation and identifiability parameters. The four topic functions distinguished by Dik (1989) are: Given Topic (GivTop), SubTopic (SubTop), Resumed Topic (ResTop) and New Topic (NewTop). The correspondences between these four topic functions and the level of activation of the discourse referents to which they are assigned, to be presented below, should not be understood as suggesting that discourse referents of a particular cognitive status will be automatically assigned to the relevant Topic function. Dik's Topic, unlike, for example, Givón's (1983a), is not coterminous with discourse referent.

The correlation between the four Topic functions and the levels of activation are fairly straightforward. The GivTop function is associated with active discourse referents. The SubTop function, elaborated by Hannay (1985b), corresponds to one of the two semi-active categories of referents distinguished by Chafe (1987), i.e. to the inferables. Recall from §6.3.1 that inferables lend themselves to both a semi-active and an unused interpretation. The SubTop function is assigned only to referents which the speaker considers or treats as semi-active, the first reading of (16), cited on p. 158, being a case in point. Unused inferables fall within the scope of the Focus function, as under the second reading of (16). The ResTop function is identified with the other semi-active category that Chafe (1987) posits, described as embracing former active referents that are assumed to be still in peripheral consciousness. Dik characterizes the ResTop function as applying especially to cases when, after several different topics have been introduced and the discourse has continued for some time about one, there is a subsequent shift to another, this other topic being the ResTop (see (31) in §6.3.3.1). One can thus presume that the distribution of ResTop will be rather limited. A point worth stressing in connection with ResTop is that this is one of the functions typically associated with the extra-clausal Theme (Chafe 1976; Givón 1983b) discussed in §6.2.

The most controversial of Dik's topic functions is NewTop. The function NewTop infringes on the domain of the Focus function in that it may be assigned to either unused or brand new discourse referents, both of which have been traditionally associated with focal information. As captured in Lambrecht's topic acceptability scale in (17), for linguists who adhere to the 'aboutness' view of topic, new referents are unacceptable as topics. This was also the former FG position, activation or semi-activation being considered a necessary property of topics. Clauses such as those in (18) and (19) were viewed as topicless.

(18) a. A tiger chased a tourist.
b. A man just got run over by a car.

(19) a. There's a man at the door.
b. There's been several whites killed at X junction.
c. There occurred a strange accident.
d. In the garden sat Mary and her sisters.

Currently the topicless analysis is maintained only for clauses such as those in (18), while the existentials and presentatives in (19) are taken to manifest the function NewTop assigned to the immediately postverbal constituents.[14] The two sets of clauses are seen to differ in that (18) comprises reports of events, expressions of single, non-complex pieces of information where none of the discourse referents is imbued with pragmatic saliency. The presentatives in (19),[15] by contrast, introduce a discourse referent which is to constitute a future topic of discourse. The difference between the two sets of clauses can be illustrated on the basis of the type of follow-up clauses that they tend to co-occur with. After the presentative (19d), for example, we are much more likely to find (20a,b) than (20c,d).

(20) a. They were having an animated conversation.
b. Mary, as usual, was holding the floor.
c. It was a beautiful day.
d. The garden was rather overgrown.

Conversely, the event clause (18b) is more likely to be continued with an utterance in which neither of the referents mentioned is a topic, that is (21a,b) rather than (21c,d).

(21) a. It's the third time that's happened this month.
b. There's a crowd gathering.
c. He's badly hurt.
d. The car drove away.

The referents of *a man* and *a car* in (18b) by virtue of being mentioned are established as discourse referents. Nonetheless, in using (18b) the primary purpose of the speaker is not to present the referents but to establish the event. Whereas the sole function of the presentatives in (19) is to introduce an entity into the file of discourse referents. A controversial aspect of Dik's treatment of (19) is that the NewTops do not meet the 'aboutness' criterion for topicality at clause level. For example, (19d) is not about *Mary and her sisters*. It is only in the subsequent clause, as in (20a), that this expression functions as a clausal topic.

Dik's analysis is intended to capture this widely accepted pragmatic difference between the clauses in (18) and (19) and also their special pragmatic status *vis-à-vis* typical topic/focus predications. The source of the special status of event reporting and presentative utterances has been traced to the *thetic/categorial* distinction, a philosophically based division of judgements, which is attributed to the nineteenth-century philosopher Franz Bretano; though by and large neglected in mainstream linguistic theory, its syntactic and pragmatic relevance has been discussed by Kuroda (1972) and recently by Sasse (1987) and Lambrecht (1988). The thetic/categorial distinction represents what is taken to be a fundamental dichotomy between two different types of logical statements, one involving two successive acts, naming an entity and making a statement about it (the *categorial*), and the other consisting of an unstructured whole expressing an event, state or situation (the *thetic*). The categorial statement is reflected in the classical bipartite subject/predicate split which corresponds to the pragmatic topic/comment opposition. Thetic statements, the prime exemplars of which are descriptions of events, existentials and presentative constructions and weather impersonals, represent an entity as included in or as part of an event rather than separate from it. Consequently thetic expressions are claimed to have no topic (and arguably no subject comparable to the fused subject/topic of categorial statements). Sasse (1987: 579) argues that they cannot be taken to possess a focus either, if focus is conceived of as an information peak, since there is no non-focal information that the would-be focus could be opposed to.

It is not quite clear to what extent the logico-semantic distinction between types of propositions can be transposed to the pragmatic distinction between utterance types (Lambrecht 1988: 162). Within FG the event-reporting utterances have been analysed as having Focus assigned to each constituent of the predication (De Jong 1981) or as having no pragmatic function assignment at all (Dik *et al.* 1981). The analysis involving no pragmatic function assignment is to be preferred on the grounds that treating the whole utterance as focal deprives the notion of focus of much of its substance. As regards presentative structures, the introduced discourse referents, while evidently not the topics of their clauses, do convey a salient piece of information, though arguably not the most salient piece of information (see Givón (1988: 270) and §6.4). Some linguists treat this salient piece of information as a clausal focus (e.g. Gúeron 1980; Kirsner 1979; Lambrecht 1988), while others, most notably Hetzron (1975: 348) and in FG Hannay (1985a: 172), consider it to warrant special pragmatic status in the form of a discourse-semantic feature (Hetzron) or pragmatic function (Hannay). The argument is that focus is involved in the specification of the relationship between a discourse referent and a predication. It has to do with the estimated difference in the pragmatic information between speaker and addressee. The pragmatic function of an entity introduced in a presentative construction, on the other hand, is specifically an introductory one. Admittedly, referents can be introduced into the discourse as clausal foci. A case in point is that of the neighbour in (22b).

(22) a. What's going to happen to your dog?
b. She's being looked after by *my neighbour*.
c. He's rather elderly but still very active and eager to have her for company, now that he's all by himself, poor dear.

However, though the *neighbour* is introduced into the discourse in (22b), and is the utterance and discourse topic of the following clauses (22c), its primary function in (22b) is to specify the identity of the person who is going to take care of the dog.

Hannay uses the term *Presentative* function for the special pragmatic function that he posits for entities introduced into the discourse by means of presentative constructions. Dik (1989) relabels it NewTop. Dik's choice of label is fortuitous from the point of view of the function of such elements in discourse, but not from the perspective of their function in the clause. The NewTop, in contrast to the other three topic functions, is not a clausal topic.

Matters of terminology aside, though we have established the correlations between different levels of activation and Dik's four topic functions, we have not as yet examined the formal exponents of these pragmatic functions, which, as stated in §6.1, provide the underlying motivation for recognizing clause-level pragmatic functions in FG. A brief overview of the type of differences in formal expression in question is presented in the following section.

6.3.3 The topic function and formal expression

The choice of topic finds reflection in the form of the topic constituent itself (morphological form, grammatical form, prosodic properties and location in the clause) and also in various characteristics of the construction in which it occurs. As regards the marking of the topic constituent, cross-linguistic investigations reveal that none of the actual forms of topic marking found in individual languages is an unambiguous marker of the topic. Nor do all the constituents identified as topics in a language exhibit the same type of marking. Both of these points may be illustrated on the basis of the use of the famous Japanese *wa* and *ga* particles. *Wa* is generally referred to as a topic particle, though in fact it can be used to mark not only a topic, as in (23), but also a theme (24) and a focus of contrast (25).

> Japanese (Tsutsui 1981: 164; Kitagawa 1982: 176)
> (23) Boku wa ima san-nen de senkoo wa keizai desu ga ...
>   I   now junior   am major   economics is but ...
>   'I am a junior now and my major is economics but ...'
>
> (24) Taroo wa Hanako ga rede-   si-ta.
>   Taro   Hanako   leave-home- do-past
>   'As for Taro, Hanako ran away from home.'
>
> (25) Tom wa ii   kedo John wa dame   da.
>   Tom   good but John   no good is
>   'Tom is okay, but John is no good.'

Not all topics are accompanied by *wa*, witness the following example from Gundel (1988: 218).

> (26) Hanashi ga   hajimaru toki   wa   eeto mazu otona no hito
>   story   subj start   time   top well first adult   person
>   tachi   ga   ippai   detekite ... sono naka de   hitori
>   subj many   appear   that among one person
>   chuugokujin ga nanka no otokonoko ga ... kare wa sosko e
>   Chinese   subj something boy   subj he   top there to
>   sono omise no toko e itte ... hajime wa   tada miteiru ....
>   that shop   place to go   first top only be looking
>   'When the story starts [top], first a lot of adults appear .... Among (them) one Chinese boy. ... He [top] goes to the shop. ... At first [top] he is just looking. ...'

The factors determining the occurrence of *wa* as opposed to *ga* have elicited much discussion.[16] The current opinion seems to be that *wa* only marks topics whose referents are either active or semi-active. The 'adults' and the first occurrence of the 'boy' in (26) therefore are marked by *ga*. It is interesting to observe that if we reverse the order of the two clauses in (23), as shown in (27), 'major' no longer represents semi-active (inferable) information and consequently cannot take *wa*.

(27) Senkoo ga/*wa keizai de boku wa ima san-nen desu ga ...
major subj/top economics is I top now junior am but ...
'My major is economics and I am a junior now but ...'

Assuming the correctness of the claim that the referents marked by *wa* are either active or semi-active, then under Dik's (1989) analysis, *wa* is a marker of GivTop, SubTop and ResTop, but crucially not NewTop.

A point of terminology worth mentioning in connection with the incompatibility of *wa* and NewTop is that topic-marking particles are often said to mark most frequently, though not exclusively, new rather than old topics. The terminological discrepancy is the outcome of different conceptions of topicality, the unitary and the scalar. Under the traditional unitary conception of topic as an 'aboutness' relation between a discourse referent and a predication, the newness or oldness of a topic does not depend on the level of activation of the referent of the topic, but on whether it does or does not correspond to the topic of the previous clause. Thus 'she' in (28a) represents an old topic relative to the previous clause, hence the sequence of clauses is an instance of topic continuity.

Pima (Langdon and Munro 1979)
(28) a. Hegai 'uuvi 'a-t 'am ṣohñi hegai ceoj c 'am ṣoṣa.
that woman 3–perf hit that man SS cry
'The woman hit the man and she cried.'

By contrast, 'he' in (28b) is a new topic, and the two clauses exemplify the phenomenon of topic shift.

(28) b. Hegai 'uuvi 'a-t 'am ṣohñi hegai ceoj ku-t (hegai ceoj) 'am ṣoṣa.
that woman S-perf hit that man DS-perf that man cry
'The woman hit the man and he (the man) cried.'

Pima, an Uto-Aztecan language, is a switch reference marking language, the relevant marking being indicated by an independent morpheme and not, as in most other switch reference languages (Haiman and Munro 1983), by a verbal affix.[17] In (28a) the morpheme *c* indicates that the topic of the clause is the same as that of the preceding one, while in (28b) *ku* indicates a change of topic. The claim as to the primary function of topic-marking particles being the coding of new topics refers to such and other instances of topic shift. In terms of activation, however, since the referent of 'he' has an antecedent in the immediately preceding clause, it is given, not new. Consequently, topic shift, for linguists who adhere to a uniform view of topic, entails a new topic; but for those like Givón who propose a topic scale or a continuum based on levels of activation, the notion, though not necessarily a misnomer, involves referents that are more often that not given or at least semi-active. This also holds for FG. This difference in terminology must be kept in mind in reading the literature on topicality and in assessing the various claims made with respect to the scope of particular topic-marking devices.

6.3.3.1 The coding of GivTop

We have just seen that the use of the topic marker as opposed to subject marker in Japanese is a form of topic coding compatible with the subdivisions of Topic suggested in FG, the line of demarcation lying between the activated/discourse-bound referents of GivTop, SubTop and ResTop and the not-yet-activated ones of NewTop. The mechanism of switch reference, on the other hand, signals primarily topic (dis)continuity rather than the level of activation of the topic. Nonetheless, though a referent associated with a 'different subject' marker may in fact be given (active), 'same subject' marking unambiguously identifies a referent as a GivTop and thus may be viewed as a GivTop marking device.

Another form of coding corresponding in the main with the FG subdivision of Topic and especially relevant for distinguishing GivTop from the other Topic functions is the morphological form of the topic constituent itself. The basic insight is that active referents tend to be coded by pronouns (independent, bound or clitic) or even omitted from verbalization altogether, while semi-active and inactive ones require lexical expression. Considerable evidence for the existence of a high degree of correspondence between the level of activation of discourse referents and their morphological form has been amassed by Givón (1983a) and his associates. These correspondences are not, however, specific to topics (referents in an 'aboutness' relation) but hold for all types of constituents. GivTops are indeed likely to be expressed by various forms of pronominal coding, but more subtle considerations are involved than mere level of activation. The factors that are claimed to determine the use of pronominal as compared to nominal anaphora pertain to the hierarchical structure of the discourse as reflected in episode boundaries (Clancy 1980) and narrative units (Fox 1987) and to the global status (e.g. central vs peripheral) of the investigated referents in discourse (Grimes 1978; Levinson 1978). Consider, for instance, the pronominal form of the italicized utterance topics *She* in (29) and *Leia* in (30), adapted from Fox (1987).

(29) She reached B deck unopposed, her flamethrower held tightly in both hands. The food locker lay just ahead. There was an outside chance the alien had left someone behind, being unable to manoeuvre itself and two bodies through the narrow ducts. A chance that someone might still be alive. *She* peered around the jamb. (*Alien*, p. 260)

(30) Slowly she [i.e. Leia] swivelled, to find an Imperial scout standing over her, his weapon levelled at her head. He reached out his hand for the pistol she held. 'I'll take that,' he ordered.
    Without warning, a furry hand came out from under the log and jabbed the scout in the leg with a knife. The man howled in pain, began jumping about on one foot. *Leia* dove for his fallen pistol.
(*Return of the Jedi*, p. 95)

Fox argues that the occurrence of pronominal as opposed to nominal forms in English narratives is strongly influenced by whether the gap between two successive mentions of the same character contains another character, not already in some confrontation or active interaction with the first character, who begins planning or performing an action. If it does, then the subsequent mention of the first character will be in nominal form, and if it does not in pronominal form. In (29) the gap between mentions of the referent in question is taken up by an off-event line description; as predicted, when the event line is resumed the referent reappears in pronominal form. In (30), the gap between the two mentions of *Leia* involves an interaction between two other characters who are not interactive with *Leia*. Thence the reintroduction of *Leia* with a full NP.

The above examples are of interest in connection with the FG distinction between GivTop and ResTop. Note that the reintroduction of these referents may be seen to constitute an instance of topic resumption. Yet these topics do not qualify as ResTop in the FG sense of the term, but rather as GivTop. Their referents are well-established discourse topics, while, as stated in §6.3.2, the ResTop function is taken to be characteristic primarily of referents which were only introduced into the discourse at some former time. Moreover, according to Dik (1989: 277), the typical patterns of marking ResTop are: a) some indication of shift of topic; b) a strong form of anaphoric marking; c) implicit or explicit indication of previous mention.

The example he gives is presented in (31), where *now* is the signal of topic shift, *John's sister Mary* is a strong form of anaphora, and *who I mentioned before* the overt reference to previous mention.

(31) John had a brother Peter and a sister Mary. [considerable episode about Peter] Now, John's sister Mary, who I mentioned before . . . .

168 *Functional Grammar*

The pronominal and nominal coding of the topics in (29) and (30) is not in conformity with that of the FG ResTop.

It is not clear whether the assignment of ResTop is to be conditioned by the forms of morphological coding that Dik lists. If this is indeed what is intended, then many instances of topic resumption will not qualify for the FG ResTop function.

6.3.3.2 NewTop

Recall that the pragmatic function NewTop is primarily associated in FG with referents introduced into the discourse by means of special presentative constructions. In many languages the basic structural characteristic of presentative constructions is the postverbal placement of the introduced discourse referent, the subject status of which is a matter of continuing dispute. The postposing of the subject after the verb, referred to as 'presentative inversion', is common cross-linguistically with a class of intransitive verbs[18] describing existence and appearance in the world of discourse, movement to a new location and change into a new state, which have come to be known as unaccusative predicates (Perlmutter 1978).[19] Examples are given below. In one from German (32b) – as also in English, Dutch, Icelandic and French – a dummy pronoun (*es* in German) occurs in initial position if this position is not otherwise filled; in another (33b) from Italian, the inversion is not accompanied by such a pleonastic element;[20] such is also the case in Spanish, Romanian, Latin and the Slavic languages.

>   German (Perlmutter and Zaenen 1984: 173)
>   (32) a.   Zwei   Kinder   spielen   im   Garten.
>   two   children   play:pres in   garden
>   'Two children are playing in the garden.'
>
>   b. Es spielen zwei Kinder im Garten.
>
>   Italian (Perlmutter 1983b: 173)
>   (33) a.   Dei   profughi   ungheresi   sono rimasti   nel   paese.
>   some   refugees   Hungarian   are remained in:the   country
>   'Some Hungarian refugees remanined in the country.'
>
>   b. Sono rimasti dei profughi ungheresi nel paese.

The postverbal constituents designating the new referents in clauses such as (32b) and (33b) display several characteristics which put into question their status as subjects. Like subjects they take nominative case (in case-marking languages) and control verbal agreement.[21] Their postverbal location, on the other hand, is atypical of subjects. Moreover, in some languages the constituents in question do not display other distributional properties associated with subjects. For instance, in German and Dutch whereas main-clause subjects are obligatorily placed in immediate postverbal position in questions, or when some other constituent is positioned in front of the verb, in presentative structures it is not the new would-be subject which comes in initial position but the dummy *es* (German) or *er* (Dutch). This is illustrated in (34) on the basis of Dutch.

Dutch (Perlmutter and Zaenen 1984: 176–177)
(34) a. Spelen er twee kinderen in de tuin?
       play   two children in the garden
       'Are there two children playing in the garden?'

    b. Vandaag hebben er twee kinderen in de tuin gespeeld.
       today   have   two children in the garden played
       'Today two children played in the garden.'

Similarly in English, the *there* of presentative and existential constructions, and not the postverbal constituent, is identified as a subject on the basis of its occurrence in question tags and in subject-raising constructions. Tag questions require that a pronoun corresponding to the subject appear in the tag. As evidenced by (35) *there* behaves like a subject in this respect.

(35) There will come better times, won't there?

That *there* has the same distribution as a subject in terms of raising can be appreciated by comparing (36) and (37).

(36) a. Alexander is a poet.
     b. Alexander is believed to be a poet.
     c. Alexander is likely to be a poet.

(37) a. There emerged a problem.
     b. There is believed to have emerged a problem.
     c. There is likely to emerge a problem.

And finally in Italian, the postverbal nominal constituent of presentative inversion constructions does not behave like a subject with respect to several control properties (Perlmutter 1983b; Calabrese 1985). For instance, as shown below, the preverbal subjects in (38) can trigger control of participial, gerundival and adverbial constructions.

Italian (Calabrese 1985: 7)
(38) a. Appena $\emptyset_i$ uscito di casa, Carlo$_i$ l'ha   vista.
         as soon   left the house   Carlo   3sg:have:3sg seen
         'On leaving the house, Carlo saw her.'

   b. $\emptyset_i$ passeggiando nel   parco, Carlo$_i$ l'ha   abbracciata.
       walking   in:the park   Carlo   3sg:have:3sg hugged
       'Walking in the park, Carlo hugged her.'

   c. Dopo $\emptyset_i$ aver conosciuto Maria, Sandro l'ha   lasciata.
       after having   known   Maria   Sandro 3sg:have:3sg left
       'After having known Maria, Sandro left her.'

The inverted nominal constituents in (39) cannot act as such controllers.[22]

(39) a. *Appena $\emptyset_i$ uscito di casa, l'ha vista Carlo$_i$.
     b. *$\emptyset_i$ passeggiando nel parco, l'ha abbracciata Carlo$_i$.
     c. *Dopo $\emptyset_i$ aver conosciuto Maria, l'ha lasciata Sandro$_i$.

The differences in the behavioral characteristics of inverted and noninverted subjects have led linguists of various grammatical persuasions, for instance RG (Perlmutter 1978, 1983b), LFG (Grimshaw 1982), GB (Burzio 1981; Calabrese 1985) and Cognitive Grammar (Lakoff 1987), to view the postverbal constituents as non-subjects.[23] In FG, on the other hand, these distinct properties are interpreted as a reflection not of the syntactic function of the postverbal term, but of its pragmatic function, namely NewTop. French presentative inversion is analysed as lacking subject assignment (Vet 1981) due to the absence of agreement (see note 19), while the postverbal terms in other Romance languages (Dik 1981) and in Germanic (Dik 1980: 108–111) and Slavic are considered to be subjects.

The formal motivation for recognizing a special pragmatic function NewTop in the cases discussed so far is the atypical postverbal location of the introduced discourse referent and its distinct behavioral characteristics. A less common means of signalling the introduction of a new discourse topic is via special morphological particles. Such a situation is described by De Vries (1989: 66–71) in Wambon, a Papuan language in which the relevant particles are the deictic: *eve*, *nomboneve* and *nombone*. As shown in (40a), the new discourse referent is placed initially, followed by the topic particle.

Wambon (De Vries 1989: 67)
(40) a. Evo   kave eve komatmbo.
         that man   top die:3sg:past
         'That man died.'

NewTop (De Vries actually uses this term) is not, however, the only form of topicality that the particles in question may indicate; De Vries states that they may also be used to signal the re-establishing of a previous topic, i.e. for a ResTop. Another point worth noting is that some of the NewTops occur predication-externally, i.e. they are separated from the predication by a short disjuncture, as in (40b).

(40) b. Evo   kave   eve   na   alive   komatmbo.
        that   man   top   pause-marker   yesterday die:3sg:past
        'That man, yesterday he died.'

Though the NewTop in (40b) resembles Dik's Theme, De Vries specifically argues against recognizing a separate predication-external (P_2) pragmatic function for such topics, claiming that the presence of the pause particle in (40b) as opposed to (40a) has no bearing on the form of the predication. Recall from §6.2 that in Modern Standard Arabic topics may also be separated from the predication by a short disjuncture. This holds for some topics in English as well. Assigning two potential structural realizations to the Wambon NewTop, a predication-internal and a predication-external one, would not, however, be incompatible with the FG claims regarding the relationship between pragmatic functions and structural positions. Given that NewTop is identified by the presence of special particles rather than positionally, and that the P_2 is a structural location, there is no reason why this pragmatic function cannot be associated with more than one location.

The formal reflexes of NewTop may also include other forms of morphological marking. The morphological marking of new discourse referents is to a large extent dependent on their referential properties as determined by parameters such as: definiteness, specificity, genericity, individuation and the presupposition of an existing referent.[24] There is no direct correspondence between the amount of coding and relative referentiality; various degrees of referentiality can be coded by a bare noun with an accompanying definiteness, referentiality or specificity marker (free or bound), e.g. *a man, the man, some man*, or by a longer descriptive phrase, e.g. *a man who will win the race, my mother's elder sister, the first person to enter the house*, etc. A number of linguists (e.g. Comrie 1981: 128; Givón 1983b: 26, 1984: 411; and Lambrecht 1987: note 27) have observed that the referential marking of a new discourse referent may be affected by the role it is to play in the discourse, a parameter often referred to as *discourse saliency* or *importance*. The type of saliency in question is seen to differ from that associated with predication-level focus in that it pertains to the potential status of a referent (or information) in the overall discourse, not just the predication.

The level of importance of discourse entities is taken to be affected by a variety of semantic and pragmatic relations. The most obvious of these relations and the most widely used (e.g. by Givón and his co-workers) is the level of topic persistence, i.e. the number of subsequent mentions of a discourse referent in discourse. The manifestation of relative importance that may bear on the identification of NewTop concerns the distinction between two types of marking of indefinite referential expressions, i.e. expressions that are assumed by the speaker to exist as unique individuals. In a number of languages, e.g. Israeli Hebrew, Hawaii Creole, Sherpa, Persian, Romance and Germanic (Givón 1984: 411), indefinite referents that are important in the discourse are marked by a form of the numeral one, while unimportant referents receive zero marking which is characteristic of non-referential expressions. The following example is taken from Givón (1983a: 26).

Israeli Hebrew
(41) a. ... az atsárti ba-xanút ve-kaníti itón-
so I-stopped at-the-store and-I-bought paper
xad ve-hitxálti li-kró *oto* ve-hayá *sham* maamár-xad
one started to-read it and-was there article-one
norá meanyén ve-ha-itón *kulo*.
very interesting and-the paper all-of-it
'... so I stopped by the store and I bought *this one paper* and I began to read *it* and *it* had a very interesting article and *the entire paper*....'

b. ...az atsárti ba-xanút ve-kaníti itón-∅
so I-stopped at-the-store and I bought *paper*
ve-haláxti ha-báyta ve-axálti másheu ve-axár-kax
and-I went- home and-I-ate something and after-that
haláxti lishón.
I went to sleep...
'... so I stopped by the store and got a paper and I went home and I ate something and then I went to sleep....'

Note that the referent marked by *xad* in (41a) persists in the following clauses, while the referent with zero marking in (41b) is not mentioned again. A similar situation is found in Turkish (Comrie 1981: 128) in which the importance of an indefinite object is indicated by assigning it the accusative case, otherwise reserved for definite objects. This is shown in (42a).

Turkish
(42) a. Hasan bir öküz-ü aldi.
         Hasan a   ox -acc bought
         'Hasan bought an ox.'

     b. Hasan bir öküz aldi.
         Hasan a   ox   bought
         'Hasan bought an ox.'

Comrie (1981: 129) states that the presence of the accusative suffix on *öküz* in (42a) as compared to (42b) advises the addressee to pay heed to the nature of this referent, which, though not yet identifiable by the addressee, will play a role in the following discourse.

In §6.3.2 we noted that the function NewTop combines properties of topicality and focality in that it introduces a future topic of discourse while simultaneously designating the most salient piece of information in the clause. These are precisely the properties that 'a paper' in (41a) and 'an ox' in (42a) are claimed to display. Moreover the two constituents are singled out for special treatment in regard to formal expression, a necessary reflex of pragmatic function assignment in FG. This special marking cannot be attributed simply to the Focus function since the corresponding unimportant referents can be focal too. Therefore, unless NewTop is exclusively tied to thetic statements,[25] as characterized in §6.3.2, i.e. statements lacking a topic/comment structure, then one would expect the two terms in (41a) and (42a) to qualify for NewTop assignment. Alternatively, discourse saliency or importance, as reflected in the two patterns of marking referentially indefinite expressions illustrated in (42), may fall outside the scope of pragmatic functions altogether. A discourse as opposed to sentence level-based notion of saliency termed *cohesiveness* has been developed within FG by Bolkestein (1985a,b). The relevant distinctions could therefore be handled with reference to this notion.

6.4 FOCALITY

Various aspects of focality have already been touched upon in the preceding two sections, so here I will just give a brief summary of the main points of the FG approach to focus, and present a short account of the subdivision of Focus proposed by the theory.

Focus, like Topic, pertains to the relationship between a discourse referent and a predication. Dik (1978: 130) defines Focus as the relatively most important or salient information in the predication relative to the pragmatic information between speaker and addressee.

The stipulation 'relatively most important or salient information' is rather vague and, as we shall see below, loosely interpreted. By virtue of the unpredictable relationship of a referent with a predication, the Focus always represents new information in the relational sense of given and new discussed in §6.3.1. But it need not be new in the referential sense. In fact, in the case of contrast or emphasis, as in (43b) or (44b), the focus may coincide with active discourse referents.

(43) a. Sonia and Joyce came to help me.
     b. *Sonia* worked *like mad*, but *Joyce* was *horribly slow*.

(44) a. I heard that Peter got married.
     b. *Peter's* married. (How amazing! I don't believe it! etc.)

Whereas the Topic function is assigned only to terms and, moreover, only single constituents, Focus may be borne by any expression (term, predicate, restrictor or operator), part of an expression (typically in the case of contrast or emphasis), several expressions, or the whole predication. The last of these situations obtains when the Focus falls on the illocutionary point of the predication, the truth value in the case of an assertion or the force of a request, promise, greeting, warning, etc., as in (45).

(45) a. Dali *did* design the bottle.
     b. Dali did *not* compose the perfume.
     c. *Do* sit down.
     d. I *do* promise to be there.
     e. Do *not* be late.

Focus on the whole predication should not be confused with the whole predication being in focus, a possibility which Dik *et al.* (1981: 51) exclude for reasons stated in §6.3.2, preferring to regard all new predications as focus neutral, i.e. lacking focus assignment altogether.

Typically the Focus denotes some element of the predication that predicates something of the Topic, i.e. it belongs to what is referred to as the *comment* or *rheme* under analyses which assume a bipartite division of the clause into a topic and a comment or a theme and a rheme (see note 5). The Topic/Focus distinction in FG does not, however, constitute a strict dichotomy. What is not Topic is not automatically Focus and vice versa. This can be illustrated on the basis of the examples in (46) and (47).

(46) a. What did the customs officer do?
     b. He went through all of my luggage.

(47) a. Where did you see *Rain Man*?
b. I saw it when I was visiting Peter in Amsterdam.

FG adopts question/answer patterns such as those in (46) and (47) (see also (11) and (12) in §6.3.1) as an operational test for focus assignment.[26] On the assumption that the Focus in a question falls on the question word,[27] Focus in an answering sentence is assigned to the expression or expressions which provide the actual answer to the question posed. And in declaratives the Focus corresponds to the elements which would constitute the essential answer if the sentence had been an answer to a question.

The use of this procedure for determining Focus requires at times some ingenuity on the part of the linguist, for the nature of the question to which a particular sentence could serve as an answer in a given context is by no means always obvious.[28] In (46b) *he* is Topic and, due to the form of the question, both the predicate and the object represent focal information. The clause thus displays a classic Topic/Focus distribution. In (47b), by contrast, as the question concerns simply the matter of location, we would expect only *in Amsterdam* to constitute the information focus, *when I was visiting Peter* to have no pragmatic function at all, and the Topic to be either *it* or *I*, but not both. Under such an analysis there is no Topic/Focus partitioning. Note, however, that the declarative in (47b) could also be an answer to (47c).

(47) c. When and where did you see *Rain Man*?

Given (47c), both *when I was visiting Peter* and *in Amsterdam* represent focal information. In speech, matters of prosody will determine which of the above two focus assignment possibilities in the case of the declarative (47b) obtains in a given instance. It was mentioned in §6.2 that FG does not equate Focus with prosodic prominence, the claim being that constituents identified as focal by means of special particles, word order or cleft-constructions need not simultaneously receive special prosodic marking. Nonetheless, prosodic prominence is interpreted as entailing Focus. Therefore, if both *when I was visiting Peter* and *in Amsterdam* receive stress, then both have been assigned Focus by the speaker irrespective of whether the question was (47a) or (47c). In the written language, if no special Focus-marking device is employed or indeed available, the determination of the intended focus assignment is to a large extent dependent on the addressee's or analyst's assessment of the significant points of development within a particular topic of discourse. This brings the notion of focus into the realm of discourse, just as in the case of topic (see §6.3).

176 *Functional Grammar*

In our discussion of topicality in §6.3.2 we noted that a relational approach to topic and focus such as that adopted in FG leads to the recognition of clauses with neither Topic nor Focus in cases where the informational content is all new, as in answer to a question like *What happened?* In FG there are also clauses with Topic but no Focus, and those with Focus but no Topic. The existence of clauses where Topic assignment is unaccompanied by Focus assignment (a theoretical impossibility under most other analyses) is due to the function NewTop being assigned to newly introduced referents in presentative constructions. Such constructions often have a Focus following or preceding the NewTop as in (48a), but they need not as in (48b). (See also the examples given in §6.3.2 and §6.3.3.2).

(48) a. There appeared a band of poachers with automatic weapons.
     b. In the heart of the tusk there was a corroded bullet.

The third possibility, the assignment of Focus but not of Topic to the constituents of a clause, occurs when there is no term within the presupposed part of the predication; recall that the Topic function in FG is assigned only to terms. Example (49b) as a response to (49a) represents such a situation.

(49) a. Who has complained?
     b. Anna has complained. Ted has complained and Lyn and Elaine have complained too.

6.4.1 The focus subdivided

The subdivision of Focus, like the subdivision of Topic, is based on the status of the information denoted by the focal element relative to the assumed pragmatic information of the addressee, not, however, in terms of activation, but in regard to the communicative point that the focus is intended to achieve. The proposed subdivision, originally presented in Dik *et al.* (1981), was strongly inspired by the analysis of the focus system of Aghem, a Grassfields Bantu language, offered in Watters (1979). The major distinctions are shown in (50) taken from Dik (1989: 336).

(50)

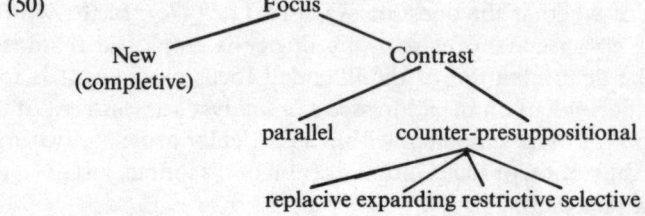

Not all of the distinctions are seen as equally relevant on a cross-linguistic basis. The claim is that if subdivisions within the category of focus can be discerned in a given language on the basis of formal expression, they will correspond to some subset of the distinctions captured in (50). A language need not, however, make any of the presented distinctions. For instance all types of (predication-internal) focus are marked by an undifferentiated focus morpheme -nde in the Papuan language Wambon (De Vries 1989: 67), and in Hungarian (Dezső 1982) by a single location, the immediately preverbal position.

The primary split within the category of Focus is between contrastive and non-contrastive information. Strictly speaking all new information is contrastive since it is opposed to all other information that might have been, but was not, expressed (Chafe 1976). The notion of contrast used in (50) refers to the narrow sense of the term, i.e. to information which the speaker assumes to be directly opposed to a restricted range of alternatives deemed to be entertained by the addressee. That contrast, thus conceived, may serve as a basis for a taxonomy of focus, is suggested by the frequently cited differences in the means of coding non-contrastive (plain, unmarked) and contrastive (marked) focus in a wide variety of languages.[29] Apart from strong stress, these differences most commonly concern order and the use of focus-marking particles. One of the manifestations of this is that many languages, for instance Haida, Hixkaryana, Wappo, Tzeltal, Malagasy, Tagalog and Cebuano, are claimed to allow fronting of verbal arguments (object and/or subject, depending on the basic order) only if they denote contrast.[30] Two cases in point, one from the Carib language Hixkaryana (Derbyshire 1977: 598) and the other from the unaffiliated Amerindian language Haida (Eastman 1986: 332), are presented below.

Hixkaryana
(51) a. Yawaka yokheko Waraka rohyaka oroke.
      axe   he-sent-it   Waraka   to-me   yesterday
      'Waraka sent the axe to me yesterday.'

    b. Waraka yawaka yokheko rohyaka oroke.
      '(It was) Waraka (who) sent the axe to me yesterday.'

    c. Rohyaka yawaka yokheko Waraka oroke.
      '(It was) to me Waraka sent the axe yesterday.'

Haida
(52) a. Nang iihlingaas laa qwiaadan.
      the   man   her   loved
      'The man loved her.'

b. Laa   uu   nang iihlingaas qwiaadan.
    her   foc   the   man   loved
    '(It is) she/her (who) the man loved.'

The Haida example in (52b) illustrates not only the fronting strategy used for marked foci, but also coding by means of a special particle *uu*[31] placed after the fronted constituent. An interesting situation is found in Efik, a Benue-Congo language described by Cook (1976), in which the presence of a contrastive element in the clause is indicated by partial reduplication of the verbal stem. The following example is taken from De Jong (1981: 105).

Efik
(53) é-tìm   ó-kó- 'bó-bób   ú-tòk   ókò'.
      Etim   past-build-preverb focus-contr house   that
      'Etim (not I) built the house.'

Turning to the FG subdivision of Focus, non-contrastive focus, referred to as *Completive Focus*, denotes information that is simply intended to fill a gap in the pragmatic information of the addressee. This is the familiar Focus determined on the basis of the question–answer test discussed on p. 175. All the other types of Focus in (50) are contrastive in one way or another. *Parallel Focus* involves an explicit contrast of two pieces of information within one linguistic expression, e.g. (see also (43b)):

(54) The *Afghans* play the buzkashi with a *goat* carcass, the *Kazahks* with a *sheep* carcass.

The focus is due to the internal relations between the contrasted pairs of constituents. In the case of *Counter-presuppositional Focus*, on the other hand, the contrast is achieved by means of the relation between the speaker's assertion and the addressee's presupposition. *Replacive Focus* consists of two steps: the rejecting of incorrect information and the substituting of correct information, as in (55b).

(55) a. Ken is in Beijing.
      b. No, he isn't in *Beijing*, he's in *Guangzhou*.

A correction presupposes a rejection, and therefore a specification of just the former may be considered as a complete statement. By contrast, a statement containing only a rejection is in principle incomplete, though this to some extent depends on the type of information involved. Compare (56a) and (56b).

(56) a. No, he's in Guangzhou.
b. No, he isn't in Beijing.

Expanding Focus is used to supplement some correct but incomplete piece of information that the speaker knows the addressee to possess by an additional piece of information considered to be of relevance under the particular circumstances of the exchange.

(57) a. The new Prime Minister has given us hope.
b. He has given us not only *hope*, but *opportunities*.
c. Yes, but he has also given us *tremendous inflation*.

In the case of *Restrictive Focus*, the addressee is assumed to be in the possession of information that is only partially correct. The Restrictive Focus delimits the information to what the speaker views as the correct part, e.g.:

(58) a. Aung San Suu Kyi is under house arrest and unable to make contact with the outside world.
b. No, she has been *imprisoned*, but not *silenced*.

And finally by means of *Selective Focus* the speaker chooses from among a set of alternatives deemed to be held by the addressee the one that is appropriate or correct.

(59) a. Is the intifadeh still on, or is it all over now?
b. It's still *on*.

For an exemplification of the different means of expression used to signal these distinctions in Aghem and some other languages I refer the reader to Dik *et al.* (1981), De Jong (1981) and Dik (1989).

One may well ask how emphasis relates to the above classification of focus. Typically, contrast is considered to be a special type of emphasis, and thus emphasis and contrast are jointly juxtaposed to plain focus under labels such as 'marked focus', 'emphasis' or, conversely, 'contrast'. Consequently most of the strategies used to code marked focus cited in the literature, including the frontings mentioned earlier, are claimed to include both emphasis and contrast. In fact, note that the cleft-construction, which generally features in the English translation of clauses with marked focus as in the Hixkaryana (51b,c), Haida (52b) and Efik (53) examples, does not allow one to determine, in the absence of contextual information, whether an explicit contrast concerning a restricted set of alternatives is involved or just an opposition to anything else that could have been entertained, accompanied by some form of emphasis. The notion of *emphasis* as opposed to *contrast* has proved to be notoriously difficult to characterize. A potentially fruitful source for such a characterization may lie in Halliday's three functions of language (see §2.3.1). De Jong (1986), among others, suggests that whereas the pragmatic functions Topic and Focus may be seen to relate to the textual (and partially ideational) level, emphasis and contrast belong to the interpersonal plane, their role being to instruct the addressee on how to process the information offered by the speaker. In the case of contrast, the addressee is invited to juxtapose the presented information with some other explicit or presupposed information, while in the case of emphasis, the addressee is advised to read into the presented information some additional meanings connected with, for example, the explanatory, emotional, unexpected or paradoxical value of the message.

Given the generally assumed underlying unity of emphasis and contrast, one would expect a taxonomy of focus such as that presented in (50) to group emphasis somehow with contrast, perhaps as the superordinate category. Neither Dik *et al.* (1981) nor De Jong (1981) addresses this issue. The only point made in connection with the FG view of emphasis is that some languages make a formal distinction between emphasis and contrast. The two languages cited in Dik *et al.* (1981) are Aghem and Dutch, both of which distinguish emphatic assertive predication focus from counter-assertive predication focus. The former involves no previous denial of the truth value of the expressed proposition, while the latter is an explicit contradiction of a previous statement and hence explicitly contrastive. In Dutch this difference is marked by the use of the emphatic particle *wel*, in the case of emphatic focus, while Aghem uses word order, namely the presence or absence of a constituent immediately after the verb. Compare (60a) and (60b).

Aghem
(60)   emphatic focus
    a.   éná   má'a   fúo   bɛ-'kɔ́   a   fin-ghɔ́.
       Inah   past-focus   give   fufu   to   friend
       'Inah *did* give fufu to his friend.'

     contrastive focus
    b.   fil   á   máà   bɛ-'kɔ́ zi.
       friends   subj   past-focus   fufu eat
       'The friends *did* eat fufu.'

Whether differences between emphasis and contrast in languages such as Aghem are to be interpreted as indicative of further subdivisions within the category of contrastive focus or of focus in general remains to be determined.

7 Form-determining expression rules

7.1 INTRODUCTION

Recall from ch. 2 that expression rules are applied to fully specified underlying predications which are successively built up from the basic predicate frame into a clausal structure and assigned syntactic and pragmatic functions. For convenience, I repeat below the previously given (see §2.3.3) example of such an underlying predication (without the decomposition of the terms).

(1) $[E_i \text{ [Dec } [X_i \text{ [Past } e_i \text{ [[give}_v \text{ (Marilyn)}_{Ag/Subj/Top} \text{ (the letter)}_{Go/Obj} \text{ (Rob)}_{Rec/Foc}]$ (surreptitiously)$_{Man}$] (during the staff meeting)$_{Loc}$ (e_i)] (allegedly)$_{Man}$ (X_i)] (in case you haven't heard)] (E_i)]

The form-determining and linearization expression rules convert the structure in (1) into the utterance in (2).

(2) In case you haven't heard, Marilyn allegedly gave the letter to Rob surreptitiously during the staff meeting.

In this chapter we will focus our attention on matters of form, leaving the details of the FG account of linearization to ch. 8.

The domain of form-determining expression rules includes the traditional set of concerns of inflectional morphology. These expression rules capture the relevant morphological processes of affixation, reduplication (partial and complete) and (regular) sound modification. In addition to these strictly morphological operations, the expression rules may introduce individual words such as adpositions, verbal auxiliaries or articles reflecting one or more of the recognized morpho-syntactic categories (often referred to as inflectional). Thus in accordance with the non-autonomy hypothesis of the subsystems of grammar (§1.2), the expression rules enable FG to provide a unified treatment of semantic distinctions which may be expressed both synthetically and analytically.

The form-determining expression rules belong to one of the most recently developed areas of FG and will be subject to various modifications. This chapter is intended to give some idea of the type of solutions that are currently being entertained, but does not pretend to be an exhaustive study of the problems involved. The discussion will begin with a few words about the interaction of form and order (§7.2). In §7.3 the basic characteristics of form-determining rules will be presented. Then §7.4 will deal with the FG treatment of agreement and cross-reference. The final section, §7.5, will be devoted to the FG account of the English verbal complex.

7.2 INTERDEPENDENCE BETWEEN FORM AND ORDER

Interdependencies between form and order are by no means rare. The effect of form on order is manifested cross-linguistically in the tendency to position shorter and less structurally complex material before longer and more elaborate language data (see §6.1.1), one of the reflexes of which is the early placement in the utterance of pronominals and/or clitics as compared to nominal forms. The converse phenomenon, form sensitive to the influence of order, can be observed in, for instance, various liaison and sandhi processes and in the presence of, or nature of, case, number, gender or person marking. For example, in a number of Australian Aboriginal languages such as Walpiri and Diyari, all the elements of a discontinuous term phrase bear case, while a continuous phrase appears only with case marking on the final element irrespective of its categorial status. To give another example, in languages such as Polish or Serbo-Croatian, an adjective or verb agrees (or may agree) in gender, number and/or person with the nearest or first element of a coordinate phrase. A particularly interesting illustration of segmental coding correlating with differences in linear order is to be found in Yagua (Payne 1985), in which a cross-referencing subject prefix *sa-* may occur on the verb only when the full NP subject is located postverbally (3), not preverbally (4b).

Yagua
(3)   Sa-   nááyi   Alchíco-ra.
      3sg-   press   Alchico-inan
      'Alchico presses it.'

(4)   a.   Jíryoonú   súúy-janu-níí.
           bushmaster   bite-past-3sg
           'A bushmaster bit him.'

      b.   *Jíryoonú   sa- súúy-janu-níí.

A similar phenomenon may be observed in written literary Arabic (Sawaie 1985) in which subject verb agreement in number is obligatory in SVO clauses and typically absent from VSO ones; (agreement in gender occurs irrespective of the location of the subject).

The FG account of the form of language expressions in cases such as the above requires a 'sandwich' application of the form-determining and linearization rules owing to the rejection of deletion and movement rules. Therefore, the Yagua clause (4a) cannot be derived from a structure underlying (3), nor can (3) be generated from a structure underlying (4a). In order to ensure the correct verb complex in both (3) and (4a), knowledge of the location of the subject (most probably as a correlate of its pragmatic function) has to be accessible to the form-determining expression rules.

7.3 LEXICAL PRIORITY

The application of the expression rules in any given instance is subject to the FG version of the Proper Inclusion Principle of TG (see Pullum 1979) called the Principle of Lexical Priority (PLP) (Dik 1989: 294, 296), which stipulates that the properties of a particular lexical item override that of the general model as presented in an expression rule. The Principle of Lexical Priority reads:

(5) Whenever a rule is encountered of the general form $M[x] = x^1$, where x^1 is the form of x under the operation M, first check the lexicon to see whether the x^1 form of x is stored there ready-made.
 (i) if a ready-made word is found, select that word;
 (ii) if a ready-made stem is found, apply the relevant rule to the stem;
 (iii) otherwise, apply the rule to the basic form of the predicate.

This principle precludes an expression rule from applying to an irregular word form, which by virtue of its irregularity must be listed in the lexicon, thereby preventing the generation of forms such as *oxes* or *catched* instead of the English *oxen* and *caught*. It also ensures the selection of the appropriate allomorph of a predicate, to which the expression rule is to be applied. This latter situation may be illustrated on the basis of the predicate *brother* in Polish which has two allomorphs, one used in the singular *brat-* and the other used in the plural and in the vocative singular *brać-* , as shown in (6).

Both of these stems have to be specified in the lexical entry for the predicate *brother* and marked for the morpho-syntactic environments in which they are used. By virtue of the PLP the expression rules will select either *brat-* or *brać-* as the stem to which the case and number affixes determined by the expression rules will be applied.

(6)
	singular	plural
Nom	brat	bracia
Gen	brata	braci
Dat	bratu	braciom
Acc	brata	braci
Instr	bratem	braćmi
Abl	bratu	braciach
Voc	bracie	bracia

Dik (1989: 299) suggests that all form-determining expression rules should conform to the following schema:

(7)   Operator [Operandum] = Value

The operator in (7) is a grammatical morpheme called a morphosyntactic or μ-operator, the nature of which will be clarified below. The operandum is a phonologically specified item of the object language, word or stem, taken from the underlying clause structure or introduced by a previous expression rule. It is specified for syntactic category (N, V or A) and may also be marked for declensional, conjugational and gender classes. The value is the output of the expression rule. To give a concrete example, the plural form of the nominal predicate *girl* would be derived as follows:

(8)   pl [girl-$_N$] = girl-s

Three kinds of μ-operators are distinguished: primary, auxiliary and contextual. *Primary* operators are present in the abstract underlying structure and as such necessarily have some semantic import. Included in this class of μ-operators are the Ω (term) and π (predicate, predication, etc.) operators mentioned earlier, and the semantic, syntactic and pragmatic functions which for the purpose of the expression rules are treated as operators. *Auxiliary* operators facilitate the operation of expression rules; they are introduced by one expression rule to trigger yet another expression rule. Case forms such as nominative, accusative, dative, etc. and infinitival and past participle verbal forms are the prime exemplars of this type of operator. A case form, say the dative, may be introduced by one of several primary operators, a recipient, experiencer, beneficiary or maleficiary. However, it does not in itself qualify for the status of a primary operator since, under the FG analysis, it has only a constant form (or forms) but no unified semantic content.[1] The same holds for the infinitive or past participle form of the verb. For example, in Polish a past participle verbal form is used in the formation of the past tense, compound future, immediate future, simplex irrealis and passive voice. Again all these different semantic sources are associated with a single segmental form. The FG analysis captures this by having the past participle introduced by each of the appropriate tense, mood and/or voice operators, and only then applying the rule specifying the actual form of the past participle. *Contextual* operators, represented between < >, specify features of the linguistic environment of the operandum which have an effect on the form of linguistic expressions. These operators are used primarily in the FG account of agreement phenomena, which will be discussed in §7.4 below.

The form of linguistic expressions, particularly in inflectional and agglutinating languages, is generally determined by the application of several μ-operators. In inflectional languages, by definition, the various operators do not tend to have their own separate phonetic realizations but fuse with each other and/or with the stem, producing semantically complex but unsegmentable so-called portmanteau forms. With nominal predicates the fused categories are typically number and case, as in the Polish examples in (6), with verbal ones person and number, person and mood, or tense and aspect (Bybee 1985: 34), though more complex combinations of tense, aspect, mood, number, person and even voice are also to be found, as for instance in Latin. To avoid arbitrary segmentation, FG derives such portmanteau expressions by the simultaneous application of the two or more operators represented in the portmanteau form. As an example of the simultaneous application of several μ-operators to a nominal stem let us consider the Polish terms *tych chłopców* and *te dziewczynki* in (9a) and (9b).

Polish
(9) a. Widziałam tych chłopców.
saw:3sg:f these:acc:m boy:pl:acc
'I saw/I've seen those boys.'

b. Widziałam te dziewczynki.
saw:3sg:f these:acc:f girl:pl:acc
'I saw/I've seen these girls.'

Every Polish nominal predicate contains a specification of number and case, the latter as a consequence of the semantic and/or syntactic function of the predicate. The accusative case of the predicates in (9) is interpreted in FG as being due to the Goal function; recall that for reasons specified in §4.4, under the FG approach to syntactic functions there is no object function in Polish. The nominal predicate itself carries inherent gender, and is classified as belonging to one of twenty-eight declensional classes and subclasses. Demonstrative pronouns are inflected for number and case; their form is determined by the gender and declensional class of the head noun. In FG demonstratives are treated as operators or more specifically as a combination of a definiteness operator (indicated by d) and a distal one (prox. for proximate; rem. for remote). Since Polish demonstratives are also obligatorily specified for number, case and gender, in order to derive the correct form of the terms in (9) all five μ-operators (definiteness, proximate, number (m for plural), case and the contextual gender operator) have to be applied simultaneously, as in (10) for example.

(10)   (d prox. m acc < N mas. > [chłopc-$_{N (decII)}$]) = tych chłopców

It is important to note that the number and case operators in (10) apply twice, so to speak; once in union with the other three operators in the realization of the demonstrative, and again in determining the fused case and number marking of the nominal predicate. This is a consequence of the FG treatment of agreement phenomena (see §7.4). As captured in the Principle of Lexical Priority in (5) above, the μ-operators either independently or in combination may be applied in yet another way, namely in choosing the appropriate form of the predicate. So if the predicate in (10) were to be one displaying allomorphy of the stem such as the predicate *brother* exemplified above in (6), the number and case operators would first have to select the form of the stem consonant with the number and case features of the operators, in this instance accusative, plural.

Another aspect of the form of morpho-syntactic categories that the expression rules must be able to reflect is sequential order. This is especially significant in the case of agglutinating languages, which are characterized by having words with a large number of grammatical morphemes realized by clearly demarcated phonological segments (usually coinciding with syllable boundaries) stacked onto each other in sequential fashion. FG seeks to provide an account of the sequencing of morpho-syntactic categories in terms of the order of primary operators in underlying clause structure and an 'inside out' application of the expression rules, starting from the operator closest to the stem. This will be illustrated in §7.5 on the basis of the FG analysis of the English verbal auxiliaries.

7.4 AGREEMENT

Agreement, the modification of the form of one element to match the properties of another element, subsumes a number of often disparate phenomena (see Moravcsik 1978; Lehmann 1982) amenable to different theory-specific analyses. In FG agreement is considered to be a purely mechanical process with no independent semantic content being displayed by the agreement marker. A typical manifestation of such agreement at clause level is the occurrence in English of -*s* on present tense verbs with third person singular subjects, as in (11c).

(11) a. I work at home nowadays.
 b. You work at home nowadays, don't you?
 c. She works at home nowadays.

The personal pronouns in (11) are obligatory, and therefore the -*s* in (11c) cannot in itself be interpreted as expressing the category of person, but only as a marker accompanying the expression of a third person singular subject. The FG approach to agreement can be captured in the following points (Dik 1989: 331):

(a) only intrinsic properties of source constituents can trigger agreement;
(b) within terms the head noun is the only source constituent, and gender is the only agreement category;
(c) apparent agreement in definiteness, number or case among the elements of a term is due to multiple application of the relevant operator or to the 'distribution' of the effect of the operator over different constituents within a domain;
(d) at clause level only terms trigger agreement, and gender, person and number are the only agreement categories;
(e) within the sphere of person marking there is a basic difference between agreement and cross-reference.

Points (b), (c) and (d) follow directly from point (a). Distinctions of gender and class, though subject to arbitrary extensions, have a broad semantic basis (e.g. sex, humanness, animacy, shape, etc.) connected with the perceived properties of the referents of nouns. Gender or class are thus intrinsic features of nouns (see e.g. Rijkhoff 1989a). Number, case and definiteness, on the other hand, are only contingent to nouns, dependent on the properties of the terms in which they are used. Therefore in FG, matchings of these features within the term are not considered as manifestations of agreement. The gender of nouns is inherited by terms[2] which by virtue of belonging to a predication have intrinsic number and person, whereas case is a contextual feature of terms determined by their function in the predication (see also the discussion after (16) below). Thus according to point (a) at the level of the clause number qualifies as a potential agreement category in addition to gender and person, but case does not. This segregation of features into features of the noun and of the term as a whole (= noun phrase) is nowadays fairly uncontroversial.

Given the FG treatment of definiteness, number and case as term operators, the fact that these categories may be borne by any member of the term, not necessarily the noun, or by the whole term, follows automatically. We have already noted that in Polish (9) and English and also many other languages definiteness is coded on a determiner or demonstrative. Latvian, Serbo-Croatian and Slovenian (Lehmann 1982: 205) show definiteness by the inflection of the adjective. And in the Amerindian language Kwakwala (Anderson 1984) it is not even the term that bears a definiteness marker since the index of definiteness is an enclitic which attaches to any word that precedes the term. This last unusual marking pattern is illustrated in (12).

```
Kwakwala
(12)  La-      i    ax?ed-ida   ts' daqa-x-a      -lu/ lqʷ/i.
      aux-pro       takes-the   woman -obj-the    dishes
      'The woman takes the dishes.'
```

Similar observations can be made in regard to the coding of case and number. For example, the sole exponent of case in German phrases with a feminine head noun such as *dieser Frau* (this:gen/dat woman) is the determiner, not the noun. As mentioned on p. 182, in several Australian languages case is marked only on the final element of a continuous term, and this element need not be a noun; in the following example from Diyari (Austin 1981) it is an adjective.

```
Diyari
(13)  Thana   ngama-rna   wapa-yi    mitha     muya-nhi.
      they    sit-part    aux-pres   country   dry-loc
      'They live in a dry country.'
```

Such marking of the final constituent of a term may also apply to number as in (14) from Yucatec (Lehmann 1982: 205).

```
Yucatec
(14)  he?   kacal-oob.
      egg   broken-pl
      broken eggs
```

If number, case or definiteness were to be interpreted as noun rather than term features the derivation of the correct forms of all the above expressions would require some type of deletion and movement rules (see Blake 1983b), both of which are strongly disfavoured in FG.

In order to have a better understanding of the FG approach to agreement, let us consider an FG analysis of structures in which the features of the noun and of the term do not always coincide. Such discrepancies in regard to number are common with collective nouns or denumerated nouns, as in the examples in (15).

(15) a. The university pays/pay in the third week of each month.
 b. Twenty thousand dollars isn't/*aren't enough.
 c. Twenty thousand students are/*is going to be there.

In (15a), though the form of the noun is singular, the verb may take either singular or plural marking depending on whether the term is interpreted as referring to the collection as a whole (intensional reference) or to the number of the collection (extensional reference). In (15b,c) the same two patterns of agreement with the same two categories of reference co-occur with a plural noun. Note that by virtue of point (b), the plural marking on the nouns in (15b,c) cannot be treated in FG as an instance of agreement of the noun with the semantically plural numerals. Since number is not an agreement feature in terms, I presume that under the FG analysis the plural form of the noun would be introduced by the expression rules as an auxiliary operator launched by the numeral, which is itself a term operator (an absolute non-proportional quantifier). A comparable analysis would also have to be posited to account for the discrepancy in case in the following examples from Polish.

Polish
(16) a. Dwadzieścia   pięć   kobiet   siedzi.
    twenty:nom:nmp five:nom:nmp woman:pl:gen sit:pres:3sg
    'Twenty-five women are sitting.'

 b. Dwudziestu   pięciu   żołnierzy   stało
    twenty:nom:mp five:nom:mp soldier:pl:gen stand:past:3sg:n
    na   podwórzu.
    in   courtyard
    'Twenty-five soldiers were standing in the courtyard.'

The numerals in (16) are in the nominative while the noun is in the genitive. The nominative case of the numerals is consistent with the subject function of the whole term. The genitive form of the nouns is conditioned by the numerals as evidenced by the nominative inflection of the noun in (16c) when there is no accompanying numerical expression.[3]

(16) c. Żołnierze   stali   na   podwórzu.
         soldiers:nom   stood:past:3pl:mp   on   courtyard
         'Soldiers were standing in the courtyard.'

As we are dealing here with an instance of government rather than agreement, an FG analysis of these case-marking facts can quite happily attribute the genitive marking to the presence of the numeral without contravening point (b). Under the proposed analysis the genitive case of the nouns in (16a,b) would be introduced by the expression rules as an auxiliary operator of the numeral quantifier, the nominative case as an auxiliary operator of the subject function. Given that case is not an agreement feature, both of these case operators must be allowed to apply several times, as stipulated in point (c), to account for the difference in case marking in (17a) and (17b), for instance.

Polish
(17) a. Pięć   pierwszych   kobiet   zostało.
         five:nom   first:gen   women:gen   remain:past:3sg:n
         'Five of the first women remained.'

    b.   Pierwsze   pięć   kobiet   zostało.
         first:nom   five:nom   women:gen   remain:past:3sg:n
         'The first five women remained.'

In (17a) the numeral is in the nominative, the ordinal and the noun in the genitive; in (17b) the nominative case is borne both by the numeral and the ordinal, the genitive case only by the noun. The two case-marking patterns reflect different scope relations which would be indicated in the underlying structure of the term by the relative order of the numeral and the ordinal operators. (Ordinals are also treated as primary operators in FG.) But how exactly the different scope relations of these primary operators are to be correlated with the correct scope of the auxiliary case operators I do not know.

The Polish examples in (16) and (17) are of interest in regard to matters of gender and number. The actual form of the nominative case reflects agreement of the numeral with the head noun in gender, non-masculine personal in (16a) and (17), and masculine personal in (16b). Gender is also indexed on the verb in (16b) and (17). (In Polish subject–verb agreement in gender occurs only in tenses built on the past participle stem of the verb and therefore there is no gender marking on the present tense verb in (16a).) The gender marking on the verb is, however, neuter, not masculine personal (see (16c)). In view of the fact that the feature marked on the verb is not displayed by the noun or numeral it would be counterintuitive to call this accommodation of the verb agreement rather than a default form conditioned by the presence of a numerically quantified term represented in the expression rules as a contextual operator. This could also be a more viable analysis of the singular marking of the verb in (16a,b) than the one based on agreement suggested for the English (15b,c). Note that the denumerated nouns in (16a,b) are plural while the verb is in the singular just as in the English (15b). However, whereas in English the number marking of the verb depends on the semantic interpretation of the whole term, in Polish the singular form of the verb with such denumerated subjects is invariant; numerals of five and above always combine with singular verbs. Since there is no opposition in number, the whole term is not so much singular as unspecified for number. Adopting this line of reasoning, the singular form of the verb would be a default form dependent on a contextual operator rather than a manifestation of agreement. In fact under an FG analysis Polish would not be considered to have subject–verb agreement at all, but rather a subject cross-referencing system.

7.4.1 Cross-reference

Cross-reference is a form of pronoun incorporation or bounding, at term level onto a nominal stem, and at clause level onto a verbal or sometimes a special auxiliary stem or catalyst particle. Whereas an agreement marker such as the English -s shown in (11c) has no independent semantic content, a cross-referencing form is a pronominal referential element. The referential properties of cross-referencing pronouns are evidenced by the fact that their presence alone, without a free pronominal or nominal form, is all that is required for a complete predication. We can see this in (18b) from the Mayan language Quiche (Norman 1978) which manifests both subject and direct object cross-referencing.

Quiche
(18) a. x-   ∅-   u-   rami-j   lee chee7   lee achih.
         asp-   3sg(O)- 3sg(S)- cut-suffix   the tree   the man
         'The man cut the tree.'

   b. x-   ∅-   u-   rami-j.
       asp-   3sg(O)- 3sg(S)- cut-suffix
       'He cut it.'

In a typical cross-referencing system such as that displayed by Quiche (18), the semantic and syntactic functions of the verbal arguments are marked exclusively by the bound pronouns. The functional information may be coded phonologically, in the form of the bound pronouns, and/or indicated by their ordering. In Quiche both of these strategies are used. One set of bound pronouns indexes transitive subjects and another intransitive subjects and direct objects (the language is ergative); the object prefix (zero for third person singular) always precedes the subject one (*u-*). Significantly, the corresponding independent forms do not bear case or adpositional marking, and display no fixed order. Since all information concerning clausal relations is indexed on the predicate, the predicate emerges as the only obligatory constituent of the predication.

In terms of the typology of morphological marking recently advanced by Nichols (1986), cross-reference is characteristic of head-marking, and agreement of dependent-marking languages. The two types of languages are seen to exhibit diverse preferences in regard to the marking of the syntactic relation of dependency between head and dependent; head-marking languages tend to mark this relation on the head, dependent-marking languages on the dependent. This distinction is claimed to reflect a fundamental difference in the syntactic bonds between the head and any overt dependents. In dependent-marking languages the relationship between the verb and the subject is taken to be one of government; the subject is syntactically governed by the verb, while the verb agrees with the subject in person and number. In head-marked languages an independent nominal or pronominal subject (or object) is assumed to be in an appositional relation to the pronominal markers on the head. Therefore it is through the bound pronominals and not by means of the independent forms that the argument requirements of a given predicate are met.

This appositional treatment of the independent forms co-occurring with cross-referencing bound pronouns, which dates back at least to Boas's (1911) analysis of the Chinookan languages, is adopted by FG. FG, however, extends the domain of cross-reference into predominantly dependent-marking languages such as Latin, Italian, Russian and Polish, and analyses traditional agreement markers as bound pronouns. As a diagnostic of cross-reference as compared to agreement, Dik (1989: 132–133) takes the ability of the predicate to stand alone in a complete predication. On the basis of this criterion, the markers of subject–verb agreement in Latin, Italian, Russian and Polish indeed emerge as cross-referencing forms.

Part of the motivation for this analysis is the general avoidance of deletion rules in FG. Dik argues that if the relationship between the subject and verb in Latin were to be considered as agreement rather than cross-reference, the derivation of subjectless clauses would require postulating an independent subject for purposes of agreement and then subsequently deleting it. Under the cross-referencing analysis, the bound pronominals are treated as the phonetic realizations of abstract semantic predicates (specified for person, number and in some languages gender features) functioning as the first restrictors of terms which may be further specified by free forms. There is, however, another analysis which does not involve deletion and which simultaneously captures the characteristics of a predominantly dependent-marking language such as Latin, Polish or Russian.

The syntactic bond between the independent and bound forms in a basically dependent-marking language is not exactly the same as in a head-marking one. In a head-marking language, the independent nominals, deprived of any specifications of function, acquire the syntactic status of subjects or objects solely by virtue of their appositional relationship to the bound pronouns. In a dependent-marking language, on the other hand, from the point of view of functional identification the cross-referencing forms on the verb are superfluous since independent forms are clearly marked for function. In other words, the independent forms do not require the bound ones, though the latter are obligatorily present. Therefore in the presence of an independent noun or pronoun, the bound forms are much more like semantically empty agreement markers than cross-referencing forms in apposition to the free forms. This duality of function of bound pronominals is explicitly catered for in LFG. In discussing grammatical and anaphoric agreement in Bantu, Bresnan and Mchombo (1987) suggest that in Chichewa the subject marker on the verb should be interpreted as a predicate with referential potential when there is no subject NP, and as an agreement affix when such a subject is present. The lack of an independent subject is thus not due to deletion, and the relationship between such a subject and the bound forms on the verb is not one of apposition. As far as I have been able to determine, there is nothing in FG to preclude an analysis along the same lines. In fact FG (De Groot and Limburg 1986) adopts a version of the claim advanced by typologists as to the diachronic evolution of independent pronominals into clitics, bound forms and finally agreement markers. Therefore, it would be strange if the theory were not to recognize the possibility of synchronic indeterminacy or duality of these markers as a reflection of some stage in their historical development.

7.4.2 A note on agreement in Achenese

Achenese is an Austronesian language which on the basis of data presented in Lawler (1977) is widely cited as displaying agreement in both active and passive clauses with the underlying rather than the surface subject. The relevant examples are shown in (19).

Achenese (Lawler 1977)
(19) a. Gopnyan ka gi-com lon.
 (S)he perf 3h-kiss me
 '(S)he already kissed me.'

b. Lon ka gi-com le gopnyan.
 I perf 3h-kiss by (s)he
 'I have already been kissed by her.'

This characteristic of Achenese agreement has been used by Relational Grammarians and specifically with reference to FG by Perlmutter (1981) as an argument for the necessity of recognizing more than one level of grammatical functions (relations in RG terminology) and hence for the superiority of RG over FG. Perlmutter's original claim has been countered by allowing the grammar to make reference to argument positions which, as suggested in §4.5.2, have the *de facto* status of grammatical functions in current FG. Nonetheless, in the light of more comprehensive data presented by Durie (1987), the FG account of Achenese agreement, or rather cross-reference, as it now would be analysed, remains far from satisfactory, particularly as compared to the neat RG solution.

Perlmutter's criticism of the FG handling of agreement in Achenese was made with reference to Dik's (1978: 117) analysis, according to which 'the verb agrees with the agent'. As argued by Perlmutter, given that the semantic function agent is used in FG only for action SoAs, Dik's generalization does not cover the analogous agreement patterns found in active and passive clauses depicting Processes, Positions or States. A case in point involving a state SoA is presented in (20).

(20) a. Gopnyan gi-nging ani? agam nyan.
 (S)he 3p- see child male that
 'She sees the boy.'

b. Ani? agam nyan gi-nging le-gopnyan.
 child male that 3p-see by (s)he
 'The boy is seen by her.'

Under previous versions of FG the account of these agreement facts required a rule consisting of a complicated disjunction of the type of semantic functions determining agreement in different SoAs, whereas the RG solution simply attributes agreement to the initial, i.e. underlying, subject. Now FG can offer an analogous analysis in terms of agreement with the first argument A^1.

Durie (1987) argues that the (a) and (b) examples in (19) and (20) are not instances of an active/passive opposition.[4] More importantly, however, he contends that cross-reference (by means of a proclitic[5]) in Achenese is not with the first argument, but only with first arguments that have the semantic status of actor as compared to undergoer in the sense of Foley and Van Valin (1984). The crucial examples are those involving different intransitive verbs, as in (21a,b) from Durie (1987: 370).

(21) a. gopnyan geu-jak.
       (s)he   3p -go
       '(S)he goes.'

    b. rhet   gopnyan.
       fall   (s)he
       '(S)he falls.'

The verb *jak* 'go' in (21a) is seen to take an actor as an A^1, while *rhet* 'fall' in (21b) takes an undergoer argument. Only the actor is cross-referenced.

In the wake of Perlmutter's unaccusative hypothesis (see note 18 in ch. 6), RG intransitive actor subjects are treated as initial 1s, while intransitive undergoer subjects are initial 2s which at a subsequent stratum are advanced to 1. Initial transitive actors are also 1s. This subdivision of initial subjects enables RG to provide a succinct statement of cross-reference: 'only initial 1s are cross-referenced'. FG must fall back on an account involving a disjunction of semantic functions. What is of interest in connection with our previous discussion of the FG treatment of cross-reference is that the single argument of an intransitive predicate enters into two different relations with the predicate depending on its semantic function; the FG equivalents of A^1 actors are in apposition to the predicate, the undergoers in a dependent/head relationship. Such an analysis will have to be extended to other languages displaying a similar semantically based system of cross-reference. The phenomenon is not unique to Achenese, being found in languages exhibiting what is commonly referred to as an *active* system of morphological marking.

7.5 THE ENGLISH VERBAL COMPLEX

Providing a non-arbitrary account of the English verbal complex has been a major goal of most grammatical frameworks ever since

Chomsky's (1957) ingenious 'affix-hopping' analysis. The nature of the problem lies in the fact that only certain combinations of verbal forms are permitted and that the permissible forms are heavily constrained with respect to order. Chomsky's treatment of the issue involved total stipulation of the morphological and linear facts in the grammar. All subsequent analyses aim to provide independent motivation for the allowable sequences of verbal forms which would relate the admissible combinations to general principles already invoked in a given framework rather than to some ad hoc rules.

The English lexical verb may take one of six morphological forms: a finite form, a bare form (with and without infinitival *to*), a present participle, a past participle and a passive participle. It co-occurs with four other verbal forms, commonly referred to as auxiliaries: modals, the perfective *have*, the progressive *be* and the passive *be*. The passive *be*, progressive *be* and perfective *have* all require a non-finite form of the verb, namely passive, present and past participle forms respectively, while the modal demands a bare lexical verb. The sequencing of the four auxiliaries must conform to the pattern in (22) and none of the auxiliaries can be used more than once.

(22) modal perfective progressive passive.

The specification of tense and agreement is marked on the lexical verb if there is no auxiliary element present. Otherwise these distinctions are coded on the first element of the auxiliary sequence; on the modal, if there is one (23a), or if there is no modal on the perfective (23b), or in the absence of the perfective on the progressive (23c) or when the progressive is lacking on the passive *be* (23d).

(23) a. He could have been being questioned when you came.
 b. He had been being questioned.
 c. He was being questioned.
 d. He was questioned.

Recall from §5.3 that in Chomsky's (1986) *Barriers*, the order of the modal and aspectual auxiliaries is specified in the phrase structure. The modal together with tense and agreement is a constituent of I, and the aspectual auxiliaries and passive *be*[6] are specifiers of the V', i.e. the lexical verb. If I is empty, i.e. there is no modal, the first auxiliary element is moved into I where it receives tense and agreement, and in the absence of auxiliary elements the lexical verb undergoes the relevant movement. This is not a very satisfactory analysis since it is basically the converse of the traditional affix-hopping transformation; instead of movement of an affix we have movement of the verb form.

A more interesting account of the data can be achieved by treating auxiliaries[7] as complement-taking verbs, an analysis originally proposed by Emonds (1976: 209) and subsequently expanded by Pullum and Wilson (1977), Gazdar et al. (1981) (within constituency grammar) and Schachter (1983) and Hudson (1984) (in dependency theory). The criteria used in the determination of the direction of dependency (e.g. co-occurrence restrictions and morphological marking) clearly identify the lexical verb as a dependent of the auxiliary. The same criteria suggest that each of the auxiliary forms on the left in the sequence in (22) are heads relative to the forms on the right. Note, for example, that the form of the perfective *have* depends on the presence of a modal, shown in (24a,b), whereas the presence of *have* does not bear on the modal.

(24) a. Claudia has/had gone to Australia (by the time we arrived).
b. Claudia may/might have/*has gone to Australia.
c. Claudia may/might go to Australia.

Analogous facts hold for all the other combinations of auxiliaries. This being the case, the morphological form of each dependent follows from the subcategorization facts specified in the lexicon. Tense and agreement marking is always on the head, which is a cross-linguistic characteristic of such marking at the level of the predication (Nichols 1986). And the relative ordering of all the elements is attributable to one of the general principles governing many facets of English constituent order, namely 'dependent sisters follow their head'.[8]

Although Dik recognizes the relations of head and dependent, the above dependency-based account of the English verbal complex cannot serve as the basis for the FG treatment of the issue. The reason for this is that in FG dependency is taken to obtain only between lexical expressions, whereas of the auxiliaries in (22), only the modal auxiliary is considered to be a lexical predicate in FG.[9] The aspectual auxiliaries are expressions of primary π operators, grammatical, not lexical, categories. Since they are not heads, they cannot have dependents whose forms they determine by virtue of the FG equivalent of subcategorization.[10] The passive auxiliary, on the other hand, is simply a semantically empty marker of the passive introduced together with the passive participle form of the verb by the expression rules. This is achieved by means of a special contextual operator $<\text{Subj not } A^1>$, as shown in (25), specifying that the appropriate context for the introduction of the relevant forms is subject assignment to a non-first argument A^1.[11]

(25) <Subj not A¹> [pred$_v$] = be$_v$ PaP pred$_v$

In view of the above, Dik (1989: 325) proposes to capture the characteristics of the English verbal complex in terms of the following sequence of μ operators:[12]

(26) { Pres/Past } (Perf) (Prog) <Subj not A¹> [pred$_v$] Inf

Modals are left out of Dik's presentation because of the additional complexities that they introduce. The *Inf* stands for infinitive, which is taken to be an auxiliary operator introduced by a prior expression rule. It is placed disjunctively with the primary tense operators, being treated as the reflex of a [-tense] option. Each of the μ operators in (26) triggers an expression rule such as (25), specifying the corresponding form of the predicate. These rules, with the exception of (25), which I will not repeat, are listed in (27) below.

(27) a. Prog[Pred$_v$] = be$_v$ PrP pred$_v$
      b. Perf[Pred$_v$] = have$_v$ PaP pred$_v$
      c. (i) Pres <1p3 Subj> [pred-$_v$] = pred-s
          (ii) Pres [pred$_v$] = pred
      d. Past[Pred$_v$] = pred-ed
      e. Inf[Pred$_v$] = to pred
      f. PaP[Pred$_v$] = pred-ed
      g. PrP[Pred$_v$] = pred-ing

The rules are applied in 'centrifugal' fashion in accordance with the order of the μ operators specified in (26). The application of the rules is shown in (28).

(28) a. PresPerfProg be$_v$ PaP call$_v$ [by 25]
      b. PresPerf be$_v$ PaP call$_v$ [by 27a]
      c. Pres have$_v$ PaP be$_v$ PrP be$_v$ PaP call$_v$ [by 27b]
      d. Pres have$_v$ Pap be$_v$ PrP be$_v$ call-ed   [by 27f]
      e. Pres have$_v$ PaP be$_v$ be-ing call-ed   [by 27g]
      f. Pres have$_v$ been be-ing call-ed   [by lexical priority]
      g. has been be-ing called   [by lexical priority]

It is obvious that this account of the formal properties of the English verbal complex rests on the ordering of the μ operators and the 'centrifugal' rule application. Dik argues that this ordering, though in the first instance motivated by descriptive convenience, finds support in semantic scope relations, as discussed in the work of Foley and Van Valin (1984), Bybee (1985) and particularly Hengeveld (1989, 1990a) presented in ch. 5. Recall from §5.2.1 that the aspectual progressive operator is a π_1 while the perfect and tense operators are π_2. Thence the relative order of these categories. Dik does not offer any further semantic evidence for the relative sequencing of the perfect and progressive. Schachter (1983: 158), however, does. He points out that the progressive denotes incomplete instantiation of an SoA, while the perfective places it in the relative past and simultaneously signals some current relevance. Given the assumption that the relative order of operators depicts scope relations, the ordering of a perfective before a progressive would entail an incomplete instantiation which is also a prior instantiation, a situation which, as argued by Schachter, simply does not make sense.[13] Turning to the passive auxiliary, Dik suggests that its innermost location may be taken to follow from the fact that subject assignment in FG concerns the presentation of an SoA, and this can be regarded as a matter more central to the nature of the SoA than completion, current relevance or anteriority.[14] This 'centrifugal' ordering of operators and rule application is not an isolated instance, but as we shall see in ch. 8, one of the manifestations of a cross-linguistic principle of order which is taken to reflect the degree of semantic bonding between a dependent and head.

8 Linearization

8.1 INTRODUCTION

The FG approach to order rests on the basic insight stemming from the last three decades of typological word order studies, namely that word order is the product of a host of interrelated and often competing factors that cannot be subsumed under one general principle, but rather must be viewed a reflex of several interacting motivations connected with the nature of human perception and cognition. Dik (1989: 337) refers to this conception of word order as the *multifunctional* theory of constituent order, the main tenets of which he captures in the following points.

- The actual constituent ordering patterns found in a language are the resultant of a number of interacting principles.
- Each of these principles is in itself functionally motivated; it is a 'natural' principle with respect to some parameter of naturalness.
- But two such principles do not necessarily define the same ordering preference. One principle may, for good reasons, prefer the order AB while another may, for equally good reasons, prefer BA.
- Therefore no language can conform to all the ordering principles at the same time or to the same degree.
- The actual 'solution' for constituent ordering in a given language will thus contain an element of compromise, and will to that extent be characterized by a certain amount of 'tension'.
- Shifts in the relative force of the different principles may lead to (sometimes radical) changes in constituent ordering.
- Where such changes relieve tension with respect to one principle, they may create new tension with respect to another.
- There is consequently no optimal, stable solution to the constituent ordering problem.[1]

The cross-linguistic factors underlying the word order patterns found in natural languages are expressed in FG by nine general principles of order which are supplemented by more specific principles reflecting the type of choices that languages tend to make from among the available options. Linear patterns in individual languages that comply with the general principles are not specified independently, but are handled with reference to the word order predictions encapsulated in the body of preferences and tendencies stated for the grammar as a whole. Language-specific aspects of order, on the other hand, are dealt with by a set of placement rules which locate constituents in predetermined, language-specific functional patterns. These functional patterns, in the case of clausal constituents, are based on the language-independent schema in (1), where S, O and V stand for subject, object and verb respectively, and the P positions designate special positions, as discussed in §6.2.

(1) P_2, P_1 (V) S (V) O (V), P_3

An analogous schema is envisaged for the term phrase (and perhaps also for the word), but has not as yet been elaborated.

In this chapter we will first (§8.2–§8.2.2.1) review the general principles of order proposed in FG concentrating on the differences between the FG formulations of familiar issues and those of other approaches, and pointing out the specific FG contributions to the area of word order typology. Of special interest in relation to this second point are Rijkhoff's (1986, 1990) principles of Head-Proximity and Domain Integrity. The second part of the chapter (§8.3–§8.3.1.2) will deal with the FG functional patterns and placement rules. We will be considering the FG claims in regard to the interplay between syntactic and pragmatic functions in the determination of order (§8.3), the status of functional patterns (§8.3.1), the role of the rules placing constituents in P_1 with respect to both inter- and intra-language word order variation (§8.3.1.1) and the functional patterns of English (§8.3.1.2).

8.2 THE UNIVERSAL PRINCIPLES OF ORDER

The relative cross-linguistic homogeneity of word order as compared to the mathematically possible combinations (Hawkins 1983: 3), like many other facets of structure, is attributed to the underlying iconic nature of language as a mediator between the world and our experience of it. The underlying iconic motivation of linearization has been expressed in the form of various principles of which the two most general ones, pertaining to temporal correspondences and semantic grouping relations, have already been discussed in §1.2.1.1, in connection with markedness, and in §5.3 in relation to the similarities in the hierarchical clausal structure proposed by FG and GB. Dik's (1989) versions of these principles are presented below.

(2)   The Principle of Iconic Ordering (PIO)
      Constituents conform to the first general principle of order (GP1) when their ordering in one way or another iconically reflects the semantic content of the expression in which they occur (Dik 1989: 340).

(3)   The Principle of Domain Integrity (PDI)
      Constituents prefer to remain within their proper domain; domains prefer not to be interrupted by constituents from other domains (Dik 1989: 343).

The PIO encompasses not only temporal order, but also generally accepted perceptions of salience and dominance involving the ego, relative authority, and also situational and textual importance connected with topicality (Allan 1987; Siewierska 1988a) and cohesiveness. The notion of *domain* referred to in the PDI denotes: the clause, the term phrase and the adjectival phrase. The PDI underlies the constraint against discontinuous constituents adopted in the form of a requirement (e.g. in GB, LFG, HPSG, RG) or treated as the unmarked case (e.g. WG, Lexicase) in most constituency- and dependency-based structural representations. The most notable departures from this norm come from languages of the Australian continent such as Djaru, Dyirbal, Garawa, Kalkatungu, Ngiyambaa, Walpiri and Walmatjari (Blake 1987), which are renowned for their discontinuous terms (NPs).[2] Discontinuity within terms and adjective phrases features prominently also in colloquial spoken Russian (Gasparov 1978; Keijsper 1985: 132–134), in Polish colloquial speech and literary prose (Siewierska 1984b) and in Latin poetry and prose (Pinkster 1988b: ch. 4). More widespread are instances of discontinuity involving: relative clause and PP extraposition, subject-raising, long-distance dependencies, parenthetical placement and, for those who believe in a VP, frontings of non-subject arguments. Some of these phenomena have already been illustrated, others will be exemplified throughout the chapter. The factors underlying these departures from the norm are typically attributable to pragmatic highlighting.[3]

The other principles characterizing cross-linguistic manifestations of order suggested by Dik may be divided into two groups:[4] those bearing on the relative order of the head and its dependents stemming from Vennemann's (1972) Natural Serialization Principle (see below), and those specifying the ordering among dependents relative to each other. Although this is not a strict dichotomy, it is a convenient one for expository purposes. We will consider the two sets of principles in turn.

8.2.1 Refining the Natural Serialization Principle (NSP)

The NSP advanced by Vennemann is an extension of the typological correlations observed by Greenberg (1963), the origins of which he in turn traces to the dependency tradition and the German typologists such as Lepsius (1880) and Schmidt (1926). The NSP stipulates that languages show a preference for serializing constituents in terms of either the head > dependent schema (VO, centrifugal) or dependent > head (OV, centripetal). Languages exhibiting linearization patterns in complete conformity with the NSP, termed 'consistent', are rare if not non-existent. Therefore the word order predictions incorporated by the NSP have been refined by supplementary principles which seek to specify among the inconsistent orderings the regularities that do obtain.

A number of subregularities of order of a high level of generality have been captured by Hawkins (1983) in the Principle of Cross-Category Harmony (PCCH). The PCCH states that languages display a quantified preference to generalize the order obtaining in one head/dependent category to that of other categories. Departures from this preference in one head/dependent category are in turn likely to induce comparable departures in other head/dependent pairs. Thus, for example, Hawkins notes that the continuum in verb position, verb-initial, verb-medial, verb-final, is reflected in the position of the noun in relation to its modifiers. This is evinced by the fact that VSO languages are more consistently noun-initial than SVO languages, in which the preposing of the subject in relation to the verb is often mirrored by the preposing of the adjective and/or genitive and/or determiner before the noun. Moreover, non-rigidly verb-final SOV languages (SOV languages which allow for the placing of some modifiers to the right of the verb) tend to have some nominal modifiers following the noun, while rigidly verb-final SOV languages generally serialize all their modifiers prenominally.

In FG the NSP is expressed as a preference for either prefield or postfield order where the *prefield* is defined as the area to the left of the head, and the *postfield* the area to the right. The prefield and the postfield are each other's *counterfield*. The principle that captures a relative interpretation of the NSP along the lines of the observations made by Hawkins is:

(4) The Principle of Cross-Domain Harmony (PCDH)
Each language has a certain degree of consistency in either using prefield or postfield ordering across the different ordering domains.

The class of word order facts covered by this principle is not, however, exactly the same as that of Hawkins's PCCH, because of Dik's restrictive interpretation of head and dependent. Recall from §1.3.2 that Dik confines the head/dependent relationship to lexical elements. Therefore operators which include articles, determiners, demonstratives, numerals and auxiliaries fall outside the head/dependent distinction in FG. Also excluded from head or dependent status are elements linking one constituent to another, referred to as *relators* among which are classed adpositions.[5] The two major characteristics of order not covered by the PCDH are the relative ordering of auxiliaries and lexical verbs, and noun and adposition order. The first of these orderings is dealt with by the Principle of Head Proximity, the second by the Relator Principles.

8.2.1.1 Head Proximity

(5) The Principle of Head Proximity (PHP)[6]
Constituent ordering rules conspire to keep the heads of different domains as close together as possible.

The PHP specifies a preference for the head of a phrase and the head of its dependent to be adjacent to each other. As far as the placement of auxiliaries relative to the head verb and its nominal dependents is concerned, the PHP predicts the following orders (lgs = languages):

(6) a. Prefield lgs   N V aux
     b. Postfield lgs   aux V N

Under analyses which consider auxiliary verbs to be heads that take lexical verbs as their dependents, the orders in (6) follow either from the PHP (there are three heads in a row) or from the NSP equivalents; observe that in (6) the dependent lexical verb is placed either to the left (6a) or the right (6b) of the head auxiliary, and the dependent nominal arguments are in turn placed to the left (6a) or right (6b) of their head, the lexical verb. In view of the fact that in FG auxiliaries are operators and not heads, the orders in (6) satisfy the PHP not by virtue of the presence of three successive heads, but by placing the auxiliary in the counterfield and thus avoiding the separation of the dependent nominal argument from its lexical head.

The PHP covers some of the ground of Hawkins's PCCH. For example, it predicts the 'leaking' of some nominal modifiers to the right of their head noun in non-rigid SOV languages to lessen the distance between the verb and the head of a postverbal dependent. This is shown schematically below, where '-' marks the location of modifiers of the noun.

(7) a. Prefield rigid lgs   - - N - -N V
    b. Prefield non-rigid lgs (i)   - - N V - - N
                               (ii) - - N V - N -

Another cross-linguistic characteristic of order which follows from the PHP is the tendency for the adjective to be adjacent to the noun irrespective of whether it occurs in the prefield or the postfield. This is captured by Hawkins (1983: 119–120) in a modified version of Greenberg's (1963) Universal 20:

(8) When any or all of the items (demonstrative, numeral and descriptive adjective) precede the noun, they (i.e. those that do precede) are always found in that order. For those that follow, no predictions are made, though the most frequent order is the mirror-image of the order for preceding modifiers. In no case does the adjective precede the head noun when the demonstrative or numeral follow.

Rijkhoff (1990: 29) suggests that adjectives which do not comply with Universal 20 may not be adjectives, a claim which finds support in the verbal status of adjectives in many African and other languages noted by various linguists. Another point worth noting raised by Rijkhoff is that in the case of head-marking languages (see §7.4.1) placement of verbal arguments at variance with the PHP does not in fact contradict this principle owing to the possibility of attributing such orders to the appositional as opposed to dependency relation between the verbal argument and the verb.

A principle analogous to the PHP, called the Head Adjacency Constraint, is formulated by Frazier (1985: 146) on the basis of a limited-window parsing strategy, which she argues facilitates on-line semantic interpretation. Frazier assumes a two-stage parsing model, in which the first stage has a limited viewing window of five or six adjacent words. She suggests that the separation of the head of a phrase from the head of its dependent leads to the construction of a phrasal package that does not form a coherent semantic unit. An extreme instance of this can be illustrated on the basis of the difficulties inherent in the parsing of a prepositional language with prenominal relative clauses, as shown in (9).

(9) Preposition Relative Clause Head N

Such languages, though extremely rare, do exist; there is one, namely Chinese, among the 326 languages in Hawkins's (1983) extended sample, for instance. Frazier states that given the word order in (9), the first-stage parser will group the preposition and relative clause together, and, if the relative clause consists of more than just a couple of words, will terminate before the head of the relative clause is reached. Since the phrase thus identified does not form a coherent semantic unit, semantic interpretation must wait until subsequent items are received.

Given the well-known correlation between prepositions and VO(X) order and postpositions and OV order (see below), the avoidance of prenominal relative clauses in prepositional VO languages provides support for the PHP in regard to the relative proximity of the V and NP of the prepositional phrase. The relative location of the preposition and head noun, however, is not covered by Head Proximity in FG, but by the Relator Principles. This is just as well because the treatment of adpositions as heads would result in numerous exceptions to the PHP. Note that Frazier's analysis, in addition to predicting the avoidance of the ordering in (9), also predicts the avoidance of postnominal relative clauses in OV languages with postpositions as in (10), which is the mirror-image of (9).

(10) Head Noun Relative Clause Postposition

Yet, as pointed out by Hawkins (1990: 241), in the language sample of Hawkins (1983), 40% of postpositional languages have postnominal relative clauses, and though in many of these languages the relative clause tends to be extraposed to the right of the postposition, in some it need not. The following example from Lakhota, attributed to Lehmann (1984), illustrates the non-extraposed ordering.

Lakhota
(11) xé   wã   Tamalpais éciya-pi   wã   él.
      mountain indef Tamalpais they-called indef   on
      'on the mountain that they called Tampalpais'.

The FG analysis of adpositions as relators rather than heads is independently motivated. Nonetheless, this analysis increases the predictive power of the PHP relative to Frazier's constraint.[7]

8.2.1.2 The relator principles

The class of relators consists of adpositions, case markers (including preclitic and postclitic ones), subordinators and conjunctions. Relators may mark a relation of dependency or coordination. In the former case the relator is taken to form a constituent with the dependent, in the latter it does not enter into a constituency relation with either of the relata. Two principles of order are suggested as affecting constructions with relators, namely:

(12) Relators have their preferred position:
(a) at the periphery of the relatum with which they form one constituent (if they do so);
(b) in between their two relata.

In the case of relators marking a dependency relation, the two relator principles predict a preference for the orders in (13) as opposed to (14).

(13) a. [[dependent] R] ... [head]
b. [head] ... [R [dependent]]

(14) a. [R [dependent]] ... [head]
b. [head] ... [[dependent] R]

For coordinations, the second of the two principles defines the order in (15) as preferred, the orders in (16) as non-preferred.

(15) [relatum] R [relatum]

(16) a. R [relatum] [relatum]
b. [relatum] [relatum] R

The two relator principles provide a means of accounting for various miscellaneous word order phenomena.[8] For example, prefield languages are predicted as showing a preference for postpositions, postfield languages for prepositions, as documented in the typological studies of Greenberg (1963), Vennemann (1972) and Hawkins (1983), among others. Prefield languages are also correctly predicted as exhibiting case suffixes rather than case prefixes.[9] With respect to embedded predications, the relator principles define a tendency to finally mark embedded predications preceding the main clause (prefield order) as in (17) from the Papuan language Tauya, and to mark initially those following the main clause (postfield order) as in (18).

Tauya (MacDonald 1988: 228)
(17) Bramani   mene-e-   na-   ?aisami   tauya-   sa   fofe - e -   ?a.
      Brahman stay-1/2- sub- ablative Tauya-   adessive come -1/2- ind
      'I came to Tauya from Brahman.' (Lit. 'From staying in Brahman I came to Tauya.')

Dutch
(18) Ik   was   te   laat   omdat   ik   me   verslapen   had.
      I   was   too   late   because   I   me   overslept   had
      'I was late because I overslept.'

Subordinating conjunctions may, however, also occur after the first word of a clause, as in the following example.

Polish
(19) Marta   wróciła   z   Australii, Ewa, natomiast, została   z   ojcem.
      Martha   returned from   Australia   Eve   whereas   remained with   father
      'Martha returned from Australia, whereas Eve remained (there) with her father.'

The same predictions hold for the location of a relative marker in prenominal and postnominal relative clauses (see Keenan and Comrie 1979) and for prenominal and postnominal genitive constructions (Limburg 1985). The predicted preferred orders in the case of genitives are exemplified below (Givón 1984: 200, 201).

Japanese   Hebrew
(20) a. watashi - no   hon -o   b.   ha-séfer shel - Yosef
         I   -gen book -obj   the-book of   - Joseph

As regards conjunctions, the occurrence of conjunctions between, rather than at the periphery of, the relata in accordance with the second of the relator principles is the norm in most languages. Nevertheless, more detailed rules of order are necessary to specify the actual location of a conjunction, for instance in English before a final conjunct. The non-preferred location of a relator in coordinations, i.e. at the periphery, occurs, for example, in Latin with the conjunction -*que* which is suffixed to the second of two conjoined terms, and in Quechua, in which the coordinator is suffixed to the first word of the second conjunct.

Although various violations of the relator principles are encountered in languages, the overall validity of the ordering predictions that they make is confirmed by the type of strategies languages employ to counter the apparent violations. One of the examples that Dik (1983c: 289) gives is the change from prepositional to postpositional marking or the allowance of preposition stranding in questioning prepositional constituents in the case of languages that place question words in P_1, a situation found in Dutch, for instance. Another repair mechanism in compliance with the relator principles is the loss of a relator in preposed subordinate clauses as in (21b).

(21) a. If you scream, you'll be sorry.
b. Scream and you'll be sorry.

The converse strategy is to add a relator on the main clause. Dik states that this frequently happens in Dutch; (22a) with such a relator is more common than (22b).

Dutch
(22) a. Als hij geld heeft, dan kan de jongen boeken kopen.
if he money has then can the boy books buy
'If he has the money, the boy can buy books.'

b. Als hij geld heeft, kan de jongen boeken kopen.
'If he has the money, the boy can buy books.'

8.2.2 Relative ordering of modifiers

The first of the principles governing the order among modifiers rather than that of modifiers relative to the head is:

(23) The Principle of Linear Ordering (PLO)
Constituents conform to (PLO) when their linear order is fixed, no matter which position they take relative to the head (Dik 1989: 341).

The PLO predicts the occurrence of linearization patterns as in (24).

(24) xyzH, xyHz, xHzy, Hxyz

The fixed orders in question may be determined by iconicity as reflected in perceptions of dominance and salience, such as those captured by Allan (1987) in his dominant descriptor hierarchies which predict a preference for orders such as:

positive > negative   hot > cold
higher > lower   vertical > horizontal
in > out   more vivid > less vivid
bigger > smaller   host > adjunct

Another type of fixed ordering is covered by:

(25) The Principle of Centripetal Orientation (PCO)
Constituents conform to PCO when their ordering is determined by their relative distance from the head, which may lead to 'mirror-image' ordering round the head (Dik 1989: 342).

The underlying iconic motivation for centripetal ordering is seen to lie in the semantic bonding to the head and the scope relations among the modifiers. Recall from §2.2.2, ch. 5 and §7.5 that this type of ordering is characteristic of the operator categories. It also provides an alternative explanation to the PHP for the sequencing of the modifiers of the noun expressed in Greenberg's Universal 20 stated in (8), as well as for the order among different type of adjectives or homosemantic adverbials. For example, identifying adjectives tend to be adjacent to the head, and the identifying value of descriptive ones decreases as we move away from the head. As shown in (26), in Polish, which permits adjectives on both sides of the head, an identifying or the most-identifying adjective is placed closest to the head noun.

Polish
(26) a. moja ulubiona krótka   czarna jedwabna (koktajlowa)
         my   favourite short   black silk   cocktail
         sukienka (koktajlowa)
         dress
    b.   moja ulubiona krótka czarna (jedwabna) sukienka (jedwabna)
    c.   moja ulubiona krótka (czarna) sukienka (czarna)
    d.   moja ulubiona (krótka) sukienka (krótka)
    e.   moja (ulubiona) sukienka (ulubiona)

The next principle is the cornerstone of all accounts of linearization based on functional notions.

(27) The Principle of Functional Stability (PFS)
Constituents with the same functional specification are preferably placed in the same position (Dik 1989: 343).

This principle provides the underlying motivation for the significance attributed to the characteristic locations of the subject and object. As regards the relative order of the subject and object, FG makes the claim that the subject always precedes the object. This is a consequence of the 'perspectival' character of the subject and object functions in FG. The argument is that since the subject imposes a primary, and the object a secondary, perspective on the SoA in the predication, one would not expect a language systematically to locate the constituent reflecting the secondary vantage point prior to the primary one.

In view of the above, Dik questions the existence of subject and/or object assignment in any language with basic object-before-subject order. And indeed most of the languages which are claimed to display such order under the FG analysis emerge as lacking either subject or object assignment. Thus the twelve languages of the Amazon area listed in Derbyshire and Pullum (1981) and Derbyshire (1986), in which the object precedes the subject (e.g. Apalaí, Apurina, Hixkaryana, Makushi, Panare and Urubu), have no active–passive opposition which, as discussed in §4.3, is the FG diagnostic for subject assignment. There is a productive passive, however, in the Malayo-Polynesian languages Toba-Batak, Gilbertese and Malagasy, in Ojibwa and in the Mayan languages Quiche, Cakchiquel, Tzeltal and Tzotzil. Most of these languages in turn may be seen to lack object assignment, an analysis which entails dealing with the direct object-like properties of Recipients and Goals in ditransitive clauses by means of predicate formation or alternatively attributing them to the A^2 rather than A^3 status of the relevant terms, along the lines sketched in §4.4.1.2. For VOS languages (e.g. Chol, Huastec, Kekchi, Mopan, Pocoman) which cannot be disposed of via lack of subject and/or object assignment, Dik (1980: 144) suggests either a synchronic or a diachronic analysis in terms of a *Theme, Predication, Tail* pattern, the would-be subject being interpreted as a tail.

Given the above considerations, the traditional classification of languages in terms of the location of the subject and object relative to the verb is not always reflected in the FG functional patterns. We will see in §8.3 that the order of major sentence constituents in some languages that lack subject and object assignment can be handled in terms of pragmatic functions and special positions. Dik (1989: 358–359) hypothesizes that one of the dominant principles affecting linearization in other subjectless and objectless languages may well be the PCO stated in (25), with an A^2 forming a closer bond with the verb than the A^1.

The last of the general principles of order covers the correlation between pragmatic functions and special positions discussed in ch. 6.

(28) The Principle of Pragmatic Highlighting (PPH)
Constituents with special pragmatic functionality (New Topic, Completive Focus, Contrastive Focus) are preferably placed in 'special positions', including, at least, the clause-initial position.

More about these special positions, especially the initial P_1 position, will be said in §8.3.1 and §8.3.1.1.

In addition to the general principles of order presented above FG posits a number of more specific principles, the most important of which concern the influence on linearization of matters of length and internal syntactic complexity; this is expressed by means of a Language–Independent Preferred Order of Constituents schema referred to as LIPOC.

8.2.2.1 LIPOC

The current[10] (Dik 1989: 351) formulation of LIPOC is:

(29) Other things being equal, constituents prefer to be placed in an order of increasing complexity, where the complexity of constituents is defined as follows:

(i) clitic < pronoun < noun phrase < adpositional phrase < subordinate clause;
(ii) for any category X: X < X co X;
(iii) for any categories X and Y: X < X [sub Y]

The specification under (ii) shows the effect of conjoining constituents of the same category, and that in (iii), the internal complexity of constituents.

LIPOC is seen to be subordinate to the more general principles of order discussed above, in particular to the PPH in (28), while simultaneously interacting with pragmatic determinants of order. Recall from the discussion of identifiability in §6.3.1 and §6.3.3.1 that the length and complexity of an element may be seen to co-vary inversely with the ease with which its referent can be identified. Thus the preference for linearizing shorter and less complex material before longer and more structurally elaborate language data is in part a consequence of the overlap between identifiability and topicality.

There is ample evidence for LIPOC. The following are just a few cases in point:

(a) the tendency for clitics to occur in second position in the utterance, known as Wackernagel's Law;
(b) the earlier placement of pronominal as compared to nominal subjects or objects in languages such as Bimoba, Cairene Arabic, German, Grebo, Ila, Karen, Twi or Uzbek, as in the Uzbek (30b), where a pronominal patient as opposed to a nominal one (30a) obligatorily precedes a Recipient/Beneficiary:

Uzbek (Sedlak 1975: 133)
(30) a. Men un-ga nlma-ni berman.
       I   him-dat apple-acc I'll give
       'I'll give him the apple.'

   b. Men u- ni sen-ga yub raman.
      I   it-acc you-dat I'll send
      'I'll send it to you.'

(c) the preference for final placement of sentential NPs observed in, for example, Blackfoot, Tuscarora, Kinyarwanda, Malagasy, Sherpa, Persian, Latin and English (see Dryer 1980 for comprehensive discussion of the phenomenon) and illustrated on the basis of Yaqui (31), a language in which nominal subjects occur clause-initially, and nominal objects preverbally, but sentential ones obligatorily in final position:

Yaqui
(31) a. Aapo hunen hia ke hu hamut tutu?uli.
he thus say Comp this woman pretty
'He says this woman is pretty.'

b. Tuisi tu?i hu hamut bwika-kai.
very good this woman sing
'It is very good that this woman sings.'

(d) the phenomena of heavy NP shift and extraposition from NP (see e.g. Mallinson and Blake 1981: 324) shown in (32) and (33) respectively.

(32) a. Fred sent to his client several brochures with all the accommodation details.
b. We elected president the most outspoken girl in our class.

(33) a. I met a man last night who reminded me of you.
b. Another book has just appeared about word order.

In regard to the ordering of nominal modifiers, Hawkins (1983: 75, 86) has made several observations as to the order of noun modifier pairs (rather than the sequencing of modifiers relative to each other) that reflect the preference for linearizing shorter constituents earlier in the utterance than longer ones.[11] His observations concern the patterns of preposing a modifier before the noun in prepositional languages, and of postposing a modifier after the noun in postpositional languages. In the case of prepositional languages, the first to be preposed is the demonstrative or numeral; then both; next comes the adjective; followed by the genitive; and finally the relative clause. This is captured in the Prepositional Noun Modifier Hierarchy (PrNMH):

(34) Prep ⊃ ((NDem v NNum ⊃ NA) & (NA ⊃ NG) & (NG ⊃ NRel))

Strictly speaking the PrNMH (as well as the PoNMH given directly below) represents a collapsing of a series of implicational universals, but the above pattern of modifier preposing can be easily deduced from it. In postpositional languages the first modifier to be postposed is the adjective; then the relative clause; then the demonstrative or numeral; and finally the genitive. The order of modifier postposing is represented in the Postpositional Noun Modifier Hierarchy (PoNMH):

(35) Post ⊃ ((AN v RelN ⊃ DemN & NumN) & (DemN v NumN ⊃ GN))

Demonstratives and numerals are typically morphologically shorter than adjectives; single adjectives tend to be shorter than genitives (the latter consisting of a noun with a genitive marker or a prepositional phrase); which in turn are shorter than relative clauses.

Given the progressive increase in length and complexity from the demonstrative to the relative clause, the PrNMH is fully consistent with the preference for placing shorter elements before longer ones. However, contrary to expectations, the PoNMH is not the mirror-image of the PrNMH. Relative clauses are the second to be postposed, not the first, and the postposing of demonstratives and numerals does not come last. Nonetheless, the principle of placing shorter and less complex constituents before longer and more structurally complex ones is partially adhered to; relative clauses tend to be postposed earlier than demonstratives or numerals.

The last set of manifestations of the short–long preference that we will be considering here involves the prehead vs posthead placement of alternative forms of a modifier correlating with reduced vs increased length and complexity. Thus behave relative clauses in, for example, Finnish, German and Tagalog (see Keenan and Comrie 1977, 1979), the inflectional and prepositional genitives in several Germanic languages as shown in (36), and simple (37a) as opposed to complement-taking (37b) adjectives in English:

(36) a. the boy's mother
      b. the mother of the boy who lives next door

(37) a. a stubborn man
      b. a man unable to admit defeat.

8.3 THE FG RULES OF ORDER

Given that linear order is viewed as a matter of expression rather than an underlying property of sentences in FG, the differences in word order flexibility displayed by languages are not elevated to the status of a typological parameter comparable to the GB bifurcation into configurational and non-configurational languages. FG does, however, posit a 'certain degree of trade off' (Dik 1989: 334) between form and order, heavy reliance on coding via the form of constituents being associated with fewer ordering restrictions and vice versa.

One of the ways that this trade-off is seen to be manifest is in the effect of syntactic as compared to pragmatic functions on ordering relations. Languages which lack syntactic function assignment (subject and/or object) are predicted to exhibit word order patterns more sensitive to pragmatic functions than those with subjects and objects. This follows in part from the form of functional patterns all of which are assumed to be based on the schema in (1), which for convenience I repeat below.

(38) P_2, P_1 (V) S (V) O (V), P_3

Observe that since subjects and objects are allocated concrete positions in the functional patterns, alternative subject or object assignment will always entail placing the non-agent or non-patient in subject or object positions. Alternative subject and object assignment is thus a means of varying the order of terms that bear specific semantic functions. Consequently, if a language can induce variations in order via subject and object assignment, it should be less likely to utilize special positions for pragmatic functions on a regular basis, because this would in a way duplicate the order-changing effect of subject and object assignment. Conversely, if a language lacks subject or object assignment, and especially both, the positioning of agents, patients, recipients, etc. will not be affected by syntactic functions. This is likely to lead to a greater reliance on special positions and to the development of additional special positions.

Considerable evidence can be adduced for the postulated interplay between syntactic and pragmatic functions in determining order. Thus most of the languages classified as having syntactically free main constituent order, for one reason or another qualify in FG as lacking at least object assignment. For instance, there is no subject or object assignment in Basque, Finnish or Hungarian, and the languages of the Australian continent such as Walpiri, Dyirbal, Yidin^y and Gunwinggu; and the following languages may be taken to lack object assignment: the Slavic languages, the Mayan languages (Cakchiquel and Quiche), Huichol, Halkomelem, Quechua, Eskimo and perhaps Latin.

The significance of the correlation between lack of syntactic function assignment and relative freedom of constituent order for the overall approach to linearization in FG is far from clear. No explicit claim is made in regard to the necessarily conditioning effect of syntactic functions on linearization in languages which have such functions. On the other hand, the nature of functional patterns leads one to expect any language that displays syntactic function assignment to be provided with a functional pattern or patterns in which the relevant syntactic functions are allocated concrete slots. The question of whether or not to incorporate syntactic function positions into functional patterns is of considerable importance in regard to the determination of appropriate functional patterns for variable word order languages which have syntactic function assignment, i.e. subject assignment, such as Latin or the Slavic languages.

The nature of the problem can be outlined on the basis of Polish. The location of the subject in Polish appears to be sensitive to the same pragmatic constraints as those affecting other constituents. Nevertheless, an evident SVX[12] preference can be discerned, which is brought to light by contrasting clauses with a preverbal and a postverbal active (given) subject in (39a,b) with those displaying analogous positioning of a given non-subject in (40a,b).

Polish
(39) [Język potoczny w zrozumieniu Ajdukiewicza, niekoniecznie oznacza język mowy codziennej.
'By colloquial language Ajdukiewicz did not necessarily mean colloquial speech.']

    a. Język potoczny *Ajdukiewicz* rozumiał... jako język
       language:acc colloquial:acc Ajdukiewicz understood as language
       normalnie używany dla formułowania określonych zagadnień.
       normally used for formulating specific issues

    b. Język potoczny rozumiał Ajdukiewicz (...) jalo język normalnie używany do formułowania określonych zagadnień.
       'Ajdukiewicz identified colloquial language with the language used in the formulation of specific issues' (Woleński 1986: 63).

(40) [Zasadniczym celem misji Cyrla i Metodego było przygotowanie Morawskiej misji kościelnej (...) ale nie stronili oni i od akcji szerzenia chrześcijaństwa wśród pogan.
'The principal aim of Cyril and Methodius' mission was to prepare the Moravian Church organization, but they did not try to avoid spreading Christianity among the pagans.]

    a. Z rąk Metodego przyjął chrzest ok. r. 884 kśiąże
       from hands Methodius accepted Christianity about y. 884 prince
       czeski Borzywój.
       Czech Borzywoj

b. Z rąk Metodego chrzest przyjął ok. r. 884 książe Czeski Borzywój.
'Around the year 884, Methodius baptized the Czech prince Borzywoj.'
(Lit. 'From the hands of Methodius the Czech prince Borzywoj accepted Christianity).'

Note that in both pairs of clauses constituents other than the ones in question are the initial topics of the respective clauses. Whereas in the case of the subject *Ajdukiewicz* the postverbal placement in (39b) is clearly perceived to be marked (see note 14), no comparable difference in markedness accompanies the postverbal placement of the given object or Goal in (40a). In fact the opposite is true; *chrzest* in preverbal position, as in (40b), is considered to be marked relative to its postverbal location.

The SVX preference can be viewed as either syntactic or pragmatic. In the former case, the preverbal positioning of the subject and postverbal positioning of non-subjects must be specified as such in the functional pattern for Polish. Since, as mentioned in §6.2, written Polish has an additional special final position for focus, the relevant functional pattern would be P_1 SVX P_ϕ, where P_ϕ is the focus position. The immediate postverbal position of subjects could then be handled by a separate functional pattern identified as deriving marked orders,[13] P_1 VSX P_ϕ.

A pragmatic interpretation of the SVX preference entails equating preverbal placement with topicality, postverbal placement as neutral in regard to pragmatic functions. The relevant functional pattern would thus be P_1 VX P_ϕ, with P_1 specified as being a topic position (see §8.3.1). The preference for preverbal subjects would then be seen as a consequence of a strong correlation between subjecthood and topicality. Assuming such an analysis, the marked nature of (39b) with a postverbal subject could be seen to follow from the failure to assign the topic function to a given subject, or alternatively from not meeting the preference for initial placement of the topic. In either instance, there would be no need to specify a subject position in the functional pattern, as the location of subjects and non-subjects alike is treated as a matter of pragmatic, not syntactic, status. Under this analysis the different perception of the markedness value of preverbal and postverbal non-subjects would be seen as a reflection of a difference in susceptibility to the topic function of non-subjects as compared to subjects rather than as a direct matter of order.

Both of these syntactic and pragmatic analyses can be accommodated within the FG rules of order. The pragmatic solution is more elegant in that it does not entail the recognition of more than one functional pattern, permits a positional identification of the P_1 position (see

§8.3.1.1), and requires a simpler set of placement rules. However, it provides a less satisfactory account of the preference for SVX order and raises the question of the number of items in P_1 (see §8.3.1.1) and the ordering preferences among these items. Moreover, it counters our expectations regarding the role of the subject function in determining order. In the absence of a clear theoretical claim as to the necessity of syntactic function positions in functional patterns, the choice of analysis must be decided on language-internal grounds. In the case of Polish a more detailed examination of the word order facts is needed before such a decision is reached. For Latin, the pragmatic solution appears to be favoured (De Jong 1986). In fact De Jong argues that the most appropriate treatment of Latin word order is by means of a set of relative, rather than absolute, positioning rules. We will resume this issue briefly in §8.3.1.2 after reviewing the overall scheme for handling constituent order in FG.

8.3.1 Functional patterns and placement rules

Since FG allows for a language to have more than one functional pattern, the ordering relations expressed in functional patterns do not represent a basic order in the sense of underlying or dominant order. The ordering of constituents in the functional patterns may be described as basic only so far as it delimits the range of significant clausal locations (special P positions) and a preferential syntactic order for syntactic functions relative to the verb. Note that semantic functions do not feature in the general functional pattern schema in (1)/(38). The assumption is that semantic functions and syntactic functions are in complementary distribution as far as the determination of order is concerned. Therefore a functional pattern will make reference to either the subject and object functions or the semantic functions of Agent, Goal, etc., but not to both. Another possibility is for specifying order in terms of the argument positions A^1, A^2, A^3.

There is no upper limit on the number of functional patterns that may be posited for a given language. This does not mean, however, that functional patterns can be multiplied at will just to meet some ordering characteristic or another. Dik (1978: 184) states that the existence of more than one functional pattern 'is not to be regarded as some sort of erratic idiosyncrasy, but as a powerful means of distinguishing clausal types'. FG practice reveals that the phrase 'clausal types' is to be interpreted rather liberally and not confined to statements, questions, imperatives, negatives, main and subordinate clauses and the like. One can presume that given the functional nature of the theory the 'non-erratic' and 'non-idiosyncratic' factors that may lead to the recognition of additional functional patterns will include considerations of text type, register and style.

That there may be marked differences in order along these dimensions has been amply documented in the literature. Some of the observed differences can be handled in FG by assigning a different weighting to various placement rules; for example, to the R2 rule, which will be discussed in §8.3.1.1. A separate functional pattern will be required to cover, for example, the SVOX as compared to SOXV preference claimed to underlie textual and stylistic variation in Russian. Keijsper (1985: 127), on the basis of her own investigations and the work of Soviet linguists such as Sirotinina (1961: 130, 1965: 74), suggests that SVO with the sentence focus falling on the last word is favoured in the formal written language and upper sociolects, while SOV order with the focus falling earlier in the utterance is dominant in casual, unplanned speech. One piece of evidence which may be adduced in support of this claim is Sirotinina's observation of the radical increase in the use of the OV pattern in the language of a single individual, from 10% in written scientific articles, to 29% in prepared lectures and 63% in spontaneous, informal speech. Another potential case in point is the frequent use of VS rather than SV order with highly active (given) nominal and pronominal subjects in Polish, and also Czech[14] and Russian, a phenomenon characteristic of expository and journalistic texts.[15] An instance of such postposing with a nominal subject was presented in (39b). In connection with our discussion in §8.3, the fact that the postverbal placement of the subject in instances such as (39b) is, although marked, basically a genre-conditioned option, may be interpreted as an argument for recognizing explicit subject positions both unmarked (preverbal) and marked (immediately postverbal) in the functional patterns for Polish.

The allocation of constituents to the designated positions in the functional patterns is achieved by a set of placement rules, such as the following.

(41) P_1 constituent ----> P_1
      Topic/Focus   ----> P_1
      Subject   ----> S
      Verb   ----> V
      Object   ----> O
      X   ----> X

The placement rules are strictly ordered and subject to this condition: once a position is occupied it cannot then be filled by another constituent of a different syntactic category.

The most important of the placement rules are those that position constituents in P_1 and other special positions, for these are the rules which specify the type of word order variations manifest in a given language. Let us therefore consider more closely the role of P_1, which is designated as a special position in all languages (see §6.2).

8.3.1.1 The P_1 position

Dik (1978: 178) describes the general pattern for the use of P_1 as follows:

(i) there are designated categories of constituents, the members of which must go to P_1;
(ii) if P_1 is not occupied by any of the special constituents meant under (i), then P_1 may be used for positioning constituents with the pragmatic function Topic or Focus.

The assumption is that P_1 may be filled only by a single constituent. Three placement rules, referred to by Dik (1980: 21) as R-rules,[16] are proposed for positioning constituents in the special P_1 position:

(42)   (R_1) P_1-constituent ---> P_1
        (R_2)   GivTopic, SubTop, Focus ---> P_1
        (R_3)   X ---> P_1

These rules, like other placement rules, are strictly ordered; so R_2 applies only if R_1 has not applied, and R_3 applies only if there is no application of R_2. The P_1-constituents placed in P_1 by R_1 include question words, subordinators, complementizers[17] and relative pronouns. R_3 is meant to account for cases not covered by R_1 or R_2 such as the initial placement of some satellite constituents or dummy elements like the English *it* or non-deictic *there* (but see §8.3.1.2). R_1 in the case of complementizers and subordinators is obligatory. And so is R_3 in strict verb-second languages, though not in other languages. R_2 is optional by virtue of the fact that the Topic and Focus functions, though closely aligned with clausal locations (P_1 or some other P-position), are not defined positionally in FG. Inherent in the optionality of R_2 is the claim that the Topic or the Focus, if not placed in P_1 (or some other special position) will occur in any location consistent with its grammatical (or semantic) relation, or its categorial status as represented in LIPOC (see §8.2.2.1).

It is important to note that R_2 makes no predictions in regard to the preference for initial placement of the Topic as opposed to the Focus. In our discussion of pragmatic functions in ch. 6 we saw that both topics and foci may be initial, though the general assumption is that the positioning of highly active, easily identifiable referents (prime candidates for GivTop) before inactive or unidentifiable ones (prime candidates for Focus) is the linguistic norm. The alleged cross-linguistic preference for topic > comment order has been questioned by Givón (1983a, 1988) and his associates, who argue that the major principle governing the pragmatics of word order is *Task Urgency*, which reads: 'A communicative task is more urgent when the information to be communicated is either less predictable or more important' (Givón 1988: 275).

The initial placement of the topic is claimed to be the most urgent task only if it represents new rather than given information, given topics being seen to favour placement further to the right – not to the left as is typically assumed to be the case – giving way to the presentation of what is thus more important, focal material. The languages cited by Givón that display linearization patterns reflecting the principle of Task Urgency include: Ute (Givón 1983c), Colloquial Mexican and Chilean Spanish (Bentivoglio 1983), Early Biblical Hebrew (Fox 1983), Klamath and Papago (Givón 1988). To this group may also belong the object-first languages mentioned in connection with obligatory subject-before-object order in §8.2.2, such as the Carib languages, the Mayan languages or Gilbertese and Malagasy. The postposing of highly active subjects in Czech, Polish and Russian illustrated earlier in (39b) may be viewed as a manifestation of the same phenomenon too.[18] Yet another language claimed to display the postposing of given topics is Latin (De Jong 1986).

On the whole, the tendency to place new before given information appears to be more characteristic of the spoken than of the written language, which could be regarded as a reflection of speaker orientation as opposed to addressee orientation (see §1.2.1.1) of speech. Some support for a crucial information-first strategy in speech as opposed to writing comes from the fact that placing the comment first appears to be the dominant strategy of the speech of young children (Bates and MacWhinney 1979: 190), who have no familiarity with the written mode of language. However, it would be premature to posit a general preference for > before given order in speech, since many languages, including colloquial spoken English (Chafe 1987), quite evidently exhibit a high instance of given > new order. Interestingly enough, whereas topic preposing is strongly associated with the initial position, topic postposing tends to involve postverbal placement, but not a concrete sentential location, say clause-final, the few subject-final languages being the major exception. Therefore, to return to our R_2 rule, many instances of topic postposing could be seen to follow from the non-application of the Topic part of R_2.

Another significant feature of R_2 is that it may be weighted differently in different languages. This assumption allows FG to use the varying strength of R_2 to account for cross-linguistic differences in the likelihood and ease of fronting phenomena. In fact a very strong R_2 is assumed to be responsible for SVO order in all the living Germanic languages except English. Dik analyses these languages as having a P_1 $V_f SOXV_i$ main clause functional pattern rather than a P_1 $SV_f OXV_i$ one with a strong tendency for the subject to go to P_1. A basic P_1 VSOX functional pattern is also posited by Lascaratou (1989) for Modern Greek. The diagnostic for a functional pattern with a postverbal, as opposed to a preverbal, subject proposed by Dik (1980: 70) is whether the subject remains preverbal if another constituent is positioned preverbally; if it does not then the language can be interpreted as P_1 VS...; if the subject continues to occupy preverbal position then the language qualifies as P_1 SV.... Note that some version of R_2 will also be responsible for SVO order in a language such as Polish if it is analysed in terms of a P_1 VX $P_\emptyset$ functional pattern.

In English, in contrast to the other Germanic languages, R_2 is claimed to be a weak rule, deriving marked orders such as OSV or VSO where P_1 is occupied by a non-subject. Initial subjects are therefore interpreted as occurring not in P_1, but in their pattern position. Observe that under the proposed analysis the P_1 position will also remain unfilled in P_1 VSO languages when none of the R-rules applies. Whether or not the subject in subject-first languages or verb in verb-first ones is or is not in P_1 is irrelevant as far as the actual ordering of constituents is concerned. However, the two analyses have different implications. If an initial subject is not in P_1, then its location is a consequence of a syntactic preference. Alternatively, if SVO order is the product of placement of the subject in P_1 via R_2, as is claimed to be the case in Dutch or German, then this positioning is pragmatically determined. Therefore the initial location of subjects is predicted as being a manifestation of two different phenomena. This analysis also leads us to expect differences in the pragmatic conditions underlying the occurrence of initial subjects and non-subjects in P_1 SVO or SOV languages.

It was suggested in §8.3.1 that, depending on text type, the strength of R_2 may differ within a language. Thus in English operational and procedural texts, for example, adverbials, including those functioning as arguments, are regularly positioned initially (Enkvist 1981), e.g.

(43) a. In a large saucepan place sugar, lemon juice and lemon rind.
      b. Into a big enamel dish put 1½ cups of heated canned tomatoes.

Therefore in such texts R_2 will receive a different weighting from that in other text types. In the case of the topic-first vs focus-first strategies, which may characterize the written as opposed to the spoken forms of some languages (interacting also with text type, see note 15), the Topic and Focus parts of R_2 could be assigned different weightings. In colloquial Spoken French, as compared to the standard written language, it is not the strength of the R_2 rule that varies, but its scope. According to Lambrecht (1987: 222–223), in the spoken language only the focus part of the rule holds, topics invariably favouring placement in either P_2 or P_3.

Given that an initial constituent may be in P_1 or in its pattern position, initial location is not a sufficient criterion for identifying P_1. The determination of whether or not a constituent is in P_1 is particularly problematic in the case of variable word order languages which appear to allow multiple placement in P_1. Some of the considerations involved are similar to those discussed in transformational theory in relation to placement in a superordinate sentence S', i.e. in C (see §5.3). Note that the same range of constituents are considered to be in P_1 as in C (wh-words, complementizers, subordinators, Topic and Focus). And just as in GB where the occurrence of three or even four successive wh-words at the beginning of the clause (44) is considered to be an argument for multiple filling of C, so in FG this phenomenon is suggestive of multiple placement in P_1.

Polish
(44) Kto   kogo   komu   polecił?
     who   whom   to whom   recommended
     'Who recommended whom to whom?'

Dik's original restriction against more than one constituent in P_1 precludes deriving orders reflecting all the various combinations of the verb and its arguments and satellites from a single functional pattern based on the schema in (38). For example, from a P_1 SVO functional pattern we can derive SVO, OSV and VSO orders, but not VOS, OVS or SOV. This being so, the FG account of linearization in variable word order languages requires that such languages be viewed as exhibiting at least two of the following characteristics:

(a) more than one functional pattern;
(b) special positions other than P_1;
(c) multiple placement in P_1 or in another special position.

Analyses of variable word order in terms of several functional patterns are subject to the same criticism of arbitrariness that is levelled at analogous additions of PS rules. Therefore, such a solution, unless clearly justified, must be seen as a last resort. Special positions other than P_1 may be discerned in a number of languages, for instance Hungarian, Serbo-Croatian, Aghem, written Czech, Polish and Russian.[19] To avoid undergeneration, the recognition of additional special positions must be coupled either with the existence of several functional patterns or with multiple placement in at least one special position.

The problem of determining whether constituents are or are not in P_1 concerns languages lacking a clearly demarcated P_1 position. Easily identifiable P_1 positions are those marked not simply linearly but positionally, for example as immediately preverbal, or preceding a clitic position, or alternatively prosodically. The prosodic marking can be illustrated on the basis of Hungarian, for which De Groot (1981) and Kiss (1981), the latter within a GB, not an FG, framework, suggest a Theme, P_1 $P_\emptyset$ V X, Tail functional pattern, where P_1 designates the Topic and $P_\emptyset$ the focus position. $P_\emptyset$ is associated with sentential stress and an accompanying high fall; P_1 is the prestress part of the sentence. Stress on the verb is less prominent than on preverbal stressed constituents, which is interpreted as suggestive of the fact that a stressed verb is not in $P_\emptyset$. This means that when the verb carries the sentence stress, the $P_\emptyset$ position is viewed as empty. $P_\emptyset$ may be occupied by only a single constituent, while P_1 is open to several constituents.

By contrast, in a language like Latin, with its preference for SOV order, P_1 cannot be identified as simply preverbal or as the prestress part of the clause. The same applies to written Czech, Polish and Russian, if these languages are analysed in terms of a P_1 SVX $P_\emptyset$ functional pattern; due to the intervening SVX sequence, presence in P_1 cannot be simply equated with lack of stress, or with immediate preverbal location. Under a P_1 VX $P_\emptyset$ analysis, on the other hand, P_1 can be identified as being simply preverbal, $P_\emptyset$ by tonic stress. Assuming such an analysis, the verb, as in Hungarian, would have to be treated as unmovable, i.e. tonic stress on the verb not entailing placement in $P_\emptyset$.

8.3.1.2 *The functional patterns of English*

For English Dik (1978: 184–187, 1980: 220) posits the three functional patterns in (45), (46) and (47):

(45) P_1 S V_f V_i O X

(46) P_1 V_f S V_i O X

(47) P_1 V_f V_i S X.

The functional pattern in (45) is suggested for main and subordinate declarative clauses. The functional pattern in (46) covers Q-word questions and inversions found with initial negative elements (48) or conditionals with *had, were* and *should* (49).

(48) a. Never have I had to borrow money from the bank.
     b. Only a couple could we find.

(49) a. Had I known you were coming ...
     b. Were he to have done it ...

The order in (47) is posited specifically for existential and presentative constructions, e.g.:

(50) a. There have been a lot of people killed.
     b. Enclosed will be a coupon, good for $25.

Recall from §6.3.2 that Hannay (1985a) posits a special presentative pragmatic function for English which Dik (1989) relabels NewTop. Part of the motivation for recognizing this special pragmatic function comes from matters of linearization. Although the third of the functional patterns posited for English (47) is intended for existential and presentative constructions, both Dik (1978: 187) and Hannay (1985a: 47) point out that some presentative constructions do not comply with the proposed schema. In (51), as compared to (50a), for example, *there* is not in P_1, but rather in what corresponds to the subject position of the declarative pattern.

(51) a. Yesterday there was an accident.
     b. At dusk there arrived three horsemen.

Similar facts hold in the case of *that*-clause extraposition, as in (52b).

(52) a. That Jane is so timid worries me greatly.
     b. It worries me greatly that Jane is so timid.

As evidence for the fact that *it* in (52b) is in the pattern position of the subject and not in P_1 Dik (1980: 218) offers its ability to undergo inversion in questions, e.g.

(53) Whom does it worry greatly that Jane is so timid?

Yet another structure which appears to display the same feature discussed by Dik is the *it*-cleft, as in (54a).

(54) a. It is you whom she loves.

Again the question test (54b) identifies *it* as being in the pattern position of the subject.

(54) b. How could it be you whom she loves?

Since in all three constructions the dummy elements are placed in subject position rather than in P_1, the relevant linearization patterns cannot be derived from a basic $P_1 \, V_f \, V_i \, S \, X$ functional pattern. Nor can they be derived from the declarative pattern in (46) in view of the fact that the postposed terms in the presentative and extraposed structures are considered to be subjects in FG. In order to ensure the derivation of all the relevant word order patterns, Hannay (1985a:177) suggests collapsing the three functional patterns in (45), (46) and (47) into the one in (55), where S_1, S_2 and S_3 are three potential subject positions:

(55) $P_1 \, (S_1) \, V_f \, (S_2) \, V_i \, O \, (S_3) \, X$

The recognition of a functional pattern in which the subject follows the object, which is the case in (55) as far as the location of the S_3 is concerned, runs counter to the FG claims concerning the primacy of the subject over the object perspective discussed in §8.2.2. Hannay therefore suggests viewing the S_3 position not as a third subject position, but as a special position for the presentative function. Assuming this line of argumentation, the functional pattern for English is:

(56) $P_1 \, (S_1) \, V_f \, (S_2) \, V_i \, O \, P_\phi \, X$.

An alternative solution is offered by Connolly (1983) who suggests substituting Dik's functional patterns by pattern schemata based on the schema in (57), in which syntactic functions are not distinguished.

(57) $P_1 \, N_1 \, N_2 \, N_3 \, N_4$

Such pattern schemata allow any constituent to be placed in any N-position. This avoids the problem of having O > S in a functional pattern, but places a greater burden on the placement rules which have to be not only ordered and prevented from positioning more than one constituent in each N, like Dik's rules, but must also be supplied with additional conditions. Connolly has elaborated the set of placement rules required for main constituent order in English and implemented them in a computer program.

Connolly suggests that his template also provides a more satisfactory way of dealing with word order in variable word order languages, since it counters the problem of undergeneration without recognizing multiple placement in any pattern position. The application of the template schema to Latin is discussed in Connolly (1983) and to Polish in Siewierska (1988a). However, only some of the pragmatic conditions underlying the various possible linearization patterns are considered. As mentioned earlier, De Jong (1986) argues that a more appropriate way of handling Latin word order is by a set of relative positions rather than a predetermined number of absolute positions. Under such an analysis, the relevant positional rules would take the form of a series of precedence preferences such as those incorporated in the various word order hierarchies that have been proposed in the literature (see e.g. Siewierska 1988a), but stated with reference to a subtle set of pragmatic functions which would include the FG subdivisions of Topic and Focus discussed in ch. 6. The expression rules would then be used to calculate the ranking of each constituent in terms of the hierarchies in question and linearize it accordingly. A similar means of handling linearization has been suggested by Uszkoreit (1986) within GPSG and endorsed by Sag (1987) for HPSG, though the range of word order phenomena envisaged as falling within the scope of their rules is much narrower than that covered by FG.

Notes

1 Functional Grammar as a theory of natural language

1 For a detailed discussion of the relevant issues from the functional point of view, see Nuyts (1983), Foley and Van Valin (1984), Dressler (1985), McCawley (1985) and especially Dik (1986). The formal paradigm is expounded in Newmeyer (1983) and in Chomsky's numerous publications.

2 The more important heuristic sources (external and internal) used in determining markedness include the following, taken from Mayerthaler (1988: 3): language acquisition (x acquired before y); speech disturbance (x lost before y); perception tests (x normally more easily perceived than y); linguistic errors (x normally evokes more mistakes than y); historical language development; pidgins and creoles; comparative grammar, and paradigmatic levelling, in all the internal sources the decisive criterion being frequency or prevalence.

3 The notion of conceptual prominence, salience, dominance or importance is used in the literature in a number of different ways some of which will be discussed in ch. 6. Gundel *et al.* (1988) use the term salience for information that constitutes the rationale for the utterance, i.e. for what in the linguistic literature is often termed focus. This usage of the term must be distinguished from the way it tends to be used in psycholinguistics and artificial intelligence where it typically denotes the focus of attention, a notion closely corresponding to topicality.

4 That iconicity is essentially addressee-oriented is not claimed as such in FG.

5 The examples are from a corpus of Australian English collected by the students of the Linguistic Department at Monash University, Melbourne, in 1980 on the basis of taped interviews. There will be other examples from this corpus scattered throughout the book.

6 Harder (1990: 142) suggests that the only aspects of *form* reflected in FG underlying structures are those that describe how content elements are combined into larger wholes. This, he argues, constitutes the domain of *content syntax*, which is a part of semantics, as opposed to *expression syntax* which deals with the actual expression of the semantic content. Under this view the FG underlying structures may be seen to reflect only the semantic organization of utterances.

7 This unclarity in regard to the semantic vs semantico-syntactic nature of the underlying structures recognized in FG creates some uncertainty in regard

8 Under Hengeveld's (1989) analysis, though not under Dik's (1989), the whole structure is embedded within an illocutionary frame which specifies the relational nature of the speech act. There is some discussion within FG in regard to the appropriateness of such a representation of illocutions (see in particular the articles in Nuyts *et al.* 1990). Dik opts for an analysis in which the basic illocutions are expressions of operators.

to the type of criteria to be used in the determination of these underlying structures. The descriptive problems arising in this connection become evident when attempting to compare the FG underlying structures with either the purely semantic or alternatively purely syntactic ones of other theoretical frameworks.

9 The power of transformations in Chomsky's models of grammar has over the years been considerably constrained. Currently transformations are required to be structure preserving in a rather strong sense (Radford 1988: 547–553). As captured in the Extended Projection Principle, transformations cannot affect the lexical (categorial, subcategorization and thematic (role) properties) or structural requirements (possession of a subject) projected from the lexicon.

10 In LFG the phrase structure component of the grammar is permitted to overgenerate widely and the non-permissible sequences are filtered out by the functional structure which acts as a mediator in the mapping between predicate argument structure and the surface categorial structure (Bresnan 1982b).

11 Most notably contrary to the analyses of linguists such as Freidin (1975), Wasow (1977) and Bresnan (1978), just to name a few, the passive in FG is not dealt with in terms of predicate formation. This will be discussed at length in ch. 4.

12 The semantic function Goal is used in FG in lieu of patient. More about this will be said in ch. 3.

13 A convenient summary of the major areas of conflict in the context of English is presented in Beaman (1984) and Biber (1986).

14 In addition to the references cited above, interesting work on linguistically based knowledge representation in the spirit of Dik has been carried out by Weigand (1986, 1989). A different approach is advocated by Nuyts (1990), Hjelmquist (1990) and Hesp (1990).

2 The organization of the grammar

1 For Semitic languages such as Modern Hebrew and Arabic more abstract lexical entries than stems or words are envisaged (Junger 1987), namely combinations of discontinuous roots and the morphophonemic patterns with which they combine.

2 The major difference is that in Chomskyan theory the subject is treated as an argument not of the verb but of the verb phrase. It is referred to as an 'external' argument as opposed to the other arguments which are 'internal'.

3 Recall from ch. 1 that the term *goal* is used in FG instead of *patient*.

4 In orthodox FG there are no avalent predicates. Mackenzie (1987: 6), however, argues for treating non-relational nominal predicates (e.g. *woman*, *girl*, *man*, etc.) as explicitly avalent.

5 I use the term *sense* here in its narrow reading as reflecting the most salient

6   characteristics of the prototypical denotata of a given language expression (Allan 1986: 99–136).
6   In what follows I will be considering only one of the senses of *bachelor*.
7   No underlying order is posited in LFG, under Falk's (1983) analysis, GPSG or HPSG or in Hudson's Word Grammar. For some discussion of the advantages arising from order-free underlying structures, see the article by Falk just cited, the articles in Gazdar *et al.* (1983) and, for a summary, Siewierska (1988a).
8   De Groot (1989: 166) suggests that in the case of category changing predicate formation rules involving different input predicates and a constant categorial output, language users may take output predicate frames as a starting point in the derivation. He does not, however, elaborate on if or how this is to be reflected in the formulation of such predicate formation rules in an FG grammar.
9   HPSG is a newer version of Gazdar *et al.*'s (1985) Generalized Phrase Structure Grammar (GPSG). The GPSG metarules which could relate clauses involving various types of gaps (displacements) are eliminated in HPSG in favour of lexical rules.
10 The FG position in regard to the argument/satellite status of English prepositional objects such as (15a,b) is not yet clear. The outlined analysis has, however, been suggested for similar alternations in the Bantu languages (see ch. 4) and as a diachronic explanation for the alternations in accusative and ablative marking of second arguments in Latin (Pinkster 1988a).
11 One of the matters which needs to be explored is whether change from argument to satellite status should be recognized as a possible predicate formation rule. Another point is whether reductions and increases in valency can involve the removal and addition solely of satellites. This may at first sight seem to be a contradiction in terms, since the notion of valency is generally assumed to encompass only arguments. Yet there may be cases which warrant extending the notion of valency reduction or increasing to cover the removal or addition of an apparent satellite. Dik *et al.* (1990) cite some relevant examples of the former situation from Ancient Greek and French involving reflexive marking, a systematic account of which can be achieved by assuming a predicate formation rule removing an underlying satellite beneficiary (or maleficiary).
12 A different approach to term formation is suggested by Mackenzie (1987: 10–11) who argues that this traditional treatment is too much like the generative semantic solution advocated by Bach (1968) and does not allow for a pragmatic view of predication comparable to the pragmatic approach to reference adopted in FG. Mackenzie points out that the FG term fulfils both a predicating and a referring function. This is by and large reflected in the term *schema*, the part to the left of the colon being associated with the referring function and the part on the right with the predicating function. He maintains that in order to represent predication as a cooperative, pragmatic action (an attempt at communication), there should be no explicit linking of the two functions of a term by means of a co-indexed variable. Thus instead of (ia), Mackenzie suggests (ib):

(i)   a. $(d1x_i : woman_N (X_i))$ 'the woman'
      b. $(d1x_i : woman_N)$.

Example (ia) reads 'one indefinite entity such that the property "woman" is predicated of that entity'; (ib), on the other hand, corresponds to a reading such as 'one indefinite entity such as I, the speaker, describe by the name "woman" '. For further details I refer the reader to Mackenzie (1987).
13 The relationship between ontological predicability, the possibility of meaningful attribution of a property or relation to an entity, and linguistic predicability, the possibility of meaningful application of a predicate to an argument, is currently being explored by Hengeveld (1990a,b) with regard to the application of non-verbal predicates to different order entities (see below and §2.3.1).
14 Rijkhoff (1989b) in fact intends his classification of term operators to also cover predication operators. And indeed a good case can be made for distinguishing the same three types of operators at the level of the predication. However, in my exposition of FG I will be following Hengeveld's (1987b, 1989) model of the layered structure of the clause, since it has been adopted in Dik (1989). The major difference between Hengeveld's and Rijkhoff's model of the clause is that Rijkhoff recognizes an additional layer in between the core and extended predication (see §2.3.2) corresponding to the predicational equivalents of quantity operators (Rijkhoff 1989b: 29–30).
15 The FG approach draws its inspiration from Brown (1985).
16 Rijkhoff (1989a) argues that due to the non-unique nature of terms (which is reflected in their ability to function in different types of predications), the identification of entities denoted by terms, as opposed to predications (see p. 36), requires not merely a specification of a deictic centre but also the presence of an identifying entity acting as a marker of location.
17 Various details of the layered model of the clause are still being elaborated. There are thus some minor differences in the number of levels recognized by particular adherents of FG and in the proposed distribution of operators and satellites over these levels. The most recent discussions on this issue are presented in Nuyts *et al.* (1990). In this book I will be following in the main the analysis given in Dik (1989).

3 States of affairs and semantic functions

1 These are not the only parameters that can be used in setting up a typology of events. For example, Halliday's (1967/68, 1985) well-known system of transitivity focuses primarily on the nature of the participants and the material vs mental or relational features of processes. Talmy (1985a) offers a cross-linguistic typology of lexicalization patterns based on the representation of *motion* (with manner/cause, path or figure) which in a later publication (1985b) he supplements with a typology of *force dynamics* incorporating both 'causing' and 'letting' with a set of unfamiliar notions (in this context) such as 'despite, 'although', 'hindering', 'helping', 'leaving alone' and 'trying'.
2 The term *Aktionsart* may be loosely defined as denoting the temporal features of the meaning of the verb in its entire paradigm (Pinkster 1983: 274, 280–286). It is thus the lexical equivalent of the grammatical category of aspect. For details, see also Comrie (1976: note 6, 41–51) and Smith (1983) with the references cited.

3   This example is from Halliday (1985: 101–102).
4   The conceptual basis underlying different means of representing the same real-world events in a single language and across languages is explored in detail within Cognitive Linguistics both in relation to lexicalization and grammaticalization. The interested reader is referred to: Lakoff (1987), Langacker (1986) and Krzeszowski (1989); and for specific issues such as the structuring of space, the representation of motion or force dynamics (see note 1), Talmy (1983, 1985a,b); or the relationship between bodily experience and mental experience, Wierzbicka (1979).
5   This is as far as Dik's (1978: 34) original classification goes. The introduction of the features [telic] and [momentaneous] is due to the influence of the work of Pinkster (1982), Vester (1983) and De Groot (1985), all heavily indebted to Verkuyl (1972) and Dowty (1979). The feature [experience] is a recent innovation. Unless stated otherwise, all references to Dik in this chapter pertain to the (1989: ch. 5) monograph.
6   A distinction similar to Vendler's, but a three-way one into Activities, Performances and States, was developed independently by Kenny (1963). Vendler's classification was originally published in an article in the *Philosophical Review* in 1957. It is therefore historically prior to Kenny's.
7   Dowty's (1979) typology is employed in Foley and Van Valin's (1984) classification of predications and also in their system of semantic functions. They do not make any substantial changes and therefore the comments on Dowty can hold equally well for them. Also related to the Dowty typology is the predicate (not predication) typology of Quirk *et al.* (1985).
8   The celebrated cosmology of the Navaho is one example of a different world view where control is a matter of relative status on a hierarchy of being, and not automatically equated with the instigating or effecting party. For details and other examples, see Klaiman (1988).
9   This approach to intentionality is due to Talmy (1985a,b).
10 Klaiman (1988: 70) states that according to DeLancey (1985), control and volition (intention) cannot be fused in Lhasa Tibetan.
11 Klaiman (1988) makes the same point in relation to the notion of 'affected entity' (the participant to which accrue the principal effects of the action denoted in the predication) which she treats in a similar way to Dik's Experiencer.
12 Telicity is a controversial notion. It is used in FG in accordance with what Dahl (1981: 81) calls the Western as opposed to the Eastern tradition.
13 The attempts at setting up typologies of predicates rather than predications with telicity as one of the basic features, such as that of Garey (1957) and Kholodovich (1963), have been unsuccessful.
14 A momentaneous SoA does have actual physical duration, but that is beside the point, the conceptualization of the event being what matters.
15 Momentaneous SoAs may co-occur with aspectual verbs under an iterative interpretation, in which case the event is viewed as a series of momentaneous events.
16 Quirk *et al.* (1985: 201) recognize a category of Stances corresponding to Dik's Positions, which they take to be intermediary between statives and dynamic verbs.
17 The correlation between the mass/count distinction and predication types was first observed by Leech (1969: 134–135, 1971: 4). It has received a

considerable amount of attention in recent years, e.g. Taylor (1977); Mourelatos (1981: 203–209); Bennett (1981: 18f); Carlson (1981: 41); Rijksbaron (1988).

18   In Chomsky's theory of grammar the subject is not a complement. This is typically the distinction drawn between the semantic term 'argument' and the syntactic one 'complement', though not in all theories.

19   This point is made by Mackenzie (1981: 302).

20   Actually δ_2, at least Duration ones, may also affect the type of SoA. Talmy (1985a: 27) notes that what he calls 'posture' verbs such as *lie, sit, stand, lean, kneel, squat, crouch, bend, bow*, etc. which denote Actions may be used in Position predications with an accompanying durative adverbial; e.g. *She knelt (when the bell rang)* vs *She knelt there for a full hour*.

21   From a syntactic point of view the FG δ_1 do not constitute a homogeneous class. The Beneficiary, Manner, Instrument, Direction, Path and Source satellites are much more argument-like in their morpho-syntactic behaviour than the satellites of Reason, Purpose or Cause (see e.g. Nichols 1986: 79). Therefore, strictly speaking, it is the first set that is regarded as the particularly problematic one.

22   This distinction is recognized in most theoretical frameworks, the major exception being classical Dependency theory (Tesnière 1959) and its successors such as Hudson's (1984) Word Grammar in which all modifiers of the predicate are viewed as direct dependants of the predicate. This analysis is motivated primarily by syntactic rather than semantic considerations.

23   In GB, as in its predecessors, subcategorization reflects the constituency relations corresponding to the configurationally defined predicate/argument structure. This means that only logical arguments are subcategorized. In Bresnan's (1982a) LFG or Gazdar *et al.*'s (1985) GPSG, on the other hand, predicates are subcategorized for the type of complements that they occur with in the surface constituent structure. Therefore, the range of subcategorized complements extends well into FG's δ_1, embracing benefactives (e.g. with *buy* or *cook*) or instrumentals.

24   For example δ_1 Manner adverbials such as *beautifully* in (27) are considered to be complements (Radford 1988: 236).

25   Different co-occurrence possibilities, such as the distribution of *that/whether* complements shown in (38)–(40) are treated in FG as a matter of placement restrictions rather than actual differences in subcategorization.

26   There is a comparable paradox within Chomskyan theory. Radford (1988: 389) in his new version of *Transformational Grammar* states that the specification of the subcategorization requirements of the predicate (plus the subject) in terms of semantic functions rather than categorial information is 'a somewhat utopian goal in the present fragmentary state of our knowledge: but it is surely the kind of ambitious goal which any serious theory of language should set itself'.

27   The same doubt has been expressed within the FG camp by Mackenzie (1981: 305).

28   The non-autonomy of the FG semantic functions and in particular the pressure from the SFH on semantic function assignment has been strongly criticized within FG by Mackenzie (1981). However, given Dik's overall stance on semantic and syntactic functions, I cannot see how the former can

be autonomous.
29 See Blake 1990, for an introductory explication of the theory.
30 This principle is adopted in Chomsky (1981: 36) as the theta-criterion.
31 In FG this problem has been discussed in relation to verbs of teaching and instructing (Workgroup on FG, 1981) which are seen to conform cross-linguistically either to a 'giving' model, where the teacher presents the thing taught to the learner as a 'gift', or to an 'operating' model, where the teacher is depicted as performing some operation on the learner by means of, or with respect to, the thing taught.
32 The types of regular conceptual distinctions underlying our use of language are discussed in the literature on cognitive linguistics of which Fillmore is nowadays a chief representative. See the references in note 4.
33 An analysis of the Instrument as a Company (comitative) satellite is excluded because the Instrument is not a joint participant, as evinced by *The car and the fender broke the window. For a more detailed discussion of the conjunction test with instrumentals, see Schlesinger (1989: 200–202).
34 The only other possible candidate for the first argument function is Processed. This too would be a very unorthodox analysis since the party actually performing the action and held responsible by others would be depicted as subject to a process.
35 Dik does not specify why FG does not recognize a default semantic function, unlike in Fillmore's (1968), Anderson's (1971, 1977) and Starosta's (1977, 1979) case grammars. I presume that this is yet another consequence of binding nuclear semantic functions to the typology of SoAs. Another possible explanation is that a default semantic function is conceptually incoherent given the basically notional character of Dik's semantic functions.
36 The term *reference* is taken from Mackenzie.

4 Syntactic functions

1 This characterization of transitivity is sometimes supplemented by semantic criteria, for instance that the verb must express a genuine action that passes over from the subject to the direct object, or that the referent of the direct object must be somehow affected as a consequence of the action expressed by the verb. Significantly, transitivity is not equated with bivalency (the presence of two arguments), since only certain kinds of A^2 (second arguments) are considered to be objects. The FG view of transitivity, which will be presented below, is along the same lines. For an alternative, discourse-based approach to transitivity see Hopper and Thompson (1980).
2 It is my impression that the difference between transitivity and bivalency is not always appreciated in FG.
3 As remarked in §1.5, the perspectivizing role of the subject and object has been examined by Bolkestein (1985a,b) and Bolkestein and Risselada (1987) who come to the conclusion that the choice of subject and object is determined by matters of relative cohesiveness, cohesiveness being a notion corresponding more closely to a broad (linguistic) sense of perspectivizing such as that relating the pairs of examples in (1)–(8) rather than to Dik's narrow conception of perspective.

4 In my analysis of the notion of perspective in linguistics I have benefited especially from the discussion in Fillmore (1977, 1981), DeLancey (1981), Kuno (1987), Bolkestein and Risselada (1987) and Ehrlich (1987). My major sources for literary approaches to perspective are Chatman (1978), Prince (1982) and Rimmon-Kenan (1983).
5 This latter usage of perspective is sometimes discussed under the label of 'narrative voice'.
6 This does not mean, however, that the oppositions exemplified in (1)–(8) cannot be viewed in FG as reflections of another wider form of perspective. The point is that they do not come under the kind of perspective relevant to the determination of the subject and object functions.
7 The term *actor* taken over from Foley and Van Valin (1984) will be used to refer to the passive agent i.e. to what under analyses other than the FG one is a demoted first argument A^1 which may be an Agent, Positioner, Force, Processed or Zero.
8 The notion of control referred to here is not that of the SoA feature control discussed in ch. 3, but the relation of referential dependence between an unexpressed entity (generally assumed to be a subject) and an expressed or implicit entity (the controller). This sense of control originates from the transformational generative literature, but is nowadays in common usage. Evidence for an implied passive actor based on control properties features prominently in current discussions of empty categories and the status of implied arguments in GB and LFG. The examples in (11) and (12) are based on Jaeggli (1986: 31) and Roeper (1987: 268).
9 The semantic presence of the actor could also be attributed to a pragmatic rule of interpretation which is the solution Dik (1983c) adopts for reflexive passives.
10 The treatment of the so-called 'topic' or 'focus' as the subject in Philippine languages is advocated by Dik in his earliest version of FG (Dik 1978). This view is shared by linguists such as: Givón (1981), Mallinson and Blake (1981), Perlmutter and Postal (1984a) and Shibatani (1988b). For an alternative interpretation of the structure of the Philippine clause, see in particular Schachter (1976, 1977) and Foley and Van Valin (1984).
11 Shibatani (1988b) argues that the verbal marking operates according to an active system. Blake (1990: 152), on the other hand, suggests that, at least in Tagalog, the goal focus in non-future tense aspects is unmarked relative to the actor focus. This he views as one of the arguments for the ergative analysis of Tagalog to be outlined in §4.3.2.1.
12 Note that the reflexive pronoun in (19) is the subject, and not a satellite as in the English translation. The restriction in question concerns the ability of the passive actor to act as a controller of a reflexive subject, not its ability to control reflexivization *per se*. Though it is sometimes claimed (e.g. Foley and Van Valin 1984: 163) that an English passive actor is never coreferential with a reflexive, this is not quite correct. Compare (ia) and (ib).

(i) a. Mary was talked to by John about *himself/*herself.
    b. The fish was bought by John for himself.

The facts of reflexivization are extremely complex and subject not only to syntactic but also to discourse constraints connected with matters of narrative voice (point of view). For a discussion of the interaction of syntactic and discourse constraints on reflexivization in English, see in particular Kuno (1987) and Zribi-Hertz (1989).

13 Implicit in the interdependence between subject assignment and passivization that FG posits is the denial of the functional unity of the various constructions that have been labelled passive. This places FG in stark contrast to the many attempts to provide a universal account of what are frequently taken to be intra- and inter-language realizations of the passive (e.g. Perlmutter and Postal 1977, 1983; Keenan 1981; Siewierska 1984a; Shibatani 1985). However, since from a functional point of view the cross-linguistic manifestations of the passive have been shown not to be uniform (see, e.g., the comparison of 'plain' and reflexive passives in European languages in Siewierska 1984a: §5.2, §7.2 and the discussion of the various semantic effects associated with different forms of passivization in Davison 1980), the lack of a unified analysis of the passive is consistent with the functional orientation of the theory.

14 For example, while the Spanish periphrastic passive in (iia) is interpreted in FG as bivalent and the product of subject assignment, the reflexive passive in (iib) is derived by a predicate formation rule similar to that given earlier in (16).

Spanish (Garcia 1975: 15)
(ii) a. Las   paces fueron firmadas   por los   embajadores.
          the:f:pl peace were sign:pap:f:pl by the:m:pl ambassadors
          'The peace was signed by the ambassadors.'

      b. Se   firmaron   las paces por los emmbajadores.
          refl sign:past:3pl the peace by the ambassadors
          'The peace was signed by the ambassadors.'

The relevant predicate formation rule derives an intransitive predicate from a transitive predicate and marks it with the reflexive *se*, which is interpreted in FG as a valency-reduction marker. The Agent in the reflexive passive clause (iib), unlike the one in the periphrastic passive (iia), is thus considered to be not an argument of the verb, but a satellite introduced at the level of the core predication (see §2.3.3).

15 Though the A^2 of the antipassive appears to be significantly more frequently overt than the A^1 of the passive (see Tsunoda 1988: 625 for relevant data from a cross-section of languages), the fact that it is backgrounded or downgraded is suggested by its morphological coding (see p. 87) and its inability to be cross-referenced on the verb. Whether it should be seen as involving a reduction in valency in all languages is not yet clear. Tsunoda (1988) provides an excellent account of this issue.

16 So far, predicate formation rules involving a change from argument to satellite status have not been proposed in FG. However, given the recent extension of the domain of predicate formation from the nuclear to the core predication, mentioned in §2.2.1.1, this may now be an option.

17 A change in semantic functions could be posited under the assumption that there is a clear connection between case marking (or other forms of coding) and semantic function, i.e. that only an absolutive (or accusative in

accusative languages) A^2 is a Goal. As pointed out to me by Machtelt Bolkestein, FG does not make such an assumption. For some discussion of this issue in the context of FG, see Pinkster (1988a).
18 Not all such pairs of clauses have this meaning difference. For instance there is no difference in completeness between *John hit the stick against the wall* and *John hit the wall with the stick*. Bolkestein (1985a) argues that there are no discernible distinctions in meaning in comparable predications in Latin.
19 Unlike the Dutch prefix *be-* (Dik 1980: 35–36), the Polish *ob-* prefix may indicate semantic distinctions other than 'completeness'.
20 There is also a grammatical tradition represented by, for instance, Curme (1931), Lyons (1968) and Green (1974) according to which the recipient in both (29a) and (29b) is an indirect object.
21 Nonetheless Kaplan and Bresnan (1982), Dowty (1982) and Dryer (1986) assign the same grammatical relation to these two terms, namely the secondary object relation mentioned above.
22 Dryer (1983: 132) maintains that the two objects in clauses such as (41) do not display identical characteristics because in the case of nominal participants the Recipient necessarily precedes the Goal; and in the case of cross-referencing pronouns, the Recipient is placed closer to the verb stem than the Goal. The first point is disputed by Kimenyi (1988: 356) who states that the order of the objects in Kinyarwanda is not fixed, but determined by pragmatic factors such as the distribution of given/new information. Given the conditioning effect of animacy and humanness on topicality and word order (see the personal hierarchy in §4.5.1), Recipients, as necessarily human, are likely to precede the Goal more often than vice versa. As regards the second point, I have not been able to establish whether the order of pronominal clitics in Kinyarwanda depends on an animacy and person hierarchy as in other Bantu languages such as Shona, Shambala and Haya (Duranti 1979). The placement of the Recipient or Beneficiary closest to the verb stem (the mirror image of the order of nominal terms) is in line with such hierarchical ordering. In any case, the fact that the two objects may not actually be identical does not necessarily entail that they must be distinguished in terms of syntactic functions rather than semantic functions.
23 Note that clauses with a Goal and Location are not among the set of double object constructions in which the two objects display the same morphosyntactic properties. When co-occurring with a Location object the Goal no longer manifests its typical characteristics, these being taken over by the Location. The Location in such cases is thus a prime candidate for a treatment in terms of object assignment. More about this will be said below. It must also be noted that the distribution of shared object properties among the discussed terms obtains only under the specified circumstances, i.e. in constructions with two prepositionless non-subject terms, not three. The problems posed by triple object constructions will be mentioned later in the text.
24 Dik (1989: 323) suggests that verbal markers such as the Bantu applicative suffix may be interpreted as signalling the presence of, say, a Beneficiary or Instrument subject or object rather than as actual markers of subject and object assignment.
25 The range of semantic functions covered by Dik's SFH does not exhaust all

the syntactic function assignment possibilities encountered in languages. Note that there is no Manner, despite the possibility of subjectivizing such terms in Kinyarwanda (see (41)). Nor is there an Accompaniment semantic function which can be a subject and/or object either in Bantu or in Nez Perce, for example. Omissions connected with the A^1 will be discussed in §4.5.2.

26 Various counterexamples can be found to this, but they are not of great significance.

27 Various versions of the personal hierarchy may be found in the literature. The form of the hierarchy given in (54) is adapted from Allan (1987).

28 Included in this discussion is also typically the Beneficiary which, like the Recipient, is obligatorily animate.

29 The situation is clear within the FG frame of reference, given that the so-called dative-subjects do not enter into subject assignment, and given the nature of the FG semantic functions. With a different set of semantic functions a case can be quite easily made for the converse order of the Goal and Recipient. Givón (1984: 141), for instance, argues for the priority of the Recipient over the Goal on the basis of the fact that in examples such as those in (iii) which he analyses as taking an A^1 Recipient and an A^2 Goal, the Recipient and not the Goal is the unmarked choice for subject.

(iii) a. The woman saw the house.
b. The man knew the answer.

In FG the A^1 in (ii) do not bear the semantic function Recipient but that of Zero[Exp]. Therefore Givón's argument in regard to the preferential treatment of the Recipient *vis-à-vis* the Goal does not hold. He is, of course, correct in ascribing superiority, in terms of accessibility to subject, to the semantic function of the A^1 in (iii) over that of the Goal. This is captured in the new version of the SFH to be discussed in §4.5.2 which includes the Zero[Exp] and other A^1 semantic functions.

30 There is very little evidence for a direct link between agentivity and familiarity. Though the preference for an active as opposed to passive perspective is cited as one of the oppositions of Cooper and Ross's (1975) extended 'Me-first' principle, the difficulty in factoring out agentivity from all the other parameters affecting the active/passive distinction casts doubt on the extent to which agentivity was indeed investigated as a separate parameter. On the other hand, the overwhelming statistical dominance of active clauses over passive ones in most languages must breed greater familiarity.

31 Dik (1989: 235-236) is very much aware of the host of considerations that may influence subject and object assignment in various languages.

32 Similar predicates govern an A^2 in the dative in Latin, German, Polish and many other languages. Unlike in Ancient Greek, however, neither the A^2 nor the A^3 Recipients can be subjectivized. Pinkster (1988a) argues that the semantic function of non-accusative A^2 in Latin depends on the lexical meaning of the predicate.

5 The layered structure of the clause

1 Foley and Van Valin (1984) attribute their model of clause structure to the work of Olson (1981).

2   For a detailed discussion of how the RRG layered model differs from the FG one, see Van Valin (1990).
3   The other major area of grammar which Foley and Van Valin (1984) use to exemplify the validity of their model of clause structure is clause linkage. Limitations of space preclude an overview of the FG contributions to this area. Mention will be made only of complementation, an issue which Foley and Van Valin handle rather unsuccessfully.
4   It is important to note that Bybee (1985) restricts her attention exclusively to inflectional manifestations of tense, aspect and modality, whereas Foley and Van Valin (1984) and Hengeveld (1989) consider also the non-inflectional expressions of these categories.
5   Foley and Van Valin (1984: 216–217) argue that a type of modality that they call *status* which corresponds to what, following Lyons (1977: 797, 804), is considered in FG to be *objective* modality tends to occur on the inner side of tense, closer to the verb stem. Bybee (1985) does not differentiate between this category of modality and subjective epistemic modality. In FG status is viewed as belonging to the same level as tense. The evidence that Foley and Van Valin present in favour of a relative ordering of status and tense is not conclusive.
6   Some aspectual distinctions are, however, neither internal nor strictly temporal. I owe this observation to Simon Dik.
7   The following characterization of the three time points is taken from Johnson (1981: 148–149).
8   This applies only to absolute tense as opposed to relative tense. See p. 118.
9   The term *quantificational* reflects the fact that these distinctions quantify over sets and series of SoAs.
10 The iterative is not traditionally regarded as a grammatical aspect entering into opposition with perfective/imperfective contrast (see e.g. Kucała 1966; Czochralski 1975: 16; Laskowski 1984: 129–131, 214–219). I have found the arguments of Majewicz (1985: 208–214) for the contrary view compelling.
11 Dik (private communications) suggests that in view of the fact that the category of verbal mood (e.g. indicative or subjunctive) can be used in a variety of circumstances, sometimes obligatorily and sometimes as a matter of choice (with semantic import), it should best be treated in FG as an *auxiliary* operator (see §7.3).
12 Though Bybee (1985) does not consider deontic modality and does not make a distinction between objective and subjective epistemic modality, her observations, in this instance, are likely to hold to both of the epistemic modalities.
13 This observation is not restricted to English. Bolkestein (1980: 73) mentions that the Latin modal verbs *debere* and *oportet*, which she suggests are like the English modal adverbs in being used to express solely subjectively modalized statements, can only occur in declarative sentences without negation and in certain types of subordinate clauses. On the other hand, the modal verb *necesse est*, which is used both in the subjective and objective senses, can occur in yes/no questions and be combined with negation. Hengeveld (1987a) discusses similar facts in Spanish.
14 This is not obligatorily reflected in linear order of string. For instance, in a variable order language such as Polish the subjective modal adverb can follow the objective, as in (ib), in which case it receives heavy stress.

(i) a. Jest to napewno możliwe, ale mało prawdopodobne.
    is   that certainly possibly, but little likely
    'That is certainly possible, but rather unlikely.'
 b. Jest to możiwe napewno, ale mało prawdopodobne.

15 As shown in Table 5.1, positive/negative polarity is treated as a π_2. Since this oposition denotes certainty as to the actuality or non-actuality of a given SoA, it represents the logical extreme of epistemic objective modality (Dik 1989: 205). Predicate negation, by contrast, is a π_1 (Dik 1989: 185–186).
16 In discussing the classification of speech acts one should distinguish a number of subcategories of speaker (e.g. author, mouthpiece, spokesman, reporter) and addressee (e.g. addressee, hearer, overhearer, bystander, audience), these distinctions being pertinent to the nature of indirect illocutions (see e.g. Levinson 1983 and the references therein). Such details will not be discussed here, and therefore the default terms *speaker* and *addressee* will continue to be used.
17 In Searle's (1975: 59, 62) terminology, the primary illocution is actually the one corresponding to the speaker's intention, whereas the illocution associated with a particular sentence type is called the secondary illocution.
18 For a detailed analysis of indirect illocutions in terms of these procedures, see, for example, Allan (1986: 211–237).
19 A comprehensive list of forms of mitigation is given in Allan (1986: 21–34).
20 Explicit performatives have the property of token-reflexivity (Lyons 1977: 726, 781), i.e. they have no truth value in the typical sense of the term, being true by virtue of merely being uttered. Clauses with illocutionary adverbs, on the other hand, are true only if the proposition that they qualify is true. Consequently the pairs of clauses under discussion differ in regard to truth conditions.
21 The performative hypothesis is due to Ross (1970) and was further developed in Sadock (1974). An extensive discussion of the many arguments for and against this hypothesis are presented in Levinson (1983: 243–263) who also gives extensive references to the literature on this topic.
22 This is only one of the functions of this affix.
23 There are a number of versions of X-bar theory. I will be referring to the system originally proposed by Chomsky (1970) and currently adhered to in revised form in *Barriers* which is extensively discussed in Radford (1988). The theory developed by Jackendoff (1977) differs from the schema presented here in regard to the maximal level of *n*, and in the rejection of non-lexical Xs. The more recent versions of X-bar advanced by Fukui (1986) and Speas (1986), on the other hand, do not adopt the assumption that all maximal projections have the same bar-level or that the projections of X must necessarily keep the same iterated bar-level up and down the structure. For a discussion of various versions of X-bar theory and a critical assessment of its role in determining the nature of phrase structure, see Kornai and Pullum (1990).
24 The treatment of *to* as a type of modal verb is not peculiar to GB. Similar analyses have been advanced in GPSG (Gazdar *et al.* 1985) and in Word Grammar (Hudson 1984), for example.
25 For further details concerning the precedence aspect of phrase structure, see Siewierska (1988a).

26 Some discussion of this matter is to be found in Bresnan (1982b) and Marantz (1984).
27 Ernst (1989) treats these adverbials together with the subject and certain nominal specifiers as tertiaries, which, given the number of levels recognized in FG, is also what they are in this theory.
28 Whether or not the semantic relations obtaining between the elements of a complex expression can serve as the basis for a cross-linguistically valid typology of complements or clause linkage in general is open to question. Lehmann (1988: 183), for example, maintains that it cannot. For an alternative view, see Givón (1980) and Foley and Van Valin (1984).
29 The truth value and attitudinal characteristics of such complements have been extensively discussed in the transformational literature. See in particular Bonney (1976) and the references there.
30 The notion of sententiality is a complex one. Lehmann (1988: 200) sets up a continuum of sententiality from the clause via non-finite constructions to the verbal noun which involves the following parameters:

(a) no illocutionary force;
(b) constraints on illocutionary elements;
(c) constraints on/loss of modal elements and mood;
(d) constraints on/loss of tense and aspect;
(e) dispensability of complements;
(f) loss of personal conjugation;
(g) conversion of subject into oblique slot;
(h) no polarity;
(i) conversion of verbal into nominal government;
(j) dispensability of subject;
(k) constraints on complements;
(l) combinable with adposition/agglutinative case affix/reflexive case affix.

6 Pragmatic functions and the pragmatics of discourse

1 Upper case will be used when reference is made specifically to FG pragmatic functions and lower case for general reference to the relevant concepts.
2 It is important to note that the FG analysis of information structure, like most other current analyses including FSP, does not take accentuation as the basis for determining whether a constituent is topic or focus. A detailed critique of this prevailing methodology is presented in Keijsper (1985).
3 Halliday's theme is to be distinguished both from Dik's theme, discussed on p. 150, and the FSP theme as defined in note 5. For a critical discussion of Halliday's pragmatic functions and certain inconsistencies in usage, see Butler (1985) and Hudson (1988).
4 We will see in §6.3.1 that topics which have the status of inferables are also stressed. Dik's analysis of topics such as the initial *this one* in (1d) will be discussed in §6.4.
5 The *theme* in the FSP tradition defined for example by Firbas (1964: 112; 1981: 52) refers to those elements that convey information derivable from the immediately relevant verbal or situational context and therefore contribute the least towards the development of the discourse (have the lowest degree of communicative dynamism). The *rheme* designates

elements specifying information not predictable from context and thus contributing the most towards forwarding the communicative function of the discourse (have the highest degree of communicative dynamism). Firbas, in addition to theme and rheme, postulates a third category of discourse elements, namely the transition. This three-way distinction is not recognized by Daneš (1974) or Sgall and his associates (1986). The FSP theme/rheme as a binary opposition corresponds to what others call *topic* and *comment*.

6   I am referring here to Western European and North American research. The Prague School FSP approach is discourse based in the way outlined on p. 147, and it, of course, is by no means recent. Much of the current work on topicality replicates various analyses of scholars of FSP; most notably Givón's (1983a) *topic continuity* is very close to Daneš's (1974) *thematic progression*. In what follows I will only point out the areas of convergence and divergence with FSP which I consider to be most relevant for our discussion.

7   The cross-linguistic validity of the view that many features of discourse and grammar are a reflection of the speaker's monitoring of the addressee's frame of mind (knowledge, experience and particularly exposure to prior discourse), to be outlined on p. 156–159, has been recently put into question by Nichols (1988: 400) who argues that Russian discourse and grammatical structure do not display the same sensitivity to cognitive functional parameters pertaining to the speaker's assessment of the addressee's knowledge as does English, for example. I am not in a position to comment on her claim.

8   The term *activation* is taken over from psychology. Recall Bock's (1982) use of the term in relation to the distinction between automatic vs controlled processing in §1.2.1.1.

9   For an FSP account of the same distinctions, see Firbas (1981: 39–41).

10 Firbas (1981: 46) maintains that this holds for all types of information, the speaker/writer being free to present non-derivable information as derivable, and derivable information as non-derivable, within certain limits.

11 According to Keijsper (1985: 55), the only thing which can make a phrase into a topic is an accent in the same predication which does not include the phrase involved in its scope.

12 Prince (1981) uses the term *familiarity* in the same sense as binary identifiability. Her familiarity is not to be confused with Ertel's (1977) mentioned in ch. 4.

13 In addition to this binary conception of identifiability, there is also a relative one which grades discourse referents according to how easy they are to identify. The matter of ease of identification is, however, of more direct relevance to topicality, particularly to forms of coding, as shown in Givón's (1983b) scales of syntactic coding, than to givenness.

14 The expression *several whites killed at X junction* in (19b) is treated as a term derived by term formation. The type of existential where it is not the entity denoted by the nominal whose existence is being asserted, but rather the whole SoA described by the nominal plus extension, is called an SoA-existential in FG. Existentials such as (19a) which receive an entity reading are referred to as E-existentials. For an extensive discussion, see Hannay (1985a).

15 The existentials (19a,b) are classed as a special type of presentative construction in FG (Hannay 1985a).
16 In addition to the two references cited in the text see, for example, Kuroda (1965, 1972), Dik (1978) and Makino (1982).
17 In the context of FG, switch reference has been discussed by De Vries (1989) in relation to two Papuan languages, Wambon and Kombai.
18 Transitive verbs may also occur in presentative structures. In English this is not very common with *there*-presentatives. The phenomenon is more widespread in German and Dutch, for example, as discussed by Perlmutter and Zaenen (1984) under the label 'indefinite extraposition'.
19 In RG unaccusative predicates are opposed to unergative ones. Unergative predicates are characterized as taking an obligatory argument bearing the semantic role of agent, experiencer or cognizer, i.e. an initial 1. The argument of an unaccusative predicate is viewed as an initial 2. Included in this group are existential and presentative predicates; predicates describing sizes, shapes, colours and smells; predicates whose subject is semantically a patient; predicates expressing involuntary emission of stimuli that impinge on the senses; aspectual predicates; and duratives.

In some languages, for example Italian (Perlmutter 1983b), unergative predicates also occur in presentative-like constructions. Lakoff (1987: 763) maintains that so far he has not found any intransitive verb in English, unaccusative or unergative, that cannot be made to fit into what he calls the presentative-existential construction, given the right locational adverbs, tense, etc.
20 Though this element has no reference it is not necessarily meaningless. Bolinger (1977) argues that the meaning of existential *there* in English, for example, is 'bring something into awareness'. Lakoff (1987: 720) sees it as designating a mental space in the sense of Fauconnier (1985) in which a conceptual entity is to be located.
21 There is neither number nor gender agreement in French presentative inversion. In English agreement in number may be suspended in existential presentatives, but only in the presence of contraction. Thus in addition to *There're problems to be solved*, we find *There's problems to be solved*. See, for example, Hannay (1985a:187) and Lakoff (1987: 727).
22 Another difference between preverbal and postverbal subjects in Italian noted by Calabrese (1985: 8) is that while a preverbal subject can always be the antecedent of a covert subject pronoun, i.e. a pronominal form expressed solely by the form of the verb, a postverbal subject cannot. Compare (ia) and (ib).

(i) a. Quando Carlo$_i$ l'ha   vista, è   arrossito.
       when   Carlo 3sg:have:3sg seen is   become red: p. past
       'When Carlo saw her, he blushed.'

    b. *Quando l'ha vista Carlo$_i$, è arrossito.

23 RG, for example, treats the inverted clauses as impersonal constructions with the apparent subject functioning as a special type of chômeur called 'brother-in-law'. The subject relation is assigned to the dummy pronoun which in the case of languages such as Italian or Latin is assumed to be

covert. For details, see Perlmutter (1983b).
24 Davison (1984: 813–814) uses such parameters to set up a scale of NP types which ranks NPs according to how easy their referents are to identify. Referentiality in language, unlike in logic, being a graded rather than an absolute distinction (see e.g. Givón 1984: ch. 11; Allan 1986: ch. 7), evidently referential NPs are viewed as enabling identification of the referent of the NP more easily than less clearly referential or non-referential ones. Ease of referent identification, as in the case of Givón's topic continuity, is seen to directly interact with topicality. The referential scale of NP types is thus simultaneously a scale of topic acceptability.
25 This is what Hannay (1985a:173) seems to be suggesting, but not Dik (1989), as far as I have been able to determine.
26 The use of questions as an heuristic device for determining focus or rheme is employed in many approaches to information structure including FSP (Adamec 1966: 28–29; Sgall et al. 1980: 40; Hajicova and Sgall (1987). The test is discussed in detail by Bogusławski (1977: 142–147). A lengthy critique of the whole procedure is presented in Keijsper (1985: 55, chs. 4 and 5).
27 It needs to be mentioned that wh-questions may have more than one focus, e.g. *Where is John?* In such cases the wh-word under some analyses qualifies as a topic or theme in FSP terms. See note 11.
28 A particular utterance may correspond to a number of different questions. As argued by Keijsper (1985: 67), the assumption that the context of utterance will prompt the 'right' question is based on considerations of very simple contexts. The same holds if we approach the matter from the point of view of speaker intentions, since the speaker can in a given context convey more than one message.
29 In connection with the placement of focal constituents, Harlig and Bardovi-Harlig (1988: 137), on the basis of work carried out mainly by Desző (1982), state that it is typologically unusual for a language to have only one position for all types of focus.
30 For some discussion of the word order characteristics of marked foci, see Harries-Delise (1978).
31 Though Eastman (1986) refers to this particle as a topic marker, it is used only to mark contrast and emphasis.

7 Form-determining expression rules

1 For an alternative view of case forms under which they are seen to have some constant, semantic content, see in particular Wierzbicka (1986).
2 This is not strictly so, since in languages there are generally fewer gender distinctions in the plural than in the singular (Lehmann 1982). In Polish, for example, masculine, feminine and neuter genders are distinguished in the singular while the plural under most analyses has only two genders (with additional subclassifications in certain instances) called masculine personal and non-masculine personal (see Kucała 1978: 174–179).
3 Polish numerals have received several quite different analyses which are conveniently summarized in Saloni and Swidziński (1985: 177–189).
4 Durie (1987: 371) states that *le* is used as a case marker when the actor follows the verb. Its occurrence is optional if the undergoer is cross-

referenced by an enclitic (see note 5) or bound to the verb.
5   There are also enclitic cross-referencing forms which may cross-reference an undergoer. However, Durie (1987: 369) states that these enclitics are typically absent.
6   The alternative analysis of passive *be* suggested by Burzio (1986) is to treat it as a raising predicate taking a small clause (see §5.3.1) complement.
7   This treatment is also extended to the infinitival *to* which under other analyses is considered to be a verbal particle, complementizer, affix or preposition.
8   In Gazdar *et al.*'s (1985) GPSG the rule reads 'a lexical item precedes its phrasal sisters'. For the range of English word order patterns captured by this single rule, see Gazdar *et al.* (1985: 110).
9   For some discussion of the English modals in the context of FG, see Goossens (1975). Note that by treating only the modal as a lexical predicate, the FG analysis resembles that of Jackendoff (1977) on which Chomsky's (1986) *Barriers* analysis is based.
10 Recall from §2.2 that since they express operators, the aspectual auxiliaries are not even in the lexicon.
11 Another possibility discussed by Dik (1983a) is to introduce the passive *be*, as well as the progressive *be* by a rule of copula support, the claim being that like the copula all of these formatives are meaningless. In such a case only the passive participle form of the verb would be introduced by the expression rule in (25).
12 For some discussion of the FG treatment of tense specifically in English and a slightly different account of the interaction between tense and aspect, see Harder (1990).
13 Schachter (1983: 161–162) points out that the incompatibility of the perfective falling within the scope of the progressive may sometimes be overcome in the case of a set of incomplete instantiations, as in (i).

(i)   ? Whenever I see you, you're always just having returned from a vacation.

14 Schachter (1983: 167–168) provides a semantic explanation for the innermost location of the passive auxiliary. He suggests that the passive auxiliary demands a semantic predicate expressing a relation between two or more entities, a condition which can be satisfied by a lexical predicate, but not a modal or the aspectual auxiliaries. Such an explanation is incompatible with the FG analysis, since the passive auxiliary is considered to be semantically empty and thus cannot exert selectional restrictions on the passive participle.

8 Linearization

1   Support for this multifunctional approach to linearization can be found in the alleged characteristics of human processing. Frazier (1985: 147), for example, states that from the perspective of language processing efficiency, there is no fixed ideal language type. What facilitates parsing is not some absolute, invariant ordering, but rather consistent adherence to an overall design, which is subject to restructuring, since a change in one parameter is

likely to induce a change in others.
2. In some of these languages the elements of the 'discontinuous' phrase may be seen as separate constituents in apposition to each other. See, for example, Blake's (1983a) discussion of Kalkatungu.
3. In constituency frameworks the discontinuous constituents are reanalysed as continuous. In the case of some of the Australian languages mentioned, arguments can be adduced for not assigning an NP structure to the noun and the adjective or demonstrative (e.g. Blake 1983a, 1987).
4. Dik does not make the proposed division.
5. For some problems connected with the head status of adpositions, see Maxwell (1984).
6. This is a simplified version of the PHP. The full version originally introduced into FG in Rijkhoff (1986) and revised in Rijkhoff (1990: 14) reads:

> The head of a domain tends to be contiguous with the head of the superordinate domain, provided this does not result in subordinate domains appearing in the counterfield as well. However, should subordinate domains also appear in the counterfield, then dependents in these subordinate domains too may occur in the counterfield.

I will not be going into the various detailed predictions following from the PHP and therefore the simplified version will suffice. It must be noted that, unlike other linguists, Rijkhoff, in discussing order in the term phrase, makes a distinction between count noun languages and numeral classifier languages.

7. For Hawkins (1990) the PHP, or rather Frazier's version of it, is just a special case of a more general parsing principle which he refers to as Early Immediate Constituent recognition (EIC). The EIC predicts a preference for linearization patterns that enable all the immediate constituents (ICs) of a mother node to be recognized as rapidly as possible. By way of illustration Hawkins offers the example of the preference for (ia) over (ib).

(i) a. I $_{vp}$[introduced $_{np}$[some friends that John had brought to the party] $_{pp}$[to Mary]]
    b. I $_{vp}$[introduced $_{pp}$[to Mary] $_{np}$[some friends that John had brought to the party]]

In (ia) the recognition of the mother VP node requires the identification of all the words up to the preposition *to*, i.e. eleven words. In (ib), on the other hand, all the constituents of the VP are established after just four words: *introduced*$_v$, *to*$_{pp}$, *Mary*$_{np}$, and *some*$_{np}$. Thus the ordering in (ib) permits earlier recognition of all the constituents of the VP than the ordering in (ia); accordingly (ib) is predicted by the EIC as being preferred to (ia). The EIC predicts the correlation between prepositions and VO languages and postpositions and OV languages, the leaking of relative clauses to the right in OV languages and the existence of various other left-to-right asymmetries including those to be discussed in connection with LIPOC in §8.2.2.1. Though the EIC makes a number of correct predictions, it is debatable whether parsing considerations such as the EIC should be seen as ultimately responsible for the relevant ordering patterns rather than factors connected with information structure, particularly in terms of a synchronic analysis. Note that even if parsing strategies have shaped matters of performance over time, i.e. in the evolutionary process of language (for which, of course, there is no evidence), this does not mean that the synchronic motivation for alternative word order patterns is not in terms of discourse function. It is of interest, however, that the claim that parsing performance is used in monitoring production performance is consistent with the observations of Gundel *et al.* (1988) in regard to the unmarked nature of listener-oriented word order patterns as compared to the marked nature of speaker-oriented ones discussed in §1.2.1.1.

8 The same predictions are made by Maxwell (1984).
9 Until recently case prefixes were assumed to be non-existent. They have been recently documented in Kordofanian languages, such as Krongo (Reh 1985).
10 This version of LIPOC is more general than Dik's (1978: ch. 9) original formulation. One of the differences is that the earlier LIPOC predicted a preference for postverbal placement of prepositional phrases as opposed to a preverbal placement of postpositional ones. Such positional preferences for the two types of adpositional phrases can indeed be discerned, but the number of exceptions to the predicted ordering were found to undermine LIPOC unnecessarily. For instance, postpositional phrases are not preverbal in SOVX languages such as Borroro, Bambara, Kpelle or Mandingo, or in alleged XOSV languages such as Apalaí, Asurini and Hixkaryana, or in the SVO Chrau, Estonian or Finnish. And in Persian, Tadzhil and Classical Greek prepositional phrases are not postverbal. Moreover, the preference for postverbal prepositional phrases and preverbal postpositional phrases is not evidently a matter of internal complexity. In any case the relevant preferences are currently accounted for by the relator principles discussed in §8.2.1.2.
11 Recall from the modified version of Greenberg's Universal 20 stated in (8) p. 205 that only the sequencing of the prenominal modifiers reflects the tendency to place shorter constituents before longer ones.
12 Recall that in FG, Polish is analysed as lacking object assignment.
13 Givón (1988) would not view this as marked since he considers rightward placement of given topics to be the norm. This will be discussed in §8.3.1.1.
14 According to Adamec (1956: 190), this type of subject postposing in Czech, which is far more prevalent than in Polish, is modelled on the German verb-second constraint. I have not been able to determine whether the same can be said for Polish. However, given the history of Polish, the German origin of this construction could lie at the heart of the genre-conditioned nature of this word order pattern in the contemporary language.
15 In my investigation of this usage (Siewierska 1987, 1988b) in works of fiction and nonfiction, texts of 50,000 words yielded three instances of postverbal nominal subjects of the relevant type in fiction as compared to 79 instances in non-fiction. The respective figures for postverbal subject pronouns established on texts of approximately 200,000 words were 29 for novels and short stories and 565 for expository texts and biographies.
16 These rules need not hold for languages which have several special positions, since question words, for example, may be placed in a special

focus position, as may other focal constituents.
17 Van der Auwera (1987) suggests that some complementizers in Dutch should be considered as being in P_2 rather than in P_1.
18 Givón (1988: 269–271) maintains that evidence for the preposing of new topics is also to be found in English, namely in existential and presentative constructions, the very constructions which are typically cited as prime exemplars of the converse preference. Under Givón's analysis the referents introduced in existential and presentative constructions emerge as exhibiting early placement in the utterance relative to the material that follows the new topics, which he sees as carrying the main predicate information in the clause. On the basis of a text study of written English performed by Fox, Givón maintains that the presence of a secondary predication in English existential and presentative constructions is the norm; in the relevant study out of 75 tokens of existential and presentative clauses there was only one which appeared without any subsequent, intonationally attached predication.
19 The enumerated languages are all variable word order ones. There are also additional special positions in relatively fixed word order languages. Recall from §6.2 that De Schutter (1987) posits an additional postverbal focus position for Dutch, and we will see in §8.3.1.2 that Hannay suggests a special position in English for his presentative function (§6.3.2).

References

BLS   Proceedings of the Annual Meetings of the Berkeley Linguistic Society
CLS   Papers from the Regional Meetings of the Chicago Linguistic Society
IULC   Indiana University Linguistic Club
WPFG   Working Papers in Functional Grammar

Adamec, Přemysl (1956) 'K rozdílum mezi českým a ruským slovosledem', *Kapitoly ze srovnávací mluvnice ruské a české. Studie syntaktické* I, Prague: Československé Akademie Véd.
—— (1966) *Porjadok slov v sovremennom russkom jazyke*, Prague: Akademica.
Aissen, Judith (1982) 'Valence and coreference', in P.J. Hopper and S.A. Thompson (eds).
Allan, Keith (1977) 'Classifiers', *Language* 53: 285–311.
—— (1986) *Linguistic Meaning*, London: Routledge & Kegan Paul.
—— (1987) 'Hierarchies and the choice of left conjuncts', *Journal of Linguistics* 23: 51–77.
Allerton, D.J. (1982) *Valency and the English Verb*, London: Academic Press.
Anderson, John M. (1971) *The Grammar of Case: Towards a Localist Theory*, Cambridge: Cambridge University Press.
—— (1977) *On Case Grammar: Prolegomena to a Theory of Grammatical Relations*, London: Croom Helm.
Anderson, Stephen R. (1984) 'Kwakwala syntax and the Government and Binding Theory', in Eung-Do Cook and Donna B. Gerdts (eds) *Syntax and Semantics 16. The Syntax of Native American Languages*, New York: Academic Press.
Aronoff, Mark (1976) *Word Formation in Generative Grammar*, Cambridge, Mass.: MIT Press.
Austin, John L. (1962) *How to Do Things with Words*, Oxford: Clarendon Press.
Austin, Peter (1981) *A Grammar of Diyari, South Australia*, Cambridge: Cambridge University Press.
Bach, Emmon (1968) 'Nouns and noun phrases', in E. Bach and R.T. Harms (eds).
Bach, Emmon and Harms, Robert T. (eds) (1968) *Universals in Linguistic Theory*, New York: Holt, Rinehart & Winston.
Bakker, Dik (1989) 'A formalism for Functional Grammar expression rules', in J.H. Connolly and S.C. Dik (eds).

Bardovi-Harlig, Kathleen (1983) 'On the claim that topics are not stressed', in John F. Richardson, Mitchell Marks and Amy Chukerman (eds) *Papers from the Parasession from The Interplay of Phonology, Morphology and Syntax*, Chicago: University of Chicago.

Bates, Elizabeth and MacWhinney, Brian (1979) 'A functional approach to the acquisition of grammar', in Elinor Ochs and Bambi B. Schieffelin (eds) *Developmental Pragmatics*, New York: Academic Press.

Beaman, Karen (1984) 'Coordination and subordination revisited: syntactic complexity in spoken and written narrative discourse', in Deborah Tannen (ed.) *Coherence in Spoken and Written Discourse*, Norwood, NJ: Ablex.

Bell, Alan (1978) 'Language samples', in J.H. Greenberg *et al.* (eds).

Bell, Sarah J. (1983), 'Advancements and ascensions in Cebuano', in D.M. Perlmutter (ed.) (1983a).

Bennett, Michael (1981) 'Of tense and aspect: one analysis', in P. Tedeschi and A. Zaenen (eds).

Bennett, Michael and Partee, Barbara (1972) 'Toward the logic of tense and aspect in English', System Development Corporation, Santa Monica, Calif. (Available from the IULC.)

Bentivoglio, Paola (1983) 'Topic continuity and discontinuity in discourse: a study of spoken Latin American Spanish', in T. Givón (ed.) (1983a).

Berman, Ruth A. (1982) 'On the nature of oblique objects in bitransitive constructions', *Lingua* 56: 101–125.

Biber, Douglas (1986) 'Spoken and written textual dimensions in English: resolving the contradictory findings', *Language* 62(2): 384–414.

Blake, Barry J. (1979a) 'Degrees of ergativity in Australia', in Frank Plank (ed.) *Ergativity: Towards a Theory of Grammatical Relations*, London: Academic Press.

—— (1979b) 'Some thoughts on case relations', MS, Monash University.

—— (1983a) 'Structure and word order in Kalkatungu: the anatomy of a flat language', *Australian Journal of Linguistics* 3: 143–176.

—— (1983b) 'Lexicase meets Diyari', MS, Monash University.

—— (1987) *Australian Aboriginal Grammar*, London: Croom Helm.

—— (1990) *Relational Grammar*, London: Routledge.

Boas, Franz (1911) 'Introduction', *Handbook of American Indian Languages*, Washington: Smithsonian Institution.

Bock, Kathryn (1982) 'Toward a cognitive psychology of syntax: information processing contributions to sentence formulation', *Psychological Review* 89: 1–47.

Bogusławski, Andrzej (1977) *Problems of the Thematic-Rhematic Structure of Sentences*, Warsaw: PWN.

Bolinger, Dwight (1977) *Meaning and Form*, New York: Longmans.

Bolkestein, A. Machtelt (1980) *Problems in the Description of Modal Verbs*, Assen: Van Gorcum.

—— (1985a) 'Discourse and case marking, three place predicates in Latin', in Chr. Touratier (ed.) *Syntaxe et Latin*, Aix-en-Provence: Université de Provience, Lafitte.

—— (1985b) 'Cohesiveness and syntactic variation: quantitative versus qualitative grammar', in A.M. Bolkestein *et al.* (eds) (1985b).

—— (1988) 'Causally related predications and the choice between parataxis and hypotaxis in Latin', in R.G. Coleman (ed.) *Proceedings of the Cambridge*

Colloquium on Modern Linguistics, Amsterdam: John Benjamins.
—— (1990) 'Sentential complements in functional grammar: embedded predications, propositions, utterances in Latin', in J. Nuyts *et al.* (eds).
Bolkestein, A. Machtelt and Risselada, Rodie (1987) 'The pragmatic motivation for syntactic and semantic perspective', in Jef Verschueren and Marcella Bertuccelli-Papi (eds) *The Pragmatic Perspective*, Amsterdam: John Benjamins.
Bolkestein, A. Machtelt, Combé, Henk A., Dik, Simon C. *et al.* (eds) (1981) *Predication and Expression in Functional Grammar*, London: Academic Press.
Bolkestein, A. Machtelt, de Groot, Casper and Mackenzie Lachlan, J. (eds) (1985a) *Syntax and Pragmatics in Functional Grammar*, Dordrecht: Foris.
Bolkestein, A. Machtelt, de Groot, Casper and Mackenzie Lachlan, J. (eds) (1985b) *Predicates and Terms in Functional Grammar*, Dordrecht: Foris.
Bonney, W.L. (1976) *Problems in the Grammar and Logic of English Complementation*, Bloomington: IULC.
Borer, Hagit (ed.) (1986) *The Syntax of Pronominal Clitics. Syntax and Semantics 19*, New York: Academic Press.
Bresnan, Joan Wanda (1978) 'A realistic transformational grammar', in M. Halle *et al.* (eds).
—— (ed.) (1982a) *The Mental Representation of Grammatical Relations*, Cambridge, Mass.: MIT Press.
—— (1982b) 'The passive in lexical theory', in J.W. Bresnan (ed.) (1982a).
Bresnan, Joan Wanda and Mchombo, Sam A. (1987) 'Grammatical and anaphoric agreement', *CLS* 22(2): 278–297.
Brinton, Laurel J. (1987) 'The aspectual nature of states and habits', *Folia Linguistica* 21:2–4, 195–214.
Brown, Cheryl (1983) 'Topic continuity in written English narrative', in T. Givón (ed.) (1983a).
Brown, Gillian and Yule, George (1983) *Discourse Analysis*, Cambridge: Cambridge University Press.
Brown, Penelope and Levinson, Stephen (1978) 'Universals in language usage: politeness phenomena', in Esther N. Goody (ed.) *Questions and Politeness: Strategies in Social Interaction*, Cambridge: Cambridge University Press.
Brown, Richard D. (1985) 'Term operators', in A.M. Bolkestein *et al.* (eds) (1985b).
Bunt, Harry (1985) *Mass Terms and Model Theoretical Semantics*, Cambridge: Cambridge University Press.
Burzio, Luigi (1981) 'Intransitive verbs and Italian auxiliaries', Ph.D. dissertation, MIT.
—— (1986) *Italian Syntax*, Dordrecht: D. Reidel.
Butler, Christopher S. (1985) *Systemic Linguistics: Theory and Applications*, London: Batsford.
Bybee, Joan L. (1985) *Morphology*, Amsterdam: John Benjamins.
Calabrese, A. (1985) 'Focus and logical structures in Italian', MS, MIT.
Carlson, Lauri (1981) 'Aspect and quantification', in P. Tedeschi and A. Zaenen (eds).
Carnap, Rudolf (1956) *Meaning and Necessity* (2nd edn), Chicago: Chicago University Press.
Chafe, Wallace L. (1970) *Meaning and the Structure of Language*, Chicago: Chicago University Press.

—— (1976) 'Givenness, contrastiveness, definiteness, subjects, topics and point of view', in C. Li (ed.).
—— (ed.) (1980) *The Pear Stories: Cognitive, Cultural, and Linguistic Aspects of Narrative Production*, Norwood, NJ: Ablex.
—— (1987) 'Cognitive constraints on information flow', in Russell S. Tomlin (ed.).
Chatman, Seymour (1978) *Story and Discourse*, Ithaca: Cornell University Press.
Chia, Emmanuel N. (1986) 'Indirect quote as the dominant style of reporting in Kom', in B.F. Elison (ed.).
Chomsky, Noam (1955) *The Logical Structure of Linguistic Theory*, Chicago: University of Chicago Press.
—— (1957) *Syntactic Structures*, The Hague: Mouton.
—— (1965) *Aspects of the Theory of Syntax*, Cambridge (Mass.): MIT Press.
—— (1970) 'Remarks on nominalizations', in R. Jacobs and P. Rosenbaum (eds) *Readings in English Transformational Grammar*, Waltham, Mass.: Ginn.
—— (1981) *Lectures on Government and Binding*, Dordrecht: Foris.
—— (1982) *Some Concepts and Consequences of the Theory of Government and Binding*, Cambridge, Mass.: MIT Press.
—— (1986) *Barriers*, Cambridge, Mass.: MIT Press.
Chung, Sandra (1978) *Case Marking and Grammatical Relations in Polynesian*, Austin: The University of Texas Press.
Chung, Sandra and Timberlake, Alan (1985) 'Tense, aspect and mood', in T. Shopen (ed.).
Clancy, P. (1980) 'Referential choice in English and Japanese narrative discourse', in W. Chafe (ed.).
Clark, Herbert H. and Haviland, Susan E. (1974) 'Psychological processes and linguistic explanation', in D. Cohen (ed.) *Explaining Linguistic Phenomena*, Washington: Hemisphere.
Cole, Peter (ed.) (1981) *Radical Pragmatics*, New York: Academic Press.
Cole, Peter and Morgan, J.L. (eds) (1975) *Syntax and Semantics 3. Speech Acts*, New York: Academic Press.
Cole, Peter and Sadock, Jerry (eds) (1977) *Syntax and Semantics 8. Grammatical Relations*, New York: Academic Press.
Comrie, Bernard (1976) *Aspect*, Cambridge: Cambridge University Press.
—— (1977) 'In defense of spontaneous demotion', in P. Cole and J. Sadock (eds).
—— (1979) 'Review of B.J. Blake: case marking in Australian languages', *Talanya* 6: 110–113.
—— (1981) *Language Universals and Linguistic Typology*, Oxford: Basil Blackwell.
—— (1982) 'Grammatical relations in Huichol', in P. Hopper and S.A. Thompson (eds).
—— (1985) *Tense*, Cambridge: Cambridge University Press.
Connolly, John H. (1983) 'Placement rules and syntactic templates', in S.C. Dik (ed.).
Connolly, John H. and Dik, Simon C. (eds) (1989) *Functional Grammar and the Computer*, Dordrecht: Foris.
Cook, Thomas L. (1976) 'Focus in Efik', Paper presented to the Twelfth West

African Languages Conference, University of Ife, Nigeria.
Cooper, William E. and Ross, John Robert (1975) 'Word order', in Robert E. Grossman, James L. San and Timothy J. Vance (eds) *Papers from the Parasession on Functionalism*, Chicago: Chicago Linguistic Society.
Cooreman, Ann, Fox, Barbara and Givón, Talmy (1984) 'The discourse definition of ergativity', *Studies in Language* 8: 1–34.
Curme, G. O. (1931) *Syntax*, Boston: Heath.
Czochralski, J.A. (1975) *Verbalaspekt und Tempussystem im Deutschen und Polnischen – eine konfrontative Darstellung*, Warsaw: PWN.
Dahl, Osten (1981) 'On the definition of the telic – atelic (bounded – nonbounded) distinction', in P. Tedeschi and A. Zaenen (eds).
Daneš, Frantisek (1974) 'Functional sentence perspective and the organization of the text', in F. Daneš (ed.) *Papers on Functional Sentence Perspective*, The Hague: Mouton.
Davison, Alice (1980), 'Peculiar passives', *Language* 56(1): 42–66.
—— (1984) 'Syntactic markedness and the definition of sentence topic', *Language* 60(4): 797–845.
Davison, Alice and Lutz, Richard (1985) 'Measuring syntactic complexity relative to discourse context', in D.R. Dowty *et al.* (eds).
De Groot, Casper (1981) 'On theme in Functional Grammar', in T. Hoekstra *et al.* (eds).
—— (1985) 'Predicates and features', in A.M. Bolkestein *et al.* (eds) (1985b).
—— (1989) *Predicate Structure in a Functional Grammar of Hungarian*, Dordrecht: Foris.
De Groot, Casper and Limburg, Machiel J. (1986) 'Pronominal elements: diachrony, typology and formalisation in Functional Grammar', *WPFG* 12.
De Guzman, V. (1983) 'Ergative analysis of Philippine languages', Paper presented at the Third Eastern Conference on Austronesian Languages, Ohio University.
De Jong, Jan R. (1981) 'On the treatment of focus phenomena in Functional Grammar', in T. Hoekstra *et al.* (1981), 89–116.
—— (1983) 'Word order within Latin noun phrases', in H. Pinkster (ed.) *Latin Linguistics and Linguistic Theory*, Amsterdam: Benjamins.
—— (1986) 'Existential/locative clauses in Latin', MS, Klassiek Seminarium, University of Amsterdam.
DeLancey, Scott (1981) 'An interpretation of split ergativity and related patterns', *Language* 57(3): 626–659.
—— (1985) 'Categories of non-volitional actor in Lhasa Tibetan', in A. Zide, D. Magier and E. Schiller (eds) *The Semantics of Participant Roles: South Asia and Adjacent Areas*, Bloomington: IULC.
Derbyshire, Desmond C. (1977) 'Word order universals and the existence of OVS languages', *Linguistic Inquiry* 8: 590–599.
—— (1986) 'Comparative survey of morphology and syntax in Brazilian Arawakan', in D. Derbyshire and G. Pullum (eds).
Derbyshire, Desmond C. and Pullum, Geoffrey (1981) 'Object initial languages', *International Journal of American Linguistics* 47: 192–214.
—— (eds) (1986) *Handbook of Amazonian Languages*, Berlin: Mouton de Gruyter.
De Schutter, Georges (1985) 'Pragmatic and syntactic aspects of word order in Dutch', in A.M. Bolkestein *et al.* (eds) (1985b).

—— (1987) 'Pragmatic positions: the case of modifying clauses in Dutch', in J. Nuyts and G. de Schutter (eds).

De Vries, Lourens (1989) 'Studies in Wambon and Kombai' Ph.D. dissertation, University of Amsterdam.

De Wolf, Charles M. (1988) 'Voice in Austronesian languages of Philippine type: passive, ergative or neither', in M. Shibatani (ed.) (1988a).

Dezső, Laszló (1977) 'Towards a typology of theme and rheme' *Akten des 12– Linguischen Kolloquiums*, Pavia Band 1, Tübingen: Max Niemeyer Verlag.

—— (1982) *Studies in Syntactic Typology and Contrastive Grammar*, The Hague: Mouton.

Dignum, Frank (1989) 'Parsing an English text using Functional Grammar', in J.H. Connolly and S.C. Dik (eds).

Dik, Simon C. (1968) *Coordination*. Amsterdam: North Holland.

—— (1975) 'The semantic representation of manner adverbials', in A. Kraak (ed.) *Linguistics in the Netherlands 1972–1973*, Assen: Van Gorcum.

—— (1978) *Functional Grammar*, London: Academic Press.

—— (1980) *Studies in Functional Grammar*, London: Academic Press.

—— (1981) 'The interaction of subject and topic in Portuguese', in A.M. Bolkestein *et al.*

—— (1983a) (ed.) *Advances in Functional Grammar*, Dordrecht: Foris.

—— (1983b) 'Two constraints on relators and what they can do for us', in S.C. Dik (ed.).

—— (1983c) 'On the status of verbal reflexives', *Communication and Cognition* 16(1/2): 39–63.

—— (1985) 'Formal and semantic adjustment of derived constructions', in A.M. Bolkestein *et al.* (eds) (1985b).

—— (1986) 'On the notion "Functional Explanation" ', *WPFG* 11.

—— (1987a) 'Linguistically motivated knowledge representation', in M. Nagao (ed.) *Language and Artificial Intelligence*, Amsterdam: North Holland.

—— (1987b) 'Generating answers from a linguistically based knowledge base', in G. Kempen (ed.) *Natural Language Generation: New Results in Artificial Intelligence, Psychology and Linguistics*, Dordrecht: Nijhoff.

—— (1987c) 'Copula auxiliarization: how and why?', in Martin Harris and Paolo Ramat (eds) *Historical Development of Auxiliaries*, Berlin: Mouton de Gruyter.

—— (1987d) 'A typology of entities', in J. van der Auwera and L. Goossens (eds).

—— (1987e) 'Embedded predications from a typological point of view', Paper for the workshop on 'Typology of Languages of Europe', European Science Foundation, Rome, 7–9 January 1989.

—— (1988a) 'Towards a unified cognitive language', in *Worlds Behind Words; Essays in Honour of Prof. Dr. F.G. Droste*, Leuven: University of Leuven.

—— (1988b) 'Some developments in Functional Grammar: predicate formation', to appear in T. van Els (ed.) *Linguistics in The Netherlands*, Washington: Georgetown University Press.

—— (1989) *The Theory of Functional Grammar. Part I: The Structure of the Clause*, Dordrecht: Foris.

Dik, Simon C., Hoffman, Maria E., de Jong, Jan R., Sie, Ing Djiang, Stroomer, Harry and de Vries, Lourens (1981) 'On the typology of focus phenomena', in T. Hoekstra *et al.* (eds).

Dik, Simon, Hengeveld, Kees, Vester, Elseline and Vet, Co (1990) 'The hierarchical structure of the clause and the typology of adverbial satellites', in J. Nuyts *et al.* (eds).
Dixon, Robert M.W. (1972) *The Dyirbal Language of North Queensland*, Cambridge: Cambridge University Press.
—— (ed.) (1976) *Grammatical Categories in Australian Languages*, Canberra: Australian Institute of Aboriginal Studies.
Doherty, Monica (1987) 'Perhaps', *Folia Linguistica* 21(1): 45–65.
Dowty, David R. (1979) *Word Meaning and Montague Grammar*, Dordrecht: Reidel.
—— (1982) 'More on the categorial analysis of grammatical relations', *Working Papers in Linguistics* 26, The Ohio State University.
Dowty, David R., Karttunen, Lauri and Zwicky, Arnold M. (eds) (1985) *Natural Language Parsing. Psychological, Computational, and Theoretical Perspectives*, Cambridge: Cambridge University Press.
Dressler, Wolfgang (1985) *Morphology*, Ann Arbor: Karoma.
Dryer, Matthew (1980) 'The positional tendencies of sentential NPs in universal grammar', *Journal of Canadian Linguistics* 25: 123–95.
—— (1983) 'Indirect objects in Kinyarwanda revisited', in D.M. Perlmutter (ed.) (1983a).
—— (1986) 'Primary objects, secondary objects and antidative', *Language* 62(4): 808–845.
Du Bois, John W. (1985) 'Competing motivations', in John Haiman (ed.) *Iconicity in Syntax*, Amsterdam: Benjamins.
Duranti, Alessandro (1979) 'Object clitic pronouns in Bantu and the topicality hierarchy', *Studies in African Linguistics* 10: 31–45.
Durie, Mark (1987) 'Grammatical relations in Acehnese', *Studies in Language* 11(2): 365–399.
Eastman, Carol M. (1986) 'Haida: exemplar of a pragmatic communicative mode', in B.F. Elison (ed.).
Ehrlich, Susan (1987) 'Aspect, foreground and point of view', *Text* 7(4): 363–376.
Elison, Benjamin F. (ed.) (1986) *Language in Global Perspective*, Dallas, Texas: Summer Institute of Linguistics.
Emonds, John (1976) *A Transformational Approach to English Syntax*, New York: Academic Press.
Enkvist, Nils Erik (1981) 'Experiential iconicism', *Text* 1(1): 97–111.
Ernst, Thomas (1984) *Towards an Integrated Theory of Adverb Position in English*, Bloomington: IULC.
—— (1989) 'A phrase structure theory for tertiaries', MS, University of Delaware.
Ertel, Suitbert (1977) 'Where do the subjects of sentences come from?', in Sheldon Rosenberg (ed.) *Sentence Production: Developments in Research and Theory*, Hillsdale, NJ: Lawrence Earlbaum.
Estival, Dominique and Myhill, John (1988) 'Formal and functional aspects of the development from passive to ergative systems', in M. Shibatani (ed.) (1988a).
Falk, Yehuda N. (1983) 'Constituency, word order and phrase structure rules', *Linguistic Analysis* 11: 331–360.
Fauconnier, Gilles (1985) *Mental Spaces*, Cambridge, Mass.: MIT Press.

Fillmore, Charles J. (1968) 'The case for case', in E. Bach and R.T. Harms (eds).
—— (1971) 'Verbs of judging: an exercise in semantic description', in C.J. Fillmore and D.T. Langendoen (eds) *Studies in Linguistic Semantics*, New York: Holt, Rinehart & Winston.
—— (1972) 'Subjects, speakers and roles', in D. Davidson and G. Harman (eds) *Semantics of Natural Language*, 2nd edn, Dordrecht: D. Reidel.
—— (1977) 'The case for case reopened', in P. Cole and J. Sadock (eds).
—— (1981) 'Pragmatics and the description of discourse', in P. Cole (ed.).
Firbas, Jan (1964) 'From comparative word order studies', *Brno Studies in English* 4: 111–126.
—— (1981) 'Scene and perspective', *Brno Studies in English* 4: 37–79.
Foley, William A. and Van Valin, Jr, Robert D. (1977) 'On the viability of the notion of subject in universal grammar', *BLS* 3: 293–320.
—— (1984) *Functional Syntax and Universal Grammar*, Cambridge: Cambridge University Press.
Foley, William A. and Olson, Mike (1985) 'Clausehood and verbal serialization', in J. Nichols and A. Woodbury (eds).
Fortescue, Michael (1984) *West Greenlandic*, London: Croom Helm.
Fox, Andrew (1983) 'Topic continuity in Biblical Hebrew narrative', in T. Givón (ed.) (1983a).
Fox, Barbara A. (1987) 'Anaphora in popular English narrative', in R.S. Tomlin (ed.).
Frazier, Lyn (1985) 'Syntactic complexity', in D.R. Dowty *et al.* (eds).
Freidin, Robert (1975) 'The analysis of passives', *Language* 51: 384–405.
Fukui, Naoki (1986) 'A theory of category projection and its implications', Ph.D. dissertation, MIT.
Garcia, Erica C. (1975) *The Role of Theory in Linguistic Analysis: The Spanish Pronoun System*, Amsterdam: North Holland.
Garey, H. (1957) 'Verbal aspect in French', *Language* 33: 91–110.
Gary, Judith (1977) 'Object creating rules in several Bantu languages', *CLS* 13: 125–136.
Gary, Judith and Keenan, Edward (1977) 'On collapsing grammatical relations in universal grammar', in P. Cole and J. Sadock (eds).
Gasparov, Boris M. (1978) 'Ustnaja reč kak semiotičeskij ob'ekt. Semantika nominacii i semiotika ustnoj reči', *Acta et Commentationes Universitatis Tartuensis*, Tartu.
Gazdar, Gerald, Pullum, Geoffrey K. and Sag, Ivan (1981) *Auxiliaries and Related Phenomena in a Restrictive Theory of Grammar*, Bloomington: IULC.
Gazdar, Gerald, Klein, Ewan H. and Pullum, Geoffrey (eds) (1983) *Order, Concord and Constituency*, Dordrecht: Foris.
Gazdar, Gerald, Klein, Ewan H., Pullum, Geoffrey K. and Sag, Ivan (1985) *Generalized Phrase Structure Grammar*, Oxford: Basil Blackwell.
Gerdts, Donna (1982) 'Causal to object advancement in Halkomelem', *CLS* 16: 83–101.
Givón, Talmy (1979) *On Understanding Grammar*, New York: Academic Press.
—— (1980) 'The binding hierarchy and the typology of complements', *Studies in Language* 4(3): 333–377.
—— (1981) 'Typology and functional domains', *Studies in Language* 5: 163–193.

—— (ed.) (1983a) *Topic Continuity in Discourse: Quantitative Cross-Language Studies*, Amsterdam: Benjamins.
—— (1983b) 'Topic continuity in discourse: an introduction', in Talmy Givón (ed.) (1983a).
—— (1983c) 'Topic continuity and word order pragmatics', in Talmy Givón (ed.) (1983a).
—— (1984) *Syntax. A Functional Typological Introduction*, Amsterdam: John Benjamins.
—— (1988) 'The pragmatics of word order: predictability, importance and attention', in M. Hammond *et al.* (eds).
Goossens, Louis (1975) 'Modality and the modals: a problem for Functional Grammar', in A.M. Bolkestein *et al.* (eds) (1985b).
Gorbet, Larry (1976) *A Grammar of Diegueño Nominals*, New York: Garland.
Green, Georgia M. (1974) *Semantic and Syntactic Irregularity*, Bloomington Indiana: Indiana University Press.
—— (1982) 'Colloquial and literary uses of inversions', in Deborah Tannen (ed.) *Spoken and Written Language: Exploring Orality and Literacy*, Norwood, NJ: Ablex.
Greenbaum, Sidney (1969) *Studies in English Adverbial Usage*, London: Longman.
Greenberg, Joseph H. (1963) 'Some universals of grammar with particular reference to the order of meaningful elements', in Joseph H. Greenberg (ed.) *Universals of Language*, Cambridge, Mass.: MIT Press.
Greenberg, Joseph H., Ferguson, Charles A. and Moravcsik, Edith A. (eds) (1978) *Universals of Human Language*, 1 *Method and Theory*, 2 *Phonology*, 3 *Word Structure*, 4 *Syntax*, Stanford Calif.: Stanford University Press.
Grice, Paul (1975) 'Logic and conversation', in P. Cole and J.L. Morgan (eds).
Grimes, Joseph E. (ed.) (1978) *Papers in Discourse*, Arlington, Texas: SIL.
Grimshaw, Jane (1982) 'On the lexical representation of Romance reflexive clitics', in J.W. Bresnan (ed.) (1982a).
Gruber, Jeffrey (1976) *Lexical Structures in Syntax and Semantics*, Amsterdam: North Holland.
Guéron, Jacqueline (1980) 'On the syntax and semantics of PP extraposition', *Linguistic Inquiry* 11: 636–678.
Gundel, Jeanette K. (1988) 'Universals of topic-comment structure', in M. Hammond *et al.* (eds).
Gundel, Jeanette K., Houlihan, Kathleen and Sanders, Gerald (1988) 'On the function of marked and unmarked terms', in M. Hammond *et al.* (eds).
Haiman, John (1985) *Natural Syntax: Iconicity and Erosion*, Cambridge: Cambridge University Press.
Haiman, John and Munro, Pamela (1983) 'Introduction', in J. Haiman and P. Munro (eds) *Switch-Reference and Universal Grammar*, Amsterdam: John Benjamins.
Haiman, John and Thompson, Sandra A. (eds) (1988) *Clause Combining in Grammar and Discourse*, Amsterdam: John Benjamins.
Hajičova, Eva and Sgall, Petr (1987) 'The ordering principle', *Journal of Pragmatics* 11: 435–454.
Halle, Morris, Bresnan, Joan W. and Miller, George (eds) (1978) *Linguistic Meaning and Psychological Reality*, Cambridge, Mass.: MIT Press.
Halliday, Michael A. K. (1967/68) 'Notes on transitivity and theme in English', *Journal of Linguistics* 3: 37–81, 199–244.

—— (1970) 'Functional diversity in language as seen from a consideration of modality and mood in English', *Foundations of Language* 6: 322–361.
—— (1985) *An Introduction to Functional Grammar*, London: Arnold.
Halliday, Michael A.K. and Hassan, Ruqaiya (1976) *Cohesion in English*, London: Longmans.
Hammond, Michael, Moravcsik, Edith A. and Wirth, Jessica R. (eds) (1988) *Studies in Syntactic Typology*, Amsterdam: John Benjamins.
Hannay, Michael (1983) 'The focus function in Functional Grammar: questions of contrast and context', in S.C. Dik (ed.) (1983a).
—— (1985a) *English Existentials in Functional Grammar*, Dordrecht: Foris.
—— (1985b) 'Inferability, discourse-boundness and sub-topics', in A.M. Bolkestein *et al.* (eds) (1985a).
Hannay, Michael and Vester, Elseline (eds) (1989) *Working with Functional Grammar: Descriptive and Computational Applications*, Dordrecht: Foris.
Harder, Peter (1990) 'Tense, semantics and layered syntax', in J. Nuyts *et al.* (eds).
Harlig, Jeffrey and Bardovi-Harlig, Kathleen (1988) 'Accentuation typology, word order and theme-rheme structure', in M. Hammond *et al.* (eds).
Harries-Delise, Helga (1978) 'Contrastive emphasis and cleft-sentences', in J.H. Greenberg *et al.* (eds) vol. 4.
Haviland, Susan E. and Clark, Herbert H. (1974) 'What's new? Acquiring new information as a process in comprehension', *Journal of Verbal Learning and Verbal Behaviour* 13: 512–521.
Hawkins, John A. (1983) *Word Order Universals*, New York: Academic Press.
—— (1990) 'A parsing theory of word order universals', *Linguistic Inquiry* 21(2): 223–261.
Hawkinson, Annie K. and Hyman, Larry M. (1974) 'Hierarchies of natural topic in Shona', *Studies in African Linguistics* 5: 147–170.
Heath, Jeffrey (1976) 'Antipassivization: a functional typology', *BLS* 2: 202–211.
Helbig, Gerhard and Schenkel, W. (1973) *Wörterbuch zur Valenz und Distribution deutscher Verben*, Leipzig: VEB Verlag Enzyklopädie.
Hengeveld, Kees (1987a) 'The Spanish mood system', *WPFG* 22.
—— (1987b) 'Clause structure and modality in Functional Grammar', in J. Van der Auwera and L. Goossens (eds).
—— (1989) 'Layers and operators', *Journal of Linguistics* 25: 127–157.
—— (1990a) 'Semantic relations in non-verbal predication', in J. Nuyts *et al.* (eds).
—— (1990b) 'Non-verbal predicability', in J. Van der Auwera and M. Kefer (eds) *Meaning and Grammar*, Berlin: Mouton de Gruyter.
Heny, Frank and Richards, Barry (eds) (1983) *Linguistic Categories, Auxiliaries and Related Puzzles*, 2, Dordrecht: D. Reidel.
Hesp, Cees (1990) 'The functional grammar computational natural language user and psychological adequacy', in J. Nuyts *et al.* (eds).
Hetzron, Robert (1975) 'The presentative movement, or why the ideal word order is V.S.O.P.,' in C. Li (ed.) *Word Order and Word Order Change*, Austin: University of Texas Press.
Hjelmquist, E. (1990) 'Context and language', in J. Nuyts *et al.* (eds).
Hoekstra, Teun, van der Hulst, Harry and Moortgat, Michael (eds) (1981) *Perspectives on Functional Grammar*, Dordrecht: Foris.

Hooper, Joan B. (1976) *An Introduction to Natural Generative Phonology*, New York: Academic Press.
Hopper, Paul J. and Thompson, Sandra A. (1980) 'Transitivity in grammar and discourse', *Language* 56: 251–300.
—— (eds) (1982) *Syntax and Semantics 15. Studies in Transitivity*, New York: Academic Press.
Huck, Geoffrey J. and Ojeda, Almerindo E. (eds) (1987) *Syntax and Semantics 20. Discontinuous Constituents*, New York: Academic Press.
Huddleston, Rodney D. (1970) 'Some remarks on case grammar', *Linguistic Inquiry* 1: 501–511.
Hudson, Joyce (1976) 'Walmadjari', in R.M.W. Dixon (ed.).
Hudson, Richard A. (1980) 'Constituency and dependency', *Linguistics* 18: 179–198.
—— (1984) *Word Grammar*, Oxford: Basil Blackwell.
—— (1988) 'Systemic Grammar [Review of Butler (1985) and Halliday (1985)]', *Linguistics* 24: 791–815.
Hupet, Michel and Costermans, Jean (1982) 'Towards a functional approach of language processing in context', in J.F. Le Ny and W. Kintsch (eds) *Language and Comprehension*, Amsterdam: North Holland.
Hyman, Larry M. and Duranti, Alessandro (1982) 'On the object relation in Bantu', in P.J. Hopper and S.A. Thompson (eds).
Jackendoff, Ray S. (1972) *Semantic Interpretation in Generative Grammar*, Cambridge, Mass.: MIT Press.
—— (1977) *X-bar Syntax: A Study of Phrase Structure*, Cambridge, Mass.: MIT Press.
—— (1987) 'The status of thematic relations in linguistic theory', *Linguistic Inquiry* 18: 369–412.
Jaeggli, Osvaldo A. (1986) 'Three issues in the theory of clitics: case, doubled NPs and extraction', in H. Borer (ed.).
Jespersen, Otto (1927) *A Modern English Grammar on Historical Principles*, vols 3 and 4, London: Allen & Unwin.
Johnson, Marion R. (1981) 'A unified temporal theory of aspect', in P. Tedeschi and A. Zaenen (eds).
Johnson-Laird, Philip N. (1981) 'Mental models of meaning', in Aravind K. Joshi, Bonnie L. Webber and Ivan A. Sag (eds) *Elements of Discourse Understanding*, Cambridge: Cambridge University Press.
Junger, Judith (1987) *Predicate Formation in the Verbal System of Modern Hebrew*, Dordrecht: Foris.
Kahrel, Peter (1985a) 'Some aspects of derived intransitivity', *WPFG* 4.
—— (1985b) 'Indirect questions and relators', in A.M. Bolkestein *et al.* (eds) (1985b).
Kalmàr, I. (1979) 'The antipassive and grammatical relations in Eskimo', in Frank Plank (ed.) *Ergativity*, London: Academic Press.
Kaplan, Ronald M. and Bresnan, Joan W. (1982) 'Lexical Functional Grammar: a formal system for grammatical representation', in J.W. Bresnan (ed.) (1982a).
Karolak, Stanisław (1984) 'Składnia wyrażeń predykatywnych', in Zuzanna Topolińska (ed.) *Gramatyka współczesnego języka polskiego. Składnia*. Warsaw: PWN.
Keenan, Edward L. (1976) 'Remarkable subjects in Malagasy', in C. Li (ed.).
—— (1978) 'The syntax of subject-final languages', in Wilfred P. Lehmann (ed.)

Syntactic Typology: Studies in the Phenomenology of Language, Hassocks, Sussex: The Harvester Press.

—— (1981) 'Passive in the world's languages', Trier: Linguistic Agency, University of Trier.

—— (1984) 'Semantic correlates of the ergative/absolutive distinction', *Linguistics* 22: 197–223.

Keenan, Edward L. and Comrie, Bernard (1977) 'Noun phrase accessibility and universal grammar', *Linguistic Inquiry* 8: 63–99.

—— (1979) 'Data on the noun phrase accessibility hierarchy', *Language* 55: 333–351.

Keijsper, Cornelia E. (1985) *Information Structure with Examples from Russian, English and Dutch*, Amsterdam: Rodopi.

Kenny, A.J.P. (1963) *Actions, Emotions and Will*, London: Routledge & Kegan Paul.

Kholodovich, Aleksander A. (1963) 'On telic and atelic verbs, on the basis of Korean and Japanese data', in *Filologia stran vostoka*, Leningrad.

Kiefer, Ferenc (1987) 'On defining modality', *Folia Linguistica* 21(1): 67–94.

Kimenyi, Alexandre (1988) 'Passiveness in Kinyarwanda', in M. Shibatani (ed.) (1988a).

Kirsner, Robert S. (1979) *The Problem of Presentative Sentences in Modern Dutch*, Amsterdam: North Holland.

Kiss, Katalin E. (1981) 'Structural relations in Hungarian, a "free" word order language', *Linguistic Inquiry* 12: 185–213.

Kisseberth, Charles W. and Abasheikh, Mohammad Imam (1977) 'The object relation in Chi-mwi:-ni', in P. Cole and J. Sadock (eds).

Kitagawa, Chisato (1982) 'Topic constructions in Japanese', *Lingua* 57: 175–214.

Klaiman, Mimi H. (1988) 'Affectedness and control: a typology of voice phenomena', in M. Shibatani (ed.) (1988a).

Kornai, András and Pullum, Geoffrey (1990) 'The X-bar theory of clause structure', *Language* 66(1): 24–50.

Koster, Jan (1982) 'Review of Dik, Studies in Functional Grammar', *De Nieuwe Taalgids* 75: 360–369.

Krzeszowski, Thomas (1989) 'The axiological parameter in idealized cognitive models', MS, Department of English, Gdańsk University.

Kucała, M. (1966) *Rozwój iteratywów dokonanych w języku polskim*, Wrocław: Ossolineum.

—— (1978) *Rodzaj gramatyczny w historii polszczyzny*, Wrocław: Ossolineum.

Kucera, Henry (1981) 'Aspect, markedness, and t_o', in P. Tedeschi and A. Zaenen (eds).

Kuno, Susumo (1976) 'Subject, theme and the speaker's empathy — a reexamination of relativization phenomena', in C. Li (ed.).

—— (1987) *Functional Syntax*, Chicago: The University of Chicago Press.

Kuroda, Sigi-Yuki (1965) 'Generative Grammatical Studies in the Japanese Language', Ph.D. dissertation, MIT. (Published 1979, New York: Garland.)

—— (1972) 'The categorial and the thetic judgement. Evidence from Japanese syntax', *Foundations of Language* 9: 153–185.

Kwee, Tjoe-Liong (1979) 'A68–FG(3): Simon Dik's funktionele grammatica geschreven in Algol68 versie nr. 03', *Publikaties van het Instituut voor Algemene Taalwetenschap* 23.

—— (1987) 'A computer model of Functional Grammar', in *Natural Language Generation. Recent Advances in Artificial Intelligence, Psychology and Linguistics*, Dordrecht/Boston: Academic Press.
Lakoff, George (1987) *Woman, Fire and Dangerous Things. What Categories Reveal about the Mind*, Chicago: University of Chicago Press.
Lakoff, George and Johnson, Mark (1980) *The Metaphors We Live by*, Chicago: Chicago University Press.
Lambrecht, Knud (1987) 'On the status of SVO sentences in French discourse', in R.S. Tomlin (ed.).
—— (1988) 'Presentational cleft constructions in Spoken French', in J. Haiman and S.A. Thompson (eds).
Langacker, Ronald W. (1986) *Foundations of Cognitive Grammar*, vol. 1, Stanford: Stanford University Press.
—— (1988) 'The nature of grammatical valence', in Brygida Rudzka-Ostyn (ed.) *Topics in Cognitive Linguistics*, Amsterdam: John Benjamins.
Langdon, Margaret and Munro, Pamela (1979) 'Subject and (switch-) reference in Yuman', *Folia Linguistica* 13: 321–344.
Larson, Richard K. (1988) 'On the double object construction', *Linguistic Inquiry* 19(3): 335–391.
Lascaratou, Cyhryssoula (1989) 'A functional approach to constituent order with particular reference to Modern Greek', Ph.D. dissertation, University of Athens.
Laskowski, Roman (1984) '(a) Podstawowe pojęcia morfologi. (b) Predykatyw', in R. Grzegorczykowa, R. Laskowski and H. Wróbel (eds) *Gramatyka współczesnego języka polskiego. Morfologia*, Warsaw: PWN.
Lawler, John M. (1977) 'A agrees with B in Achenese: a problem for relational grammar', in P. Cole and J. Sadock (eds).
Leech, Geoffrey (1969) *Towards a Semantic Description of English*, London: Longman.
—— (1971) *Meaning and the English Verb*, London: Longman.
Lehmann, Christian (1982) 'Universal and typological aspects of agreement', in Hansjakob Seiler and Franz Josef Stachowiak (eds) *Die Techniken und ihr Zusammenhang in Einzelsprachen*, Tübingen: Gunter Narr.
—— (1984) *Der Relativsatz. Typologie senier Strukturen, Theorie senier Funktionen, Kompendium senier Grammatik*, Tübingen: G. Narr (LUS 3).
—— (1988) 'Towards a typology of clause linkage', in J. Haiman and S.A. Thompson (eds).
Lehmann, Wilfred P. (1973) 'A structural principle of language and its implications', *Language* 49: 47–66.
Lepsius, R. (1880) *Nubische Grammatik*, Berlin.
Levinson, Stephen C. (1978) 'Participant reference in Inga narrative discourse', in John Hinds (ed.) *Anaphora in Discourse*, Edmonton, Canada: Linguistic Research, Inc.
—— (1983) *Pragmatics*, Cambridge: Cambridge University Press.
Lewis, Geoffrey L. (1967) *Turkish Grammar*, Oxford: Clarendon Press.
Li, Charles (ed.) (1976) *Subject and Topic*, New York: Academic Press.
Li, Charles and Thompson, Sandra A. (1976) 'Subject and topic: a new typology of language', in C. Li (ed.).
Lichtenberk, Frantisek (1982) 'Individuation hierarchies in Manam', in P.J. Hopper and S.A. Thompson (eds).

Limburg, Machiel J. (1985) 'On the notion "relator" and the expression of the genitive relation', in A.M. Bolkestein et al. (eds) (1985b).
Longacre, Robert E. (1976) *An Anatomy of Speech Notions*, Lisse: Peter de Ridder Press.
Lyons, John (1968) *Introduction to Theoretical Linguistics*, Cambridge: Cambridge University Press.
—— (1977) *Semantics*, vols 1 and 2, Cambridge: Cambridge University Press.
McCawley, James D. (1968a) 'Concerning the base component of a transformational grammar', *Foundations of Language* 4: 243–269.
—— (1968b) 'The role of semantics in a grammar', in E. Bach and R.T. Harms (eds).
—— (1985) 'Review of [Newmeyer 1983]', *Language* 61: 668–679.
MacDonald, Lorna (1988) 'Subordination in Tauya', in J. Haiman and S.A. Thompson (eds).
Mackenzie, J. Lachlan (1981) 'Functions and cases', in T. Hoekstra et al. (eds).
—— (1987) 'The representation of nominal predicates in the Fund', *WPFG* 25.
Majewicz, Alfred F. (1985) *The Grammatical Category of Aspect in Japanese and Polish in a Comparative Perspective*, Poznań: Wydawnictwo Naukowe Uniwersytetu Adama Mickiewicza.
Makino, Seiichi (1982) 'Japanese grammar and functional grammar', *Lingua* 57: 125–173.
Mallinson, Graham and Blake, Barry J. (1981) *Language Typology: Cross-Linguistic Studies in Syntax*, Amsterdam: North Holland.
Marantz, Alec P. (1984) *On the Nature of Grammatical Relations*, Cambridge, Mass.: MIT Press.
Masica, Colin P. (1976) *Defining a Linguistic Area, South Asia*, Chicago: University of Chicago Press.
Matthews, G. H. (1965) *Hidatsa Syntax*, The Hague: Mouton.
Matthews, Peter H. (1981) *Syntax*, Cambridge: Cambridge University Press.
Maxwell, Daniel N. (1984) 'A typologically based principle of linearization', *Language* 60: 251–285.
Mayerthaler, Willi (1988) *Morphological Naturalness. Linguistica Extranea, Studia 17*, Ann Arbor: Karoma.
Miller, Philip (1986) 'On certain formal properties of Dik's Functional Grammar', *Belgian Journal of Linguistics* 1: 171–222.
Mithun, Marianne (1987) 'Is basic word order universal?', in R.S. Tomlin (ed.).
Moravcsik, Edith (1978) 'Agreement', in J. Greenberg et al. (eds), vol. 4.
Mourelatos, Alexander P. (1981) 'Events, processes and states', in P. Tedeschi and A. Zaenen (eds).
Moutaouakil, Ahmed (1984) 'Le focus en Arabe: vers une analyse fonctionnelle', *Lingua* 64: 115–176.
—— (1989) *Pragmatic Functions in a Functional Grammar of Arabic*, Dordrecht: Foris.
Muysken, Pieter (1988) 'Taalkunde in F-groot en F-klein', *Tijdschrift voor Taal- en Tekstwetenschap*.
Nakajima, Heizo (1982) 'The V^4 system and bounding category', *Linguistic Analysis* 9(4): 341–378.
Newmeyer, Fredrick J. (1983) *Grammatical Theory: Its Limits and Possibilities*, Chicago: The University of Chicago Press.
Nichols, Joanna (1986) 'Head-marking and dependent-marking', *Language* 62: 56–119.

—— (1988) 'Nominalization and assertion in scientific Russian prose', in J. Haiman and S.A. Thompson (eds).
Nichols, Joanna and Woodbury, Anthony (eds) (1985) *Grammar Inside and Outside the Clause*, London: Cambridge University Press.
Noonan, Michael (1985) 'Complementation', in T. Shopen (ed.).
Norman, William N. (1978) 'Advancement rules and syntactic change in Mayan', *BLS* 4: 458–476.
Nuyts, Jan (1983) 'On the methodology of Functional Language Theory', in S.C. Dik (ed.) (1983a).
—— (1988) 'Aspekten van een kognitief-pragmatische taaltheorie', Ph.D. dissertation, University of Antwerp. (Shortened English version to appear: Amsterdam: John Benjamins.)
—— (1989) 'Functional Procedural Grammar: an overview', *WPFG* 31.
—— (1990) 'Linguistic representation and conceptual knowledge representation', in J. Nuyts *et al.* (eds).
Nuyts, Jan and de Schutter, G. (eds) (1987) *Getting One's Words into Line*, Dordrecht: Foris.
Nuyts, Jan, Bolkestein, A. Machtelt and Vet, Co (eds) (1990) *Layers and Levels of Representation in Language Theory. A Functional View*, Amsterdam: John Benjamins.
Oehrle, Richard (1975) 'The grammatical status of the English dative alternation', Ph.D. dissertation, MIT.
Okamoto, Shigeko (1981) 'The notion of givenness and the use of pronouns and ellipsis', *BLS* 7: 222–223.
Olson, Michael L. (1981) 'Barai clause junctures: towards a functional theory of interclausal relations', Dissertation, Australian National University, Canberra.
Palmer, Frank R. (1983) 'Semantic explanations for the use of the English modals', in F.R. Heny and B. Richards (eds).
Parks, Douglas R. (1976) *A Grammar of Pawnee*, Garland Studies in American Linguistics, New York: Garland Publishing.
Payne, Thomas E. (1982) 'Role and reference related subject properties and ergativity in Yup'ik Eskimo and Tagalog', *Studies in Language* 6(1): 75–106.
—— (1985) 'Referential distance and discourse structure in Yagua', *Working Papers. Summer Institute of Linguistics* vol. 29, University of Northern Dakota.
Perlmutter, David M. (1978) 'Impersonal passives and the unaccusative hypothesis', *BLS* 4: 157–189.
—— (1981) 'Functional Grammar and Relational Grammar: points of convergence and divergence', in T. Hoekstra *et al.* (eds).
—— (ed.) (1983a) *Studies in Relational Grammar 1*, Chicago: Chicago University Press.
—— (1983b) 'Personal vs impersonal constructions', *Natural Language and Linguistic Theory* 1: 141–200.
Perlmutter, David M. and Postal, Paul M. (1977) 'Towards a universal characterization of passivization', *BLS* 3: 395–417.
—— (1983) 'Some proposed laws of basic clause structure', in D.M. Perlmutter (ed.) (1983a).
—— (1984a) 'The 1-advancement exclusiveness law', in D.M. Perlmutter and C.A. Rosen (eds).

—— (1984b) 'Impersonal passives and some relational laws', in D.M. Perlmutter and C.G. Rosen (eds).
Perlmutter, David M. and Rosen, Carol G. (eds) (1984) *Studies in Relational Grammar 2*, Chicago: Chicago University Press.
Perlmutter, David M. and Zaenen, Anne (1984) 'The indefinite extraposition construction in Dutch and German', in D.M. Perlmutter and C.G. Rosen (eds).
Pinkster, Harm (1982) *On Latin Adverbs*, Amsterdam: North Holland.
—— (1983) 'Tempus, aspect and aktionsart in Latin', in H. Temporini and W. Haase (eds) *Aufstieg und Niedergang der Römischen Welt*, Berlin: Walter De Gruyter.
—— (1988a) 'Non-accusative second arguments of two-place verbs in Latin', *Cuadernos de Filologia Clásica* 21: 235–245.
—— (1988b) *Lateinische Syntax und Semantik*, Tübingen: Francke Verlag.
Prince, Ellen F. (1978) 'A comparison of wh-clefts and it-clefts in discourse', *Language* 54: 883–906.
—— (1981) 'Toward a taxonomy of given/new information', in P. Cole (ed.).
—— (1984) 'Topicalization and left-dislocation: a functional analysis', in S. White and V. Teller (eds) *Annals of the New York Academy of Sciences vol. 433, Discourses in Reading and Linguistics*.
Prince, Gerald J. (1982) *Narratology*, Berlin: Mouton.
Pullum, Geoffrey K. (1979) *Rule Interaction and the Organization of Grammar*, London: Garland.
Pullum, Geoffrey and Wilson, Deirdre (1977) 'Autonomous syntax and the analysis of auxiliaries', *Language* 53: 741–788.
Quirk, Randolf and Greenbaum, Sidney (1973) *A University Grammar of English*, London: Longman.
Quirk, Randolf, Greenbaum, Sidney, Leech, Geoffrey and Svartvik, Jan (1972) *A Grammar of Contemporary English*, London: Longman.
—— (1985) *A Comprehensive Grammar of the English Language*, London: Longman.
Radewa, Sabina (1984) *Govoritie li Bylgarcki? Zwięzły kurs języka bŀugarskiego*, Warsaw: Wiedza Powszechna.
Radford, Andrew (1981) *Transformational Syntax*, Cambridge: Cambridge University Press.
—— (1988) *Transformational Grammar*, Cambridge: Cambridge University Press.
Reh, Mechtild (1985) *Die Krongo Sprache (nìino mó-dì)*, Berlin: Dietrich Reiner Verlag.
Reichenbach, Hans (1947) *Elements of Symbolic Logic*, New York: Macmillan.
Reinhart, Tanya (1982) 'Pragmatics and linguistics: an analysis of sentence topic', *Philosophica* 27(1): 53–94.
Rijkhoff, Jan (1986) 'Word order universals revisited: the principle of Head Proximity', *WPFG* 14.
—— (1989a) 'Toward a unified analysis of term operators', MS, University of Amsterdam.
—— (1989b) 'The identification of referents', in J.H. Connolly and S.C. Dik (eds).
—— (1990) 'Explaining word order in the noun phrase', *Linguistics* 28: 5–42.
Rijkhoff, Jan, Bakker, Dik, Hengeveld, Kees and Kahrel, Peter (1990) 'A method of language sampling', MS, University of Amsterdam.

Rijksbaron, Albert (1988) 'Aristotle and the classification of states of affairs in FG', (unpublished paper), University of Amsterdam.
Rimmon-Kenan, Shlomith (1983) *Narrative Fiction. Contemporary Poetics*, London: Methuen.
Roeper, Thomas (1987) 'Implicit arguments and the head – complement relation', *Linguistic Inquiry* 18(2) 267–310.
Romero-Figueroa, Andrés (1985) 'OSV as the basic word order in Warao', *Lingua* 66: 115–134.
Ross, John R. (1970) 'On declarative sentences', in R.A. Jacobs and P.S. Rosenbaum (eds) *Readings in English Transformational Grammar*, Waltham (Mass.): Ginn.
Rude, Noel (1982) 'Promotion and topicality of Nez Perce objects', *BLS* 8: 463–483.
Sadock, Jerry M. (1974) *Towards a Linguistic Theory of Speech Acts*, New York: Academic Press.
Sag, Ivan (1987) 'Grammatical hierarchy and linear precedence', in G.J. Huck and A.E. Ojeda (eds).
Saloni, Zygmunt and Swidziński, Marek (1985) *Składnia współłczesnego języka polskiego* (2nd edn), Warsaw: PWN.
Sasse, Hans-Jürgen (1987) 'The thetic/categorial distinction revisited', *Linguistics* 25(3): 511–80.
Sawaie, Mohammed (1985) 'An aspect of verb subject concord in Arabic', MS, University of Virginia, Oriental Languages Department.
Schachter, Paul (1976) 'The subject in Philippine languages: topic, actor topic or none of the above', in C. Li (ed.).
—— (1977) 'Reference related and role related properties of subjects', in P. Cole and J. Sadock (eds).
—— (1983) 'Explaining auxiliary order', in F. Heny and B. Richards (eds).
Schank, Roger and Abelson, Robert C. (1977) *Scripts, Plans, Goals and Understanding: An Inquiry into Human Knowledge Structure*, Hillsdale, NJ: Lawrence Erlbaum.
Schlesinger, I.M. (1989) 'Instruments as agents: on the nature of semantic relations', *Journal of Linguistics* 25: 189–210.
Schlyter, Suzanne (1982) 'Adverbial position in French contrasted with those in Swedish: stress, focus and subjectivity', in Nils E. Enkvist and Viljo Kohonen (eds) *Approaches to Word Order*, Abo: Publications of the Abo Akademi Foundation.
Schmidt, W. (1926) *Die Sprachtfamilien und Sprachenkieise der Erds*, Heidelberg.
Searle, John R. (1969) *Speech Acts*, London: Cambridge University Press.
—— (1975) 'Indirect speech acts', in P. Cole and J. Morgan (eds).
Sedlak, Philip A. (1975) 'Direct/indirect object word order', *Working Papers in Language Universals*, 18, California, Stanford University.
Sgall, Petr, Hajičová, Eva and Buráňová, E. (1980) *Aktuální členění věty v češtine*, Prague: Academia.
Sgall, Petr, Hajičová, Eva and Panevová, J. (1986) *The Meaning of the Sentence in its Semantic and Pragmatic Aspects*, Dordrecht and Prague: Reidel and Akademia.
Shibatani, Masayoshi (1985) 'Passives and related constructions', *Language* 61(4): 821–848.

—— (ed.) (1988a) *Passives and Voice*, Amsterdam: John Benjamins.
—— (1988b) 'Voice in Philippine languages', in M. Shibatani (ed.) (1988a).
Shopen, Timothy (ed.) (1985) *Language Typology and Syntactic Description*, vol. 3, Cambridge: Cambridge University Press.
Siewierska, Anna (1984a) *The Passive: a Comparative Linguistic Analysis*, London: Croom Helm.
—— (1984b) 'Phrasal discontinuity in Polish', *Australian Journal of Linguistics* 4: 57–71.
—— (1987) 'Postverbal subject pronouns in Polish in the light of topic continuity and the topic/focus distinction', in J. Nuyts and G. de Schutter (eds).
—— (1988a) *Word Order Rules*, London: Croom Helm.
—— (1988b) 'Subject postposing in Polish as a textual dimension', Paper presented at the annual Societas Linguistica Europea Conference, Freiberg, July 1988.
Silverstein, Michael (1976) 'Hierarchies of features and ergativity', in R.W.M. Dixon (ed.).
Sirotinina, O. B. (1961) 'O porjadke slov v russkom jazyke. Voprosy teorii i metodiki izučeniji russkogo jazyka', *Trudy vtoroj naučnoj konferencii kafedr russkogo jazyka pedagogičeskich institutov Povolz'ja*, Kujbyšev.
—— (1965) *Porjadok slov v russkom jazyke*, Sarotov: Izd. Sarotovskogo Universiteta.
Smith, Carlota (1983) 'A theory of aspectual choice', *Language* 59: 479–501.
Sommers, H.L. (1987) *Valence and Case in Computational Linguistics*, Edinburgh: Edinburgh University Press.
Speas, Margaret (1986) 'Adjunctions and Projections in Syntax', Ph.D. dissertation, MIT.
Sridhar, S. N. (1976) 'Dative subjects, rule government and relational grammar', *Studies in the Linguistic Sciences*, 6(1): 130–151.
Starosta, Stan (1977) 'The one per cent solution', in W. Abraham (ed.) *Valence, Semantic Case and Grammatical Relations*, Amsterdam: John Benjamins.
—— (1979) 'The end of phrase-structure as we know it', *University of Hawaii Working Papers in Linguistics* 11(1): 59–76.
Stockwell, Robert P. (1980) 'Summation and assessment of theories', in Edith A. Moravcsik and Jessica R. Wirth (eds) *Syntax and Semantics 13. Current Approaches to Syntax*, London: Academic Press.
Svartvik, Jan (1966) *On Voice in the English Verb*, The Hague: Mouton.
Talmy, Leonard (1983) 'How languages structure space', in H. Pick and L. Acredolo (eds) *Spatial Orientation, Theory, Research and Application*, New York: Plenum Press.
—— (1985a) 'Lexicalization patterns: typologies and universals', *Berkeley Cognitive Science Report Series*, Berkeley.
—— (1985b) 'Force dynamics in language and thought', in *Parasession on Causatives and Agentivity*, Chicago Linguistic Society (21st regional Meeting), University of Chicago.
Taylor, Barry (1977) 'Tense and continuity', *Linguistics and Philosophy* 1: 199–220.
Tedeschi, Philip and Zaenen, Anne (eds) (1981) *Syntax and Semantics 14. Tense and Aspect*, New York: Academic Press.
Tesnière, Lucien (1959) *Elements de Syntaxe Structurale*, Paris: Klincksieck.

Thompson, Sandra A. (1985) 'Grammar and written discourse: Initial vs Final purpose clauses in English', *Text* 5(1/2): 55–84.
—— (1986) 'The passive in English: a discourse perspective', in R. Channon and L. Shockey (eds) *Festschrift for Isle Lehiste*, Dordrecht: Foris.
Tomlin, Russell S. (1983) 'On the interaction of syntactic subject, thematic information and agent in English', *Journal of Pragmatics* 7: 411–432.
—— (ed.) (1987) *Coherence and Grounding in Discourse*, Amsterdam: John Benjamins.
Trithart, Lee (1975) 'Relational Grammar and Chichewa subjectivization rules', *CLS* 11: 615–625.
—— (1979) 'Topicality: an alternative to the relational view of the Bantu passive', *Studies in African Linguistics* 10: 1–30.
Tsunoda, Tasaku (1988) 'Antipassives in Warrungu and other Australian languages', in M. Shibatani (ed.) (1988a).
Tsutsui, Michio (1981) 'Topic marker ellipsis in Japanese', *Studies in the Linguistic Sciences* 11(1): 163–179.
Uszkoreit, Hans (1986) 'Constraints on order', *Linguistics* 24(5): 883–889.
Van der Auwera, Johan (1981) 'Tagalog "ang" – an exercise in universal grammar', in S. Daalder and M. Gerristen (eds) *Linguistics in The Netherlands*, Amsterdam: North Holland.
—— (1987) 'Complementizers as P_2 fillers', in J. Nuyts and G. de Schutter (eds).
Van der Auwera, Johan and Goossens, Louis (eds) (1987) *Ins and Outs of the Predication*, Dordrecht: Foris.
Van der Korst, Bieke (1986) 'Twelve sentences: a translation procedure in terms of Functional Grammar', *WPFG* 19.
Van Dijk, Teun A. (1977) *Text and Context*, London: Longman.
Van Valin, Robert D. (1990) 'Layered syntax in role and reference grammar', in J. Nuyts *et al.* (eds).
Vendler, Zeno (1957) 'Verbs and times', *Philosophical Review* 66: 143–160.
—— (1967) *Linguistics in Philosophy*, Ithaca, NY: Cornell University Press.
Vennemann, Theo (1972) 'Analogy in generative grammar, the origin of word order', in L. Heilmann (ed.) *Proceedings of the Eleventh International Congress of Linguistics*, Vol. 2, Bologna: Il Mulino.
—— (1974) 'Words and syllables in natural generative grammar', *Language* 50: 347–374.
Verkuyl, Hendrik J. (1972) *On the Compositional Nature of Aspect*, Dordrecht: Reidel.
Vester, Elseline (1983) 'Instrument and Manner Expressions in Latin', Ph.D. dissertation, University of Amsterdam.
Vet, Co (1981) 'Subject assignment in the impersonal constructions of French', in A.M. Bolkestein *et al.*
—— (1986) 'A pragmatic approach to tense in Functional Grammar', *WPFG* 16.
Vlach, Frank (1981) 'The semantics of the progressive', in P. Tedeschi and A. Zaenen (eds).
Wanner, Eric and Maratsos, Michael (1978) 'An ATN approach to comprehension', in M. Halle *et al.* (eds).
Wasow, Thomas (1977) 'Transformations and the lexicon', in P.W. Culicover, T. Wasow and A. Akmaijau (eds) *Formal Syntax*, New York: Academic Press.

Watters, John R. (1979) 'Focus in Aghem: a study of its formal correlates and typology', in L. Hyman (ed.) *Aghem Grammatical Structure*, Los Angeles: University of Southern California.
—— (1980) 'Review of S.C. Dik's *Functional Grammar*', *Lingua* 50: 155–189.
Weigand, Hans (1986) 'An overview of the conceptual language Koto', MS, Department of Mathematics and Computer Science, Free University, Amsterdam.
—— (1989) *Linguistically Motivated Principles of Knowledge Representation*, Dordrecht: Foris.
Weiner, E. Judith and Labov, William (1983) 'Constraints on the agentless passive', *Journal of Linguistics* 19: 29–58.
Wierzbicka, Anna (1979). 'Ethno-syntax and the philosophy of grammar', *Studies in Language* 3(3): 313–383.
—— (1986) 'The meaning of a case: a study of the Polish dative', in R.D. Brecht and J.S. Levine (eds) *Case in Slavic*, Columbus, Ohio: Slavic Publishers.
Williams, Edwin (1980) 'Predication', *Linguistic Inquiry* 11: 203–238.
—— (1983) 'Against small clauses', *Linguistic Inquiry* 14: 287–308.
Wise, Mary R. (1986) 'Grammatical characteristics of PreAndine Arawakan languages of Peru', in D. Derbyshire and G. Pullum (eds).
Wójcik, T. (1973) *Gramatyka języka rosyjskiego. Studium kontrastywne.* Warsaw: PWN.
Woodbury, Anthony C. (1977) 'Greenlandic Eskimo, ergativity and Relational Grammar', in P. Cole and J. Sadock (eds).
Ziv, Yael and Sheintuch, Gloria (1979) 'Indirect objects reconsidered', *CLS* 15: 390–403.
Zribi-Hertz, Anne (1989) 'Anaphor binding and narrative point of view: English reflexive pronouns in sentence and discourse', *Language* 65(4): 695–727.
Zubin, David (1979) 'Discourse function of morphology. The focus system in German', in T. Givón (ed.) *Syntax and Semantics 12. Discourse and Syntax*, New York: Academic Press.

Language index

Achenese 193–195
Aghem 153, 176, 179, 180, 224
Amerindian 177, 188
Amharic 86
Apalaí 211
Apurina 211
Arabic 151, 153, 171, 183, 212
Australian 86, 87, 122, 182, 188, 202, 215
Austronesian 193

Bantu 74, 97–105, 109, 110, 143, 176, 193
Basque 153, 215
Benue-Congo 178
Bimoba 212
Blackfoot 213
Bulgarian 126

Cakchiquel 101, 211, 215
Campa 122
Carib 177, 221
Cebuano 83–85, 93, 177
Chichewa 99, 109, 193
Chi-Mwi:ni 101
Chinese 43, 164, 206
Chinookan 192
Choctaw 86
Chol 211
Czech 121, 153, 216, 217, 221, 224

Diegueño 130
Diyari 182, 188
Djaru 202
Dutch 152, 153, 168, 169, 180, 208, 209, 222

Dyirbal 88, 90, 92, 202, 215

Efik 178, 179
English 6, 7, 13, 30–33, 37, ch. 3 *passim*, 77–80, 84, 96–97, 106, 110, 112, 128, 133, 135, 143, 149–152, 156–158, 161, 163, 167, 169, 174–179, 188, 191, 213, 221, 222, 224–226
Eskimo 81, 93, 215; West Greenlandic 81, 130

Finnish 214, 215
French 18, 59, 129, 168, 170, 223

Garawa 202
German 55, 168, 169, 188, 203, 212, 214, 222
Germanic 170, 172, 214, 222
Gilbertese 211, 221
Grebo 212
Greek 15, 58, 119, 222; Ancient 108–110
Greenlandic *see* Eskimo
Gunwinggu 215

Haida 177–179
Halkomelem 215
Hawaii 172
Haya 99
Hebrew 15, 94, 108–110, 172, 208; Early Biblical 221
Hibena 105
Hidasta 130
Hiligaynon 83
Hindi 86

Hixkaryana 177, 179, 211
Huastec 211
Huichol 101, 102, 215
Hungarian 27, 28, 86, 94, 151, 153, 168, 177, 215, 224

Icelandic 168
Ila 212
Ilocano 83
Italian 168–170, 192

Japanese 94, 95, 164, 166, 208

Kalkatungu 88, 202
Kapampangan 83
Karen 212
Kekchi 211
Kinyarwanda 98–100, 102, 103, 105, 110, 213
Klamath 221
Kobon 15
Kom 143
Kwakwala 188

Lardil 86
Latin 15, 128, 168, 185, 192, 193, 202, 208, 213, 215, 216, 218, 221, 224, 227
Latvian 188
Luiseño 122
Luyia 99

Macro-Siouan 126
Makushi 211
Malagasy 177, 211, 213, 221
Manam 101
Mandarin 119
Maori 109
Mashi 99
Mayan 101, 191, 211, 215, 221
Mojave 86
Mopan 211

Nani 86
Nez Perce 101, 102
Ngiyambaa 202

Panare 211
Papago 221
Papuan 170, 177, 207
Pawnee 126, 127
Persian 172, 213

Philippine 74, 82–85, 90–94
Pima 165
Pocoman 211
Polish 22, 43, 71, 80, 94, 95, 117–120, 122, 125, 126, 134, 143, 153, 182–186, 188–193, 202, 208, 210, 216–219, 221–224, 227
Polynesian 211

Quechua 208, 215
Quiche 101, 191, 192, 211, 215

Romance 94, 106, 170, 172
Romanian 168
Russian 43, 119, 153, 192, 193, 202, 219, 221, 224

Serbo-Croatian 153, 182, 188, 224
Sherpa 94, 144, 172, 213
Shona 101
Siouan 126, 130
Slavic 94, 106, 168, 170, 215, 216
Slovenian 188
Spanish 119, 136, 168, 221

Tagalog 83–85, 91–93, 177, 214
Tauya, 207
Thai 31
Tigre 86
Toba-Batak 211
Turkish 29, 136, 172, 173
Tuscarora 213
Twi 212
Tzeltal 101, 177, 211
Tzotzil 101, 211

Urubu 211
Usan 15
Ute 86, 221
Uto-Aztecan 165
Uzbek 212

Walmadjari 122
Walpiri 182, 202, 215
Wambon 15, 170, 171, 177
Wappo 177
Warungu 86–89, 93

Yagua 182, 183
Yalarnnga 87, 88
Yaqui 213
Yidin^y 88, 215
Yucatec 188

Name index

Abashheikh 101
Abelson 157
Aissen 101
Allan 24, 26, 31, 202, 209
Allerton 58, 59
Anderson, John 23, 62, 66, 73
Anderson, Stephen 188
Aronoff 20
Austin, John 37, 124, 130
Austin, Peter 188

Bakker 18
Bardovi-Harlig 149
Bates 221
Bell 17, 82, 85
Behagel 115
Bennet 117
Bentivoglio 221
Berman 108, 212
Blake 63, 65, 82, 86–88, 189, 202, 213
Boas 192
Bock 7, 8, 159
Bolinger 1
Bolkestein 19, 30, 107, 128, 141, 173
Bresnan 12, 82, 95, 139, 193
Brinton 54
Brown 131, 134, 154
Bunt 31
Burzio 170
Butler 2
Bybee 115, 125, 127, 185, 198

Calabrese 169, 170
Carnap 25
Chafe 46–48, 51, 53, 62, 69, 70, 155–158, 160, 177, 221

Chia 143
Chomsky 1, 13, 16, 29, 30, 60, 101, 115, 138, 139, 141, 196
Chung 109, 124
Clancy 166
Clark 158
Comrie 2, 16, 29, 38, 51, 52, 65, 75, 101, 116, 119, 121, 171–173, 208, 214
Connolly 17, 226, 227
Cook 87, 98, 178
Cooper 105
Cooreman 82, 84, 93

Davison 147
De Groot 27, 28, 46, 51, 151, 193, 224
De Guzman 82
De Jong 36, 162, 178–180, 218, 221, 227
De Schutter 14, 152
De Vries 170, 171, 177
De Wolf 82
Delancey 76, 105
Derbyshire 177, 211
Dezső 148, 149
Dignum 18
Dik 1, 4, 8, 10, 12–15, 17, 19, 20, 22–27, 29–31, 35, 36, 38, 39, 42, 44–47, 49–58, 60, 61, 63, 65, 67, 70–72, 74, 75, 85, 86, 88, 90, 92, 94, 99, 102, 103, 105, 108, 114, 116–119, 123, 124, 132, 139, 141, 146, 148–152, 154, 155, 160, 162, 163, 165, 167, 168, 170, 171, 173, 174, 176, 179, 180, 183, 184, 187,

192, 194, 197, 198, 199, 200, 202, 204, 208–212, 215, 218, 220, 222–226
Dixon 88
Doherty 127
Dowty 12, 46, 47, 52–54, 69, 88, 95
Dryer 84, 95, 99, 100, 213
Duranti 99
Durie 194, 195

Eastman 177
Emonds 197
Enkvist 222
Ernst 139
Ertel 76, 107
Estivasl 90

Falk 139
Fillmore 48, 55, 62, 66, 68–70, 72, 105, 107
Foley 2, 12, 14, 48, 69, 82, 85, 114, 115, 122, 123, 127, 136, 195, 198
Fortescue 130
Fox 166, 167, 221
Frazier 205, 206

Gary 98, 99
Gasparov 202
Gazdar 139, 197
Givón 2, 84, 105–107, 116, 147, 148, 162, 166, 171, 172, 208, 221
Gorbet 130
Greenbaum 39, 139, 140
Greenberg 1, 17, 203, 205, 207, 210
Grice 131, 154, 156
Grimes 166
Grimshaw 170
Gruber 62, 69, 70
Gúeron 163
Gundel 5, 6, 8, 147, 155, 164

Haiman 2, 165
Halliday 2, 14, 15, 39, 62, 65, 70, 95, 107, 112, 124, 127, 128, 149, 180
Hannay 157, 158, 160, 163, 225, 226
Harlig 149
Harries-Delisle 148
Hassan 107
Haviland 158
Hawkins 17, 201, 203–207, 213, 246

Hawkinson 101
Heath 86, 87
Helbig 55
Hengeveld 35, 36, 39, 113, 116, 123–125, 127, 130, 132, 136, 142–144, 198
Hetzron 163
Hooper 20
Hopper 84
Huddleston 68
Hudson, Joyce 122
Hudson, Richard 10, 23, 197
Hyman 99, 101

Jackendoff 20, 66, 129
Jespersen 1, 95
Johnson 24, 105
Johnson-Laird 24
Junger 27

Kahrel 17, 28, 86
Kalmar 93
Kaplan 95
Karolak 57, 59
Keenan 16, 66, 71, 80, 98, 99, 208, 214
Keijsper 149, 202, 219
Kiefer 127
Kimenyi 98, 100
Kirsner 163
Kiss 22, 194, 224
Kisseberth 101
Kitagawa 164
Klaiman 47
Koster 1
Kucera 121
Kuno 2, 76, 107
Kuroda 162
Kwee 18

Labov 84
Lakoff 105, 170
Lambrecht 148, 158, 159, 161–163, 171, 223
Langacker 122
Langdon 165
Larson 101, 102
Lascaratou 222
Lawler 193, 194
Leech 128

Name index

Lehmann 186, 188, 206, 241
Lepsius 203
Levinson 131, 166
Lewis 136
Li 87, 150, 172
Lichtenberk 101
Limburg 17, 37, 193, 208
Longacre 66
Lyons 31, 33, 36, 38, 123, 126, 127, 135

McCawley 24, 25
MacDonald 208
Mackenzie 230–231
MacWhinney 221
Majewicz 117, 122
Mallinson 213
Marantz 88
Mashi 99
Masica 50
Matthews, G. 130
Matthews, Peter H. 61
Mayerthaler 5
Mchombo 193
Miller 1
Moravcsik 186
Mourelatos 52
Moutaouakil 36, 151, 153
Munro 165
Muysken 1
Myhill 90

Nakajima 139
Newmeyer 4
Nichols 2, 61, 192, 197
Noonan 142, 144
Norman 101, 191
Nuyts 14, 18, 24, 36

Oehrle 97
Okamoto 157
Olson 122, 127

Palmer 127
Parks 127
Partee 117
Payne 82, 182
Perlmutter 10, 63, 80, 82, 99, 168–170, 194, 195
Pinkster 202

Postal 10, 63, 80, 82, 99
Prince 152, 155, 157, 158, 216, 217
Pullum 183, 197, 211

Quirk 139, 140

Radewa 126
Radford 60, 144
Reichenbach 117
Reinhart 154
Rijkhoff 17, 33–36, 187, 201, 205
Rijksbaron 52–55
Risselada 107
Roeper 80
Rosen 10
Ross 105
Rude 101

Sag 30, 227
Sasse 162
Sawaie 183
Schachter 82, 197, 199
Schank 157
Schenkel 55
Schlesinger 66
Schlyter 129
Schmidt 203
Searle 36, 37, 124, 130, 131
Sedlak 212
Sheintuch 95
Shibatani 2, 80, 82–85, 93
Siewierska 6, 80, 83, 105, 202, 227
Silverstein 105
Sirotinina 219
Sommers 59, 61, 62, 66, 71, 108
Sridhar 50
Starosta 23, 62, 63, 65
Stockwell 62
Svartvik 84

Talmy 66, 112
Taylor 53
Thompson 2, 84, 150
Timberlake 124
Trithart 99, 109
Tsunoda 86, 89, 93
Tsutsui 164

Uszkoreit 227

Van der Auwera 76
Van der Korst 18
Van Dijk 154
Van Valin 2, 12, 14, 48, 69, 82, 85, 114, 115, 122, 123, 127, 136, 195, 198
Vendler 14, 46, 47, 51, 53, 54, 69, 143
Vennemann 20, 202, 203, 207
Vet 113, 170
Vlach 121
Watters 108, 153, 176

Weiner 84
Williams 142
Wilson 197
Wise 122
Woodbury 81

Yule 154

Ziv 95
Zaenen 168, 169
Zubin 76, 107

Subject index

absolutive 81, 86–88, 90–93
accomplishment 45–47, 51, 67
accusative 50, 77, 82, 83, 86, 91–93, 108, 141, 172, 173, 184–186
achievement 14, 47, 51
action 37, 43, 45–48, 53–54, 66, 67, 69, 105, 108, 167, 194
action-process 46–47
activation 8, 156, 158–161, 163, 165, 166, 176
active/passive 79, 82, 195 *see also* passive, subject assignment
activity 28, 45–47, 67, 86
adjective 25, 129, 136, 142, 182, 188, 202, 203, 205, 210, 213, 214
adjunct 55, 61, 80, 114, 137, 140, 209 *see also* satellite
adposition 10, 55, 97, 136, 192, 204, 206, 207, 212
Agent 9, 13, 27, 28, 42, 64–70, 74, 79, 83, 88, 90–93, 104, 105, 108, 111, 112, 194, 215, 218
agentivity 41, 43, 46–49, 54, 69, 80
agreement 5, 9, 55, 73, 77, 138, 168, 170, 182, 183, 185, 186–197
Aktionsart 43, 44, 116
animacy 48, 63, 64, 111, 187
antipassive 78–79, 86–93
applicative 102–104
apposition 193, 195, 205
argument 9; *see also* complement; position 9–10, 12, 24, 75–76, 96, 110, 194, 218; structure 9–12, 23–24, 27–30, 66–67, 139
argument/satellite 44, 55–62
article 22, 172, 181, 204, 219

aspect 12, 23, 38, 46, 51, 114–122, 130, 137, 138, 140, 185, 196–198; conative 118, 119; habitual 119, 121; imperfective 38, 116–121; iterative 38; perfective 38, 116–121, 196, 197, 199; phasal 116–121; progressive 51, 54, 118–121, 196, 198, 199, 214; prospective 118–119; quantificational 38, 116–119, 121, 130; resultative 118, 120
atelic *see* telicity
auxiliary operator 184, 189, 190, 198
auxiliary verb 10, 195–199, 204

backgrounding 84, 86, 105, 156
Beneficiary 9, 44, 56, 58, 72, 83, 92, 94, 96, 98–104, 107, 111, 184, 212

Case Grammar 14, 16, 23, 68, 73
case marking 9, 151, 168, 182, 190, 207
clause 10–12, 35–42, 113–115
classifier 31, 33
clitic 100, 134, 150, 153, 166, 182, 193, 212, 224
collective nouns 189
comparative 9, 29
complement 23, 55, 61, 71, 137 *see also* argument
complementation 115, 135, 140–145, 197, 214
conative *see* aspect
constituent order *see* linearization
contextual operator 185, 191, 197
contrast 7, 174–180
control 45–51, 54, 56, 64, 66, 68, 69

controller 74, 80, 85
coordination 90, 128, 207, 208
copula 35
core predication 31, 39, 41, 58, 104, 113, 114, 121, 124, 139, 140
cross-category harmony (PCCH) 203–205
cross-reference 50, 55, 101, 182, 187, 191–195

dative 29, 50, 71, 79, 87, 89, 93, 94, 101, 108, 184
dative-shift 79, 93, 94, 101
declarative 41, 132, 134, 143, 175, 225, 226
definiteness 32, 34, 44, 107, 158, 171, 186–188
demonstrative 22, 185, 186, 188, 204, 205, 213, 214
deontic *see* modality
dependency 10, 197, 204
dependent-marking 192
direct object *see* object assignment
discourse topic 154, 155, 163, 167, 170
double object 95–101, 106
dynamicity 45, 46, 53–54, 68, 71
dynamism *see* dynamicity

embedded clause 18, 34, 138, 207
empathy 76, 107
empty category 138, 141
ensemble 31, 33
epistemic *see* modality
epistemological *see* modality
ergative 74, 77, 78, 80–83, 86–88, 90–93, 192
ergativity 70, 88, 91, 92
event 37, 45, 46, 51, 55, 66, 67, 105, 162
existential construction 161–162, 169, 225
experience 45, 47, 49–50, 66, 106, 116
Experiencer 50, 65–69, 71, 112, 184
expression rules 10, 12, 13, 18, 20, 23, 42, 55, 147, ch. 7 *passim*, 227
extended predication 12, 30, 39–41, 88, 90, 105, 107, 113, 114, 123, 140–142, 147, 195, 206
extraposition 202, 213, 225

familiarity 76, 107, 111, 221
focality 40, 146, 148, 173
Focus 9, 40, 42, 89, 140, 148, 149, 153, 156, 158–160, 162–164, 171, 173, 174–181, 211, 217, 219–221, 223, 224, 227
focus constructions in Philippine languages 83–85, 91–93
focus position 153, 217, 224
Force 67–69, 71, 74, 108, 111, 112
foregrounding 84, 157, 159
formal paradigm 1, 3
FPG *see* Functional Procedural Grammar
functional explanation 2, 3–8, 15
functional paradigm 1–4, 15
functional pattern 13, 201, 211, 215–226
Functional Procedural Grammar (FPG) 14, 18
fund 12, 20, 31

GB *see* Government and Binding
gender 23, 182–188, 190, 193
Generalized Phrase Structure Grammar (GPSG) 227
genitive 107, 189, 190, 203, 208, 213, 214
givenness 107, 148–150, 152, 156–159, 160, 165, 166, 168, 217–221
Given Topic (GivTop) 160, 165–168, 220, 221
given/new 155–160, 221
Goal 9, 13, 16, 27, 28, 41, 51, 64, 66, 69–71, 74, 79, 83, 84–106, 110, 111, 144, 185, 217, 218
Government and Binding (GB) 3, 16, 23, 24, 60, 73, 81, 95, 101, 115, 137–141, 143, 144, 145, 170, 202, 214, 223, 224
GPSG *see* Generalized Phrase Structure Grammar
grammaticalization 64, 65

habitual *see* aspect
head 10, 30, 32–35, 136, 167, 186–188, 190, 192, 193, 195, 197, 199, 201–206, 209, 210

Head-Driven Phrase Structure Grammar (HPSG) 23
headmarking 192, 205
head proximity (PHP) 204–206, 210, 246–247
HPSG *see* Head-Driven Phrase Structure Grammar

iconicity 6, 105, 209
identifiability 34, 155, 158–160, 212
illocution 36, 39, 114, 123, 130, 131, 133–135
illocutionary force 12, 36, 41, 42, 114, 124, 126, 130, 131, 142, 143, 151
illocutionary frame 11, 114, 132
illocutionary operator 36, 39, 40, 116, 130–136, 143
illocutionary satellite 39, 40, 116, 130–136
imperative 4, 48, 85, 132, 134, 143, 218
imperfective *see* aspect
incorporation 30, 58, 89, 191
indefiniteness 34
indicative 79, 138, 144, 145, 148, 180
indirect object 64, 65, 75, 95, 96, 99, 100, 131, 132, 142, 143, 144
indirect speech 143–145
inferential 17, 126, 127, 157
infinitive 138, 141, 184, 198
inflection 125, 128, 132, 137–139, 188, 189
Instrument 9, 18, 38, 56, 58, 63, 65, 68, 72, 78, 83, 87, 96, 98, 99, 102–104, 107, 108, 110
interrogative 4, 29, 132, 134

layered structure; of clause 10–11, 36–39, ch. 5 *passim*; of term 34–35; in GB 137–138
Lexical Functional Grammar (LFG) 12, 23, 24, 73, 82, 95, 139, 170, 193, 202
lexical priority 183, 186
lexicon 20, 22, 23, 31, 183, 197
LFG *see* Lexical Functional Grammar
linearization 13–16, 27, 42, 139, 181, 183, 187, 197, ch. 8 *passim*

LIPOC 211–214, 220
Location 38, 57, 61–66, 72, 78, 83, 85, 87, 92, 99, 100, 107–111
locational operator 33–35

Manner 38, 41, 48, 54, 56, 58, 60, 65, 72, 80, 98, 99, 102–104, 110, 129, 133, 135, 139, 140
markedness 5, 6, 8, 202, 217
maximal projection 137, 141
meaning 23–26, 28, 46, 58, 59, 67, 94, 119, 128, 131
meaning postulate 24–25, 67
modality 36, 38, 39, 114–116, 123–136; deontic 125; epistemic 124–126, 128, 129, 136, 139, 143; epistemological 39, 123–125, 127, 129, 130, 134–136; evidential 114, 116, 125, 126, 129, 130; objective 116, 123–130, 134; quotative 126; subjective 39, 114, 116, 125, 126, 128, 129, 136, 139, 143
momentaneous 51–52, 232
mood 23, 81, 123–125, 131, 132, 134, 136, 185

Natural Language Using system (NLU) 1, 14, 17, 18
Natural Serialization Principle (NSP) 202–204
negation 38, 116, 128, 140
newness 148, 150, 165, 168–171, *see also* given/new
New Topic (NewTop) 160, 161, 163, 165, 166, 168, 170–173, 176, 211, 225
NLU *see* Natural Language Using system
nominative 29, 50, 82, 83, 86, 91, 93, 151, 168, 184, 189, 190
NSP *see* Natural Serialization Principle
nuclear predication 35, 38–41, 43, 44, 55, 56, 59, 72, 77, 113, 124, 129, 139, 140, 142
number marking 34, 186, 191
numeral 33–34 172, 189, 190–191, 204–205, 213, 214

object *see* object assignment

278 *Functional Grammar*

object assignment 19, 39, 74–76, 78, 79, 88, 92–95, 99, 100, 101–104, 106, 107, 111, 210, 211, 215
operator 13, 16, 20, 23, 36, 41, 114, 118, 151, 174, 184, 186, 187, 189–191, 197–199, 210
operator/satellite 20, 38–39, 114, 116, 137

P_1 13, 22, 150, 152, 153, 201, 209, 211, 215, 217–220, 222–226
P_1-constituent 220
P_2 13, 22, 150, 152, 153, 171, 201, 215, 223
P_3 22, 150, 152, 153, 201, 215, 223
passive 13, 30, 57, 71, 74, 76, 79–86, 88, 90–93, 97, 101, 103, 108, 184, 194–197, 199, 211, 236
passive actor 80–82, 84–86, 97
patient 64–66, 69, 70, 212, 215
PCCH *see* Cross Category Harmony
perfective *see* aspect
personal hierarchy 6, 32, 83, 103, 105–108, 111, 112, 187, 190
perspective 40, 41, 43, 74–79, 82, 90, 95, 96, 99, 106, 210
PHP *see* head proximity
phrase structure 30, 115, 139, 196
placement rules 13, 201, 218–220, 226
Positioner 67–70, 74, 108, 112
possession 69, 179
possessor 34, 66
postposition 206–208, 213, 214
pragmatic function 19, 30, 40, 42, 90, ch. 6 *passim* 183, 201, 211, 215, 220, 225
Prague School 1, 147
predicate 22, 24; basic 25, 27, 104, 137, 181; derived 27, 30
predicate formation 12–15, 23, 27–30, 35, 57, 58, 81, 82, 86, 88–90, 92, 94, 103, 104, 211
predicate frame 9, 11, 23, 24, 27, 28, 30, 32, 35, 40, 44, 58, 67, 77–79, 81, 82, 94, 102, 104, 181
predicate operator 38, 39, 114, 116, 118–121
predicate satellite 38, 39, 116
predication 10–12, 35–42, 113–115

predication operator 38, 39, 116, 121–123
predication satellite 90, 116
preposition 30, 84, 95, 96, 98, 102–103, 142, 205, 206, 208, 213, 214
presentative construction 161–163, 168–170, 176, 225, 226
presentative function 163, 226
Process 45–47, 53, 67–69, 120
Processed 28, 64, 67, 69, 70, 108, 111, 112
progressive *see* aspect
proposition 10–12, 36, 37, 39–41, 59, 113–116, 125–127, 135, 140–142
proposition operator 39, 40, 116, 123–130
proposition satellite 39, 40, 116, 123–130
prospective *see* aspect
Purpose 35, 43, 58, 60, 72, 134, 162, 184

Quality 33–35, 58, 72
quantifier 33–35, 129, 189, 190
question 11, 97, 105, 127, 140, 223
question/answer test 175
quotative *see* aspect

Reason 58, 60, 72
Recipient 9, 27, 42, 64, 65, 67, 69–71, 79, 83, 92, 94, 95, 96–104, 106, 108–111, 184, 212, 215
recursion 32, 137
Reference 70, 111
referentiality 107, 171
reflexivization 29, 85, 86, 90, 98
Relational Grammar (RG) 10, 16, 23, 30, 65, 73, 75, 76, 81, 88, 89, 95, 97, 100, 102, 103, 109, 170, 194, 195, 202
relative clause 205–206, 213–214
relativization 84, 97, 98, 100, 105
relator 22, 204, 206–209
relator principles 204, 206–209
Resumed Topic (ResTop) 160, 165–168, 171
restrictor 32, 33, 113, 174
resultative *see* aspect
RG *see* Relational Grammar

Role and Reference Grammar
(RRG) 2, 14, 16, 114, 124, 139
RRG *see* Role and Reference
Grammar

satellite *see* argument/satellite; *see* operator/satellite
selectional restrictions 24–27, 44, 47, 77
semantic function 9, 24, 62–72, 78, 104–112
Semantic Function Hierarchy (SFH) 9, 27, 55, 76, 104–111
semi-indirect speech 142–143
sententiality 241
SFG *see* Systemic Functional Grammar
SFH *see* Semantic Function Hierarchy
Situation 45, 47, 54
SoAs *see* state of affairs
Source 66, 67, 70, 72, 83, 105
specifier 137, 196
speech act 10, 11, 36–39, 42, 113–115, 117, 134, 142, 156
State 45–47, 53, 55, 56, 63, 67, 69
state of affairs (SoA) 43–45; typology of 45–55, 77
stepwise lexical decomposition 26
subcategorization 23, 60, 61, 197
subject *see* subject assignment
subject assignment 30, 74, 76, 79–93, 103, 104, 106–110, 170, 197, 199, 211, 216
subjunctive 136, 138, 144
Sub Topic (SubTop) 158, 160
syntactic function 18, 24, 40, 57, 73–112, 170, 185, 215, 216, 218
Systemic Functional Grammar (SFG) 14, 15, 39

Tail 9, 146, 150–153, 211, 224 *see also* P_3
telic *see* telicity
telicity 45–46, 51–54, 56, 118

tense 38, 41, 114–118, 122, 128–130, 137, 138, 140, 144, 184, 185, 187, 190, 196–199
term 31–35, 187–191
term formation 12, 31, 32
term operator 188–189
TG *see* Transformational Grammar
Theme 9, 69, 70, 146, 149–153, 160, 164, 171, 174, 211, 224 *see also* P_2
thetic/categorial 162
Topic 7, 9, 40, 42, 76, 83, 107, 137, 148–151, 153–156, 159–168, 170–176, 180, 211, 217, 219, 220, 221, 223, 224, 227
topic continuity 165
topic position *see* P_1
topic shift 165, 167
topicality 40, 107, 146, 148, 153–155, 162, 165, 166, 171, 173, 176, 202, 212, 217
Transformational Grammar (TG) 136, 141, 183
transitivity 70, 73, 74, 88

unaccusativity hypothesis 168, 195, 243
underlying clause 10, 36, 184, 186
underlying predication 17, 20, 50, 94, 181
underlying structure 9–13, 23, 33, 35, 36, 81, 101, 139, 142, 184, 190
valency 55, 61, 71, 74, 80, 82, 86, 88–90, 94, 104; qualitative 28, 74, 80, 86, 89, 94; quantitative 28, 74, 80, 86, 88, 89
valency extension 28
valency reduction 28
verb phrase 136, 137
verbal complex 182, 195, 197, 198

Word Grammar 23
word order *see* linearization

X-bar theory 136, 240

Zero 63, 67, 69, 108, 110–112